CONCEPTUAL DEVELOPMENT

Piaget's Legacy

The Jean Piaget Symposium Series
Available from LEA

OVERTON, W. F. (Ed.) ● The Relationship Between Social and Cognitive Development

LIBEN, L. S. (Ed.) ● Piaget and the Foundations of Knowledge

SCHOLNICK, E. K. (Ed.) ● New Trends in Conceptual Representation: Challenges to Piaget's Theory?

BEARISON, D. J. & ZIMILES, H. (Eds.) ● Thought and Emotion: Developmental Perspectives

LIBEN, L. S. (Ed.) ● Development and Learning: Conflict or Congruence

FORMAN, G. & PUFALL, P. B. (Eds.) ● Constructivism in the Computer Age

OVERTON, W. F. (Ed.) ● Reasoning, Necessity, and Logic: Developmental Perspectives

KEATING, D. P. & ROSEN, H. (Eds.) ● Constructivist Perspectives on Developmental Psychopathology and Atypical Development

CAREY, S. & GELMAN, R. (Eds.) ● The Epigenesis of Mind: Essays on Biology and Cognition

BEILIN, H. & PUFALL, P. (Eds.) ● Piaget's Theory: Prospects and Possibilities

WOZNIAK, R. H. & FISCHER, K. W. (Eds.) ● Development in Context: Acting and Thinking in Specific Environments

OVERTON, W. F. & PALERMO, D. S. (Eds.) ● The Nature and Ontogenesis of Meaning

NOAM, G. G. & FISCHER, K. W. (Eds.) ● Development and Vulnerability in Close Relationships

REED, E. S., TURIEL, E., & BROWN, T. (Eds.) ● Values and Knowledge

AMSEL, E. & RENNINGER, K. A. (Eds.) ● Change and Development: Issues of Theory, Method, and Application

LANGER, J. & KILLEN, M. (Eds.) ● Piaget, Evolution, and Development

SCHOLNICK, E. K., NELSON, K., GELMAN, S. A., & MILLER, P. H. (Eds.) ● Conceptual Development: Piaget's Legacy

CONCEPTUAL DEVELOPMENT

Piaget's Legacy

Edited by

ELLIN KOFSKY SCHOLNICK
University of Maryland, College Park

KATHERINE NELSON
City University of New York Graduate Center

SUSAN A. GELMAN
University of Michigan, Ann Arbor

PATRICIA H. MILLER
University of Florida, Gainesville

LEA
1999

LAWRENCE ERLBAUM ASSOCIATES PUBLISHERS
Mahwah, New Jersey   London

Lawrence Erlbaum Associates, Inc., Publishers
10 Industrial Avenue
Mahwah, New Jersey 07430

Cover design by Kathryn Houghtaling Lacey

Library of Congress Cataloging-in-Publication Data

Conceptual development : Piaget's legacy / edited by Ellin Kofsky
   Scholnick . . . [et al.].
      p. cm. -- (The Jean Piaget Symposium series)
   Papers originally presented at the 28th Annual Symposium of the
Jean Piaget Society in 1996.
      Includes bibliographical references and indexes.
      ISBN 0-8058-2500-2 (hardcover : alk. paper)
      1. Cognition in children--Congresses. 2. Piaget, Jean, 1896--
-Congresses.   I. Scholnick, Ellin Kofsky.   II. Series.
BF723.C5C655 1999
155.4' 13--dc21   99-17339
                                                                        CIP

Books published by Lawrence Erlbaum Associates are printed on acid-free paper, and their bindings are chosen for strength and durability.

Printed in the United States of America
10   9   8   7   6   5   4   3   2   1

To Bärbel Inhelder as she wanted to be remembered.

The structures Piaget demonstrated in the so-called "classical" theory of cognitive development provide an overall architecture of knowledge . . . I was first interested in the way such a development occurs through dynamic constructive processes that ensure the transition from one structural level to another. . . . Given the architecture of knowledge Piaget provided, and which defines the epistemic subject, I tried to study psychological processes more amenable to direct observation in particular problem-solving situations. (Inhelder & De Caprona, 1990, p. 41)

Instead of praising Piaget for what he accomplished, the best tribute we can pay to his memory is to go forward. With this idea in mind, . . . we have undertaken to complement the study of knowledge by that of discovery processes in the child, taking into account recent contextual evolution. (Inhelder, 1992, p. xiv)

This volume is written in this spirit and pays homage to a joint legacy.

REFERENCES

Inhelder, B. (1992). Foreword. In H. Beilin & P. B. Pufall (Eds.), *Piaget's theory: Prospects and possibilities* (pp. xii-xiv). Hillsdale, NJ: Lawrence Erlbaum Associates.
Inhelder, B., & De Caprona, D. (1990). The role and meaning of structure in genetic epistemology. In W. F. Overton (Ed.), *Reasoning, necessity, and logic: Developmental perspectives* (pp. 33-44). Hillsdale, NJ: Lawrence Erlbaum Associates.

Contents

Foreword

Michael Chandler
President, The Jean Piaget Society

Ordinarily the themes that have governed the by now 28 Annual Symposia of the Jean Piaget Society, and the volumes that have arisen out of these proceedings, have been freely chosen. This volume, overtaken as it was by history, is not like that. 1996—the year in which Ellin Scholnick, Katherine Nelson, Susan Gelman, and Patricia Miller organized the 26th Annual Symposium of the Jean Piaget Society and began work on this volume—was also the centenary of Piaget's birth. Not surprisingly, everyone, or at least everyone who counts themselves as somehow having seen further by standing on Piaget's shoulders, automatically recognized the importance of not letting this celebratory occasion go unmarked. In consequence, celebrations of one sort or another were being planned in Argentina, Brazil, Canada, France, Japan, Mexico, Portugal, Spain, and the United Kingdom, as well as in Switzerland, where there were three. A crowd of what would prove to be nearly 10,000 scholars strong was already beginning to mill about in search of direction, and for many, the June meetings of the Jean Piaget Society were seen as an obvious hub around which much of this activity would likely turn.

Compelled by these circumstances, the broad focus of this volume, and the Annual Symposium out of which it grew, was never in serious doubt. Piaget's centenary without Piaget as its theme was hardly conceivable. Still, simply recognizing whose party it was meant to be hardly amounts to a plan. Not every tribute, after all, is automatically a fitting tribute. Possibilities rushed to mind. Why not something genuinely commemorative—something that would preserve and call to remembrance all those accomplishments that, taken together, earned Piaget his special place in history? A fool's errand, you realize on a moment's reflection. The job of trying to take the full measure of Piaget, as John Flavell reminded us in a different festschrift (1996), is analogous to trying to assess the impact of Shakespeare on English—impossible. The impact is too monumental to embrace and, at the same time, often too omnipresent to detect. Forget about "full" measures, you counter, what about just the early years, or the final years? Although perhaps of a more tractable size, such piecemeal efforts seem no less wrong-headed. Piaget's oft repeated worst nightmare was that he would merely end up collecting about him true believers—"followers" whose misplaced veneration would suffocate his live ideas and turn them into dead relics. Clearly then, simply deciding that the centenary of Piaget's birth is an occasion worth marking is not at all the same thing as knowing how, in particular, such a celebration ought to go.

The way in which the editors of this volume have chosen to probate Piaget's legacy is by examining how we, as its current beneficiaries, have undertaken to spend the inheritance bequeathed to us. They have done this by focusing attention upon contemporary thoughts about the course of conceptual development—an obvious centerpiece of Piaget's own life's work—through an exploration of its nature, its foundations, and the sources of its novelties. They have pursued this course, both in the structure of the Annual Symposium that they organized, and in the outline of the volume before you, by beginning each of its sections with an overview of Piaget's own position, and following up with the contributions of a panel of notable experts whose own research has helped to hone the cutting edge of their respective fields. What becomes evident from a close reading of these dozen chapters is the degree to which Piaget's ideas have served to scaffold contemporary thinking about every aspect of conceptual development.

Of course, as Webster's unabridged dictionary helps to make clear, not all scaffolds are created equal. Some are of the "catafalque" variety, and are used primarily for "exposing the remains of eminent persons to public view." Others are scaffolds in the embryologic sense, and are understood only as temporary bridgewords that are later "modified or replaced by [more] adult structures" that are literally built upon the bones of their progenitors. Some, as is the custom in the building trades, view the scaffolding left by Piaget as a kind of makeshift catwalk intended only as castaway means for "the supporting of workmen" as they go about the serious business of building what are meant to be more enduring theoretical edifices of their own. Others still appear to regard Piagetian structures in more macabre ways, viewing them as someting more akin to "stage platforms for the execution of a criminal." Piaget, I venture to suggest, would have regarded all of these uses as preferable to any plan to employ the conceptual timbers, planks, and boards that he left behind as the raw materials out of which to construct a church in his name.

Conceptual Development: Piaget's Legacy is no such church. What it is instead is an unusually well-crafted assemblage of state-of-the-art commentaries upon the evolving ways in which both children, and the developmentalists who study them, undertake to represent the novel workings and changing contents of growing minds.

To talk of "Piaget's legacy," as is done throughout this volume, is, of course, only a shorthand means for describing a bequest accumulated through the collaborative efforts of an entire family of coworkers. Principal among those who worked to build up this sizable inheritance was Bärbel Inhelder, who, to our collective sorrow, died on February 16, 1997, while this volume was itself under construction. The editors have chosen to dedicate this work to her working memory.

REFERENCES

Flavell, J. H. (1996). Piaget's legacy. *Psychological Science, 7*, 200-203.

Chapter 1

Piaget's Legacy: Heirs to the House That Jean Built

Ellin Kofsky Scholnick
University of Maryland, College Park

The Jean Piaget Society periodically returns to examine its intellectual roots. Recently, the society celebrated its founding with a symposium: Piaget's Theory: Prospects and Possibilities (publication edited by Beilin & Pufall, 1992; for editors' remarks, see Beilin & Pufall, 1992, pp. 311–326). At the end of his life, Piaget and his colleagues were in the midst of modifying his theory. Contributors to the symposium suggested that this late work clarified the central aims of the theory, provided a more specific analysis of developmental change than did Piaget's earlier work, and modified ideas about logical structure. Many past criticisms of Piaget had been unwarranted because they were misreadings of the substance and aims of the theory or these criticisms could be handled by extrapolations from the latest version of the theory (Beilin, 1992; see also Chapman, 1988; Lourenco & Machado, 1996). These modifications in Piaget's theory provided another example of the ongoing cycle of equilibration. These changes opened up new possibilities by widening the scope of the theory and by providing opportunities to increase its conceptual coherence. This assessment of Piaget was internal to the theory, and the source of the modification was partially internal to the theory, too. Piaget and his colleagues reorganized and modified the theory to close some gaps, and the product was evaluated by those working within the Genevan tradition.

In 1996, the 100th anniversary of Piaget's birth provided another occasion to celebrate. Another symposium, entitled Conceptual Development: Piaget's Legacy, explored Piaget's work from a different perspective, an external one. While Piaget's theory was changing, so was the field of developmental psychology. Because genetic epistemology looks for parallels between the history of science and the cognitive development of the child, scientific progress should produce shifts in both our epistemological framework and our understanding of the child's epistemology and ontology. Chapman (1988) observed:

> Genetic epistemology is itself a science in development. . . . The genetic epistemologist traces the development of a given science up to its current point of development from the point of view of the researcher's own knowledge at its current point of development. Future developments in both are, of course, possible. (p. 201)

Accumulating data, increasingly sophisticated instrumentation, and new or revised paradigms produced different readers and different readings of the Piagetian corpus than did those inspired by the theory at the foundation of the Jean Piaget Society. We now know more about development, and we conceptualize it differently because of work in and outside genetic epistemology.

Inhelder and de Caprona (1997) contrasted two perspectives on cognitive development. One explores the universal epistemic subject's attempts to establish a coherent logical framework for understanding the basic categories of existence and fundamental physical laws. The second examines the psychological subject's attempts to achieve goals. The Piagetian oeuvre was assimilated into changing paradigms of the epistemic and psychological subject. Some developmental researchers returned to their study of function, that is, the vicissitudes of forging and implementing procedures to achieve goals. Their research provided new data on children's ability to assemble, deploy, and refine strategies (Siegler, 1996). Those interested in epistemology shifted from tracing the mastery of logic to analyzing the organization of domain-specific knowledge, from studying deduction to exploring induction, from focusing on physical concepts to describing the ontogeny of biological, social, and psychological categories (Flavell & Miller, 1998; Scholnick, in press; Wellman & Gelman, 1998). As a result, we know more about the child's narrative skill, script repertoire, psychological acumen, and ontological theories than we did 30 years ago. This knowledge has revised our picture of the epistemic subject's capacity for theory construction.

The earlier symposium volume explored how Piagetian theory was modified to provide a new perspective on development. This new book samples the diverse ways that the field of cognitive development has changed and the ways that Piagetian theory and research have contributed to the change. It is no coincidence that several contributors to this volume also wrote chapters in the newest edition of the *Handbook of Child Psychology* (Damon, 1998). Here I consider their current research and theories as legacies of the Piagetian tradition, and point out what they inherited.

CATEGORIES OF INHERITORS

What is the legacy? Imagine the Genevan work as a house left to different types of heirs. Some select furniture that fits their own houses. The furniture remains intact, but now appears in a new context. Others choose some furniture, but reupholster it: They borrow a task or a phenomenon and translate it. They may draw different architectural designs for each piece they borrow. For these two groups, Piaget's legacy consists of behavior to be explained and tasks to be explored. The legacy is a storehouse of concepts, and the Piaget Society could produce a series of volumes for each area that Piaget furnished: such as categorization, conservation, causality, and so forth. Many early heirs belonged to these two groups, but not most of the contributors to this book.

A third group takes the house, and remodels it to create a modern dwelling. Rooms are subdivided, extensions are added, and new building material is incorporated. The legacy they draw upon is not the mind's inventory of conceptual furniture, but the cognitive structure in which we represent and situate concepts—the language that we use to describe the mind and its development. Piagetian theory provides the foundation and the bricks for building a new theoretical structure for cognitive development. These researchers use Piaget's theory as a starting point for deep reformulations that result in the discovery of phenomena and issues that might not be expressible in Piagetian structuralism.

Finally, some inheritors raze the house and discard the furniture and the potential building material; they preserve only the land on which the house stood. They seem to destroy or ignore the legacy, yet if the original house had not been built, how could they know what functioned poorly or what aspects of the design were insufficient for the changing purposes of its inhabitants? Moreover, to explain cognitive development, they must explain issues that are central to Piaget's theory: the nature of cognitive representation, the origin of knowledge, the sources of change.

ISSUES IN CONCEPTUAL DEVELOPMENT

The 1996 symposium organizers were interested in how the current generation of developmentalists defined Piaget's legacy. Which type of heir were they and why? How did they use Piaget's legacy? The organizers invited Piagetians, neo-Piagetians, and researchers working in other frame-works to participate. The symposium focused on conceptual development, which was interpreted in different ways: as an analysis of the nature and growth of representation, concepts, and categories. The speakers addressed a set of related questions fundamental to genetic epistemology. Their an-swers reflected different uses of the Piagetian tradition to describe the nature and ontogeny of conceptual life:

How should we represent the workings and contents of the mind?

How does the child construct a mental model during the course of development?

What is the developmental origin of this model? What accounts for the novelties that are the products and producers of developmental change?

MENTAL REPRESENTATION

In the initial chapters of this book, the authors analyze the nature of concepts, categories, and conceptual representation. Case (chap. 2) maps the territory on which various theoretical structures were built and continue to rise. In his view, three paradigms have dominated developmental re-search: associationism, the rationalist tradition in which Piaget worked, and sociocultural approaches. Each framework offers an incomplete pic-ture of development. Associationism divorces function from structure and specific environmental influences from the social system in which individu-als learn. The sociocultural tradition neglects the constraints imposed by an individual's nature and developmental state and fails to specify the particulars of social learning. Rationalists ignore problems in the use of rationality and neglect the cultural traditions that define and shape ration-ality. To remedy these problems, researchers have formulated hybrid ap-proaches. For example, neo-Piagetian theory weds associationism and ra-tionalism by reupholstering elements of each approach (Case & Okamoto, 1996). Case argues the need for an integrative and complete framework and notes some beginning attempts to create new designs for development.

Therefore, we might expect that the four other chapters in Part I (chaps. 3–6) would illustrate the transformation of Piagetian material into a new structure blending the authors' theoretical traditions with Piaget's. How-ever, the writers do not use Piaget's legacy in the same way because their paradigms are not equally hospitable to genetic epistemology, and they select diverse aspects of Piaget's work.

The Piagetian legacy is most visible in the work in the concepts-as-theories position, which also lies in the rationalist tradition (Gopnik & Meltzoff, 1997; Wellman & Gelman, 1998). Researchers in this tradition have held that children operate with intuitive causal theories of specific domains, theories that enable them to make sense of experience, to go beyond perceptual experience, and to generalize from past experience to new material. Therefore, like Piaget, these researchers attempt to characterize the theoretical interpretation that individuals impose on experience. As in genetic epistemology, this interpretation rests on deployment of a set of basic, universal categories, but there are crucial differences. The concepts-as-theories approach endows infants with richer and more elaborated representational processes and conceptual frameworks than did Piaget. Very young infants have the ability to construct theories, validate them, and reason with them. They also begin with an intuitive conceptual core around which their theories are organized. Researchers also attempt to account for children's understanding of domain-specific contents, such as biology and mentation, rather than positing a general interpretive structure incorporating contents such as time and space or category structure. Because researchers differed in the exclusivity of their adherence to nativism and domain specificity, they also differed in how extensively they use Piaget's theory.

In this book, Meltzoff and Moore[1] (chap. 3) present work that most closely draws on the Piagetian tradition. They examine core themes in Piaget's (1952b, 1954) theory of sensorimotor development: the origin of representation and the foundation for the concept of object permanence. Piaget invented tasks to measure object permanence and used imitation as an index of infants' representational prowess. He also tracked the construction of representational capacity and object understanding during infancy and explored the ways that concepts of object permanence and space were linked. According to Meltzoff and Moore (p. 53), "classical Piagetian theory makes explicit predictions about these domains, and modern empirical research bears directly on the classical framework."

Meltzoff and Moore choose the representational rug and the permanence piece of Piaget's furniture. They pick apart and reweave the tapestry but maintain a developmental, constructivist framework in which qualitative changes proceed in a predictable sequence. They contend that the capacity for representation, as indexed by imitation, is present at birth, but not the concepts of object identity and object permanence. Newborns begin by applying inherent representational skills to experiential data to sculpt distinctive objects that maintain their identity over various changes in location. Infants represent movements very early, and these movement schemata form the foundation for individuating objects. They can use trajectory information to construct the unchanging identity of a moving

---

[1]Elsewhere, Gopnik and Meltzoff (1997, p. 82) presented an elaborate characterization of sensorimotor children's theory of the world, a theory that generates predictions and that is revised when predictions fail. They claimed that from the beginning children have a theory of the world based on trajectories of objects; later, this theory is revised. In chapter 2, children do not construct an abstract theory until object permanence is achieved.

object. An infant realizes that because an object in motion always looks the same, it must be the same object. Understanding movement paths and object identity subsequently enables infants to link observations of an object as it appears, disappears, and reappears. When an object disappears from view along a defined path, an infant expects its re-emergence.

These conceptual changes lay the foundation for a radical change in the nature of representation, a *theory* of the object's fate during its disappearance. When infants understand that objects exist in a coordinated spatiotemporal framework independent of the observer, they can go beyond perceptual data to imagine that an object persists in an unseen location. Thus, early representation is transformed from a purely perceptual to a conceptual, imaginative process. Conceptual development reflects babies' discovery of the cues that specify the objects and their attempts to coordinate and transform this information into a new explanatory framework.

Although the birth of the representational infant may provide a new layout for cognitive development, the nursery still looks the same except that some pieces are in place earlier and different language is used to describe the conceptual underpinnings. Meltzoff and Moore use many pieces of Piaget's furniture to refurbish Piaget's dwelling. Infants accomplish the same tasks, such as differentiating and coordinating featural and spatial information, and undergo qualitative transformations that allow them to transcend sensory data to build a conceptual world.

Meltzoff and Moore explore representational change. Others in the concepts-as-theories tradition take representational capacity for granted and concentrate on conceptual development in older children, domain-specific concepts, and the structure of categories. They use Piaget's analysis as a platform for rethinking the nature and scope of categories and concepts. Although, according to Keil and Lockhart (chap. 5), these researchers "draw different conclusions from Piaget concerning the nature of conceptual development. . . . at the same time, in true Piagetian tradition, it will be powerfully evident how his ideas seemed to have formed an almost necessary scaffold for more current notions" (Keil & Lockhart, p. 103).

Categorization plays a key role in coordinating and extending knowledge in Piaget's theory (Inhelder & Piaget, 1964; Piaget, Henriques, & Ascher, 1992). Gelman and Diesendruck (p. 79) raise two of the same questions as Piaget: "What are the logical structures implicit in children's grouping of objects? How do conceptual hierarchies get constructed and change over time?" Gelman and Diesendruck even use two phenomena discussed by Piaget, nominal realism and perceptually driven categorization, as the starting point for their analysis. But their definition of categories differs radically from Piaget's, and their discussion illustrates how cognitive science provides a different view of the epistemic subject's framework for constructing an ontology and deploying it to make sense of experience.

Although Piaget (1966) was initially interested in children's understanding of specific concepts, his later work (Inhelder & Piaget, 1964) explored children's grasp of the general principles and structuring activities underlying categorization. Piaget employed a classical definition of categories in which every instance in a class possessed features that were necessary and sufficient for membership. All and only the members of the class possessed the criterial features. The logic of categorization was universally applicable to all contents and to all levels of a taxonomy. The principles for organizing knowledge and generating deductions were constructed during childhood and were the foundation for other concepts, like number.

Rosch (1983; Medin, 1989) argued that most categories did not have a classical structure. Natural categories are not defined by necessary and sufficient features; instead, membership and definitions are graded. Membership depends on clusters of correlated features. Some features are found in more category members than are others, and some instances in the class possess more key features than do other members.

Rosch also demonstrated that classes in a taxonomy differ in accessibility. Category definitions group together similar instances and distinguish these instances from other groups. The higher the level of the hierarchy, the fewer the commonalities in a category; thus such a category seems less cohesive than a lower level one but has greater distinctiveness. One level of a hierarchy, the basic, achieves the best balance of cohesiveness and distinctiveness and therefore is the most accessible. Rosch also shifted the basis of categorization from a mental act of coordinating correspondences between instances according to general principles to the detection of specific similarities in the external structure of specific domains. Categories reflected the way that nature carved the world at its joints.

Although Gelman and Diesendruck adopt Rosch's description of graded categories, they depart from her empiricist analysis to return to a rationalist framework. People use a rich causal theory based on their knowledge of specific domains to construct categories that help them identify instances and explain their appearance. Thus, like Piaget (Inhelder & Piaget, 1964; Piaget, et al., 1992), Gelman and Diesendruck claim that categories are constructed, not just detected. However categories do not result from application of general logical rules. They reflect domain-specific theories. Whereas Piaget studied the universal properties of categories, this approach emphasizes comprehension of specific concepts.

Research on the origin of particular ontologies leads Gelman (chap. 4) to conclude that even very young children assume that each natural kind is defined by an essence or design plan that determines its appearance. The concept of an eagle, for example, includes ideas about how talons enable eagles to survive as predators.

Although essentialism is a universal assumption, its elaboration and use are content specific. Not all conceptual tasks require it, not all domains are consistent with it, and children must specify the nature of the causal theory that it entails.

A characteristic methodology tracks the use of essentialist notions. In contrast to Piaget who asked children whether there were more ducks or birds on a pond, in this approach, a child ponders whether the duck's possession of an omentum implies that an emu has an omentum, too, or whether, after surgery on a duck to make it resemble an emu, it will behave like an emu and give birth to little emus.

The revision of the nature of categorization alters Piaget's (1985) story of development. Because conceptual structures are organized around the causes and mechanisms that link some putative essence to the actual perceptual and behavioral properties of living organisms, conceptual development entails children's increasing grasp of causes and mechanisms. Keil and Lockhart (chap. 5) simultaneously describe these causes and mechanisms and trace conceptual change. Like Gelman and Diesendruck, they note the diversity of concepts. Gelman and Diesendruck explore the ways that the external features of the task, the level of the hierarchy, and the domain affect conceptual structure, whereas Keil and Lockhart emphasize the heterogeneous composition of the internal structure of any given concept. Concepts are networks of relations that contain feature correlations, logical connections, and causal links. These three aspects are not necessarily coordinated in a principled way in children or adults. How unlike Piaget's analysis!

Piagetians have postulated a developmental pathway from perceptual similarity to abstract rules and causal theories. Keil and Lockhart reject this narrative because all three aspects of concepts coexist from the beginning. Infants' "original competencies" include the capacity to detect perceptual regularities, derive rules and explanatory mechanisms, and represent them in a schematic knowledge structure. Babies operate with skeletal theories that constrain the kinds of mechanisms, permissible data, and principles that are deemed relevant. They possess rudimentary tools to elaborate and revise initial theories. Infants simply need to fill in the perceptual details and select the specific causal mechanisms that link perceptual data to intuitions. The choice is based on a set of local heuristics. Each domain highlights particular mechanisms. Through experience, "inchoate fragments of local mechanisms may come to gradually cohere into larger and larger bodies of explicitly statable mechanisms and even rules and principles that can be shared socially" (p. 126). What begins as an implicit, hybrid structure becomes more coherent and explicit.

This description of the endpoint of development sounds Piagetian, a sequence of transformations of knowledge to achieve a broader, deeper, and more cohesive structure than earlier, accompanied by a metatheory explaining why the successive transformations are broader, deeper, and more cohesive. But it is not Piagetian. The changes are often local reorganizations of knowledge, not changes in representational format or in the conceptual activities brought to bear on the material. There is no set developmental progression. The modification of knowledge structures is neither orderly nor universal but content driven and contextually determined. Children do not invent a biological theory independently, but use available intuitive and formal bodies of knowledge. Because children differ in their exposure to content areas, their concepts vary in cohesiveness and detail. Only experts in a discipline develop a full-blown theory, and even for them, gaps and inconsistencies prompt further intellectual and scientific refinement.

Piaget provided a framework for characterizing development as a quest for understanding the meaning of concepts. These descriptions of children's search for conceptual cohesion and explicit understanding may be inspired by Piaget, but assumptions about the conceptual apparatus, the mechanisms of change, and the course of development are departures from the Piagetian tradition.

The final author in Part I rejects the Piagetian legacy entirely. Although Klahr (chap. 6) discusses the balance beam task that Piaget (1976) described, he doubts that Piaget's theory can be incorporated into the architecture of a modern theory of conceptual development, and he wants to raze the house. Klahr sees psychology as unnecessarily burdened by the shadow of the massive edifice of Piagetian theory. He uses the metaphor of assimilation and accommodation to attack Piaget's (1985) description of developmental change and to explain the futility of using Piagetian conceptual structures and processes to characterize development.

Klahr poses two arguments. First, any cognitive theory must describe how individuals encode the outside world in a format compatible with its structure and their own knowledge state. Cognitive theories must also explain changes in representation resulting from experience. These issues are so generic that it is fatuous to claim that they are uniquely Piagetian. Second, computational theories cannot digest Piaget's theoretical insights so that they can be dissolved, decomposed, and intermingled with those approaches. Assimilation has its limits. Organisms can process only what they have the capacity to digest, and the product of the assimilation bears the imprint of the digestive organism, not just of the nutrients it has assimilated. Piaget's ideas cannot be assimilated into the language of information processing or connectionism that springs from an associationist tradition.

One example that Klahr cites is the use of the term, structure. In Piaget's (1970b) theory, *structure* refers to an epistemological framework that he represented in logicomathematical formalisms. Klahr uses *structure* to refer to the conceptual habitat or system necessary to represent content, execute processes, and learn. Although many information-processing researchers have not thought that the habitat develops, neo-Piagetians (Case, 1992; Case & Okamoto, 1996) described changes in speed and capacity, and Karmiloff-Smith (1992) postulated transformation of the representational format.

Klahr depicts development as change in the computational programs employed to solve tasks, not as change in the architecture of cognition. He describes two genres of computational theories. In the information-processing approach, a set of instructions (stimulus condition–action statements) is assembled to execute a task. Simulations of changes in the instructions enable teasing apart the underlying mechanisms, such as more differentiated stimulus coding or new links between encoding and actions. In the connectionist approach (Bechtel & Abrahamsen, 1991), performance is modeled through an associative neural network that connects stimulus encodings and response. Weights on stimulus–response connections are modified by experience.

Accounts of performance on the balance beam illustrate the differences in the way that mental life is modeled. Piaget (1976) explained successful predictions in terms of a single insight, appreciation of proportionality, which depended on appreciation of the formal properties of the INRC group. In an information-processing analysis, expert solution of the problem entails encoding comparisons of weight and distance across arms. There are four types of comparisons: The weights on each arm are equal and placed at an equal distance from the fulcrum; the weights differ, although they are placed at the same distance; the weights are equal, but placed at different distances from the fulcrum; and both the weights and their locations vary. Each comparison produces a different set of actions. Computation occurs only when the heavier weight is placed nearer the fulcrum on one arm and the lighter weight is farther from the fulcrum on the other arm. The expert multiplies the weight and distance for each arm, compares the two products, and chooses the larger product.

In one connectionist simulation (McClelland, 1995), each configuration is encoded in nodes corresponding to each separate property of the balance beam: weights, distances from the fulcrum, and arms. The presentation of a particular problem activates corresponding nodes. The nodes are connected to a set of responses: left arm up, left arm down, or balanced beam. The excitation of each node is passed along connections to response nodes, and the most strongly excited response node wins out. A correct response increases the strength of the connection between each excited node and the response. The system learns the response to each numerical configuration separately at a pace determined by the number of examples to which the system is exposed. The rate of change from one learning example to the next is also governed by the connectionist modeler's algorithm for determining how the system modifies itself to strengthen correct responses and to eliminate errors. These descriptions illustrate the divide between structural and computational approaches in terms of representation and response-generating mechanisms. The creation of a new, holistic conceptual structure is replaced by strengthening of connections between existing elements.

CONCEPTUAL CHANGE

In contrast, like Piaget, the authors of parts II and III are particularly concerned with the origin of novelty. They use three mechanisms to account for qualitative change: reorganization of a dynamical system, engagement in cultural practices, and paradigm shifts. These explanations are linked to different aspects of Piagetian theory and they produce varied stories of development.

Dynamical Systems Approaches

García (chap. 7) lives in Piaget's house with windows to a shifting scientific landscape. These alterations provide the inspiration for rearranging the house and thereby refining and redefining the basic tenets of genetic epistemology. He draws on the ideas of systems theory (Gottlieb, 1997; Thelen & Smith, 1994) to reassess the Piagetian analysis of the definition of change, the forces that produce change, and the content that changes.

In his view, Piagetian theory and systems theory define change similarly. Development involves nonlinear and structurally discontinuous evolution that proceeds by successive reorganizations of complex interpretive systems. Systems theory, however, postulates disparities among the elements, organizing principles, and mechanisms of the biological, cognitive, and social systems. García suggests that consideration of these different levels of analysis permits a more precise formulation of Piaget's (1970a) assertions about the limited roles of biology and environment in prompting cognitive development. The biological and social systems constrain the possibilities for cognitive change, but they do not shape the nature of the change. When the cognitive system generates new possibilities, the other systems influence which potential is realized. Shifts in the other systems perturb the cognitive system, but do not determine how cognition is reconfigured to respond.

Framing the influence of society and biology in systems language is a shift at the margin of the theory. Piaget and García (1991) introduced a more dramatic change by attempting to incorporate functionalism into their structuralist theory. They redefined the nature of the system that developed. The language of dynamical systems provides added support for the assertion that cognitive structures have an active dynamic that works toward internal consistency. Structures are not static, coherent frameworks into which schemes are embedded, but systems of activities that produce coherence. Piaget and García also expanded the content of structures to blend the logic that imposes internal coherence on conceptual schemes with the grasp of the causal structure of the external world. García challenges Piaget's heirs to investigate the interconnections of causal and logical understanding during development. Thus, García selects the framework of systems theory as a new way to arrange Piagetian conceptual furniture, but he leaves the basic design of the house intact. He reconfigures Piaget's legacy to accommodate the changes, but preserves the basic structure of the theory.

Oyama (chap. 8) also draws on systems theory to explain developmental change. Like Piaget and García, Oyama posits an active organism who attempts to adapt to the world by continual changes in the conceptual system into which experience is assimilated. Each assumes that the phases of ontogenetic and evolutionary development have some universal regularities, but despite sharing these general assumptions about the principles of development, Oyama presents a divergent view of the causes of change, the course of change, and the content that changes.

Oyama doubts that development is exclusively the product of interiorization of actions and objects in the external world and internal coordination of interiorized representations. Instead, there is a dynamic interplay in which interactions with the environment shape the self, while the self reconfigures the environment. Whereas García sees society and biology as boundary conditions that constrain but do not shape development, Oyama eliminates the boundaries. Causal influences inside and outside the skin have such powerful reciprocal effects on each other that the influences belong in the same framework, not at separate levels of analysis.

Because Oyama sees development as more dynamic than does García, her beliefs about the course of change differ. Dynamics imply constant change. Cognitive systems are variable; their form of organization is evanescent. Sometimes the system reaches relative equilibrium and coherence, but systems continually break up and then reconfigure themselves in response to shifting situational demands. Whereas Piaget (1987) was convinced that a series of accidents could not produce the objective, necessary knowledge that he wished to explain, Oyama argues that accidents and contingencies in the external world cause developmental change and that cognition does not evolve toward an abstract logical framework of necessary principles.

Hence she proposes a different model of cognition, one that blurs the distinction between structure and process. Whereas Piaget's thinking lies in the cognitivist tradition that models the mind in terms of internal systems, Oyama describes cognition as a host of related internal activities and external resources to support them. Understanding is based on a grasp of "more or less reliably occurring patterns, rather than precisely enduring (or even precisely recurring" structures; Oyama, p. 191). The new theories and data that perturbed the Piagetian paradigm led Oyama to a new theoretical organization.

Miller and Coyle (chap. 9), like Oyama, continue Piaget's quest to resolve central issues of developmental change, such as the emergence of novelty, the nature of developmental sequences, and the generality of developmental transformations. Like Piaget, Miller and Coyle assume that children are active problem solvers whose choice of goal-directed strategies is partially determined by their self-reflective analysis of the consequences of behavior. Like Piaget, they consider the individual to be the unit of analysis, but they use a different strategy for looking at change: close examination of the process. Microgenetic analysis was not in Piaget's tool kit, although it interested Inhelder (Inhelder & de Caprona, 1997; Inhelder, Sinclair, & Bovet, 1974). Miller and Coyle synthesize a line of empirical work that was pursued intensively after Piaget's death. The research was designed to track the development of the psychological subject, devising and implementing means to achieve goals.

Miller and Coyle describe changes in specific task strategies, changes that result from massed exposure over a short time; therefore their definitions of the content, causes, and course of change differ from Piaget's. The analysis often focuses on isolated laboratory tasks in narrow domains. Shifts in strategies for handling tasks of memory, attention, problem solving, academic content, and a few Piagetian concepts have been studied. The changes result from massed practice or from structured interventions. The content and time period are narrow. The shifts in strategies are not expected to produce radical cognitive reorganizations, although such reorganizations might occur.

The analysis of change is also different from Piaget's analysis. It is a description of regularities in the birth and demise of particular strategies. Piagetians might describe the progressive adequacy and complexity of later strategies, but microgenetic analyses explore the nature of transition states, variability in performance in the same individual, the same task, and across tasks, and variability in sequence of changes.

Microgenetic analyses yield descriptions of change, but they do not necessarily specify the mechanisms of change or the representational content that supports change. The microgenetic method is a tool, not a theory. Researchers must fit their data into some theoretical superstructure. Siegler (Siegler & Shrager, 1984), for example, proposed an associative model of a changing knowledge base to account for changes in behavior on addition tasks. Presently, the empirical data are more consistent with connectionist and dynamical systems models than with genetic epistemology. Children adopt seemingly effective strategies without any impact on performance.

Their developmental course is winding and variable. Much progress results from growing automaticity in executing strategy components. Other theoretical strategies that encompass both the epistemic and the psychological subject may prove to be more fruitful than at present.

Sociocultural Perspectives

García retains three aspects of the Piagetian analysis of change: system, invariant sequences, and constructivism. Dynamical systems theorists have maintained a commitment to qualitative change in systems, although they redefined systemic change. Researchers using microgenetic approaches have simply examined the emergence of novelty. The three representatives of the second perspective on developmental change blend the sociocultural and rationalist traditions. Thus they retain a commitment to qualitative change, the grounding of succeeding stages on earlier ones, and constructivism. They also share Piaget's (1962) interest in symbolic representation, but they stress the role of cultural traditions in supplying the conceptual material and practices that produce qualitative transformations. Their version of constructivism is also co-constructive. The children who incorporate social practices create the individual variations that other social agents may incorporate. Despite these similarities, the representatives of the sociocultural perspective differ in what they take from Piaget's theory and how radically they modify his ideas.

Voneche (chap. 10) describes the intellectual tradition that Piaget inherited and the legacy that he left. His enduring legacy is the choice of children as instruments for studying epistemology. Piaget's theory legitimated research charting changes in the child's epistemological stance. Voneche intends to live in this house, yet he wants to rearrange the furniture because he questions Piaget's method of using children as evidence for his own brand of epistemology, which embodied a particular theory of logic and science. Voneche also questions reliance on equilibration as the explanation of developmental change. He argues that Piaget's theory is essentially normative, but the norms for science and logic that serve as the endpoint of development are culturally and historically situated. So are children.

> [I]t is much more complicated to know which child is the epistemic subject. After all, childhood, as a separate period of life, is largely dependent on the culture and its particular demands, and, even in Western societies, it is culturally dated. (p. 249)

Voneche, therefore, acknowledges the formative role of cultural institutions and practices in motivating and providing the materials for development. Consequently, he notes problems with Piaget's theory. How can a universal theory of development handle diverse patterns of sociohistorical change? By what mechanisms does culture exert its influence?

Saxe and Nelson (chaps. 11 & 12) study two different symbol systems and present different answers to these questions, answers reflecting different uses of the Piagetian tradition. Saxe explores the room in Piaget's (1952a) house devoted to mathematical reasoning and uses Piaget's (1952a) mathematical analyses, for instance, how appreciation of many-to-one correspondences underlies understanding ratios. Like Piaget (1970a), he believes that development produces a series of increasingly organized, coherent, and abstract representations. This legacy provides the lens for analyzing the content and sequence of change, but Saxe modifies the Piagetian perspective on the causes of change and the sources of new understanding by stressing the functional meaning of conceptual content.

Saxe notes that cultures vary in their numerical notation systems, which, in turn, vary in the ease with which they can be used to perform different mathematical tasks. Saxe's (1981) studies of the use of a body-part notation among the Oksapmin supported this claim. In this book, he describes societies with diverse systems of economic exchange engage in distinctive cultural practices that affect the nature and use of children's mathematical understanding. Saxe observed the emergence of arithmetic competence in unschooled Brazilian boys who earned a living by selling candy. Their income depended on setting a viable markup above the wholesale price of candy. Saxe analyzes the ontogenetic sequence in which a novice seller, totally dependent on cultural practices to determine the criteria for sufficient profit and on wholesalers and other vendors to perform the calculations, becomes an expert who devises reliable, sometimes novel, algorithms for computing prices and adjusting to frequent inflationary changes. The expert's appreciation of the market economy also enables him to foresee how price changes might affect his customers' buying practices.

An older Brazilian vendor arrives at some of the same mathematical principles as Piaget's Swiss teenagers: The Brazilian adolescent constructs a mathematical theory. The transformation to an adept merchant is not solely the result of self-regulated change in mathematical understanding arising from retail transactions: Progress is shaped by the activities that candy selling entails. Specific mathematical skills and familiarity with Brazilian currency are required. In the inflationary economy of Brazil, even candy selling involves exchanging large denominations. Selling is a social practice. Skilled practitioners provide assistance and general rules to guide novice sellers.

Saxe redefines the sources of change to include social purposes as well as intellectual curiosity. Conceptual change results from achieving the goal of making a profit. This goal makes mathematics meaningful. The meaning is provided by others through a set of activities that they support while children learn. As children execute the prestructured activity, they begin to induce the formal principles that the activities embody. Thus, formal analysis is infused with its derivation from social practices.

Nelson (chap. 12), like Saxe, draws on some Piagetian beliefs about the nature of change. She, too, assumes that children acquire their concepts through active exploration of the world. Symbolization originates in the internalization of action systems. Cognitive change is driven by children's attempts to make sense of the world. Growth results from children's generalizations about and abstractions from the meanings they impose, but it is also constrained by the experiential base from which abstractions and generalizations arise.

Like Saxe, Nelson departs from Piaget in describing the sources of change. The social environment structures the practices in which children engage and provides the symbolic tools for understanding the nature of the practices. These practices are usually designed to achieve personal ends. Saxe describes qualitative changes in logicomathematical skills. Although acknowledging children's increasing grasp of logical and physical concepts, Nelson emphasizes the centrality of their growing comprehension of the social events in which they participate. By focusing on social content and social communication, she thoroughly transforms the Piagetian legacy.

Children engage in daily routines like bathing and social events like birthday parties. Children use the order that adults impose on these events and the meanings that adults attribute to them to construct a model of the self in society. The event representations supply the material from which understanding of the nature of categories, causes, and contingencies is built.

Event representations also provide the conceptual foundation for language, a tool for social communication. Language then fundamentally alters conceptual life by expanding the content and power of children's models of the world and by infusing these models with cultural meanings. Language begins as another way of internalizing observed actions, then becomes a means of coordinating actions into narratives and maps of the psychological and social world. Then mastery of written symbols enables the construction of the tools of formal analysis so prized by Piaget (Inhelder & Piaget, 1958, 1964). Qualitative conceptual change reflects qualitative change in children's grasp of the symbolic and communicative power of language.

Paradigm Shifts

Carey (chap. 13) also works in the constructivist tradition, but she claims that the source of conceptual change is internal and reflects shifting theoretical commitments to accounts of the nature of things. She reupholsters some of Piaget's furniture—concepts of life, object identity, and causality—and rearranges them within the concepts-as-theories approach. Like Keil and Gelman, she explores the development of domain-specific concepts, most notably biology, and she asserts that progress in development reflects alterations in the structure of children's theories, not changes in their logical skill. Unlike Gelman and Keil, however, she is particularly intrigued by the emergence of novelty.

Fodor (1985) doubted that a new theory could arise from a previous one unless it was commensurate with its origins. Consequently, he rejected accounts of qualitative change in favor of nativism. Carey's explanations of qualitative change encompass both nativism and development. Like Piaget (1970a), she rejects sociocultural influence as the sole source of new ideas. What enables lessons to be assimilated into an unprepared or inhospitable system? Although growth in processing resources enables increasingly broad consideration of material, what guides selection of the specific ideas that produce theory change? She rejects equilibration for the same reason. Contradictions can prompt rejection of previously held notions, but what guides children to new formulations and prepares the cognitive system to assimilate them? She concedes that some new schemata can arise, as Piaget (1985) claimed, through differentiating old concepts or conversely through coalescing previously distinctive entities (or principles) into a single concept. Yet how do children select the right way to parse concepts or to subsume them? Moreover, equilibration does not account for changes that arise from reanalyzing a concept's basic structure to arrive at a new conceptual core.

Carey does not deal with radical incommensurablity in which the initial and the transformed theories are completely different in kind. She tries to account for the local changes in conceptual content, changes that eventually produce radical theory change. She asserts that infants are endowed with a rich conceptual base enabling construction and modification of theories. Infants appreciate the general nature of causality. They can also draw on a generic essentialist framework to individuate different kinds into typologies with unique causal mechanisms that explain the workings and appearances of things. Thus infants "know" in general what a theory must explain and what explanation is. They also grasp a host of domain-specific principles in mechanics, psychology, and number, principles that can be used to construct theories. Many of these principles were derived from Piaget's theory, although Carey offers another developmental timetable and framework for them.

Carey suggests children use two tools to revise concepts: analogy, which was discussed by Piaget (Piaget et al., 1992), and bootstrapping. Bootstrapping occurs when the later theory contains enough earlier material that the earlier can provide links to the new theory. She describes children as constructing a ladder grounded in the concepts of T1 [the earlier theory], getting to a new place, and then kicking the ladder out from under. . . . [Facts that were provided by the old theory] provide fodder for disequilibration. . . . They become articulated in the concepts of T2, internal contradictions are resolved, and then the ladder is kicked out from under. (p. 316)

Many contemporary developmentalists have described their use of Piaget's theory in the same way. They built on his foundation, but their theories have evolved in directions that are locally incommensurable with their origin. They have claimed that the Piagetian ladder, a tool that is external to the building, was then discarded and that the new level that was reached bears no imprint of the original foundation or of the means by which the heights were scaled. Yet Piaget's theory is more than a strap or a ladder. Bootstrapping requires some overlap between the foundational system and the new one. The old material is blended with the new, provides entry to the new, and may be retained in the new. Carey's quote illustrates the blend as she draws on Piaget's theory of equilibration. On close inspection, many researchers used the boards in Piaget's house to build new stairs in the house. They then constructed new upper stories and burrowed beneath the old foundations to explore key Piagetian ideas, such as representation, metacognition, and qualitative change, from different and enriching perspectives. They combined new material with old to reshape the architecture and to add structural potential. Not all the old material disappeared, nor was it exhausted. Piaget's legacy is so vast that researchers continue to return to it to find new furniture to sit on and reupholster and new designs for development.

REFERENCES

Bechtel, W., & Abrahamsen, A. (1991). *Connectionism and the mind: An introduction to parallel processing in networks.* Cambridge MA: Basil Blackwell.

Beilin, H. (1992). Piaget's new theory. In H. Beilin & P. B. Pufall (Eds.), *Piaget's theory: Prospects and possibilities* (pp. 1–17). Hillsdale, NJ: Lawrence Erlbaum Associates.

Beilin, H., & Pufall, P. (1992). In conclusion: Continuing implications. In H. Beilin & P. B. Pufall (Eds.), *Piaget's theory: Prospects and possibilities* (pp. 311–326). Hillsdale, NJ: Lawrence Erlbaum Associates.

Beilin, H., & Pufall, P. (Eds.). (1992). *Piaget's theory: Prospects and possibilities.* Hillsdale, NJ: Lawrence Erlbaum Associates.

Case, R. (1992). Neo-Piagetian theories of intellectual development. In H. Beilin & P. B. Pufall (Eds.), *Piaget's theory: Prospects and possibilities* (pp. 61–104). Hillsdale, NJ: Lawrence Erlbaum Associates.

Case, R., & Okamoto, Y. (1996). The role of central conceptual structures in the development of children's thought. *Monographs of the Society for Research in Child Development, 61*(1–2), Serial No. 265.

Chapman, M. (1988). *Constructive evolution: Origins and development of Piaget's thought.* Cambridge, England: Cambridge University Press.

Damon, W. (1998). *Handbook of child psychology* (5th ed.). New York: Wiley.

Flavell, J. H., & Miller, P. (1998). Social cognition. In D. Kuhn & R. S. Siegler (Eds.), *Handbook of child psychology: Cognition, perception, and language* (Vol. 2, pp. 851–898). New York: Wiley.

Fodor, J. A. (1985). Fodor's guide to mental representation: The intelligent auntie's vademecum. *Mind, 94,* 76–100.

Gopnik, A., & Meltzoff, A. N. (1997). *Words, thoughts and theories.* Cambridge, MA: MIT Press.

Gottlieb, G. (1997). *Synthesizing nature-nurture: Prenatal roots of instinctive behavior.* Mahwah, NJ: Lawrence Erlbaum Associates.

Inhelder, B., & de Caprona, D. (1997). What subject for psychology? *Genetic Epistemologist, 25,* 1, 4–5.

Inhelder, B., & Piaget, J. (1958). *The growth of logical thinking from childhood to adolescence.* New York: Basic Books.

Inhelder, B., & Piaget, J. (1964). *The early growth of logic in the child.* London: Routledge & Kegan Paul.

Inhelder, B., Sinclair, H., & Bovet, M. (1974). *Learning and the development of cognition.* London: Routledge & Kegan Paul.

Karmiloff-Smith, A. (1992). *Beyond modularity: A developmental perspective on cognitive science.* Cambridge, MA: MIT Press.

Lourenco, O., & Machado, A. (1996). In defense of Piaget's theory: A reply to ten common criticisms. *Psychological Review, 103,* 143–164.

McClelland, J. L. (1995). A connectionist perspective on knowledge and development. In T. Simon & G. S. Halford (Eds.), *Developing cognitive competence: New approaches to process modeling* (pp. 157–204). Hillsdale, NJ: Lawrence Erlbaum Associates.

Medin, D. L. (1989). Concepts and conceptual structure. *American Psychologist, 44,* 1469–1481.

Piaget, J. (1952a). *The child's concept of number.* New York: Norton.

Piaget, J. (1952b). *The origins of intelligence in children.* New York: International Universities Press.

Piaget, J. (1954). *The construction of reality in the child.* New York: Basic Books.

Piaget, J. (1962). *Play, dreams and imitation in childhood.* New York: Norton.

Piaget, J. (1966). *The child's conception of physical causality.* London: Routledge & Kegan Paul.

Piaget, J. (1970a). Piaget's theory. In P. H. Mussen (Ed.), *Carmichael's handbook of child development* (pp. 703–732). New York: Wiley.

Piaget, J. (1970b). *Structuralism.* New York: Basic Books.

Piaget, J. (1976). *The grasp of consciousness.* Cambridge, MA: Harvard University Press.

Piaget, J. (1985). *The equilibration of cognitive structures: The central problem of intellectual development.* Chicago: University of Chicago Press.

Piaget, J. (1987). *Possibility and necessity, Vol. 2: The role of necessity in cognitive development.* Minneapolis: University of Minnesota Press.

Piaget, J., & García, R. (1991). *Towards a logic of meanings.* Hillsdale, NJ: Lawrence Erlbaum Associates.

Piaget, J., Henriques, G., & Ascher, E. (1992). *Morphisms and categories: Comparing and transforming.* Hillsdale, NJ: Lawrence Erlbaum Associates.

Rosch, E. (1983). Prototype classification and logical classification: The two systems. In E. K. Scholnick (Ed.), *New trends in conceptual representation: Challenges to Piaget's theory* (pp. 73–86). Hillsdale, NJ: Lawrence Erlbaum Associates.

Saxe, G. B. (1981). Body parts as numerals: A developmental analysis of numeration among the Oksapmin of New Guinea. *Child Development, 52,* 306–316.

Scholnick, E. K. (in press). Representing logic. In I. E. Sigel (Ed.), *Theoretical perspectives in the development of representational (symbolic) thought.* Mahwah, NJ: Lawrence Erlbaum Associates.

Siegler, R. S. (1996). *Emerging minds: The process of change in children's thinking.* New York: Oxford University Press.

Siegler, R. S., & Shrager, J. (1984). Strategy choices in addition and subtraction: How do children know what to do? In C. Sophian (Ed.), *Origins of cognitive skills* (pp. 229–293). Hillsdale, NJ: Lawrence Erlbaum Associates.

Thelen, E., & Smith, L. B. (1994). *A dynamic systems approach to the development of cognition and action.* Cambridge, MA: MIT Press.

Wellman, H. M., & Gelman, S. A. (1998). Knowledge acquisition in foundational domains. In D. Kuhn & R. S. Siegler (Eds.), *Handbook of child psychology: Cognition, perception, and language* (Vol. 2, pp. 523–574). New York: Wiley.

Part I

HOW SHOULD WE REPRESENT THE WORKINGS AND CONTENTS OF THE MIND?

Chapter 2

Conceptual Development in the Child and in the Field: A Personal View of the Piagetian Legacy

Robbie Case
University of Toronto and Stanford University

Although Piaget has had a dominating influence on our understanding of children's intellectual development, important research on this topic has also been conducted in several other theoretical frameworks throughout this century. A number of schemes have been proposed for classifying these frameworks (Beilin, 1983; Case, 1997; Overton, 1984, 1990). The scheme that I use in the present chapter is one that distinguishes three distinct traditions, each with its own epistemology, pioneers, and tradition of progressive inquiry. When Piaget assumed a role of leadership in one of these traditions he moved it forward in a direction that was extremely productive. By the same token, however, he increased the tension between this tradition and the other two. The legacy that he has left us, then, is a dual one: On the one hand, we have a greatly expanded body of data and a considerably more powerful theory than before his monumental oeuvre. On the other hand, we have a pressing need to acknowledge the record of the other two traditions and to move forward in a direction that takes account of their contribution to the field as well as his.

THE EMPIRICIST TRADITION

Piaget used the empiricist tradition as a foil throughout his career. The epistemological roots of this tradition lie in British empiricism as articulated by Locke and Hume (1955/1748). According to the empiricist position, knowledge of the world is acquired by a process in which the sensory organs first detect stimuli in the external world and the mind then detects the customary patterns or conjunctions in these stimuli. Developmental psychologists who have accepted this view have tended to view the goals of psychology as being to describe the process by which new stimuli are discriminated and encoded (perceptual learning), the way in which correlations or associations among these stimuli are detected (cognitive learning), and the process by which new knowledge is accessed, tested, and used in other contexts (transfer). The general method that they have favored includes the following steps: make detailed empirical observations of children's learning in conditions that can be reliably replicated, generate clear and testable explanations for these observations, and conduct carefully controlled experiments to test these hypotheses and to rule out any rival hypotheses.

Early attempts to apply this perspective were designed to show that the laws of learning in young children were identical to those in other species (Thorndike, 1914; Watson, 1914). Later work was aimed at documenting and explaining the changes that took place in children's capability for learning at older ages. The paradigm that was used most extensively was one in which children were presented with pairs of sensory stimuli that varied along a number of dimensions (e.g., form, color, pattern) and were asked to figure out which stimulus feature was associated with receipt of a small reward (e.g., square stimulus on top of container = raisin inside container; circular stimulus on top = nothing inside). On each trial, children were allowed one guess as to which stimulus would be rewarded. When they had succeeded in picking the correct stimulus on some predetermined number of trials, they were said to have acquired the concept. At that point, a different stimulus attribute was selected, and a fresh sequence of experimental trials was initiated.

The results from these studies were interesting. Although preschool children could learn to select a stimulus on the basis of its shape, color, or pattern by the age of 3 to 4 years and could learn to change the basis for their selection when the criterion was changed, they did so in a slow and laborious manner, with the result that their learning curves looked much like those exhibited by lower primates (Kendler, Kendler, & Wells, 1960). By the age of 5 to 6 years, children's original learning became much more rapid. They also became capable of relearning much more rapidly, typically in one or two trials, but only if the new criterion required attention to the same general stimulus dimension (e.g., shape; Kendler & Kendler, 1962). If chidren were required to shift to a different dimension, particularly one that was perceptually less salient than the first dimension, the capability for rapid relearning did not emerge until the age of 7 to 10 (Mumbauer & Odom, 1967; Osler & Kofsky, 1966).

When these phenomena were first observed, the change in children's learning on such tasks was hypothesized to be part of a larger pattern, which White (1967) referred to as the "5 to 7 shift." In keeping with learning theories of the time, Kendler and Kendler (1962) proposed that the pattern was caused by a shift from unmediated to verbally mediated learning. The notion was that children under the age of 5, like lower primates, can learn to differentiate objects that are associated with reward from other objects. Because they do not covertly label each object by using dimensional terms (e.g., square), they have to learn about each object in a local fashion: They gradually build up a set of associations between the particular perceptual features of each positive stimulus and the receipt of a reward. By contrast, because older children and adults do engage in such covert verbal labeling, they are capable of much more rapid initial learning. They are also capable of much more rapid relearning, since they need only substitute one dimensional term for another rather than learn a whole new set of associations. This same change, from unmediated to verbally mediated learning, was believed to have a wide variety of other consequences for children's cognition, especially the sort required in school (Kendler & Kendler, 1967; Rohwer, 1970).

In interpreting the data in this fashion, investigators in this tradition were asserting that a distinctive *pattern* may be discerned in young children's conceptual understanding, one that is present across a wide variety of different local exemplars, and that this pattern reflects a fundamental difference, not just in the content of children's conceptual knowledge, but in the way that knowledge is organized. It was not these assumptions that separated the empiricist position from Piaget's but rather the interpretation of this pattern. For learning theorists, what differentiated 6- to 10-year-olds from adults was their history of verbal learning—not some general logicomathematical structure. In fact, in the learning theory tradition, a good deal of work was devoted to showing that children *could* encode the relation to be learned in the required fashion with a little instruction, but did not do so spontaneously (Kendler & Kendler, 1967). This latter datum was interpreted as indicating a "performance" rather than a "structural" deficiency in children's verbal mediation.

In retrospect, what can be said about the early work on children's concept formation in this tradition? From a theoretical point of view, the harvest was relatively meager, but that is not to say that there was no harvest at all. First, the data gathered were extremely reliable and formed a lasting part of the general corpus that subsequent investigators felt obliged to explain in building a model of the change that takes place in children's cognition in this age range (Case, 1985; Gholson, 1985). Second, the experimental paradigm that was used embodied a number of methodological canons that proved enduring. Of particular importance were several notions: There is much to be learned, in studying any complex conceptual structure, by examining the manner in which children encode its constituent elements; there is also much to be gained by selecting a carefully circumscribed learning task and varying its parameters; finally, there is much to be learned about the different capabilities of different age groups by observing their performance in multiple-trial tasks in which learning can be directly observed. This paradigm, and the epistemological assumptions on which it is based, has been preserved and strengthened in this tradition in the post-Piagetian era (Siegler, 1978, 1997).

THE RATIONALIST TRADITION

The second theoretical tradition in which children's conceptual structures have been studied is the one that Piaget inherited. This tradition drew its inspiration from Continental rationalism rather than from British empiricism. In reaction to British empiricists, philosophers such as Kant (1961/1796) suggested that knowledge is acquired by a process in which the human mind imposes order on the data that the senses provide; the mind does not merely detect order in these data. Examples of concepts that played this foundational role in Kant's system were space, time, causality, and number. Without some pre-existing concept in each of these categories, Kant argued, it would be impossible to make sense of the data of sensory experience: to see events as taking place in space, for example, or as unfolding through time, or as exerting a causal influence on each other. He therefore believed that these categories must exist in some a priori form rather than being induced from experience.

Developmental psychologists who were influenced by Kant's view tended to see the study of children's cognitive development in a fashion different from those who were influenced by empiricists. Developmental psychologists began by exploring the foundational concepts with which children come equipped at birth; then they documented any changes in these concepts with age. The first developmental theorist to apply this approach was Baldwin (1968/1894). According to Baldwin, children's conceptual schemata progress through a sequence of four universal stages, which he termed the stages of "sensorimotor," "quasilogical," "logical," and "hyperlogical" thought, respectively. In any given stage, Baldwin believed, new experience is "assimilated" to the existing set of schemata, much as the body assimilates food. He saw transition from one form of thought to the next as driven by "accommodation," a process by which existing schemata are broken down and then reorganized into new and more adaptive patterns. Finally—and here he was attempting to go beyond Kant—he saw children's conceptual understanding in each of Kant's categories as something that they constructed, not something that is inborn.

The only primitive elements that Baldwin recognized at birth were entities that he called "circular reactions." These reactions led to the formation of habits. As children encountered the limitations of their existing habits, Baldwin believed, they renewed their interest in a situation and actively experimented with new approaches. This behavior required active attention, which, being itself limited, set a limit on the complexity of the new responses that they could create. He also believed, however, that the span and power of children's attention increased with age and gave them new capabilities. Between the age of birth and 4 months, children could focus on only one circular reaction; between 4 and 8 months, they could focus on two circular reactions and coordinate them. After 8 months, they could focus on multiple reactions, and so on.

What caused children's span of attention to increase? Here Baldwin cited cortical coordination: a maturational factor under which he subsumed the development of brain cells, the development of fibers connecting different parts of the brain, and the myelinization of these fibers. He called for subsequent generations of biologists to explore these changes and to chart the process by which lower order schemata are broken up and assembled into higher order schemata, in each of the categories that Kant had outlined. The name that he proposed for the research effort aimed toward this goal was "genetic epistemology."

Piaget's (1960, 1970) acceptance of Baldwin's challenge and his reworking of Baldwin's theory led to the "classic" theory of his middle years. The most important feature that Piaget added to Baldwin's theory was the notion of a "logical structure": a coherent set of logical operations that can be applied to any domain of human activity and to which any cognitive task in the domain must ultimately be assimilated. Piaget hypothesized that the form of children's structures is different at different stages of their development and that this difference gives the thought of young children its unique and progressively more coordinated character. To highlight the importance of these structures, he relabeled Baldwin's second and third stages of development and called them the stages of "pre-operational" and "operational" thought, respectively. He also divided the stage of operational thought into the "concrete" and "formal" periods and added additional substages to each of the resulting epochs. Finally, he made other adjustments that were necessary to give the revised system coherence, such as increasing the emphasis on reflexive abstraction as an underlying developmental mechanism and decreasing the emphasis on increased attentional power and cortical coordination.

Together with his collaborators at the University of Geneva, Piaget conducted a vast number of empirical studies designed to reveal the details of children's conceptual understanding in each of Kant's categories at different stages and the process by which this understanding is arrived at. His basic procedure was to present children with a wide variety of simple problems or tasks to see how they responded to them, then to interview them to determine the reasoning on which these responses were based. A final step was to look for a common pattern in children's reasoning at different ages and to treat this pattern as a clue about the underlying logical structure.

As Piaget modeled these structures, he devised tasks that he hoped would document their existence directly (Inhelder & Piaget, 1958, 1964). Two of the most famous were conservation (a task based on early work by Binet, 1900) and class inclusion. The class inclusion task is similar in certain respects to the concept-learning task investigated by empiricists. Both tasks present children with a simple set of stimuli that can be classified in different ways (by shape, color, etc.). Both tasks require children to overcome their "natural" or "habitual" way of classifying the stimuli. Both tasks require children to sustain a focus on subordinate stimulus values, without losing sight of a superordinate classification. Finally, both tasks are passed for the first time during the same general age range: 7 to 10 years. The interpretation that each group of theorists developed to explain the developmental change, however, was quite different. For learning theorists, the switch to a new form of response was seen as the result of applying a learned set of labels to stimuli and forming associations among them; in short, the change was the result of a verbally mediated process of associative learning. For Piaget, the switch was seen as the result of acquiring a new logical structure: one in which superordinate and subordinate categories were differentiated and integrated. This structure, in turn, was seen as emerging from an internal process of reflection, not from a process driven directly by empirical experience.

THE SOCIOHISTORIC TRADITION

The third epistemological tradition in which children's conceptual development has been studied has its roots in the sociohistoric epistemology of Hegel, Marx, and the modern continental philosophers (Kaufmann, 1980). According to the sociohistoric view, conceptual knowledge does not have its primary origin in the structure of the objective world (as empiricist philosophers suggested) or in the structure of subjects and their spontaneous cogitation (as rationalist philosophers suggested). It does not even have its primary origin in the interaction between the structure of the subject and the structure of the objective world (as Piaget maintained). Rather, it has its primary origin in the social and material history of the culture of which the subject is a part and in the tools, concepts, and symbol systems that the culture has developed for interacting with its environment.

Developmental psychologists who accepted the sociohistoric perspective viewed the study of children's conceptual understanding in a fashion different from empiricists or rationalists. They began their study of children's thought by analyzing the social and physical contexts in which human cultures found themselves and the social, linguistic, and material tools that they developed over the years for coping with these contexts. Then they examined the way in which these intellectual and physical tools were passed from one generation to the next, in different cultures and different eras.

The best known of the early sociohistoric theories was Vygotsky's (1962). According to Vygotsky, children's thought must be seen in a context that includes both its biological and its cultural evolution. Three of the most important features of human beings as a species are that they have language, that they fashion their own tools, and that they transmit the discoveries and inventions of one generation to the next, via language and institutions such as schooling. From the perspective of Vygotsky's theory, the most important milestone in children's early development is the acquisition of language, not the construction of some logical structure or the exposure to a set of universal stimuli and labels for them. Children first master language for social (interpersonal) purposes. Next, they internalize this language and use it for intrapersonal (self-regulatory) purposes. Finally, as these changes take place, their culture recognizes their new capabilities and begins an initiation process that includes an introduction to the forms of social practice in which they will engage as adults.

In modern literate societies, this initiation process normally includes the teaching of such skills as reading, writing, and arithmetic in primary school, followed by such subjects as science and formal mathematics in secondary school. Followers of Vygotsky often saw the acquisition of the first set of skills as causally related to the appearance of the concrete logical competencies that children develop in middle childhood and the second set as causally linked to the emergence of the formal competencies that appear in adolescence.

Early research in the sociohistoric tradition led to interesting findings. One of the most provocative was that adults in a traditional agricultural society, especially those who have not attended school, tend to score at a much lower level than adults who *have* attended school, on tests of mnemonic and logical capabilities such as syllogisms (Luria, 1976; Vygotsky, 1962). To Vygotsky, this finding indicated that modern schooling, not some universal process of reflexive abstraction, is the major instrument of cognitive growth. This inference has not gone unchallenged in recent years. Nevertheless, the datum is important and has led to follow-up studies that have continued to this day (Cole, 1991). In most early studies, there were strong schooling effects, not just on the tasks that Luria and Vygotsky had used, but on tasks that had been used in the other two traditions as well (Cole, Gay, Glick, & Sharp, 1971; Goodnow, 1962; Greenfield, Reich, & Oliver, 1966). Although the results differed somewhat from study to study, the general pattern was that children moved through the shift to "concrete" operational thought at a considerably later age if they did not attend school;

very often, too, they failed to show the teenage shift to a more abstract or "formal" type of response. The shift that they did show in this latter period was one that could be understood only by studying their culture, beliefs, and socialization practices (Greenfield, 1966). The methods used for this sort of study further differentiated this tradition from the others. If the empiricist tradition took physics as its model of a well-developed science and the rationalist tradition took evolutionary biology as its model, the third tradition increasingly turned to anthropology for its inspiration. As is indicated in Table 2.1, the resulting view of human cognition was different from those of the other two traditions along a variety of dimensions.

DIALOGUE BETWEEN THE EMPIRICIST
AND RATIONALIST TRADITIONS

Early Empiricist Critiques of Piaget's Theory

Until the late 1950s, North American psychology was dominated by empiricism of a rather extreme form: the school of logical positivism. Although the influence of this school was rather short lived in philosophy, its hold on North American psychology lasted much longer and served to justify the radical behaviorism that developed in North America. During the late 1950s and early 1960s, however, North American behaviorism came under fire from within North America as well as without. The most common criticism was that behaviorism failed to do justice to the organization of human behavior and to the complex inner processes responsible for generating it (Bruner, Goodnow, & Austin, 1956; Chomsky, 1957; Miller, Gallenter, & Pribram, 1960; Newell, Shaw, & Simon, 1958). At the same time as this criticism was being voiced, computers were emerging as a new economic force, and a new discipline, whose province was the design of computer software, was being created. Eventually, investigators from the newly formed discipline of computer science joined hands with psychologists, linguists, and other social scientists in an effort to describe the cognitive processes that are necessary to generate and control complex human behavior. This event became known as the cognitive revolution and the new discipline became known as cognitive science (Gardner, 1985).

Interestingly, although theories of learning underwent a profound transformation at this time, the underlying epistemology on which they were based changed relatively little. By and large, North American investigators still presumed that the ultimate locus of knowledge was the empirical world and that the acquisition of knowledge by psychologists should follow the canons of experimental physics. In the field of cognitive development, the result was an interesting ambivalence. On the one hand, there was a great surge of interest in the sort of work that Piaget had pioneered (Flavell, 1963).

TABLE 2.1
Comparison of the Three Views of Knowledge and Their Embodiment in Philosophy, Psychology, and Education

Psychological Constructs	Empiricist	Rationalist	Sociohistorical
Knowledge	Repertoire of patterns or problems that an individual has learned to detect and operations that one can execute on them.	Structure created by the human mind and evaluated according to rational criteria, such as coherence, consistence, and parsimony.	Creation of a social group as it engages in its daily interaction and praxis and both adapts to and transforms the environment around it.
Learning	Process that generates knowledge; begins when one is exposed to a new pattern or problem and continues as one learns to respond to that pattern and generalize one's response to other contexts.	Process that takes place when the mind applies an existing structure to new experience to understand it.	Process of being initiated into the life of a group, so that one can assume a role in its daily praxis.
Development	Cumulative learning.	Long-term, transformational change that takes place in the structures into which new experience is assimilated.	The emergence and training of the symbolic and tool-using capacities that make social initiation possible.
Intelligence	Individual trait that sets a limit on the maximum rate at which cumulative learning takes place.	Adaptive capability that all children possess to apply and modify their existing cognitive structures; this capability grows with age (and is transformed).	Distributed across a group and intimately tied to the tools, artifacts, and symbolic systems that the group develops.
Motivation	Internal state that is subject to external influence and that affects the deployment of attention.	Natural tendencies that draw human beings of all ages toward epistemic activity.	Identification: i.e., the natural tendency of the young to see themselves as being like their elders and to look forward to the day when they assume their elders' role.
Education	Process by which the external conditions that affect children's learning and motivation are carefully arranged and sequenced so that socially desirable goals may be achieved.	Child-centered process: involves the provision of an environment that stimulates children's natural curiosity and constructive activity and promotes active reflection on the results of that activity.	Process by which a community takes charge of its young and moves them from a peripheral to a central role in its daily practices.

31

On the other hand, as Piaget (1963) noted, his theory was often read in North America with empiricist glasses. Thus, many investigators found the manner in which his theory was formulated to be excessively abstract, vague, and difficult to operationalize. They also found it too impregnated with general philosophical arguments and difficult to verify or falsify. They had problems with the substance of the theory as well: In particular, they thought that the general logical structures that Piaget hypothesized probably did not exist and that such cognitive structures as did exist were more likely to be the result of empirical learning than of "reflexive abstraction." Finally, they viewed Piaget's method of interviewing children as too clinical and subjective and his methods of sampling and data analysis as too unsystematic.

Subsequent Developments of the Empiricist Critique

During the decade that followed these first critiques, work on Piaget's theory in the empiricist tradition continued, and dissatisfaction mounted over the theory's assumptions about the role of logicomathematical structures in children's thought. Thus, when Gelman and Baillargeon reviewed the theory in 1983, they were able to cite at least five different strands of empirical research—all of which were by now well developed—that called Piaget's general view of these structures into question. The relevant data included the following: data on intertask correlations, which were often substantial but which did not assume a pattern that bore any obvious relation to the structures Piaget had hypothesized; data on the sequence of cognitive development, which rarely showed logicomathematical structures emerging before the conceptual competencies they were supposed to generate; data on preschool cognition, which often demonstrated the presence of logical competencies years before many Piagetians would have predicted; data on the training of concrete operational concepts, which likewise indicated that they could often be acquired during the preoperational period; and data on logical competencies in adolescence and adulthood, which often demonstrated the *absence* of logical competencies at an age where they would have long since been expected.

In suggesting which aspects of Piaget's theory were likely to prove lasting, Gelman and Baillargeon cited his emphasis on the active nature of children's cognitive processes, his suggestion that these processes were organized into coherent (although not necessarily logical) structures, and his elucidation of concepts such as assimilation and accommodation. Elsewhere, Gelman also mentioned the many tasks that Piaget's group had created and the provocative data that they had generated as significant and enduring contributions (Gelman, 1979). The aspects of Piaget's theory that were seen as having received *no* support and as being unlikely to last were his view of the role played by children's logicomathematical structures in their cognitive development and his view of the stage-like nature of children's cognitive growth. This general evaluation was pervasive in North America in the late 1970s and early 1980s. The dilemma with which it left investigators, however, was perplexing. How could they create a child development theory that eliminated the weaknesses of Piaget's theory without also eliminating its strengths? How could they characterize the development of children's conceptual understanding in a fashion that captured its specificity without also eliminating any ability to capture its overall shape? How could they create a weaker and less logic-bound characterization of children's conceptual structures, which did not also weaken the powerful heuristic utility of Piaget's account?

NEW MODELS OF CHILDREN'S CONCEPTUAL UNDERSTANDING

In response to this dilemma, several different lines of inquiry have been pursued in the last 2 decades. Four of these seem particularly important for understanding the other chapters in this book. The first of these (often referred to as neo-Piagetian theory) had its origins in an attempt to integrate the core assumptions of the empiricist and rationalist traditions. The other three had their origins in attempts to preserve the core assumptions of one of the three classical traditions, but to develop a theory that met the criticisms leveled at the existing theory from other quarters.

Conceptual Development as a Local Process, Limited by General Constraints

The first line of theoretical inquiry to emerge became known as neo-Piagetian theory. This enterprise involved a direct attempt to build a bridge between the assumptions and methods that had underpinned Piaget's research program and the assumptions and methods of empiricism. Neo-Piagetians accepted Piaget's position that children constructed their own understanding of the world and that reflexive abstraction played an important role in this process. They also accepted Piaget's contention that development was a very general process in which changes that cannot be tied to any form of specific external stimulation played an important role. Finally, they accepted the implicit methodological canons underlying Piaget's research, including the notion that the best way to develop a balanced view of children's intellectual capabilities was to examine their cognition on a broad spectrum of tasks, which spanned all the major categories of human understanding articulated by Kant, as well as any other categories on which reliable data were available.

At the same time, however, neo-Piagetians also agreed with empiricists that much of children's knowledge of the world was acquired in a fashion more piecemeal than that indicated by Piaget, and that local task factors, specific experience, and associative processes played a crucial role in this process. They also accepted the notion of examining and explaining children's performance in specific contexts in great detail and of modeling the process of learning. Finally, they accepted the necessity of defining their constructs and task situations in operational terms. The notion of a scheme, for example, was defined in the first neo-Piagetian system as an ordered pair of responses, s-r (Pascual-Leone, 1970).

Different neo-Piagetian theorists proposed somewhat different views of the general architecture of the cognitive system and the way in which that system develops. Nevertheless, everyone subscribed to a core set of propositions, which included the following: Children's cognitive development does show a general pattern of growth across many different domains, but not because of the existence of system-wide logicomathematical structures. Rather, the local structures that children construct are all subject to a common, system-wide constraint in attentional capacity, and this constraint gradually lifts with age. Different theorists focused on different aspects of children's capacity, such as their short-term memory, their working memory, or their information-processing speed (Biggs & Collis, 1982; Case, 1985; Demetriou, Efklides, & Platsidou, 1993; Fischer, 1980; Halford, 1982, 1993; Pascual-Leone, 1970). They also used different metrics for calibrating the load that any given task places on children's information-processing capacity. Finally, several theorists returned to Baldwin's notion about the neurological bases of these changes (Case, 1992; Fischer & Rose, 1993; Pascual-Leone, Hamstra, Benson, Khan, & Englund, 1990) and used mathematical techniques drawn from dynamic systems thought to model the sudden transitions that could take place as neurological and task-specific variables reached critical levels (Case, 1996; Fischer & Kennedy, 1997; Van der Maas & Molenaar, 1992; Van Geert, 1994).

Not surprisingly, the conservation task and the class inclusion tasks were two of those analyzed in great detail. According to Pascual-Leone (1969), these tasks were deliberately designed by Piaget to insure that children would activate a set of *misleading* schemes in response to the questions posed. Because the tasks contained these misleading features, the correct response could be generated only by active problem solving, not simply by the application of past learning. To overcome the misleading schemes activitated by these tasks, three general prerequisites were deemed necessary. First, children needed a learned repertoire of other schemes that were relevant to the task and that took account of the problem question as it was presented. Second, they needed an information-processing capacity of a particular size, typically a size that was not acquired until 6 to 10 years of age. Third, they needed a cognitive style of field independence that allowed them to integrate the various task-specific schemes and reach a logical conclusion, even in the face of the misleading scheme. Without such a style, their acquisition of conservation was considerably delayed.

In support of this analysis, neo-Piagetian theorists gathered several new kinds of data. Among the most important were these: (1) Tests of children's information-processing capacity do reveal an increase with age (Case, 1972b; Pascual-Leone, 1970). (2) Subjects whose information-processing capacity develops in an unusually rapid or slow manner show a corresponding acceleration or delay in acquiring new conceptual understandings of the sort studied by Piaget (Case, 1985; Crammond, 1992). (3) Subjects whose information-processing capacity is normal but who have a field-dependent cognitive style do not pass the most misleading of Piaget's tasks until 1 to 2 years after other children (Globerson, 1985; Pascual-Leone, 1969, 1974). Finally, the age at which conceptual tasks are passed can be reduced by 2 years by training studies that chunk two task-relevant (i.e., not misleading) schemes together (Case, 1972a). Conversely, it can be increased by 2 years by task modifications that increase the number of schemes that must be coordinated to arrive at a successful task solution (Case, 1972b; Pascual-Leone & Smith, 1969).

In keeping with the methods of the rationalist tradition, such demonstrations were attempted not just for logical tests such as conservation or classification. They were also attempted for a very broad range of other tasks. Finally, an attempt was made to analyze the data from the concept-learning studies cited earlier to show that they, too, showed a similar pattern. In this case, the suggestion was that—to focus on a single dimension—children had to abstract its relevance by focusing on at least two lower order schemes (e.g., square—no reward; circle—reward). For this reason, initial learning does not become rapid until children have an information-processing capacity of two units (which is typically acquired at 6 years). In addition, if children are to decenter from this dimension and focus on some other, less salient dimension, they need an an additional information-processing capacity of one unit. Because a capacity of this size does not become available until 7 or 8 years (Case, 1972b; Pascual-Leone, 1970), relearning does not normally become rapid until this age.

CONCEPTUAL DEVELOPMENT AS A SEQUENCE
OF THEORETICAL REVOLUTIONS

In contrast to the first line of work, which attempted to integrate the assumptions of the empiricist and rationalist traditions, the second line of work stayed squarely in the rationalist tradition itself. Rather than turning to information-processing theory for inspiration, theorists who took this second direction turned to two other sources: Chomsky's work on the acquisition of the structures of natural language and Kuhn's (1962) work on theory change in science. According to Chomsky (1957), the reason that children come to understand and speak language as rapidly as they do is that they have an innate language acquisition device: one that is modular in nature and that sensitizes them to the relevant features in their environment. According to Kuhn (1962), progress in science does not take place evenly but in spurts: Relatively short periods of revolutionary change are punctuated by long periods of "problem solving" in the general paradigm that any new theory affords.

Putting these two notions together, investigators in this second group suggested that the human mind is best conceived of as a loosely connected set of modules, each of which is specialized for executing a particular function in the same way as is the system for natural language (Carey, 1985; Fodor, 1982; Gardner, 1985). Certain theorists in this school believed that children possess "naive theories" of the world at birth, theories whose properties are universal (Spelke, 1988). Other theorists in this school emphasized the innate property of theories less strongly (see Wellman & Gelman, 1997). Regardless of the degree to which they took an innatist stance, however, theorists in this school agreed that, by the preschool years, children possess a coherent, albeit naive, theory of the world, which they then re-work as they enter their years of formal schooling (Carey, 1985). Such re-workings take place in one of two fashions: Existing concepts can be related in new ways as children gain experience with the world or experience in trying to understand adult explanations. (This change is analogous to the sort that occurs during stable periods in science, when new data are being gathered and the problems with the existing theoretical structure are being worked out.) Alternatively, existing conceptual structures can be radically restructured. This change corresponds to the one that takes place during scientific revolutions. When this second, revolutionary form of transformation occurs, three cognitive changes were hypothesized to take place in close synchrony: a change in the phenomena that children see as needing explanation in the domain; a change in the nature of what counts as an explanation in their eyes; and a change in the concepts that form the core of such explanations (Carey, 1985).

To understand this transformation, theorists in this school developed interesting new tasks. In one task, children were told about an imaginary new human organ (e.g., an omenta) and given some information about how it worked. They were then asked what other things they think might possess an omenta (A sheep? A worm? A cloud? A rock? Carey, 1985). In another task, they were told about a biological process with which they had some firsthand knowledge (e.g., breathing) and were asked about the range of objects to which this process applies (Does a worm breathe? Does a rock breathe? Do clouds breathe? Carey, 1988). In still another task, children were shown a situation in which one animal was made to look like another by the application of paint and were asked whether they thought it was "really" still the same kind of animal or whether it had changed into an animal that was more in line with its new appearance (Keil, 1986, 1994). These questions were interspersed with questions of the sort posed by Piaget in his work on children's naive concepts, namely, questions about what sorts of objects are and are not alive.

The general results from these first studies were similar across all the tasks. At the age of 4, children presumed that animals that most resemble humans tend to have the same organs and processes as humans, but that objects that do not look like humans (e.g., snakes) do not. They also assumed that, when the appearance of an animal changes, its behavior tends to change also. By the age of 8 to 10 years, children's view of the natural world was quite different. Now they presumed that most organs found in humans are found in all other animals and not in inanimate objects, regardless of their visual similarity to humans. They also presumed that plants share certain underlying processes with humans (e.g., the need for air) and that changes in the appearance of any living thing do not affect its behavior unless they affect these underlying biological processes.

The foregoing changes fit well with one set of changes documented by Piaget, the change from an "animistic" to a more "scientific" way of explaining natural phenomena. This change normally occurs somewhere between the ages of 5 and 7 years. Theorists in this school sided with Piaget, not with empiricists, in asserting that animistic responses involve a genuine *mis*understanding by children, not simply an absence of empirical experience with the object being talked about or a lack of familiarity with the type of question being posed (Carey, 1985). The theory–theory explanation for these changes was also *different* from Piaget's in two important respects: first, in the locus of conceptual change proposed and second, in the particular *kind* of domain-specific change proposed. Change did not occur as a function of some system-wide transformation, such as the development of "concrete operations" or an increase in information-processing capacity but instead was domain specific. An animistic response was not replaced by a more "logical" one; instead, a psychological theory was restricted in its domain of application to mental phenomena, and a new theory was constructed to account for phenomena biological in nature.

As was the case with neo-Piagetian theory, there was much variety among these theory-theorists, and their theories continued to evolve, in response to the diversity on the one hand and to new data (e.g., data showing early evidence of biological knowledge) on the other. One investigator who has contributed to this evolution is Keil, whose most recent work is summarized in chapter 3. (For a review of this and other recent work in this tradition, see Wellman & Gelman, 1997.)

Conceptual Development as the Acquisition of Expertise

A third view of conceptual structures proposed in the post-Piagetian era had its origins in the empiricist tradition in work on expert systems. Early studies of chess experts revealed—somewhat to everyone's surprise—that these individuals did not appear to have a set of general problem-solving heuristics or spatial memory more powerful than those of novices. To be sure, they can perform powerful feats of memory; for example, if shown a chessboard for only a few seconds, they can reproduce the entire configuration of pieces without error. However, this is true only if the pieces are placed in a configuration that they might typically assume in a real chess game. If the pieces are randomly placed on the board, the ability of experts to remember their positions is no better than that of novices (DeGroot, 1966). This study, and others like it, convinced many investigators that the most important feature that distinguishes chess experts from others is that they possess a huge repertoire of chess patterns that they can recognize (e.g., a horizontal line of squares with no piece on it) and good moves that they can make in response to these patterns (e.g., move a rook to this file). This notion of expertise fit well with attempts to simulate the performance of chess experts on a computer. Provided with about 10,000 chess patterns, computer programs did a very good job of simulating expert performance, beating human novices in the same general fashion and in the same number of moves as would a real expert and losing to grand masters in a similar fashion as well.

This early work on expertise was soon extended to domains of knowledge less perceptually based, such as medicine and physics. Studies in these domains also found that the distinguishing feature of experts was the vast network of specific knowledge that they possessed rather than a powerful set of general heuristics or strategies. Equipped with this specific knowledge, experts classified new problems in a fashion different from novices, typically with regard to their deep principles rather than their superficial features (Chi & Rees, 1983). Once the problems were classified in this fashion, experts solved them with *less* effort and *less* elaborate problem-solving processes than did novices. Again, attempts to create expert systems on a computer were more successful when they built a huge repertoire of specific knowledge and a powerful way of representing that knowledge than when they tried endowing the system with powerful problem-solving strategies. The work reported by Klahr in chapter 6 fits into this general category. Klahr's work has a number of interesting features. One of the most interesting is that—in addition to endowing children with thousands of elementary rules or "production systems" (ordered if–then pairs)—he also endows them with the capability for reviewing production systems that have recently fired in sequence and then extracting second-order regularities in them. In effect, his rules for finding these regularities consitute one possible version of the process that Piaget referred to as reflexive abstraction.

A second line of recent work in the empiricist tradition has taken a different perspective on children's cognition. Rather than construing children's minds as populated by a vast repertoire of if–then rules, this second group of theorists has represented children's minds as containing a vast networks of nodes, none of which individually has any symbolic content. The association strengths of the links connecting the nodes in the network are adjusted after every learning trial to optimize the fit between various stimulus and response conditions (McClelland, Rumelhart, & Hinton, 1987).

The general architecture that most such models presume is illustrated in Fig. 2.1. A layer of units is directly stimulated by input from the external world at the bottom of the figure. Another layer of units is responsible for producing some sort of output at the top of the figure. Between is a layer of hidden units, which are connected to the layers above and below them with facilitatory and inhibitory links of various strengths. To get such a network to respond in a rule-like fashion, one presents the system with a series of stimuli exemplifying a concept and forces it to make a choice. One then presents feedback on the adequacy of this choice, followed by another example. In short, one exposes the system to much the same situation that children were confronted with in the classic concept-learning experiments described at the beginning of the chapter.

Remarkably, such systems respond in much the same fashion as do young children: They gradually acquire the ability to correctly identify all exemplars of the concept in question. The learning algorithm with which connectionist systems are most frequently programmed and that enables them to accomplish this feat is called the backward propagation rule. This algorithm begins at the top level in the hierarchy (i.e., the level closest to the output) and adjusts the weights of the hidden units in such a fashion as to increase the likelihood that, if a new set of trials, which is the same as the set of trials to date, is produced, then the correct answer is given on as many trials as possible. From a mathematical point of view, the algorithm conducts a sort of nonlinear regression analysis by using the response to be predicted as the dependent variable.

This sort of model has proved remarkably successful in simulating certain types of perceptual and motor learning. It has also been applied to the simulation of complex cognitive behaviors, including those studied in the developmental literature. Three cognitive developmental tasks that have been modeled are the learning of the past tense in linguistics (Rumelhart & McClelland, 1987), the concept-learning task described at the beginning of the chapter (Kruske, 1992), and the balance beam task (McClelland, 1995). Although the model's fit to complex tasks such as the balance beam has been questioned, other learning algorithms have been proposed to improve this

Output patterns

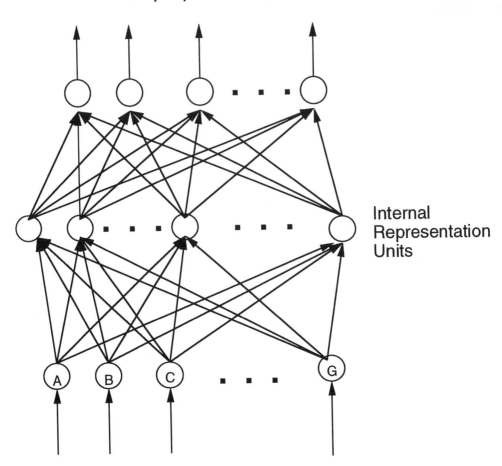

Internal
Representation
Units

Input patterns

FIG. 2.1. Pattern of nodes and connections used in simulated learning in a connectionist system. The nodes at the bottom are turned on by specific inputs. Those at the top are turned on by the weighted sum of inputs from below them. Any given connection may be either positive or negative. The values of the weights are adjusted in the course of learning to maximize the probability that a particular value of the input (say input detectors ABC on DEF off, and G on) generates a pattern of output that is considered "appropriate."

fit, including "cascade correlation" (Shultz, 1991) and a wake–sleep algorithm (Hinton, Dayan, Frey, & Neal, 1995). Finally, new approaches that combine elements of symbolic and connectionist models have been proposed (Siegler & Shraeger, 1997). Interestingly, these new approaches, like Klahr's, involve the postulation of a second-level system that abstracts features directly from the first (see Klahr & Wallace, 1976; Klahr, this volume). (For a review of these approaches, see Case, 1997.)

**Conceptual Development as Initiation
into a Community of Praxis**

The fourth line of inquiry in the post-Piagetian era had its roots in the sociohistoric tradition. The general starting point from which this work took off was Vygotsky's and Luria's demonstration that the performance of adults in a traditional agricultural setting, on a set of mnemonic and logical tasks, is a function of their degree of exposure to modern schooling. Several important questions were raised by this finding. First, how general is this effect? Does it apply across the board and produce a change in the full range of intellectual performance of which individuals are capable, or is it restricted to school-type tasks? Second, what aspect of schooling is responsible for producing this effect? Is it the acquisition of new symbol systems, such as those involved in literacy and numeracy (Olson, 1977)? Is it exposure to the new form of instruction, one that originally evolved to teach these systems (Greenfield & Bruner, 1966)? Is it the mastery of the formal systems of Western thought, the ones that the new symbolic systems were designed to represent?

A good deal of work has been devoted to pursuing these questions in recent years. Although many questions remain to be answered, the pattern of findings that has emerged is remarkably coherent. In the work devoted to analyzing the acquisition of literacy and its cognitive consequences, early studies suggested that the acquisition of literacy—both in a culture and in an individual child—produces a transformation in cognitive structures revolutionary in its consequences and applicable to the full range of activities in which a literate individual engages (Olson, 1977). Subsequent work, although continuing to reinforce the notion that literacy is important, has suggested that its effects are much more differentiated than previously thought, as a function of the local social, economic, and institutional contexts (Olson, 1994).

The classic study that led to this conclusion was conducted by Cole and his colleagues in Liberia, with the Vye. What made the Vye so interesting for Cole's purpose was that, some time during the late 18th century, they had developed a script of their own. Of even greater interest, this script is still taught today, in several different institutional contexts. In one context (secular schools), it is taught by means of a form of schooling that resembles the Western one; once acquired in this context, the script is then used for Western purposes. In another context (religious schools), the script is taught by means of chant and recitation, so that it can be used for further reading, memorization, and recitation of the Koran. In a third (family) context, it is taught informally, so that it can be used by relatives who are separated but want to stay in touch with each other by writing letters. Cole and his collaborators demonstrated that each of these contexts leads to a unique pattern of cognitive consequences. No universal transformation takes place that differentiates the thinking of those who are literate from those who are not. Rather, the particular transformation that takes place is a function of the context in which literacy is acquired and the use to which it is put (Scribner & Cole, 1981).

In the face of this and other evidence implicating such factors as economic exchange and authority as mediating variables (Street, 1984), even those who still viewed literacy as the gateway to higher cognitive functioning took a much more differentiated view of the process by which this transformation occurs and the aspects of literate practice that are crucial for it (Olson, 1994). The same view applies to the acquisition of other paper-based cultural systems, such as those involved in the use of arithmetic (Damerow, 1995; Hoyrup, 1994) or cartography (Olson, 1994, chap. 10). Although interesting cognitive consequences often do appear to be associated with the acquisition of these systems, the nature of the effects that they produce appears to be a function of the context and purpose of their use (e.g., the use of writing for scientific records and discourse in science). In short the effects appear to be the result of the cultural practices that literacy permits. By itself, literacy does not appear sufficient to produce a conceptual transformation.

Literacy is apparently also not *necessary* for the acquisition of sophisticated conceptual structures. Neisser (1976) was one of the first to make this point. Drawing on the work of Gladwyn (1970) with the Pulawatt, Neisser pointed out that the navigational competence of this group was remarkable. With the knowledge acquired from their elders, young Pulawatt men traveled thousands of miles across uncharted stretches of ocean in small outrigger canoes and arrived precisely at their intended destination. This remarkable achievement did not appear to depend on any formal logical system of the sort that Piaget postulated or on literacy or the use of modern Western artifacts such as a compass or a map. On the other hand, it clearly *did* depend on the acquisition of a complex knowledge structure: one that entailed principled and sophisticated understanding of celestial movements in the region and that utilized this understanding for navigational purposes (Oatley, 1977).

If the conceptual capabilities of adults are particular to their geographic locale and historical period, social transmission must play a vital role in the developmental process. In our own culture, of course, much of this transmission takes place through schooling. As mentioned previously, one early hypothesis about modern schools had to do with their decontextualized nature. The notion was that protracted formal schooling—which originally emerged as a vehicle for teaching children to read and write— also exposed children to a form of learning that was unique and extremely powerful, one in which the conceptual content that must be mastered was learned in a context remote from that in which it must ultimately be applied. In an essay on this topic, Greenfield and Bruner (1966) suggested that this decontextualized form of learning produced a corresponding decontextualization of children's thought, that is, the ability to apply that thought in a logical, principled fashion across a wide variety of contexts.

Just as the presumed superiority of Piaget's formal structures was challenged by cross-cultural investigations, however, so was the presumed superiority of formal schooling. The most widely cited studies were those that concerned the development of children's conceptual understanding of whole numbers and the base system that underlies their use. These understandings showed a typical pattern of development during the early school years. This development progressed from an understanding of how small whole numbers work to an understanding of groupings and exchanges to an understanding of the principles underlying such operations as multiplication and division (Resnick, 1989). If formal schooling had any advantage, it should manifest itself in this precise and relatively decontextualized domain, but this did not appear to be the case. Studies with unschooled children who worked as street vendors in Brazil showed that these children's understanding of the number system proceeded normally in such unschooled contexts (Carraher, Carraher, & Schliemann, 1985). Indeed, children who grew up in this environment often displayed an understanding of numerical principles and operations *superior* to that displayed by children who learned mathematics in school. These latter children sometimes applied the algorithms that they learned in a rote or unprincipled fashion, whereas children who grew up as street vendors rarely if ever made mistakes of this sort. If the problem that was presented was *unique* to a schooled setting (as is the case for certain kinds of ratio problems), schooled children did show some competencies superior to those of street vendors (Saxe, 1988). By and large, however, the informal learning in the market was every bit as powerful as, and perhaps more powerful than, the decontextualized learning provided by the academy.

These results, and others like them, have been used by Lave and her colleagues (Lave, 1988; Lave & Wenger, 1991) to argue for the superiority of contextually based "apprenticeship" over formal learning. A major feature of apprenticeship is that it involves some sort of "scaffolding" of cognition, a concept first explicated by Wood, Bruner, and Ross (1976).

Rogoff (1990) has suggested that most intellectual comptencies can be seen as acquired by a scaffolding process. Other investigators have looked at naturally occurring variation in a culture in this and other social processes of the sort that Vygotsky specified, processes such as the internalization of affective regulation via inner speech (Diaz, Neal, & Amaya-Williams, 1992), tutoring (Brown & Campione, 1994; Inglis & Biemiller, 1997), and collaboration (Damon & Phelps, 1993). (For a review of recent work in these areas, see Rogoff, 1990.)

To summarize: early workers in the sociohistoric tradition accepted Vygotsky's notion that children's conceptual development depended on the acquisition of an intellectual and physical technology, one normally acquired in school and dependent on the acquisition of literacy and numeracy. Recent workers in this tradition have continued the emphasis on the importance of mastering the intellectual technology that the culture provides, but they have painted a picture a good deal more complex and context specific. Not only is there no formal structure that applies across all contexts, but literate structures are not necessarily superior to other structures and may even lead to practices that are less rather than more sophisticated. The same picture holds for the institutions with which literacy has been associated and the historical practices that have developed in them. Although they may offer certain advantages, they may also offer certain disadvantages that are equally important to understand.

Comparing the New Models
and Abstracting Common Principles

As is no doubt apparent, the epistemological differences that divide different schools of thought in the post-Piagetian era are still considerable, as are the different schools' pictures of the process of conceptual growth. In view of the continuing commitment to different epistemologies, it is perhaps not surprising that the methods employed to explore the different positions also continue to be distinctive, that each still looks to different disciplines and metaphors for its inspiration, and that each group occasionally fires methodological broadsides across the bows of another (see Klahr, chap. 6, this volume).

For expertise-theorists, the growth of knowledge is still largely seen as being under the control of local learning factors, and the relation between learning and development is still seen as the one indicated under the empiricist rubric in Table 2.1. This view applies whether the favored models are symbolic or connectionist. What has changed, however, largely as a result of developments in cognitive science, is the sophistication of the knowledge models that can be proposed in this tradition and the ease with which these models can be simulated on a computer.

A similar point may be made for theory-theorists. Theorists in this school still largely view children's knowledge as qualitatively different from that of adults and still subscribe to most of the general propositions listed under the rationalist rubric in Table 2.1. Their attempts to model the structure of children's conceptual understanding have, however, been greatly enriched by contemporary analyses of theory change in science and by the new database concerning foundational knowledge in young children.

Contemporary sociohistoric theorists still largely see conceptual change in the fashion outlined in the table, too. As a result of developments in cognitive anthropology, however, their models have become less Eurocentric and more contextualized. Their analysis of cognitive benefits and drawbacks has also become more balanced, and they have begun to examine the socialization processes that facilitate different forms of cognition in much greater detail.

Of the four groups reviewed, neo-Piagetian theorists have made the most explicit attempt to cross the epistemological boundaries indicated in the table. Even in this group, however, most theorists still lean strongly in either the empiricist or rationalist direction. The principal factors that unite them are their commitment to the notion that task and domain-specific factors in development must be modeled with rigor and precision, their commitment to the notion that—notwithstanding its specificity—development is still strongly influenced by factors of a general-maturational nature, and their commitment to the notion that the dynamic interplay of these factors propels development through a set of powerful reorganizations that cannot simply be reduced to cumulative learning.

To say that large differences still separate the different traditions is not to say that the process of dialogue has had no effect. On the contrary, if we look at the general structure of the new theories in each tradition and compare them with their predecessors, we see a number of important points of convergence. In contrast to the state of affairs 20 years earlier, contemporary theorists in each school are now agreed that the notion of a system-wide cognitive structure should be replaced by a notion of more specific structures, that children's cognitive structures should not be modeled as systems of logical operations but as systems for making meaning (Piaget also made this move in his later years [Piaget & García, 1991]), and that children's physical and social experience should be assigned a much more central role in explaining the process of structural change than Piaget's theory gave it.

For theorists in the empiricist tradition, the move to this middle ground has meant a move away from an atomistic view of knowledge toward a view in which broad structural and disciplinary coherencies are given more emphasis and some mechanism for reflecting on them is acknowledged. For theorists in the rationalist tradition, the move to this middle ground has meant a move away from system-wide analyses toward a detailed consideration of factors that are domain specific. For theorists in the sociohistoric tradition, the new position has entailed a similar movement: away from a general unilinear model of social, economic, and intellectual change toward a model in which all three of these variables are viewed in more particular terms.

In light of the trend toward greater convergence, we may see a still greater convergence in the future. This direction is the one that I have pursued in my own work. Starting with a point of view that was generally classified as neo-Piagetian, I have attempted to show that a Piagetian notion of general conceptual structure, as well as Baldwinian notions of attentional capacity and cortical integration, are necessary to explain the full pattern of human intellectual development. When these central conceptual structures are examined in detail, they are also seen to differ from Piaget's in ways that have been proposed in the other traditions. They are domain or module specific or both, as suggested by contemporary theory-theorists. They can be modeled as semantic networks as proposed by contemporary empiricists. They contain content that is culturally specific and are hence open to influence by schooling and social class as contemporary sociohistoric theorists have suggested. Finally, they are created by a hierarchical learning process that includes important associative as well as conscious, reflexive components (Case, 1996).

Readers interested in this particular synthesis are referred to the recent monograph that my colleagues and I have published (Case & Okamoto, 1996). The general points with which I would like to end, however, are ones that transcend this or any other particular attempt at integration. Stated in their simplest form, they are as follows: Piaget's contribution to the rationalist tradition was so monumental that it temporarily obscured the important contributions that had been made to that tradition in the past, as well as contemporary and previous contributions made in other traditions. In the post-Piagetian era, there has been a reflowering of interest in these other traditions, as well as a renewed interest in the rationalist tradition, in certain ideas that Piaget had inherited from Baldwin, but had deemphasized. The current era is thus particularly lively and is characterized by exciting developments in each of these traditions in isolation, as well as by an increased interest in drawing all three traditions together, to forge a vision of children's conceptual growth that is multidimensional yet coherent.

REFERENCES

Baldwin, J. M. (1968). *The development of the child and of the race.* New York: Kelly. (Original work published 1894)

Beilin, H. (1983). The new functionalism and Piaget's program. In E. K. Scholnick (Ed.), *New trends in conceptual representation* (pp. 3–40). Hillsdale, NJ: Lawrence Erlbaum Associates.

Biggs, J., & Collis, K. (1982). *Evaluating the quality of learning: The SOLO taxonomy.* New York: Academic Press.

Binet, A. (1900). *La Suggestibilité.* Paris: Schleicher et frères.

Brown, A. L., & Campione, J. C. (1994). Guided discovery in a community of learners. In K. McGilly (Ed.), *Classroom lessons* (pp. 229–272). Cambridge, MA: MIT Press.

Bruner, J. S., Goodnow, J. J., & Austin, G. A. (1956). *A study in thinking.* New York: Wiley.

Carraher, T. N., Carraher, D. W., & Schliemann, A. D. (1985). Mathematics in the streets and schools. *British Journal of Developmental Psychology, 3,* 21–29.

Carey, S. (1985). *Conceptual change in childhood.* Cambridge, MA: MIT Press.

Carey, S. (1988). Reorganization of knowledge in the course of acquisition. In S. Strauss (Ed.), *Ontogeny, phylogeny, and historical development* (pp. 1–27). New York: Ablex.

Case, R. (1972a). Learning and development: A neo-Piagetian interpretation. *Human Development, 15,* 339–358.

Case, R. (1972b). Validation of a neo-Piagetian capacity construct. *Journal of Experimental Child Psychology, 14,* 287–302.

Case, R. (1985). *Intellectual development: Birth to adulthood.* New York: Academic Press.

Case, R. (1992). The role of the frontal lobes in the regulation of cognitive development. *Brain and Cognition, 20,* 51–73.

Case, R. (1996). Modelling the dynamic interplay between general and specific change in children's conceptual understanding. In R. Case & Y. Okamoto, The role of central conceptual structures in the development of children's thought, *Monographs of the Society for Research in Child Development, 61* (Serial No. 246; pp. 156–188).

Case, R. (1997). The development of conceptual structures. In D. Kuhn & R. S. Siegler (Eds.), *Handbook of child psychology, Vol. 2: Perception, cognition, and language* (pp. 745–800). New York: Wiley.

Case, R., & Okamoto, Y. (1996). The role of central conceptual structures in the development of children's thought. *Monographs of the Society for Research in Child Development, 61* (Serial No. 246).

Chi, M. T. H., & Rees, E. (1983). A learning framework for development. *Contributions to Human Development, 9,* 71–107.

Chomsky, N. (1957). *Syntactic structures.* The Hague, Netherlands: Mouton.

Cole, M. (1991). Cognitive development and formal schooling: The evidence from cross cultural research. In L. C. Moll (Ed.), *Vygotsky and education: Instructional implications and applications of sociohistorical psychology* (pp. 89–110). New York: Cambridge University Press.

Cole, M. (1997). *Cultural psychology.* Cambridge, MA: Harvard University press.

Cole, M., Gay, J., Glick, J. A., & Sharp, D. D. (1971). *The cultural context of learning and thinking.* New York: Basic Books.

Crammond, J. (1992). Analyzing the basic developmental processes of children with different types of learning disability. In R. Case (Ed.), *The mind's staircase: Exploring the conceptual underpinnings of children's thought and knowledge* (pp. 285–302). Hillsdale, NJ: Lawrence Erlbaum Associates.

Damerow, P., Englund, R. K., & Nelson, H. J. (1995). The first representations of number and the development of the number concept. In R. Damerow (Ed.), *Abstraction and representation: Essays on the cultural evolution of thinking* (pp. 275–297). Dordrecht: Kluwer.

Damon, W. (1997). Learning and resistance: When developmental theory meets educational practice. In E. Amsel & K. Renninger (Eds.), *Change and development: Issues of theory, method, and application* (pp. 287–310). Mahwah, NJ: Lawrence Erlbaum Associates.

Damon, W., & Phelps, E. (1993). Peer collaboration as a context for cognitive growth. In S. Strauss & L. Landsmann (Eds.), *Culture, cognition, and schooling.* Hillsdale, NJ: Lawrence Erlbaum Associates.

DeGroot, A. (1966). Perception and memory versus thought: Some old ideas and recent findings. In B. Kleinmuntz (Ed.), *Problem solving.* New York: Wiley.

Demetriou, A., Efklides, A., & Platsidou, M. (1993). The architecture and dynamics of developing mind. *Monographs of the Society for Research in Child Development, 58* (5–6, Serial No. 234).

Diaz, R. M., Neal, C. J., & Amaya-Williams, M. (1992). The social origins of self-regulation. In L. Moll (Ed.), *Vygotsky and education*. New York: Cambridge University Press.

Fischer, K. W. (1980). A theory of cognitive development: The control and construction of hierarchies of skills. *Psychological Review, 87,* 477–531.

Fischer, K. W., & Rose, S. P. (1993). Development of coordination of components in brain and behavior: A framework for theory and research. In G. Dawson & K. W. Fischer (Eds.), *Human behavior and the developing brain* (pp. 3–66). New York: Guilford Press.

Fischer, K. W., & Kennedy, B. (1997). Tools for analyzing the many shapes of development: The case of self-in-relationships in Korea. In K. A. Renninger & E. Amsel (Eds.), *Change and development: Issues of theory, method, and application* (pp. 117–152). Mahwah, NJ: Lawrence Erlbaum Associates.

Flavell, J. H. (1963). *The developmental psychology of Jean Piaget*. Princeton, NJ: Van Nostrand.

Fodor, J. (1982). *The modularity of mind*. Cambridge, MA: MIT Press.

Gardner, H. (1985). *The mind's new science: A history of the cognitive revolution*. New York: Basic Books.

Gelman, R. (1979). Why we will continue to read Piaget. *Genetic Epistemologist, 8*(4), 1–3.

Gelman, R., & Baillargeon, R. (1983). A review of some Piagetian concepts. In P. H. Mussen (Ed.), *Carmichael's handbook of child development* (4th ed., Vol. 3, pp. 167–230). New York: Wiley.

Gholson, B. (1985). *The cognitive developmental basis of human learning: Studies in hypothesis testing*. New York: Academic Press.

Gladwyn, T. (1970). *East is a big bird: Navigation and logic on a Pulawatt atoll*. Cambridge, MA: Harvard University Press.

Globerson, T. (1985). Field dependence/independence and mental capacity: A developmental approach. *Developmental Review, 5,* 261–273.

Goodnow, J. J. (1962). A test of milieu differences with some of Piaget's tasks. *Psychological Monographs, 36* (Whole number 555).

Greenfield, P. M. (1966). On culture and conservation. In J. S. Bruner, R. R. Oliver, & P. M. Greenfield (Eds.), *Studies in cognitive growth* (pp. 225–256). New York: Wiley.

Greenfield, P. M., & Bruner, J. S. (1966). Culture and cognitive growth. *International Journal of Psychology, 1,* 89.

Greenfield, P. M., Reich, L. M., & Oliver, R. R. (1966). On culture and equivalence, II. In J. S. Bruner, R. R. Oliver, & P. M. Greenfield (Eds.), *Studies in cognitive growth* (pp. 270–319). New York: Wiley.

Halford, G. S. (1982). *The development of thought*. Hillsdale, NJ: Lawrence Erlbaum Associates.

Halford, G. S. (1993). *Children's understanding: The development of mental models*. Hillsdale, NJ: Lawrence Erlbaum Associates.

Hinton, G. E., Dayan, P., Frey, B. J., & Neal, R. M. (1995). The "wake–sleep" algorithm for unsupervised neural networks. *Science, 268,* 1158–1161.

Hoyrup, H. (1994). Varieties of mathematical discourse in pre-modern socio-cultural contexts: Mesopotamia, Greece, and the Latin middle ages. In J. Hoyrup (Ed.), *In measure, number and weight: Studies in mathematics and culture* (pp. 1–22). Albany: State University of New York Press.

Hume, D. (1955). *An inquiry concerning human understanding*. New York: Bobbs-Merrill. (First published in 1748)

Inglis, A., & Biemiller, A. (1997, March). *Fostering self-direction in mathematics: A Cross-Age Tutoring Program*. Paper presented at the annual conference of the American Educational Research Association, Chicago, IL.

Inhelder, B., & Piaget, J. (1958). *The growth of logical thinking from childhood to adolescence.* New York: Basic Books.

Inhelder, B., & Piaget, J. (1964). *The early growth of logic in the child.* London: Routledge & Kegan Paul.

Kant, I. (1961). *Critique of pure reason* (F. Max Müller, Trans.). New York: Doubleday Anchor. (First published in 1781)

Kaufmann, W. (1980). *Discovering the mind: Goethe, Kant and Hegel.* New York: McGraw-Hill.

Keil, F. C. (1986). On the structure-dependent nature of stages of cognitive development. In I. Levin (Ed.), *Stage and structure: Reopening the debate* (pp. 144–163). Norwood, NJ: Ablex.

Keil, F. C. (1994). The birth and nurturance of concepts by domains: The origins of concepts of living things. In L. A. Hirschfeld & S. A. Gelman (Eds.), *Mapping the mind: Domain specificity in cognition and culture* (pp. 234–254). New York: Cambridge University Press.

Kendler, H. H., & Kendler, T. S. (1962). Vertical and horizontal processes in problem solving. *Psychological Review, 69,* 1–16.

Kendler, T. S., & Kendler, H. H. (1967). Experimental analysis of inferential behavior in children. In L. P. Lipsitt & C. C. Spiker (Eds.), *Advances in children's development and behavior* (pp. –). New York: Academic Press.

Kendler, T. S., Kendler, H. H., & Wells, D. (1960). Reversal and nonreversal shifts in nursery school children. *Journal of Comparative and Physiological Psychology, 53,* 83–88.

Klahr, D., & Wallace, J. G. (1976). *Cognitive development: An information-processing view.* Hillsdale, NJ: Lawrence Erlbaum Associates.

Kruse, J. K. (1992). ALCOVE: An exemplar-based connectionist model of category learning. *Psychological Review, 99,* 22–44.

Kuhn, T. S. (1962). *The structure of scientific revolutions.* Chicago: University of Chicago Press.

Lave, J. (1988). *Cognition in practice.* New York: Cambridge University Press.

Lave, J., & Wenger, E. (1991). *Situated learning: Legitimate peripheral participation.* Cambridge, MA: Cambridge University Press.

Luria, A. R. (1966). *Higher cortical functions in man.* New York: Basic Books.

Luria, A. R. (1976). *Cognitive development: Its cultural and social foundations.* Cambridge, MA: Cambridge University Press.

McClelland, J. L. (1995). A connectionist perspective on knowledge and development. In T. J. Simon & G. S. Halford (Eds.), *Developing cognitive competence: New approaches to process modeling* (pp. 157–204). Hillsdale, NJ: Lawrence Erlbaum Associates.

McClelland, J. L., Rumelhart, D. E., & Hinton, G. E. (1987). *The appeal of parallel distributed processing: Explorations in the microstructure of cognition* (Vol 1). Cambridge, MA: MIT Press.

Miller, G. A., Galanter, E., & Pribram, K. H. (1960). *Plans and the structure of behavior.* New York: Holt, Rinehart & Winston.

Mumbauer, C. C., & Odom, R. D. (1967). Variables affecting the performance of preschool children in intradimensional, reversal and extradimensional shifts. *Journal of Experimental Psychology, 75,* 180–187.

Neisser, U. (1976). *Cognition and reality: Principles and implications of cognitive psychology.* San Francisco: Freeman.

Newell, A., Shaw, J. C., & Simon, H. A. (1958). Elements of a theory of human problem solving. *Psychological Review, 65,* 151–166.

Oatley, K. (1977). Inference, navigation and cognitive maps. In P. N. Johnson-Laird & P. Waron (Eds.), *Thinking: Readings in cognitive science.* Cambridge, England: Cambridge University Press.

Olson, D. R. (1977). From utterance to text. *Harvard Educational Review, 47,* 257–281.

Olson, D. R. (1994). *The world on paper: The conceptual and cognitive implications of writing and reading.* New York: Cambridge University Press.

Osler, S. F., & Kofsky, E. (1966). Structure and strategy in concept attainment. *Journal of Experimental Child Psychology, 4,* 198–209.

Overton, W. (1984). World views and their influence on psychological theory and research: Kuhn-Lakatos-Laudon. In H. W. Reese (Ed.), *Advances in child development and behavior.* New York: Academic Press.

Overton, W. F. (1990). The structure of developmental theory. In P. van Geer & L. P. Mos (Eds.), *Annals of theoretical psychology.* New York: Plenum.

Pascual-Leone, J. (1969). *Cognitive development and cognitive style.* Unpublished doctoral dissertation, University of Geneva, Geneva, Switzerland.

Pascual-Leone, J. (1970). A mathematical model for the transition rule in Piaget's development stages. *Acta Psychologica, 32,* 301–345.

Pascual-Leone, J. (1974, July). *A neo-Piagetian process-structural model of Witkin's psychological differentiation.* Paper presented at the symposium on cross-cultural studies of psychological differentiation in the meeting of the Internal Association for Cross-Cultural Psychology, Kingston, Ontario, Canada.

Pascual-Leone, J., Hamstra, N., Benson, N., Khan, I., & Englund, R. (1990). *The P300 event-related potential and mental capacity.* Paper presented at the fourth international evoked potentials symposium, Toronto, Ontario, Canada.

Pascual-Leone, J., & Smith, J. (1969). The encoding and decoding of symbols by children. A new experimental paradigm and a neo-Piagetian theory. *Journal of Experimental Child Psychology, 8,* 328–355.

Piaget, J. (1960). *The psychology of intelligence.* Totowa, NJ: Littlefield Adams.

Piaget, J. (1963). Forward. In J. H. Flavell (Ed.), *The developmental psychology of Jean Piaget.* New York: Van Nostrand.

Piaget, J. (1970). Piaget's theory. In P. H. Mussen (Ed.), *Carmichael's handbook of child development* (pp. 703–732). New York: Wiley.

Piaget, J., & García, R. (1991). *Toward a logic of meanings.* Hillsdale, NJ: Lawrence Erlbaum Associates.

Resnick, L. B. (1989). Developing mathematical knowledge. *American Psychologist, 44,* 162–169.

Rogoff, B. (1990). *Apprenticeship in thinking. Cognitive development in social context.* New York: Oxford University Press.

Rohwer, W. D. (1970). Implications of cognitive development for education. In P. H. Mussen (Ed.), *Carmichael's handbook of child development* (pp. 1379–1454). New York: Wiley.

Rumelhart, D. E., & McLelland, J. C. (1987). Learning the past tenses of English verbs: Implicit rules or parallel distributed processing? In B. MacWhinney (Ed.), *Mechanisms of language acquisition* (pp. 195–248). Hillsdale, NJ: Lawrence Erlbaum Associates.

Saxe, G. (1988). The mathematics of street vendors. *Child Development, 59,* 1415–1425.

Scribner, S., & Cole, M. (1981). *The psychology of literacy.* Cambridge, MA: Harvard University Press.

Shultz, T. Z. (1991). Simulating stages of human cognitive development with connectionist models. In L. Biumbaum & G. Collins (Eds.), *Machine learning: Proceedings of the eighth international workshop* (pp. 105–109). San Mateo, CA: Morgan Kauffman.

Siegler, R. (1978). The origins of scientific reasoning. In R. S. Siegler (Ed.), *Children's thinking: What develops* (pp. 109–149). Hillsdale, NJ: Lawrence Erlbaum Associates.

Siegler, R. S. (1997). *Emergent minds.* Cambridge, MA: Cambridge University Press.

Siegler, R. S., & Shraeger, J. (1997, April). *A model of strategy discovery.* Paper presented at the biennial meeting of the Society for Research in Child Development, Washington, DC.

Spelke, E. S. (1988). Where perceiving ends and thinking begins: The apprehension of objects in infancy. In A. Yonas (Ed.), *Perceptual development in infancy: The Minnesota symposia in child psychology* (pp. 197–234). Hillsdale, NJ: Lawrence Erlbaum Associates.

Street, B. (1984). *Literacy in theory and practice.* New York: Cambridge University Press.

Thorndike, E. L. (1914). *Educational psychology* (Vol 3). New York: Teachers College Press, Columbia University.

Van der Maas, H. L. J., & Molenaar, P. C. M. (1992). Stagewise cognitive development: An application of catastrophe theory. *Psychological Review, 99,* 395–417.

Van Geert, P. (1994). *Dynamic systems of development: Change between complexity and chaos.* Hemel Hempstead, Herefordshire, England: Harvester Wheatsheaf.

Vygotsky, L. S. (1962). *Thought and language* (E. Hanfmann and G. Vaker, Trans.). Cambridge, MA: MIT Press. (Original work published in 1934)

Watson, J. S. (1914). *Behavior, an introduction to comparative psychology.* New York: Holt, Rinehart & Winston.

Wellman, H. M., & Gelman, S. A. (1997). Knowledge acquisition. In D. Kuhn & R. S. Siegler (Eds.), *Handbook of child psychology, Vol 2: Perception, cognition, and language* (pp. 523–574). New York: Wiley.

White, S. H. (1967). Some general outlines of the matrix of developmental changes between five and seven years. *Bulletin of the Orton Society, 20,* 41–57.

Wood, D. J., Bruner, J. S., & Ross, G. (1976). The role of tutoring in problem-solving. *Journal of Child Psychology and Psychiatry, 17,* 89–100.

Chapter 3

A New Foundation for Cognitive Development in Infancy: The Birth of the Representational Infant

Andrew N. Meltzoff
M. Keith Moore
University of Washington, Seattle

Philosophers and psychologists have historically made assumptions about the initial state of the human mind because there were no tools to investigate it empirically. These assumptions colored their theories about human nature. One reason for the excitement about modern infancy research is that long-held assumptions can now be tested. The new findings have revealed many surprising facts and have provoked considerable discussion. They have implications reaching beyond the study of infancy and impact developmental psychology, cognitive science, and neuroscience in general.

What has infancy research discovered? Two phenomena are showcase examples: infant imitation and object permanence. These phenomena stand out for three reasons. First, they concern two of the most important entities in an infant's world: people and things. Second, Piagetian theory makes explicit predictions about these domains, and modern empirical research bears directly on the classical framework. Third, the phenomena have engendered competing interpretations by different schools of human development.

At nearly every scientific meeting of developmental psychologists, one hears two diametrically opposed views on the recent findings in infancy:

Professor Rampant Nativist: The findings on early imitation and object permanence (and much else) agree. Classical Piagetian theory is dead. There is no need for an elaborate developmental theory because infants are born with the knowledge that we used to think developed.

Professor Status Quo: Whatever is shown by these recent empirical tests, it is about something else, something different from what Piaget was after. Let's not throw out the baby with the bathwater. It doesn't seem to me that we have to revise all that much about the sensory-motor period.

Our aim is to break this impasse. In this chapter, we articulate a new way of looking at the problem. Our position embraces innate structure while being thoroughly developmental. It elevates the power of infants' perception and their capacity for representation, yet is conservative about attributing complex concepts to young infants. Against Professor *SQ*, we argue that modern research has demonstrated that young infants, even newborns, cannot be reduced to a collection of sensory-motor habits. We think that there is a powerful representational capacity before language develops. Against Professor *RN*, we argue that the modern findings do not refute, but rather underscore, conceptual change in infancy. In our laboratory, we have found that newborns are not as competent as 18-month-olds or even 9-month-olds, and we think that the observed changes cannot be attributed to the lifting of performance constraints or to maturational changes. We think they are due to genuine conceptual development in the preverbal period.

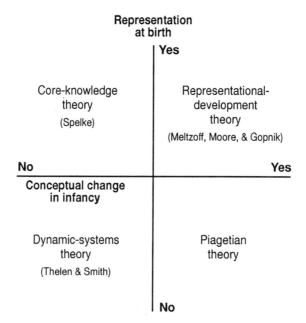

FIG. 3.1. A simplified theory space distinguishing four contemporary views of infancy on the dimensions of representational capacity and conceptual development.

Figure 3.1 places our position in a theory space that distinguishes four theories of infancy according to their views on early representation and conceptual change. Obviously a more complex space could be envisioned, but this is sufficient to make the point.

The classical Piagetian position is located in Quadrant D. Piaget's theory holds that infants have no representational system at birth and that a profound restructuring occurs in the way that infants understand the world over the first 18 months of life. Spelke's core-knowledge thesis is the extreme opposite: It holds that there is innate representation and no conceptual change; the core concepts of adults are present in infants in unchanging form (Spelke, 1994; Spelke, Breinlinger, Macomber, & Jacobson, 1992). Thelen and Smith's (1994) dynamic systems theory shares the Piagetian view that there is no early representation, but differs from Piaget in eschewing conceptual change in infancy. Thelen and Smith are far more conservative than Piaget because they do not go beyond the sensory-motor coordinations of infants and do not see these as giving rise to concepts (the very entities whose origins and development Piaget was striving to explain with genetic epistemology). Although Piaget discussed mental structures that underlie and generate apparently diverse surface behavior, Thelen and Smith focus more on the surface behavior itself. For them, all problems are unique; the account of infants' response to these problems should be in terms of the dynamics of each specific situation. To explain infant behavior at a conceptual level is misguided: In their view, there is behavioral reorganization but not conceptual change in infancy.

Our position is located in Quadrant B. It postulates both an initial representational capacity *and* conceptual change in the preverbal period. We call our view the representational-development theory because it envisions a rich initial state with a qualitative restructuring of representation as a function of interaction with the world. Our position is a particular instance of a broader theory of cognitive and linguistic development that has been put forward elsewhere (Gopnik & Meltzoff, 1997).

To illustrate our viewpoint, consider the two test cases of object permanence and imitation. We do not think that there is an innate understanding of object permanence as advocated by Spelke. No one, not even modern nativists, has reported manual search for objects hidden by occluders before 8 months, the same age discovered by Piaget (1954). This finding does not easily fit with the core-knowledge thesis. Various attempts have been made to reconcile this fact; for example, younger infants have innate knowledge about permanence but cannot use this knowledge in action (Spelke, 1994). We think that the change in search behavior marks a significant development in infants' understanding about objects that are invisible and cannot be fully explained by changes in motor skills, means–ends capacity, memory, or the integration of innate knowledge into the

action system. Despite this developmental view of infant object permanence, we think that the findings on early infant imitation imply a rich
initial state. Young infants can imitate facial gestures (demonstrating early
intermodal coordination) and even more importantly can perform deferred imitation, which demonstrates a form of nonverbal representation
and recall memory. A capacity for intermodal coordination and representation seems to be available at birth.

SKETCH OF A NEW FOUNDATION

We cannot get new theorizing off the ground if the dichotomy between a
theory's being either nativist or developmental is allowed to creep in. Every
theory of development must make some commitments about infants'
original state. This state may be sensory-motor reflexes without representation (as Piaget postulated) or something more sophisticated (as we
postulate). In either case, there is an initial state from which development
proceeds. The issue is not either-or, but specifying both the initial structure
and what develops.

In this chapter, we adduce data and arguments to show that the youngest
infants are not confined to a purely sensory–motor level of functioning.
They use what we call *representational persistence*. The evidence for such early
representation derives primarily from recent findings about imitation, especially deferred imitation during the 1st year of life, but also from recent
work on objects. We show that infants pick up information from observation
alone, before and without acting on objects. This information persists over
lengthy delays and can be accessed in the absence of the original stimulus.

We next argue that young infants are deeply concerned about maintaining the numerical identity of people and objects in a dynamically changing
world. Numerical identity refers to an object's being the self-same one over
encounters in space and time. One of infants' first cognitive acts is to
determine whether a person or thing is the same individual over different
encounters—the idea that James (1890) colorfully captured as "Hollo!
thingumbob again!" In our view, the criteria that infants use to determine
numerical identity changes with development. Spatiotemporal parameters
are the earliest criteria used for numerical identity. Stationary objects are
initially identified by their place (location in space) and moving objects by
their trajectory (speed and direction of movement). With development, two
further identity criteria are coordinated with the spatiotemporal ones. Infants
begin to use featural criteria (what an object looks like) and functional criteria
(what it does and how it can be used). Interestingly, infants' concern with
identity cuts across both people and things (Meltzoff & Moore, 1992, 1995,
1998). The evidence suggests that infants use imitation to probe whether a
person before them is the same individual whom they previously encoun-

tered; analogously, they use manipulatory actions to probe whether an inanimate object is the same one that they encountered previously. Finally, we offer a reinterpretation of Baillargeon's and Spelke's reports of young infants' reactions to object disappearances (e.g., Baillargeon, 1993; Baillargeon, Spelke, & Wasserman, 1985). Rather than being based on an innate or early-developing object permanence, infants' visual responses can be accounted for by mechanisms for keeping track of object identity. The primary identity criteria are spatiotemporal: trajectory for moving objects and place for stationary ones. Using such spatiotemporal parameters allows infants to function both prospectively, predicting where and when the same object will be seen, and retrospectively, reidentifying objects after movements or breaks in perceptual contact. Because of this prospective functioning, discrepancies from expected outcomes can occur and recruit increased attention. We argue that such discrepancies are sufficient to account for the preferential-looking effects that have been reported for occlusion events in early infancy. Object permanence is not necessary.

One of Piaget's most important legacies was his insistence on cognitive development in infancy. The modern empirical findings have revealed a more sophisticated initial state than Piaget had assumed, but have also underscored psychogenesis. In our view, the ability to act on the basis of stored representations is the starting point, not the crowning achievement, of psychological development in infancy. By making this shift, we can understand a host of recent empirical findings, including modern work on imitation and object permanence, without attributing to young infants complex reasoning about the existence and locations of invisible entities— an understanding that Piaget rightly saw as a developmental construction.[1]

DEFERRED IMITATION AND REPRESENTATION

In classical developmental theory, deferred imitation is inextricably bound to the development of mental representation. The onset of deferred imitation was thought to be 18 months of age, during Stage 6 of Piaget's sensory-motor period (Piaget, 1962), but new empirical findings have demonstrated that deferred imitation does not first arise at the end of infancy. This discovery is of interest because it potentially illuminates the character of early representation. As with any new behavioral "fact," what is most important is not its simple existence, but the nature, generality, and limitations of the phenomena. Next we critically analyze the recent studies on deferred imitation to discern what inferences (if any) can legitimately be drawn about early representation.

---

[1]In a subsequent section, the theoretical constructs of representation, numerical identity, and object permanence are further defined and their interrelation examined in detail.

Deferred Imitation Without Motor Practice

In assessing deferred imitation, it is important to distinguish between infants: (a) forming a representation of an event from observation alone without motor involvement and (b) repeating their own behavior or motor habits after a delay. For Piaget (1952, 1962), only the former qualified as deferred imitation. At stake is whether infants must motorically produce the act at Time $t1$ for it to be preserved at Time $t2$.

Meltzoff (1985, 1995b) addressed this issue by using an "observation only" design in which infants were shown target acts on objects *but not allowed to touch or handle the objects* at Time $t1$. A delay was then imposed. After the delay, the objects were presented to the infants, and deferred imitation was assessed. Thus, infants could not be repeating their own actions with the objects, because interaction with them had been barred at $t1$. With this design, deferred imitation of actions on objects has been documented in infants as young as 6 to 9 months of age (Barr, Dowden, & Hayne, 1996; Heimann & Meltzoff, 1996; Meltzoff, 1988b).

Deferred Imitation of Novel Acts

If imitation after a delay in the pre-18-month-old age range were restricted to highly familiar behaviors and well-practiced routines, it would limit the inference that could be drawn. It would suggest that pre-18-month-old infants can recognize which of their own behaviors should be applied to particular objects, but that observational learning alone is not an avenue for acquiring new behavior.

Several experiments have addressed these issues and have found no such limitations. Meltzoff (1988a) showed infants an adult who leaned forward and pressed a panel with his forehead. The infants were not allowed to play with the panel and were sent home for a 1-week interval. Both control infants (who did not see the display) and experimental infants were then brought back to the laboratory and presented with the object. The findings were that this novel use of the forehead was exhibited by 0% of the controls; thus the object in and of itself did not prompt head touching. However, 66% of the infants who saw the display reproduced the act after the week's delay. Other work showed that infants imitated not only novel single actions but novel event sequences after a delay (e.g., Bauer & Hertsgaard, 1993; Bauer & Mandler, 1992).

Also examined was whether early deferred imitation is a trial and error process in which infants run through acts at Time $t2$ and eventually recognize the one they saw used with a particular object. A microanalysis of the response pattern at Time $t2$ showed that this was not the case—the adult's action on the object was essentially the first thing that infants did with the object after the delay (Meltzoff, 1985, 1988a).

Length of Delay

Piaget's (1962) classic observation of Jacqueline's deferred imitation (of a temper tantrum) occurred after a delay of more than 12 hours. Because the original perceptual input had long since disappeared, Piaget was convinced that this response was no longer a simple sensory-motor coordination, but that some representative element was involved. If young infants were limited to imitation after delays on the order of seconds or minutes, such a conclusion would not be demanded. Young infants' imitation might be a perceptually grounded process, perhaps involving the decay of sensory traces.

Recently, researchers have investigated the length of delay that can be tolerated by young infants, with surprising results. Infants as young as 6 to 9 months of age successfully imitated after 24 hours, 12-month-olds performed deferred imitation after 4-week delays, and infants in the second year succeeded after 4 months or longer (e.g., Barr et al., 1996; Bauer & Wewerka, 1995; Heimann & Meltzoff, 1996; Klein & Meltzoff, 1999; Meltzoff, 1988a, 1988b, 1995b). Once formed, representations evidently tend to persist and can be used as the basis of subsequent action.

Deferred Imitation Is Generalized Across Contexts

The utility of deferred imitation requires more than long-lasting representations; it also demands a generalizability and availability of the represented acts for application in new situations. A striking example of inflexible rigidity and lack of generality in early mnemonic processes was uncovered by Rovee-Collier (1990) in her research on infants kicking their legs to make mobiles move. She found that 6-month-old infants showed robust memory if and only if they were trained and subsequently tested in the same environmental context. If something as simple as the crib liner was altered between Time *t1* and *t2*, infant performance on the memory test dropped to chance, and they "stare blankly" at the mobile (Rovee-Collier, 1990). If a similar constraint operated in imitation, this would distinguish early deferred imitation from the type classically reported in 18-month-olds, which is generalizable across contexts. For young infants, observed acts would be inaccessible outside the context in which they were formed.

To test the generalizability of early deferred imitation, Meltzoff and colleagues conducted several studies that involved a change of context. In a test involving 12-month-olds, one adult showed target acts in an infant's home, and infants successfully imitated when a different adult presented the test objects in a laboratory room 1 week later (Klein & Meltzoff, 1999). Other studies have corroborated these findings across a range of changes in context, including changes from day-care centers to home (Hanna & Meltzoff, 1993) and from oddly decorated tents to normal rooms (Barnat, Klein, & Meltzoff, 1996). Evidently, deferred imitation in young infants is not rigidly context bound. The requirement for generalizability seems to be that the shape of the object observed at Time *t1* is preserved at *t2*. This suggests that early representations are "object-organized": Infants code more than the human actions in isolation; the stored representation includes the object together with the act performed on it.

Deferred Imitation in the First Months of Life

In light of the evidence so far presented, there might be a temptation to tinker slightly with the classical developmental sequence and to allow deferred imitation and representation at about 1 year instead of 1.5 years. However, these capacities seem to be part of the initial state, at least when simple body actions are presented. Facial imitation in the first 2 months of life appears to meet many of the foregoing criteria for inferring that it is representationally mediated: It has been demonstrated using an observation-only design, with novel gestures, and over long delays.

One study used the observation-only design with facial gestures. Infants sucked on a pacifier while an adult demonstrated mouth opening and tongue protrusion (Meltzoff & Moore, 1977). This technique was developed to block infants from coaction, imitating while the display was in the perceptual field. The adult then stopped the demonstration, assumed a neutral face, and only then removed the pacifier. The results showed that 3-week-old infants imitated the gestures in the subsequent response period. Many other studies have also reported early facial imitation when the gesture was no longer visible (Fontaine, 1984; Heimann, Nelson, & Schaller, 1989; Heimann & Schaller, 1985; Legerstee, 1991; Meltzoff & Moore, 1989).

Young infants have also been shown to imitate across longer delays. In a recent study, four groups of 6-week-old infants saw different gestures on Day 1 and returned on Day 2 to see the adult with a neutral pose (Meltzoff & Moore, 1994). The target gesture was not shown on Day 2. What differed across the groups was not their current perception, but what they remembered from the past. The results showed that 6-week-old infants differentially imitated the gestures they saw 24 hours earlier.

Finally, it has been shown that 6-week-old infants were able to imitate novel gestures, such as tongue protrusion to the side versus straight tongue protrusion (Meltzoff & Moore, 1994). Tongue protrusion to the side does not occur at high baseline rates. It is interesting that such young infants did not imitate this novel act on their first try but seemed to correct their behavior over successive efforts (see Meltzoff & Moore, 1997, for a comprehensive review of the data, mechanisms, and development of early imitation).

Implications of Deferred Imitation for Representation

Deferred imitation in pre-18-month-old infants might have been either nonexistent or highly constrained. Infants might not have tolerated long delays, imitated novel acts, or generalized across a change in context. No such constraints were found. We believe that a strong reading of these results is warranted. The findings support three inferences about the nature and scope of early representations:

1. *They can be formed from observation alone.* Infants create representations at *t1* without having to perform an act themselves and moreover do so for nonhabitual, novel acts. This finding shows that infants are not just storing and bringing to mind their own past behavior. Observation without synchronous motor action is sufficient to form representations.
2. *They persist.* Even after relatively brief observation periods, infant representations are long-lived, persisting mental entities.
3. *They are a sufficient basis on which to organize action.* Objects or people may be sitting passively on a second encounter, but appropriate actions toward them can be based on representations of past encounters. Perceptually derived representations from *t1* are sufficient to generate motor production at *t2*.

It is also important to be clear about what we are *not* claiming. We do not argue that the imitative capacities of neonates are equivalent to those of 2-year-olds without any further development. Having a powerful initial state does not preclude development (indeed, it allows it). Elsewhere, we have characterized important developmental changes in imitation in the first 2 years of life (Meltzoff, 1995a; Meltzoff & Moore, 1995, 1997). From our viewpoint, young infants may be able to perform deferred imitation and still not engage in other representationally based behaviors such as symbolic play and other activities requiring a full differentiation between signifier and signified. The crux of the argument so far is simply this (and no more): *The ability to act on the basis of a stored representation of perceptually absent stimuli is the starting point of infant development, not its culmination.*

If young infants are representational in the sense we claim, we need to take this fact seriously in analyzing their behavior in domains other than imitation. For example, the claim that young infants are representational has profound implications for theories of infant object permanence.

THE NEED FOR MORE DIFFERENTIATED
THEORETICAL CONCEPTS

The foregoing characterization of the initial state suggests that we need to develop a more differentiated set of theoretical concepts than are currently in play. In particular, we need to more carefully define the concepts of representation, identity, and permanence.

The deferred imitation findings suggest that infant representations can be formed from brief observations, can persist over lengthy delays, and can be accessible after loss of perceptual contact. We call this *representational persistence*. The problem of object permanence, we contend, is not whether infants can maintain the object in mind. Representational persistence insures this. The problem of object permanence is whether the persisting representation refers to an object as being located in an invisible portion of the external world. An infant can have a representation in mind but not think the object continues to exist in the external surround.

Representation Without Object Permanence

Positive evidence for representation has often been mistaken as evidence for object permanence. For example, when infants saw something being hidden and the object was then surreptitiously replaced by another, infants' puzzlement on recovery of the featurally changed object was taken as evidence of permanence (e.g., LeCompte & Gratch, 1972). This conclusion does not, however, follow logically. The affect could simply be due to the mismatch between present perception and the persisting representation of the object that had disappeared, with no implications for permanence. Surprise or puzzlement at reappearance need not indicate that infants think the object resides behind the occluder while it is out of sight.

Conversely, the apparent lack of object permanence was taken as evidence against any form of mental representation. Once permanence is differentiated from representation, we can also see that this conclusion does not necessarily follow. For example, in classical Piagetian theory, representation was hypothesized to emerge late, partly because in early infancy object disappearance led to no search for even the most desirable toy. Out of sight was said to be out of mind. For an infant with representational persistence, object disappearance causes perceptual contact to cease, but does not necessarily cause the representation of the object to cease. Out of sight is not out of mind to an infant with representational persistence. Nonetheless, even if the object is in mind (as we contend), infants can still have a problem of object permanence; namely, is this persisting representation in mind linked to a hidden location where that particular object now exists?

Differentiating Two Types of Identity

The capacity for representation raises questions of object identity: Is this animate or inanimate object (*O*) now present to perception the same as *O'* previously encountered and now represented?

As both Piaget (1954, 1962) and philosophers (e.g., Strawson, 1959) have argued, there are two meanings of the phrase "*a* is the same as *b*." One meaning concerns the notion of an object's being the same thing over different encounters in space and time. Two different objects cannot be the same in this sense. Another meaning concerns appearances, such that the features of this object are the same as the features of that object. Many objects may be "the same" in this sense. Philosophers have referred to the first notion as numerical identity and to the second as featural or qualitative identity.[2]

There have been scores of visual habituation and conditioning studies investigating qualitative identity in infancy (e.g., Cohen, 1979; Fagan, 1990; Kuhl, 1983, 1994; Quinn & Eimas, 1996). These studies have demonstrated that young infants are proficient at recognizing one pattern as the same as or similar to another. Piaget himself was interested in qualitative identity, albeit from a different perspective. In his sensory-motor framework, objects were qualitatively the same if infants can do the same actions on them: "These objects are suckable or shakable," and so forth.

Piaget was also concerned with the development of numerical identity in infancy. Numerical identity does not require asking whether this looks the "same as" that, but rather whether this is the "same one" again. In a celebrated example, Piaget (1954) reported that Lucienne saw him in the garden and then quickly turned around and looked for papa in the office window, without fully understanding that these were appearances of the same person (a confusion about numerical identity after an invisible displacement, or so Piaget claimed).

Modern researchers have begun to focus on numerical identity, and like Piaget, have documented that young infants make interesting errors. It is not that young infants are clueless about numerical identity, but that their criteria for tracing object identity changes with development (e.g., Bower, 1982; Meltzoff & Moore, 1995, 1998; Moore, Borton, & Darby, 1978; Xu & Carey, 1996).

---

[2]The label "numerical" identity is used because the concept concerns one underlying individual (despite multiple appearances). There is no implication that an organism tracing numerical identity understands anything about numbers, addition, arithmetic, etc. The word "numerical" should not lead to confusion on this score.

Object Identity as a Developmental Precursor
to Object Permanence

For adults, object permanence and numerical identity are mutually implica-
tive. We cannot interpret an object as being permanent over a disappear-
ance-reappearance unless we have got the original one back. Also, we cannot
say that such events are two encounters with the same individual without its
having continued to exist between encounters. Adults cannot have object
permanence without identity or object identity without permanence.

If we adopt a developmental model, it becomes clear that the relation
between identity and permanence may be different for infants than for
adults. *In fact, maintaining object identity seems to be a prerequisite to developing
permanence* (Moore, 1975; Moore & Meltzoff, 1978). Repeated hidings and
unveilings would not contribute to developing permanence unless there
was a previous notion of numerical identity. Without numerical identity,
the (re)appearance of an object that has disappeared is merely another
object. Unless appearance is understood as a *re*appearance of the same
thing, there is no question of where it was when out of sight, and thus,
no experiential data from which to develop a notion of permanence. A
developmental prediction is that infants wrestle with problems of maintaining the numerical identity of objects over disappearance-reappearances
before they begin wrestling with the problem of object permanence.

INFANTS' REACTIONS TO OBJECT OCCLUSIONS: EVIDENCE OF REPRESENTATION, IDENTITY, OR PERMANENCE?

There is a long tradition of manual search studies with infants. The results
show that manual search for objects hidden by occluders does not occur
much before 8 months. Investigators have questioned whether manual
search masks infant competence by taxing motor skills, means–ends understanding, and so on. For this reason, theorists have turned to visual
responses to assess permanence.

Two different types of visual responses have been measured, spatially
directed looking and preferential looking. The findings using the two
measures are at least superficially at odds with one another, with the preferential-looking effects seeming to show permanence at young ages,
whereas spatially directed looking does not. Why should two visual measures
lead to different answers? The difference cannot be put down to manual
skill problems because the visual system is used in both cases. The theory
we propose offers a resolution to this dilemma. We show that preferential-looking effects can be reinterpreted on the basis of mechanisms that
do not require object permanence.

Overattribution of Permanence Based
on Anticipatory Looking

Young infants who fail manual search tasks often respond with anticipation to objects disappearing behind an occluder. This fact is not new or controversial: Piaget (1952, 1954) noted this in many observations of visual tracking. If a moving object disappears behind a stationary occluder, 4- to 5-month-olds do not simply orient to the object after it reappears but anticipate by shifting their attention to the trailing edge of the occluder before the object emerges (Bower, 1982; Moore et al., 1978; van der Meer, van der Weel, & Lee, 1994). Such anticipations suggest that young infants are forming prospective expectations about object (re)appearances by using the initial trajectory of movement to specify where and when to look. A key question is whether these anticipations are formed by extrapolating the object's visible trajectory from before occlusion or by reasoning about the object's invisible movement while it is behind the screen.

The permanence interpretation is that the object continues to exist behind the screen, and the screen merely blocks its view. A failure to emerge constrains its location to a definite part of space (behind the screen). On this account, what unifies the components of the occlusion event (object movement → disappearance → no movement → reappearance of object → further movement) is a concept of the physical entity that continues to exist in the world—the enduring object. Anticipatory looking to the other side of the screen is based on the permanence of the object behind the screen. We think that this interpretation is too strong to apply to the looking behavior.

A more conservative interpretation of anticipatory looking is based on object identity, not permanence. The identity interpretation is that an infant extrapolates the initial trajectory (defined by the object's already seen speed and direction) beyond the screen to anticipate where and when the same object will next be visible (in this case, the trailing boundary of the screen). The two encounters on either side of the screen are interpreted as manifestations of the same object because they lie on two *visible* portions of the same trajectory. *The crucial point, which is at once logical and developmental, is that recognizing this sameness does not force young infants to infer existence between encounters.* Young infants need not understand that the object resides behind the screen to succeed. What allows infants to treat the disparate components as a unitary event is the maintenance of object identity—the two encounters are interpreted as manifestations of one and the same object. On the identity account, prospective looking to the other side of the screen is based on extrapolating the visible, preocclusion trajectory of the object.

Thus, both the permanence and identity accounts predict looking across occluders. Success on anticipatory-looking tasks does not warrant the inference of object permanence. To ascribe object permanence on this basis is a case of overattribution.

Using the Split-Screen Technique to Disentangle Identity and Permanence

How, then, can we use visual behavior to differentiate the permanence and identity accounts? One relevant approach is referred to as the split-screen technique. With this technique, infants are presented with a moving object disappearing behind the first of two separated screens and then emerging from behind the second screen without appearing in the gap between the screens. If a single object did this, it would violate object permanence.

For infants who understand permanence (hereafter *permanence infants*), the object must exist at every point along its path of motion. It cannot move from Screen 1 to Screen 2 without passing through the space between. Failure to appear in the gap between the screens coupled with a reappearance from behind the second screen presents a conflict. On some portion of its trajectory, the object apparently did not exist.

For infants who understand object identity but not permanence (hereafter *identity infants*), recognizing it as the same object does not depend on continued existence. The object emerging from the second screen can be reidentified as the original one because it is on the original trajectory with the same features. Thus, the split-screen event does not present a conflict for identity infants.

In principle, the permanence and identity infants can be differentiated from one another. Only permanence infants can interpret the failure to appear as specifying that the original object remains behind the first screen and therefore that the object emerging from the second screen must be a second one. Moreover, only permanence infants experience the split-screen event as a violation of understanding, with possible conflict responses (see Moore & Meltzoff, 1998, for an examination of conflict responses in permanence infants).

FIVE-MONTH-OLDS MAINTAIN NUMERICAL IDENTITY ACROSS OCCLUSIONS BUT NOT PERMANENCE

A study was designed to test whether: (a) young infants interpreted object occlusions in terms of identity but *not* permanence and (b) if so, when the permanence interpretation developed. Moore et al. (1978) used the split-screen situation with 5- and 9-month-old infants (see Fig. 3.2). Infants' sensitivity to a violation of permanence was tested by having the object

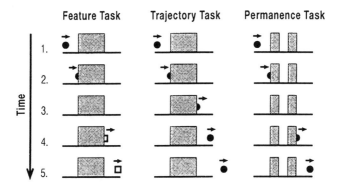

FIG. 3.2. Visual tracking tasks used in the Moore et al. (1978) study to diagnose infants' understanding of object identity (based on featural and trajectory rules) and object permanence.

disappear behind the first of two split screens, not appear in the gap between the screens, and then re-emerge from the second screen, still on the original trajectory with its original features. It thus appeared that a single object did not exist along some part of its movement so as to violate permanence (Fig. 3.2, Permanence Task). The empirical question was how infants responded to the event.

Permanence infants should see this as a violation event. They should monitor the edges of the first screen for the object that must have stopped behind it; moreover, when the same-looking object emerges from the second screen, they should treat it as a different one and look for the original.

Identity infants should *not* see the Permanence Task as a violation event, because they do not yet understand permanence. The object that emerges from the second screen can readily be reidentified as the same one that disappeared at the first screen (because the visible event maintains the object's trajectory and features). If, as per the hypothesis, young infants conserve object identity over occlusions, they would be sensitive to identity violations. Two identity criteria that infants might use are the object's features and its trajectory. As shown in Fig. 3.2, infants' reliance on features as an identity criterion was tested by changing the object's features while it was out of sight behind a screen. It emerged as if it was the same object on the same trajectory but now with a different appearance. Infants' reliance on trajectory as an identity criterion was tested by having the featurally identical object emerge too soon in light of the initial speed.

The results showed that 9-month-old infants were sensitive to both the permanence and identity violations. For both the identity and permanence tasks, they looked away from the visible object emerging from the screen and looked back along the path as though seeking the original. The object that emerged from the screening events was not treated as the same one as the original under all three experimental conditions: a featurally different object emerging at the correct time, a featurally identical object emerging too soon to be on its initial trajectory, and an object that did not pass through the gap between the screens. Moreover, 9-month-olds successively monitored the edges of the first occluder as if peering around it to find the hidden object. In sum, the 9-month-olds' visual behavior was in accord with an understanding of object permanence and also treated both featural and trajectory changes as bearing on identity.

The 5-month-old infants behaved like the 9-month-olds on the identity tasks, but differed substantially on the permanence task. On the permanence-violation task 5-month-olds did not monitor screen edges and did not look back.

According to these results, 5-month-olds understand object identity but not permanence; 9-month-olds understand both. This notion conforms with theoretical predictions that infants can maintain object identity across occlusions before they are sensitive to issues of permanence. It is noteworthy that the spatially directed visual measures suggest a change in the understanding of object permanence at about 9 months, a finding that fits with the results from manual search studies. That two widely divergent response systems, visual and manual, yield the same story increases our confidence in the conclusions.

TESTS OF EARLY PERMANENCE USING THE PREFERENTIAL-LOOKING TECHNIQUE

Other researchers have used a different type of visual behavior to assess early object permanence, preferential looking. Preferential looking to novelty is a robust measure and has been shown over a range of ages and phenomena (e.g., Bornstein, 1985; Cohen, 1979; Fagan, 1990). In this section, we analyze several studies of object occlusion by Baillargeon and Spelke which used this measure.

These results are often interpreted as revealing an understanding of object permanence earlier than the 9-month-old period (but see Bogartz, Shinskey, & Speaker, 1997; Fischer & Bidell, 1991; Haith, 1998). We offer a different interpretation. We explain how the looking-time effects could arise without attributing complex reasoning or knowledge of object permanence. In each case, we show that infants striving to maintain identity rather than permanence succeed on the tasks administered. Clearly, there are also other studies using the preferential-looking technique to test infants' understanding of object occlusions, and we think our analysis can be generalized to account for many of them (for a more extended treatment see Meltzoff & Moore, 1998).

A Reinterpretation of Baillargeon's Split-Screen Studies

Baillargeon conducted a series of studies with the split-screen situation. In one of the studies, infants were initially habituated to both a tall and a short object moving repetitively behind a solid screen. This screen was then replaced by one with a gap in the top (Fig. 3.3). Alternate trials were presented with the short and tall object moving as before, but no object appeared in the gap. The tall object created what was called an "impossible" (violation) event because it should have appeared in the gap. The short object provided a nonviolation control because it was too short to appear in the gap.

Results showed that 5.5-month-olds (Baillargeon & Graber, 1987) and 3.5-month-olds (Baillargeon & DeVos, 1991) looked longer at the tall-object (violation) event. Baillargeon proposed a strong reading of the findings and suggested that infants believed that the object continued to exist while moving behind the screen and maintained its height while invisible; therefore, infants reasoned that it should reappear in the gap and were surprised that it did not. The results were interpreted as showing infants' understanding of permanence of objects and their properties such as height.

From our viewpoint, this interpretation is too strong: It attributes an understanding of permanence to infants on the basis of their having expectations about (re)appearances in the visible world (at the gap). Such expectancies are not sufficient, as we have argued, to tell us about object permanence. We suggest an alternative interpretation of these findings based on the idea that young infants are concerned about conserving object identity rather than permanence. As we have seen from studies of anticipatory looking, young infants extrapolate the trajectories of moving

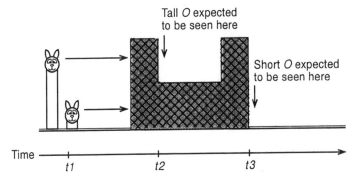

FIG. 3.3. Our reanalysis of Baillargeon's test of early permanence. In the text, we reinterpret increased looking to the tall object (O) as a case of discrepancy from expectations based on identity, not permanence.

objects to anticipate where and when the same object will next be visible. Figure 3.3 shows how such trajectory extrapolation would lead to differential expectations in the tall- and short-object conditions. For the tall object, infants expect appearance at the boundary marked as $t2$. For the short object, they expect appearance at the boundary marked as $t3$. The short object fulfills the infants' expectations, but the tall one does not. This discrepancy in expectation in the tall-object condition would produce the increased looking that was obtained without requiring permanence.

A Reinterpretation of Baillargeon's Drawbridge Studies

Baillargeon also conducted studies investigating the hiding of stationary objects (Baillargeon, 1987, 1991; Baillargeon et al., 1985). In the original study done with Spelke, 5-month-old infants were habituated to a screen that rotated up and down in the manner of a drawbridge. After habituation, a box was put behind the screen. Infants were shown two events in alternation. In one, the screen rotated up until it contacted the box where it stopped and then reversed direction to reveal the box (nonviolation condition). In the other, the screen rotated up and passed through the space that the box should have occupied until the screen lay flat on the table. No box was seen in the empty place (violation condition).

Results showed that infants looked longer at the violation than at the nonviolation event. The authors proposed a strong reading of the findings and suggested that infants thought the box continued to exist behind the rotating occluder, thought the box retained its solidity, and therefore were surprised when the screen passed through the box.

The identity-based analysis also applies to this case. Once again, infants can succeed without understanding the permanence of the absent object. A spatiotemporal identity criterion for stationary objects is its place (location in space), which parallels the role of trajectory for moving objects. In the violation condition of this study, the box was first seen stationary in a place. It was occluded as the screen rotated up and was absent when the screen lay flat on the table. Over multiple trials, there were repeated disappearances and reappearances. Infants would be expected to set up a representation of the box in place, especially after repeated exposures. If this representation persisted over short intervals, infants would expect to see the same box, identified by its place, whenever the place is visible. When the screen was rotated down to reveal no box in place, there is a mismatch between perception and representation. This discrepancy yields longer looking. The discrepancy concerns two situations that were fully visible. Sensitivity to this discrepancy does not require any knowledge of what is *behind* the screen during occlusion, which is the crux of object permanence. Thus, detecting the discrepancy between the pre- and postdisappearance scenes requires representational persistence, but object permanence is unnecessary. To infer object permanence in this case is an example of the overattribution of permanence.

REINTERPRETING THE STUDIES OF EARLY OBJECT PERMANENCE

It is often considered a puzzle that infants show object permanence when tested by visual attention measures but not by manual search measures. This puzzle has led some theorists to postulate separate modules that do not communicate with each other. The infant "knows" where the object is but cannot use this underlying knowledge to act, because the action module is isolated from the module controlling visual attention (Spelke, 1994).

We argue that there is no fundamental tension between the visual and search measures. The visual measures do not show that infants understand object permanence in the first place. Infants do not act to recover objects in the classic object permanence tests because they do not know where the objects are. The Moore et al. (1978) findings on spatially directed looking are consistent with this view, because they showed that infants do not visually search for absent objects until 9 months of age. We argue that the apparent anomaly posed by the preferential-looking effects is resolved by differentiating the notion of object identity from object permanence. In our view, young infants seek to maintain the identity of objects across disappearances and anticipate where and when reappearances occur. The increased looking to occlusion events is due to a discrepancy when expectations are not fulfilled. Such increased looking does not rely on permanence, a hypothesis that, in turn, is consistent with the evidence of the lack of early permanence from the other two measures, spatially directed visual search and manual recovery (see also the manual search studies by Moore & Meltzoff, 1998).

We underscore that we are not attributing the Spelke–Baillargeon effects to experimental artifact; we accept their looking-time results and offer a reinterpretation based on what we believe to be less cognitively demanding mechanisms. It is equally important not to lose sight of the commonalities underlying the identity and permanence accounts of early preferential looking. Both views hold that infants go beyond surface appearances by using representations of the past to interpret present scenes. What is at issue is not whether infants are representational, but the content of representations attributed to them.

The permanence interpretation is that infants represent the absent object as being located in the invisible space behind the screen. The identity interpretation is that a representation of the once-visible object and its spatiotemporal parameters is maintained, and this representation can be used to anticipate future contact points and to reidentify the object as the same one again. For both, a representation persists in mind in the absence of sensory contact. Nonetheless, *there is a logical distinction between the persistence of infant representations and infants' representation of the persistence of external objects.*

NEW FOUNDATIONS FOR INFANT COGNITIVE DEVELOPMENT

Sensory-motor development is essential to infants, but early cognition neither reduces to, nor is wholly dependent on, such development. Prereaching infants are engaged in detecting regularities, forming expectations, and anticipating future states of affairs on the basis of representations that allow them to bring experience to bear on the present. As a whole, the research discussed in this chapter suggests that there is no purely sensory-motor stage of infancy. Others have also drawn this inference (e.g., Bertenthal, 1996; Gopnick & Meltzoff, 1997; Karmiloff-Smith, 1992; Mandler, 1988; Munakata, McClelland, Johnson, & Siegler, 1997; Meltzoff, 1990; Meltzoff, Kuhl, & Moore, 1991, Meltzoff & Moore, 1998; Mounoud & Vinter, 1981), although these positions vary among themselves. Thus far, we have adduced data showing that young infants have some representational capacities from the beginning of postnatal life. In this section, we draw general theoretical implications that follow from the kind of representational being we argue that infants are.

Representational-Development Theory

In the foregoing sections, we have argued for development within the domain of objects, in that an understanding of object identity precedes an understanding of object permanence. We now consider the possibility that development occurs in the representational substrate itself, which would have consequences across many domains.

We think there are two kinds of representation that young infants use, and these suggest a developmental order: representing objects and events that were previously perceived but no longer visible (hereafter *PP-representations*) and representing invisible objects and events that were never perceived (hereafter *NP-representations*).

An example of "previously perceived, but no longer visible" is representing a moving object disappearing at a screen edge. The object, movement, and disappearance event were all once visible. An example of "never perceived" is a moving object coming to a stop behind the screen. The transition from moving to stopping, the stopped object, and its location behind the screen were all never seen. Both PP- and NP-representations refer to objects and events no longer perceived, but there is an important difference in the level of cognition ascribed to infants capable of one or the other. We think that the capacity for representations of never-perceived events develops later than does the capacity for representing previously perceived events.

Both the work on imitation and that on object occlusions suggest that infant representations are not short lived. Such representational persistence allows object representations formed at Time $t1$ to be compared to subsequent transformations of the object at Time $t2$, a process we call *pre-post comparison*. When confronted with disappearance–reappearance events, young infants using pre-post comparisons could detect changes in an object's featural appearance, time of arrival, or direction and speed of movement.

One of the simplest cases of future-oriented behavior documented in young infants is anticipating that a moving object can be re-encountered beyond the trailing boundary of the occluding screen. In our terms, the perception of the moving object before it disappears at the screen edge sets up a PP-representation that includes the object's spatiotemporal and featural descriptors. The spatiotemporal descriptor (the trajectory defined by the object's already seen speed and direction) allows the prediction of potential next contact points in the visible world. We do not think that infants employ high-level reasoning to make this extrapolation of a visible trajectory. It seems more likely to be grounded in basic perceptual processing of the dynamic visual world (Meltzoff & Moore, 1998).[3]

In our framework, this prospective behavior can be generated from a PP-representation because the information specifying future contact points is already encoded in the representation of the initial encounter. An NP-representation is unnecessary. Even recognition that the postdisappearance object is the same one as the one that disappeared can be mediated by a PP-representation, by comparing the trajectory and features of the perceived object with the one in representation. Thus the PP-representation supports both predictive looking and postdictive recognition of identity.

We can now see why diagnosing infants' understanding of occlusion events presents such a profound challenge. Pre-post analyses of disappear-

---

[3]Psychophysical work with adults has shown that trajectories of moving objects are extracted at an early stage in visual processing (Watamaniuk & McKee, 1995; Watamaniuk, McKee, & Grzywacz, 1995). Lee (1980; van der Meer et al., 1994) has provided a model for how such perceived trajectories can be extrapolated forward in time without involving high-level cognition. Other work with adults has described how the adult perceptual system functions to keep track of the identity of objects in the visual field (Kahneman, Treisman, & Gibbs, 1992; Treisman, 1992). See Meltzoff and Moore, 1998, for a fuller discussion of these topics.

ance events can be accomplished with either PP- or NP-representations. The challenge is to determine whether infants represent the once-moving object as having stopped *behind* a screen while occluded (NP-representation) or simply make comparisons between the pre- and postocclusion states, both of which are visible (PP-representation).

In the split-screen occlusion event, infants employing PP-representations would anticipate contact in the gap between the screens at the time specified by the object's previously visible movement. Failure to appear in the gap presents a discrepancy when using PP-representations (Meltzoff & Moore, 1998).

Infants using NP-representations would have more than expectancies about the visible world. For such infants, disappearance at the first screen edge engenders a representation of the object as located in the invisible (and never seen) space behind the screen. Infants using NP-representations could interpret the object's failure to emerge as indicating that it remained there. Such representation would enable spatially directed responses such as reaching into the hidden space or peering around the boundaries of an occluder to see the hidden object, both of which have been observed in 9-month-olds. We believe that at least part of the explanation for the developmental change between 5 and 9 months of age is a shift from relying on PP-representations to a state in which both PP- and NP-representations can be used to parse disappearance events.

SUMMARY

We have argued that new theoretical foundations are needed to account for cognitive development in infancy. There is currently no new theory with the scope and grandeur of Piaget's, but six building blocks can be discerned from the arguments and data presented in this chapter.

1. Young infants are not confined to sensory-motor habits. Representations of objects and events can be set up after brief encounters. They can be formed from perception alone without concurrent action, as shown by work on deferred imitation using the observation-only design.

2. Representations persist and are accessible after lengthy delays; we call this phenomenon "representational persistence."

3. Representational persistence differs from object permanence. Object permanence concerns the continued existence of a physical object in the external world. Representations can persist in mind without implying this understanding.

4. The world is dynamically changing. One of young infants' chief cognitive concerns is maintaining the numerical identity of objects. Representational persistence coupled with spatiotemporal identity criteria (place for stationary objects, trajectory for moving objects) constitute a representational system that functions to keep track of the identity of perceived objects.

5. The representational system functions prospectively (by predicting where and when the same object can be seen) and retrospectively (by reidentifying an object as the same one after movements or disappearances-reappearances). Discrepancies from expectations based on representational persistence and identity are sufficient to account for the preferential-looking effects reported by Spelke and Baillargeon. Object permanence is unnecessary.

6. At a general level, there is developmental change in the nature of representation itself. There is development from representational persistence for objects and events that were previously perceived but no longer visible (PP-representations) to representations of invisible objects and events that were never perceived (NP-representations).

In a nutshell, we postulate a richer initial state than Piaget had envisioned, but we also embrace conceptual development. To paraphrase Piaget (1970), there is no structure without genesis but also no genesis without structure. By elevating the mental capacities of young infants, we do not abolish the need for psychogenesis. This insight is Piaget's lasting legacy.

ACKNOWLEDGMENTS

The order of authorship is alphabetical; the theoretical work is a coequal endeavor. We are deeply indebted to Pat Kuhl and Alison Gopnik for many valuable conversations on the topics addressed here. Pat Kuhl, Katherine Nelson, and Ellin Scholnick provided insightful comments on an earlier draft of this chapter. We thank Craig Harris and Calle Fisher for help on the empirical work. Work on this chapter was supported by a grant from the National Institutes of Health (HD-22514).

REFERENCES

Baillargeon, R. (1987). Object permanence in 3½- and 4½-month-old infants. *Developmental Psychology, 23,* 655–664.
Baillargeon, R. (1991). Reasoning about the height and location of a hidden object in 4.5- and 6.5-month-old infants. *Cognition, 38,* 13–42.

Baillargeon, R. (1993). The object concept revisited: New directions in the investigation of infants' physical knowledge. In C. Granrud (Ed.), *Visual perception and cognition in infancy* (pp. 265–315). Hillsdale, NJ: Lawrence Erlbaum Associates.

Baillargeon, R., & DeVos, J. (1991). Object permanence in young infants: Further evidence. *Child Development, 62,* 1227–1246.

Baillargeon, R., & Graber, M. (1987). Where's the rabbit? 5.5-month-old infants' representation of the height of a hidden object. *Cognitive Development, 2,* 375–392.

Baillargeon, R., Spelke, E. S., & Wasserman, S. (1985). Object permanence in five-month-old infants. *Cognition, 20,* 191–208.

Barnat, S. B., Klein, P. J., & Meltzoff, A. N. (1996). Deferred imitation across changes in context and object: Memory and generalization in 14-month-old infants. *Infant Behavior and Development, 19,* 241–251.

Barr, R., Dowden, A., & Hayne, H. (1996). Developmental changes in deferred imitation by 6- to 24-month-old infants. *Infant Behavior and Development, 19,* 159–170.

Bauer, P. J., & Hertsgaard, L. A. (1993). Increasing steps in recall of events: Factors facilitating immediate and long-term memory in 13.5- and 16.5-month-old children. *Child Development, 64,* 1204–1223.

Bauer, P. J., & Mandler, J. M. (1992). Putting the horse before the cart: The use of temporal order in recall of events by one-year-old children. *Developmental Psychology, 28,* 441–452.

Bauer, P. J., & Wewerka, S. S. (1995). One- to two-year-olds' recall of events: The more expressed, the more impressed. *Journal of Experimental Child Psychology, 59,* 475–496.

Bertenthal, B. I. (1996). Origins and early development of perception, action, and representation. *Annual Review of Psychology, 47,* 431–459.

Bogartz, R. S., Shinskey, J. L., & Speaker, C. J. (1997). Interpreting infant looking: The event set × event set design. *Developmental Psychology, 33,* 408–422.

Bornstein, M. H. (1985). Infant into adult: Unity to diversity in the development of visual categorization. In J. M. R. Fox (Ed.), *Neonate cognition: Beyond the blooming, buzzing confusion* (pp. 115–138). Hillsdale, NJ: Lawrence Erlbaum Associates.

Bower, T. G. R. (1982). *Development in infancy* (2nd ed.). San Francisco: Freeman.

Cohen, L. B. (1979). Our developing knowledge of infant perception and cognition. *American Psychologist, 34,* 894–899.

Fagan, J. F., III. (1990). The paired-comparison paradigm and infant intelligence. In A. Diamond (Ed.), *Annals of the New York Academy of Sciences: The development and neural bases of higher cognitive functions* (Vol. 608, 337–364). New York: New York Academy of Sciences.

Fischer, K. W., & Bidell, T. (1991). Constraining nativist inferences about cognitive capacities. In S. Carey & R. Gelman (Eds.), *The epigenesis of mind: Essays on biology and cognition* (pp. 199–235). Hillsdale, NJ: Lawrence Erlbaum Associates.

Fontaine, R. (1984). Imitative skills between birth and six months. *Infant Behavior and Development, 7,* 323–333.

Gopnik, A., & Meltzoff, A. N. (1997). *Words, thoughts, and theories.* Cambridge, MA: MIT Press.

Haith, M. M. (1998). Who put the cog in infant cognition? Is rich interpretation too costly? *Infant Behavior and Development, 21,* 167–179.

Hanna, E., & Meltzoff, A. N. (1993). Peer imitation by toddlers in laboratory, home, and day-care contexts: Implications for social learning and memory. *Developmental Psychology, 29,* 701–710.

Heimann, M., & Meltzoff, A. N. (1996). Deferred imitation in 9- and 14-month-old infants: A longitudinal study of a Swedish sample. *British Journal of Developmental Psychology, 14,* 55–64.

Heimann, M., Nelson, K. E., & Schaller, J. (1989). Neonatal imitation of tongue protrusion and mouth opening: Methodological aspects and evidence of early individual differences. *Scandinavian Journal of Psychology, 30,* 90–101.

Heimann, M., & Schaller, J. (1985). Imitative reactions among 14–21 day old infants. *Infant Mental Health Journal, 6,* 31–39.

James, W. (1890). *Principles of psychology.* New York: Holt, Rinehart & Winston.

Kahneman, D., Treisman, A., & Gibbs, B. J. (1992). The reviewing of object files: Object-specific integration of information. *Cognitive Psychology, 24,* 175–219.

Karmiloff-Smith, A. (1992). *Beyond modularity: A developmental perspective on cognitive science.* Cambridge, MA: MIT Press.

Klein, P. J., & Meltzoff, A. N. (1999). Long-term memory, forgetting, and deferred imitation in 12-month-old infants. *Developmental Science, 2,* 102–113.

Kuhl, P. K. (1983). Perception of auditory equivalence classes for speech in early infancy. *Infant Behavior and Development, 6,* 263–285.

Kuhl, P. K. (1994). Learning and representation in speech and language. *Current Opinion in Neurobiology, 4,* 812–822.

LeCompte, G. K., & Gratch, G. (1972). Violation of a rule as a method of diagnosing infants' levels of object concept. *Child Development, 43,* 385–396.

Lee, D. N. (1980). The optic flow field: The foundation of vision. *Philosophical Transactions of the Royal Society of London, 290,* 169–179.

Legerstee, M. (1991). The role of person and object in eliciting early imitation. *Journal of Experimental Child Psychology, 51,* 423–433.

Mandler, J. M. (1988). How to build a baby: On the development of an accessible representational system. *Cognitive Development, 3,* 113–136.

Meltzoff, A. N. (1985). Immediate and deferred imitation in fourteen- and twenty-four-month-old infants. *Child Development, 56,* 62–72.

Meltzoff, A. N. (1988a). Infant imitation after a 1-week delay: Long-term memory for novel acts and multiple stimuli. *Developmental Psychology, 24,* 470–476.

Meltzoff, A. N. (1988b). Infant imitation and memory: Nine-month-olds in immediate and deferred tests. *Child Development, 59,* 217–225.

Meltzoff, A. N. (1990). Towards a developmental cognitive science: The implications of cross-modal matching and imitation for the development of representation and memory in infancy. In A. Diamond (Ed.), *Annals of the New York Academy of Sciences: The development and neural bases of higher cognitive functions* (Vol. 608, pp. 1–31). New York: New York Academy of Sciences.

Meltzoff, A. N. (1995a). Understanding the intentions of others: Re-enactment of intended acts by 18-month-old children. *Developmental Psychology, 31,* 838–850.

Meltzoff, A. N. (1995b). What infant memory tells us about infantile amnesia: Long-term recall and deferred imitation. *Journal of Experimental Child Psychology, 59,* 497–515.

Meltzoff, A. N., & Moore, M. K. (1977). Imitation of facial and manual gestures by human neonates. *Science, 198,* 75–78.

Meltzoff, A. N., & Moore, M. K. (1989). Imitation in newborn infants: Exploring the range of gestures imitated and the underlying mechanisms. *Developmental Psychology, 25,* 954–962.

Meltzoff, A. N., & Moore, M. K. (1992). Early imitation within a functional framework: The importance of person identity, movement, and development. *Infant Behavior and Development, 15,* 479–505.

Meltzoff, A. N., & Moore, M. K. (1994). Imitation, memory, and the representation of persons. *Infant Behavior and Development, 17,* 83–99.

Meltzoff, A. N., & Moore, M. K. (1995). Infants' understanding of people and things: From body imitation to folk psychology. In J. Bermúdez, A. J. Marcel, & N. Eilan (Eds.), *The body and the self* (pp. 43–69). Cambridge, MA: MIT Press.

Meltzoff, A. N., & Moore, M. K. (1997). Explaining facial imitation: A theoretical model. *Early Development and Parenting, 6,* 179–192.

Meltzoff, A. N., & Moore, M. K. (1998). Object representation, identity, and the paradox of early permanence: Steps toward a new framework. *Infant Behavior and Development, 21,* 201–235.

Moore, M. K. (1975, April). *Object permanence and object identity: A stage-developmental model.* Paper presented at the meeting of the Society for Research in Child Development, Denver, CO.

Moore, M. K., Borton, R., & Darby, B. L. (1978). Visual tracking in young infants: Evidence for object identity or object permanence? *Journal of Experimental Child Psychology, 25,* 183–198.

Moore, M. K., & Meltzoff, A. N. (1978). Object permanence, imitation, and language development in infancy: Toward a neo-Piagetian perspective on communicative and cognitive development. In F. D. Minifie & L. L. Lloyd (Eds.), *Communicative and cognitive abilities—Early behavioral assessment* (pp. 151–184). Baltimore: University Park Press.

Moore, M. K., & Meltzoff, A. N. (1998). *New findings on object permanence: A developmental difference between two types of occlusion.* Manuscript submitted for publication.

Mounoud, P., & Vinter, A. (1981). Representation and sensorimotor development. In G. Butterworth (Ed.), *Infancy and epistemology: An evaluation of Piaget's theory* (pp. 200–235). Brighton, England: Harvester Press.

Munakata, Y., McClelland, J. L., Johnson, M. H., & Siegler, R. S. (1997). Rethinking infant knowledge: Toward an adaptive process account of success and failures in object permanence tasks. *Psychological Review, 104,* 686–713.

Piaget, J. (1952). *The origins of intelligence in children.* New York: International Universities Press.

Piaget, J. (1954). *The construction of reality in the child.* New York: Basic Books.

Piaget, J. (1962). *Play, dreams and imitation in childhood.* New York: Norton.

Piaget, J. (1970). *Structuralism.* New York: Harper & Row.

Quinn, P. C., & Eimas, P. D. (1996). Perceptual organization and categorization in young infants. In C. Rovee-Collier & L. P. Lipsitt (Eds.), *Advances in infancy research* (Vol. 10, pp. 1–36). Norwood, NJ: Ablex.

Rovee-Collier, C. (1990). The "memory system" of prelinguistic infants. In A. Diamond (Ed.), *Annals of the New York Academy of Sciences: The development and neural bases of higher cognitive functions* (Vol. 608, pp. 517–542). New York: New York Academy of Sciences.

Spelke, E. (1994). Initial knowledge: Six suggestions. *Cognition, 50,* 431–445.

Spelke, E. S., Breinlinger, K., Macomber, J., & Jacobson, K. (1992). Origins of knowledge. *Psychological Review, 99,* 605–632.

Strawson, P. F. (1959). *Individuals: An essay in descriptive metaphysics.* London: Methuen.

Thelen, E., & Smith, L. B. (1994). *A dynamic systems approach to the development of cognition and action.* Cambridge, MA: MIT Press.

Treisman, A. (1992). Perceiving and re-perceiving objects. *American Psychologist, 47,* 862–875.

van der Meer, A. L. H., van der Weel, F., & Lee, D. N. (1994). Prospective control in catching in infants. *Perception, 23,* 287–302.

Watamaniuk, S. N. J., & McKee, S. P. (1995). Seeing motion behind occluders. *Nature, 377,* 729–730.

Watamaniuk, S. N. J., McKee, S. P., & Grzywacz, N. M. (1995). Detecting a trajectory embedded in random-direction motion noise. *Vision Research, 35,* 65–77.

Xu, F., & Carey, S. (1996). Infants' metaphysics: The case of numerical identity. *Cognitive Psychology, 30,* 111–153.

Chapter 4

A Reconsideration of Concepts: On the Compatibility of Psychological Essentialism and Context Sensitivity

Susan A. Gelman
University of Michigan, Ann Arbor

Gil Diesendruck
University of Arizona

INTRODUCTION

In this chapter we focus on the representation of concepts. As researchers studying concept development, we are indebted to Piaget for raising fundamental questions that current scholars continue to grapple with, including: When do basic ontological distinctions emerge? What are the logical structures implicit in children's groupings of objects? How do conceptual hierarchies get constructed, and how do they change over time? How does the meaning of a word change as the underlying conceptual understanding changes? What is the content of children's concepts and, correspondingly, the nature of children's understanding of the world at large (what we might now call *implicit theories*)? (See, for example, Inhelder & Piaget, 1964; Piaget, 1929.)

Although Piaget's answers to these questions have been in considerable dispute, and his developmental claims about concepts have come under close critical scrutiny (see R. Gelman & Baillargeon, 1983; Markman & Callanan, 1984, for detailed reviews), there were two broad insights in his work on concepts that we explore here in some detail. These insights might seem at first to pose a paradox. On the one hand, Inhelder and Piaget (1964), in *The Early Growth of Logic in the Child*, noted that, for young children, concepts (or preconcepts) are highly sensitive to context, especially perceptual aspects of context. In forming graphic collections, for example, children are guided by the spatial configuration of objects in the array and "allow themselves to be guided by what they can perceive" (p.

45) rather than making use of a coherent core concept. Although the role of perception in early concepts is under debate (S. A. Gelman & Medin, 1993; Jones & Smith, 1993), none would argue with Piaget's observations that children are overcome by appearances on many cognitive tasks.

On the other hand, in his discussion of nominal realism, Piaget (1929) noted that children treat certain categories as having an essence or "intrinsic character" (p. 73): "[I]n learning the names of things the child at this stage believes it is doing much more. It thinks it is reaching to the essence of the thing and discovering a real explanation" (pp. 61–62). Piaget further made clear that children's notion of essence is not a visible, perceptual notion: "[I]n the primitive stage the name of a thing is part of the thing. But this does not mean that it is inscribed on or materially represented in the thing. It is part of the essence of the thing" (p. 75).

The seeming paradox in Piaget's account is how children can be perceptually driven and yet impute essences.[1] This question has recently reemerged, in the form of how psychological essentialism can be reconciled with the context-sensitive nature of concepts. A growing literature has argued that children treat concepts as having essences and at times even override salient perceptual information (S. A. Gelman, Coley, & Gottfried, 1994; Medin, 1989). On the other hand, even for adults, concepts are highly flexible, sensitive to context, variable depending on the task, and influenced by perceptually immediate (online) properties (Barsalou, 1993; Jones & Smith, 1993). Thus, there seems to be a logical contradiction akin to Piaget's: One proposal is that essences are at the core of concepts; the other proposal is that perceptual features are core or, in the extreme, that concepts have no core. Accordingly, a number of scholars have suggested that essentialism is incompatible with context sensitivity (Braisby, Franks, & Hampton, 1996; Malt, 1994; L. B. Smith & Heise, 1992).

In this chapter we argue that the contradiction is only apparent: Psychological essentialism *is* compatible with the context sensitivity noted in recent years by cognitive scientists and with the attention to perceptual features noted by Inhelder and Piaget. First, we briefly summarize the arguments for essences and for contextually driven variability. Next, we provide a resolution that can account for both the importance of essences and the variability in performance. To do so, we clarify what is meant by

---

[1]The dual characterization of children as both perceptually driven and imputing essences need not be a paradox *for Piaget*, for at least two reasons. First, the kinds of concepts he considered in the two cases were very different: spontaneous superordinate groupings (in the case of graphic collections) versus reasoning about the names of individuals and basic-level categories (in the case of nominal realism). Second, reference to essence in discussions of nominal realism is clearly a metacognitive understanding, elicited by extended discussions with children about the origins and ontological status of names (e.g., Benelli, 1988; Markman, 1976), unlike the claims about concept formation. Thus, we see no logical disparity in Piaget's own writings on these matters.

essentialism, demonstrate the limits of relying on perception as providing a conceptual core, and examine some of the consequences of claiming that concepts have no core. Finally, we attempt to characterize what is represented in a concept and what implications this suggestion has for concept development in general.

BACKGROUND

Essences and Theories

In the past 25 years, theorizing about how people represent concepts and word meanings has undergone two major shifts (Medin, 1989). The traditional view, assumed by Inhelder and Piaget (1964) as well as by numerous psychologists, linguists, and anthropologists, was that concepts can be represented by a set of properties that are singly necessary and jointly sufficient for picking out all and only those instances of the concept. For instance, we can characterize *bachelor* as *unmarried, marriageable male* (E. E. Smith & Medin, 1981). Inhelder and Piaget (1964) stated that a class necessarily includes "Properties which are specific to the members of the given class and which differentiate them from members of other classes" (p. 17). Implicit in the traditional view were other assumptions (see also Johnson-Laird & Wason, 1977): (1) Concepts are arbitrary constructions. Thus, the best way to study concepts is to examine knowledge-free, context-free domains, to abstract away from confounding influences of language, encyclopedic knowledge, and the like. (2) All concepts are (fundamentally) alike. (3) Concept boundaries are clear-cut, and the best way to study concepts is to examine where people draw the boundaries.

The first shift moved away from a traditional, defining-features view to propose that membership in a category is probabilistically determined. All three implicit assumptions of the traditional view were challenged: (1) Concepts encoded in natural language are not arbitrary, but reflect real-world feature correlations (Rosch, 1978). (2) Relatedly, all concepts are not alike. The use of arbitrary concepts invented in the laboratory, although useful for precise tests of various representational accounts, often obscured the structure of concepts in natural language. (3) Category boundaries are not clear-cut; rather, probabilistic models (such as prototypes) determine category membership.

The second shift moved to incorporate commonsense theories into models of categorization.[2] The major limitation of the prototype view was its reliance

---

[2]The theory view does not *replace* prototype theory; instead, it argues for its insufficiency. Prototypes are accurate descriptions of the information that people use to identify instances on many tasks (a point to which we return later). Importantly, however, the prototype is not the full story.

on similarity as an explanatory mechanism. Not only are there epistemological problems with defining similarity in a theory-neutral way (Goodman, 1972), but also much of categorization behavior requires appeal to more knowledge-rich, explanatory models (i.e., theories). Adults' concepts are influenced by theoretical belief systems and cannot be characterized by statistical information alone (Heit & Rubinstein, 1994; Keil, 1989; Murphy & Medin, 1985; Rips & Collins, 1993; see Murphy, 1993, for review). How subjects incorporate different features varies, depending on their theories about the domain (Wisniewski & Medin, 1994). The probability of incorporating novel instances is also dependent on theoretical beliefs rather than statistical correlations (Medin & Shoben, 1988). Thus, in some cases a property equally true of two different concepts is more central to one than the other (e.g., *curved* is more central to boomerangs than to bananas, even though in all our experience, *curved* is equally true of both concepts). The extent to which features are weighted in classification judgments is influenced by causal understandings: Properties that are causes are viewed as more central to a concept than properties that are effects (Ahn & Lassaline, 1996). This point again demonstrates that correlations alone cannot account for the centrality and significance of features in a concept (see also Ahn, Kalish, Medin, & Gelman, 1995; Keil, 1989; White, 1995).

The theory-based model of concepts is argued to be a *contributor to* concept development rather than its *outcome* (see Wellman & Gelman, 1992). Indeed, without theoretical commitments of some sort, it may be difficult for children to develop concepts at all. Murphy (1993) noted that theories help concept learners in three respects: (1) Theories help identify those features that are relevant to a concept, (2) theories constrain how (e.g., along which dimensions) similarity should be computed, and (3) theories can influence how concepts are stored in memory. The implication is that concept learning may proceed more smoothly with the help of theories, even though the theories themselves are changing developmentally.

Children appear to use theoretical knowledge in their classifications from a young age. In a by-now-classic series of studies, Keil (1989) asked children to consider animals and objects that had undergone transformations leading them to appear to be something else—such as a raccoon that underwent an operation so that it looked and acted like a skunk. Second-graders realized that animal identity was unaffected by superficial transformations (e.g., the animal was judged to be a raccoon). Even younger children demonstrated a similar understanding when considering items that were transformed to resemble something from a different ontological category (e.g., preschoolers reported that a porcupine that was transformed to look like a cactus was still a porcupine) or that were transformed by means of a costume. Gelman and Wellman (1991) similarly found that preschool children appreciated that for some objects, insides are more important than outsides for judgments of identity and functioning (e.g., a dog without its insides cannot bark and is not a dog, whereas a dog without its outsides can bark and is a dog).

Similarly, Barrett, Abdi, Murphy, and Gallagher (1993) noted: "Concept learning involves more than simply keeping a running tally of which features are associated with which concept" (p. 1612), and presented data suggesting that children's intuitive theories help determine which properties and which feature correlations children attend to in their classifications. For example, in a task that required children to categorize novel birds into one of two novel categories, first- and fourth-grade children noticed the association between brain size and memory capacity and used that correlation to categorize new members. Specifically, exemplars that preserved the correlation were more often judged to be category members and to be more typical of the category. The children did not make use of features that correlated equally well but were unsupported by a theory (e.g., the correlation between structure of heart and shape of beak).

These studies provide further support for the argument that similarity is insufficient to account for human categorization (see also Cassirer, 1923, cited in Nelson, 1974). The conclusion is further bolstered by research suggesting that classifications may at times privilege information that is nonobvious or that even runs counter to observable features. S. A. Gelman and Markman (1986) demonstrated that categories have an *inductive* function even for preschool children; they have the potential to generate novel inferences. For example, on one item, children learned a new property of a brontosaurus ("a dinosaur") and a rhinoceros (that they had cold blood and warm blood, respectively) and were asked which property was true of a triceratops ("a dinosaur"). Children reported that the triceratops had cold blood like the brontosaurus, even though it more closely resembled the rhinoceros. The results of this and other related experiments showed that by 2½ years of age, children base inferences on category membership, even in the strong case when outward appearances conflict (S. A. Gelman & Coley, 1990). Thus, children expect certain labels—and the categories to which they refer—to capture properties well beyond those they have already encountered. A variety of control studies showed that these effects were not simply a response bias arising from hearing the same word for the two category members. For example, children do not base inferences consistently on novel labels (Davidson & Gelman, 1990) or generalize accidental properties, such as an animal's age, on the basis of category membership (S. A. Gelman & Markman, 1986).

In addition to basing inductive inferences on category labels, children use essential properties as an index to naming. Diesendruck, Gelman, and Lebowitz (1998) conducted a study that capitalized on a well-known word-learning error studied by Markman and others (Markman, 1989; Merriman

& Bowman, 1989). Children have a powerful tendency to assume that each object has only one label, the *mutual exclusivity* assumption. For example, if young children know that a poodle is a dog, they sometimes deny that it is a poodle or an animal. Diesendruck et al. predicted that children would overcome this mutual exclusivity tendency if they learned that dogs and poodles (for instance) share nonobvious properties. Three- to five-year-olds learned new words for a series of animals, then were tested on their interpretations of the new words. For example, children saw two distinct kinds of squirrels (a standard squirrel and a flying squirrel) and heard: "This one [the flying squirrel] is a squirrel; it's a mef. This one [the standard squirrel] is a squirrel; it's not a mef." Before teaching the new word, the experimenter described how the two instances were alike. In the "insides" condition, internal, hidden properties were described (e.g., "has the same stuff inside . . . the same kind of bones, blood, muscles, and brain"). In the control condition, superficial similarities were described (e.g., "is the same size . . . it lives in the same zoo in the same kind of cage").

The labeling phase alone provided all the information that children needed to construct the hierarchy accurately. We know from past work, however (e.g., Gelman, Wilcox, & Clark, 1989) that children tend to collapse such a hierarchy into two mutually exclusive sets. The question is whether the brief description of internal similarities is sufficient to alter subjects' patterns of word learning. Indeed, the results demonstrated a clear-cut condition effect. When the similarities were superficial, children showed their usual pattern of treating the two labels (e.g., "squirrel" and "mef") as mutually exclusive. In contrast, describing internal similarities helped children overcome the error. Diesendruck (1997) has recently replicated this finding in Brazil, with Portuguese-speaking children of widely varying socioeconomic backgrounds. Again, there was the same weakening of mutual exclusivity in the "insides" condition.

These data converge to provide a picture of preschool children as attending to theory-relevant properties even when they are subtle and relatively nonobvious. Medin (1989) invoked the notion of "psychological essentialism" to account for findings such as these. Philosophers have long proposed that the categories we use are supported by essences—an underlying reality or true nature that we cannot directly observe but that gives an object its identity (Locke, 1959/1894; Schwartz, 1977). In contrast to this metaphysical claim about the structure of reality, the psychological claim is that ordinary people *believe* (probably incorrectly; Dupré, 1993; Mayr, 1991; Sober, 1994) that the categories of ordinary language are of this sort. In other words, psychological essentialism is the proposal that people (children and adults) maintain a dual assumption: (1) that the world has a natural order that is not imposed by the observer; (2) that the symbolic system humans use to represent the world (namely, concepts and words) maps onto this natural order. Psychological essentialism posits that people believe categories are *real*, in several senses: They are discovered (vs. invented), they are natural (vs. artificial), they predict other properties, and they carve up nature at its joints.

This notion of *essence* is clearly distinct from Piaget's reference to *essence* (in his discussion of nominal realism) yet is also intriguingly similar. Whereas Piaget's focus was on the presumed reality of the *name*, the consubstantiality of name and object, and children's difficulty in separating name from object, Medin's writings have emphasized the structure of the *categories* involved and the link between essence (as an explanatory construct) and theory. Thus, Piaget's claim is about language; Medin's claim is about categories (and language only indirectly). Nonetheless, both share a common realist theme: Under both views of essence, a human construction (either category or category name) is presumed to have a reality beyond the human creator.[3]

Essentialist concepts and theory-laden concepts are related but distinct notions. The set of theory-laden concepts is broader than (and superordinate to) the set of essentialist concepts, and there are theory-laden concepts that are not essentialist. For example, Murphy and Medin (1985) convincingly made the case that we use theories to classify items such as trash cans, but we need not appeal to essentialism in such cases. On the other hand, people may appeal to essences without having detailed theoretical belief systems (Atran, 1990). Thus, psychological essentialism does not imply full-fledged explanatory theories, but rather theoretical commitments in the sense of adherance to nonobvious (theorized) entities to account for observable structure.

Variability and Context Sensitivity

There are at least two major challenges to the claim that children hold essentialist beliefs about the core of concepts. One fundamental objection argues against the very notion that concepts have mentally stable represented cores. A variation of this objection asserts that whereas concepts may have more or less determining components, perceptual features are just as important as (or more important than) nonperceptual ones.

The claim that concepts are not stably represented takes the form that concepts are constructions in working memory and shift with the surround-

---

[3]Piaget's findings of nominal realism have been confirmed in several controlled studies (e.g., Benelli, 1988; Brook, 1970; Williams, 1977). However, more sensitive tasks have revealed that even preschool children have some capacity to reason about names as arbitrary and distinct from the objects to which they refer (Markman, 1976; Rosenblum & Pinker, 1983). In any case, the validity of nominal realism is separate from the claims of psychological essentialism advanced in this chapter: Although nominal realism presupposes that young children are essentialist, the reverse is not the case.

ing context. Barsalou (1993) suggested that people hold conceptual cores in long-term memory, but because such cores do not affect behavior, the term *concept* should be saved for the dynamic temporary representations in working memory that do control behavior. Such representations allow for the widely noted flexibility and linguistic vagary of concepts. We review some of these phenomena in the remainder of this section.

The features that are most salient vary with linguistic context (e.g., weight vs. sound of a piano; McCloskey & Glucksberg, 1978). When asked to define concepts, subjects generate variable responses from one occasion to the next (Barsalou, 1993a). The prototypes that subjects generate can be manipulated consistently by contextual cues (e.g., telling subjects to rate typicality of birds from the point of view of the average U.S. citizen vs. from the point of view of the average Chinese citizen; Barsalou, 1991). Hierarchies are not fully transitive (Hampton, 1982); this finding suggests inconsistency across uses.

Similarly, Jones and Smith (1993) argued that categorization and labeling are best predicted by online, context-specific considerations. Cognitive acts are a result of dynamic processes, not of structural representations. In their view, "concepts are not represented entities that exist as a unit . . . there is no set intension (definition in the head) or extension (category in the world). Both are transient and emergent in the task at hand" (p. 136).

One reason that concepts have been presumed to be stable representations is that most tasks focus on *taxonomization* as the primary function of categories (Barsalou, 1993). In the traditional account, people are intuitive taxonomists engaged in the categorization of the world on the basis of the discovery of essential features of different classes. Once discovered, such features serve to identify and allow inferences about other exemplars of the same category. Yet concepts are clearly used for a variety of functions aside from taxonomization (see also Gelman & Medin, 1993). Concepts are also used for effective communication, for goal-oriented classifications, and for building world models. In these tasks, concepts do not necessarily capture the taxonomic essence of categories, but instead help establish and describe referents (e.g., when a waitress refers to a customer who ordered a ham sandwich as "the ham sandwich at the corner table"; Barsalou, 1993). Similarly, people commonly violate ontological distinctions, such as those between animate and inanimate entities, in their object naming (e.g., using the label *bear* to refer to both real and toy bears; Jones & Smith, 1993; Landau, Jones, & Smith, 1992).

The suggestion that concepts are contextually based is closely related to the claim that perceptual features are crucial determinants of children's representations (Inhelder & Piaget, 1964). Barsalou (1993) proposed that perceptual symbols constitute the core of concepts. Through processes involving selective attention, introspection, and compositional analyses, perceptual symbols get combined to give rise to abstract concepts. Moreover, perceptual symbols serve as the basis for linguistic ones, and the flexibility of concepts arises from interactions among such symbols (Barsalou, 1993). In a study by Olseth and Barsalou (1995), adults were asked to judge whether a property was a physical part of an object (e.g., whether a claw is a part of a chair). Subjects were given numerous pairs of property and object, some true and some false, and their verification time was measured. The authors found that perceptual properties of the pairs (e.g., distance between the center of the object and the part) significantly accounted for the variance in correct verification time, even when the experimenter did not explicitly instruct subjects to create an image of the property–object pair. Olseth and Barsalou (1995) concluded that conceptual representations have perceptual content that is spontaneously used by adults.

In a similar vein, Eimas (1994) claimed that "nonperceptual knowledge ... finds its origins and basis in the same processes of perception and categorization that make possible the initial perceptually driven categorical representations; thus it too is perceptually based" (p. 86). Likewise, Jones and Smith (1993) argued that children's performance on cognitive tasks is determined by their weighting of perceptual dimensions, attention to physical regularities, and consideration of context-specific contingencies. These processes function online to focus children's attention on the dynamic similarity space; thus they do not resort to some kind of deeper conceptual knowledge. Perceptual categories derived from these processes, though, can represent conceptually relevant abstract knowledge (e.g., surface gradient differences between natural and manufactured kinds; L. B. Smith & Heise, 1992).

One of the most commonly cited sources of evidence for the primacy of perceptual properties in children's concepts is that of children's lexical extensions. In one standard procedure, researchers introduce children to a target object labeled with a novel word and then present them with a set of test objects, similar to the target in some property but different from it in others. Children are asked to identify a referent of the novel word among the test objects. When provided with items that are either taxonomically, thematically, or perceptually similar (e.g., same shape) to the target object, children most commonly choose the object similar in shape to the target object as the referent of the novel word (Baldwin, 1992; Imai, Gentner & Uchida, 1994).

Summary

The evidence sketched in this section demonstrates that concepts are highly variable and context sensitive. Jones and Smith (1993) proposed that this demonstration argues against the role of essences or theories in two major ways: Concepts have no stable core (i.e., no essence), and perceptual features (vs. nonobvious features) are most central.

A RESOLUTION OF THE PARADOX

In the following sections, we argue for a resolution of the apparent contradiction between early essentialism and early context sensitivity. The resolution rests on four main points: (1) First, we clarify what is meant by psychological essentialism and what it does *not* entail. Contrary to common depictions, essentialism is a skeletal heuristic rather than a detailed set of scientific beliefs. (2) Next, we outline a sample of the major distinctions among concepts and argue that different kinds of concepts require different theories to account for their structure. (3) Third, we cast a critical eye on the role of perceptual features, in particular, shape, as prime determinants of conceptual structure. We argue that the power of perceptual features often derives from their status as markers of theory-relevant information. (4) Finally, we examine what is stable in the variability and context sensitivity of concepts. We suggest that the variability in the information that people use is patterned, predictable, and consistent with the notion of a theory-based core.

What Is Psychological Essentialism? A Clarification

Resolving the paradox between the essences-are-core and the concepts-have-no-core positions first requires a clarification of what is meant by psychological essentialism. To quote Medin (1989), psychological essentialism entails the following:

> People act as if things (e.g., objects) have essences or underlying natures that make them the thing that they are. Furthermore, the essence constrains or generates properties that may vary in their centrality. One of the things that theories do is to embody or provide causal linkages from deeper properties to more superficial or surface properties. (p. 1476)

At first blush, essentialism may sound like a return to the defining-features view of categories outlined earlier. It is not, and to see why, we must clarify what essentialism does *not* entail. Essentialism does not entail that people know (consciously or unconsciously) what the essence is. Medin and Ortony (1989) referred to this unknown-yet-believed-in entity as an "essence placeholder." People may implicitly assume, for example, that there is some quality that bears share that confers category identity and causes identifiable surface features, and they may use this belief to guide inductive inferences and explanations without being able to identify any feature or trait as the bear essence. This belief can be considered an unarticulated heuristic rather than a detailed theory.

Furthermore, an essence is rarely consulted to determine category membership, for the simple reason that people often do not know (or cannot readily access) the relevant information. For example, we may believe gender to be determined by nonobvious features (such as chromosomes), but in most cases we need to rely on outward (clothed) appearance and voice to make a gender classification. A related point is that the folk essence may include concepts that have no scientific counterpart (e.g., *soul* in Western philosophy, *kunam* among the Tamil; Daniel, 1985). Indeed, Atran (1990) argued that even those living in cultures with no scientific tradition assume that essences exist. Moreover, some have argued that essentialism and current biological theory are incompatible (Hirschfeld, 1996; Mayr, 1991; Sober, 1994).

These initial points of clarification imply that essentialism is difficult (perhaps impossible) to study *directly*. Psychological essentialism posits that people believe in the existence of essences, not that people have detailed knowledge about the content of essences or that the world is organized in accord with essences. Studies demonstrating that people classify instances based on nonessential features or that people cannot specify an essence or that people's representation of a concept does not match that of science do not offer evidence against psychological essentialism. They are valuable for examining what kinds of information are used on certain tasks, but they do not constitute tests of psychological essentialism as a theory of concepts.

In sum, contrary to common depictions, essentialism is a skeletal principle (Medin, 1989; see also R. Gelman, 1990; R. Gelman & Williams, 1997, for a discussion of skeletal principles) rather than a detailed set of beliefs, scientific or otherwise. It is a guiding assumption in the mind of the cognizer (a "stance," "construal," or "heuristic"; Keil, 1995), rather than a fixed set of features contained in the concept. In this sense, we are sympathetic to the portrayal of essentialism as a metaconceptual belief about conceptual structure (Malt, 1990). However, *metaconceptual* does not mean epiphenomenal or divorced from conceptual structure; essentialism is a metaconceptual construal with extended conceptual implications. Although essentialism does not *specify* particular conceptual content, it constrains and generates such properties (to use Medin's [1989] terminology), and guides further knowledge acquisition. The essence, when unknown, may serve as a motivator and source for conceptual change (see Waxman & Braig, 1996). Because the (unknown) essence, not any particular set of features, is regarded as necessary, essentialist categories can incorporate anomalies and thus better account for conceptual change than can models of concepts that presume the existence of fixed features. Because essentialism is a placeholder notion, it provides stability in the face of conceptual change and context sensitivity: What is stored is not *what* the essence is, but *that* it exists.

A second point is that perceptual features are closely linked to the essence; thus, essentialism is not a claim that perceptual features are unimportant. Essences are often correlated with and predictive of perceptual features. According to a somewhat oversimplified folk portrayal, XY chromosomes *cause* the observable properties of a male. Because we typically do not have direct access to the essence, the correlated observable properties become crucial to many tasks (see Keil, 1989). This linkage between observable properties and assumption of underlying causal (essential) properties can provide an account of why perceptual prototypes, although insufficient for characterizing many categorization decisions (e.g., Keil, 1989; Rips & Collins, 1993), are so prevalent in online processing of concepts.

Domain Specificity and Conceptual Variation

Sensitivity to distinctions among categories promises to bring order to the inconsistency that appears when we try to characterize conceptual structure in a way that encompasses the full variety of all forms of human categorization. For example, does the concept *things to take from a burning house* differ from the concept *dogs*, or are they indistinguishable in structure? Common sense tells us that, at the very least, they differ in the perceptual similarity among instances, richness of stored knowledge, inferences that can be made, stability over time, position in a hierarchy, and so forth. Moreover, we suggest that the concept of *dogs*, but not the concept of *things to take from a burning house*, is treated as having an essence. Although Medin (1989) allowed for the possibility that all natural language concepts (including, e.g., wastebasket) are essentialist (see also Carey, 1995), we suspect instead that different categories have fundamentally different kinds of structure for children and adults.

At least three factors are relevant: category domain, category level, and linguistic expression. *Domain differences* have consequences for a variety of tasks that tap essentialist reasoning. Radical transformations result in judgments of category change for artifacts, but stability for animals (Keil, 1989); thus animals—but not artifacts—retain some essential qualities that persist despite external appearance changes. Information about internal parts is used when extending novel labels for animals but not for artifacts (Diesendruck et al., in press), thus suggesting that the relevance of nonobvious internal parts (a close stand-in for essences) is domain specific. Inductive inferences are more powerful for animal categories than for artifact categories (S. A. Gelman, 1988). Children are also more likely to attribute immanent (inherent) causes for animals than for artifacts (S. A. Gelman

& Gottfried, 1996). In categorization, adults also distinguish between the two domains. They believe that membership in animal categories is more "absolute" than membership in artifact categories (Kalish, 1995), and that animal categories have defining features to a larger extent than artifact categories do (Malt, 1990). In general, these findings support the notion that children and adults hold essentialist beliefs about living kinds but not about artifacts. Explanations for the domain differences vary: They may reflect an innate domain-specific module for reasoning about living kinds (Atran, 1995), a teleological or essentialist construal that finds a better match with some domains in the world than with others (Keil, 1995), or an assumption that entities without external similarities (i.e., natural kinds) must have internal essential causal properties (S. A. Gelman et al., 1994).

At this point, very little is known about how *category level* intersects with judgments of essentialism, although some evidence is suggestive. The distinction between basic-level categories (e.g., dog) and superordinate-level categories (e.g., animal) may be particularly relevant. Inhelder and Piaget's (1964) studies in which children produced graphic collections typically used materials for which basic-level sorts were not possible; for taxonomic responding, superordinate groupings were required. In contrast, Piaget's findings of nominal realism emerged when children were reasoning about the names of individuals and *basic-level* categories. Similarly, although there appears to be no endorsement of H_2O as the essence of *water* when the word is used in a relatively broad sense (including pond water, polluted water, etc.), H_2O may be the essence of *water* when the word is used in a restricted sense (pure water; Malt, 1994, although her interpretation differs). Furthermore, Atran et al. (1996) found that the "generic-species" level (e.g., oak, robin) is favored for drawing inductive inferences by both people raised in Michigan and the Itzaj Maya people of Guatemala.

Linguistic expression is also predictive of category structure: Essentializing may be more likely to occur when a concept is encoded in language than when it is not. Certainly, hearing a familiar name can foster essentializing (S. A. Gelman & Markman, 1986), although not every word carries with it essentialist assumptions (Davidson & Gelman, 1990). The reasons for the importance of lexicalization are not entirely clear; concepts so important as to be essentialist may be prime candidates for lexicalization because of their salience, frequency, and stability. Instead, perhaps having a name helps fix the concept in people's minds, transmit it to new generations, and so reify its existence. Linguistic form class also appears to be important, although to date this possibility is underexplored. Markman (1989) suggested that nouns are more likely than adjectives to capture essentialist kinds (see also Waxman & Markow, 1995).

Altogether, it appears that essentialism is most likely to appear for basic-level living kinds that are referred to by common nouns, at least among adults. A major source of confusion in the literature is that the dimensions of domain, level, and linguistic expression have generally been ignored in discussions of the validity of psychological essentialism. The scope of essentialism can be exaggerated when derived from studies of natural kind categories, especially basic-level animal categories with familiar common nouns as names. Conversely, the role of perception can be misleading when focused on nonlexicalized categories for which essences or theories are barely possible. For example, Landau, Smith, and Jones (1988) found that children had a strong tendency to extend labels on the basis of perceptual features such as shape—a finding that is not surprising because the stimuli in that study were simple novel objects (e.g., U-shaped piece of plywood), about which children had little knowledge. Similarly, Mervis, Johnson, and Scott (1993) reported a study in which subjects sorted on the basis of shape; yet the task was a silhouette identification task, in which shape and size were the only dimensions available. If the only information that children receive concerns shape, texture, and size, then frequent use of shape is unsurprising. In contrast, when children reason about real-world living kinds, issues of ontology, essence, and kind become important.

Role of Shape

The notion that words capture theory-based categories or essences is called into question by recent studies (reviewed earlier) suggesting that shape is a crucial component of children's semantic representations and even overrides ontological distinctions. In this view, children have a general shape bias in their interpretations of novel count nouns, such that a new word (e.g., a *dax*) is assumed to refer to a set of objects that share a common shape (Baldwin, 1992; Imai, Gentner, & Uchida, 1994; Landau et al., 1988; Landau, Jones, & Smith, 1992). One interpretation of the bias is that ontological status is irrelevant, at least in naming and perhaps in conceptualization (e.g., toy bears and real bears are both *bears* because they have a common shape; Jones & Smith, 1993).

However, children may attend to shape not because it is the basis on which words are extended, but rather because it is an indirect indicator of category membership; it correlates with and "is often . . . a good source of information about" what kind of thing an object is (Soja, Carey, & Spelke, 1992). For example, shape (more than color, texture, or parts) is an excellent predictor of whether an animal is a pig, cat, or horse. The word *pig* does not refer to the property *pig shaped*, but instead suggests that shape is a good index of which particular kind an animal belongs to. More generally, the power of perceptual features often derives from their status as markers of theory-relevant information. If this interpretation is correct, then when children directly receive information about theoretical kind, this information should influence which features are used.

Ample evidence shows that shape cannot be the central determinant of children's nonlinguistic classifications. In these examples, fundamental conceptual distinctions—often ontological—are more predictive than shape. By 9 months of age, infants sort together different basic-level animal categories (e.g., dogs and fish) and separate birds with outspread wings from airplanes (Mandler & McDonough, 1993; see also Ross, 1980, for evidence of superordinate classifications in children 12–24 months of age). Ten-month-olds classify together containers differing in shape and distinguish between same-shaped objects that differ in their capacity to contain (Kolstad & Baillargeon, 1996). By the age of 2 years, children weight substance more heavily than shape on a match-to-sample task on which the items are nonsolid masses (Soja, Carey, & Spelke, 1991). By 3 and 4 years of age, children treat plants and animals as belonging to a single category (living things), despite the extreme differences in shape between, say, a cow and a tree (Backscheider, Shatz, & Gelman, 1993; Hickling & Gelman, 1995). Conversely, children treat humans and apes as belonging to distinctly different categories, despite their greater similarity (Coley, 1993; Johnson, Mervis, & Boster, 1992). Preschool children also overlook similarity in shape when making predictions about how statues versus live animals move (Massey & Gelman, 1988).

Particularly crucial for the shape–bias hypothesis are its implications for language. Below the age of 2½, children make many overextension errors (e.g., calling a round ball "moon"), and these errors are often described as being shape based (Clark, 1973). However, in previous analyses there were few attempts to tease apart shape from taxonomic relatedness as the basis of children's overextensions. More recently, Gelman, Croft, Fu, Clausner, and Gottfried (in press) examined the relative role of taxonomic relatedness and shape in children's overextensions, using two tasks, productive labeling and comprehension. Subjects were 2, 2½, and 4 years of age.

The results argued against a shape bias in overextensions in three ways. First, children were typically correct in comprehension. Even when presented with objects of the same shape *and* same taxonomic kind (e.g., an orange, when asked for "an apple"), most children refrained from extending a word erroneously. Second, in both comprehension and production, when children did overextend, it was typically to items that matched the target word in both shape *and* taxonomic relatedness. Third, in comprehension, children were as likely to overextend on the basis of taxonomic relatedness alone as on shape alone. For example, when asked for an "apple," children picked a banana as often as they picked a baseball. All these findings suggest that shape has no special priority in young children's semantic representations. Both superordinate-level taxonomic relatedness and shape are salient in children's early word meanings.

If, as we suggest, shape is not central to children's naming, then why are ontological distinctions commonly ignored in ordinary language use? Soja et al. (1992) suggested that children do not name shape per se but attempt to name what the shape represents. A toy bear is called a "bear" because it represents a bear, not because it is shaped like a bear. Indirect support for this argument comes from the observation that objects not designed to represent another kind of thing are rarely mislabeled (e.g., footballs are rarely called "eggs"). Gelman and Ebeling (1998) have conducted a pilot study designed to test this hypothesis more directly. Subjects were 47 preschool children (2;5 to 3;11). They saw line drawings roughly shaped like various nameable objects, such as a bear. For half the subjects, we described each line drawing as depicting a shape that was created *intentionally*—for example, someone painted the picture. For the remaining subjects, we described the same drawing as depicting a shape that was created *accidentally*—for example, someone spilled paint. For each item, subjects first heard the brief story, then were shown the corresponding line drawing and asked, "What is this?" Children's open-ended responses were coded as naming the shape (e.g., "a bear"), naming the actual materials (e.g., "paint"), or other (e.g., "this looks like a bear," "I don't know").

We hypothesized that subjects' use of shape as the basis of naming would be influenced by the representational status of the pictures: When the drawings were intended, subjects should name the shapes; when the drawings were unintended, subjects should not name the shapes (e.g., describing the literal materials instead). In other words, the hypothesis was that when children name in accordance with shape, it is not because shape is paramount, but rather because shape is a representation. When the shape does not stand for a kind—as with accidental paint spills—shape is no longer relevant. The findings fit the predictions: 2- and 3-year-olds named on the basis of shape (e.g., referring to the bear-shaped drawing as a "bear") significantly more often when the shape was intended than when it was not.

A final issue is taxonomic level. Most earlier studies examining the shape bias have pitted shape against superordinate category membership (e.g., food). For example, given a target picture of a round cake, subjects were permitted to choose among a hat (shape match), a pie (superordinate-level taxonomic match), or a gift (thematic match) (Imai et al., 1994). The taxonomic match was not from the same basic-level category as the target (e.g., a heart-shaped cake). However, it is well known that children's earliest words typically name basic-level object categories and that children have relative difficulty reasoning with superordinate-level categories (Markman & Callanan, 1984). Thus, pitting shape against superordinate-level categories provides a particularly stringent test of whether shape wins out over taxonomic kind in children's word learning. Moreover, if children search for a basic-level match but cannot find one (because there is no basic-level match in the experimental array), they may rely on shape because it is typically a strong predictor of basic-level category membership.

A more sensitive test involves pitting shape against basic-level category membership. Golinkoff et al. (1995) have conducted a set of experiments examining children's extensions of novel words in which the taxonomic choices were of the same basic-level category as the targets (e.g., if the target was a high-heeled shoe, the taxonomic match was a boot). The other choices matched in perceptual similarity or thematic relatedness. Corresponding to our predictions, 2-year-olds in their studies generalized novel nouns to members of the same basic-level category and overrode perceptual similarity.

To summarize, shape is not the sole or even primary factor in children's naming and classification. On tasks that provide information only about perceptual dimensions (e.g., sorting of simple, novel artifacts that vary only in shape, texture, and color), shape is an especially salient dimension. However, its salience derives largely from its value as an index or predictor of other information (Medin, 1989; Soja et al., 1992; Waxman & Braig, 1996). When ontological knowledge and theoretical beliefs are available and when they conflict with shape, children often sort and name on the basis of these other factors.

Stability in Conceptual Representation

What is stable in the representation of concepts? Barsalou (1993) has argued that stability is in the long-term knowledge, rather than in the concepts that draw on such knowledge. Jones and Smith (1993) proposed a more extreme position, that nothing is stable: "Concepts have no constant structure, but are instead continually created. There is, in brief, a dynamic conceptual space of which the dynamic similarity space is part" (p. 130). There are at least two problems, however, with arguing that concepts are not stable. First, at the very least there is stability in what gets linked to a word. Phonetic representations are stored in long-term memory, and we treat some meanings linked to these representations as importantly the *same*, but others as mere homophones (e.g., brown flying *bat* and baseball *bat*). Second, there appear to be constraints on which kinds of information get stored with a word or concept (Markman, 1989). Such constraints provide conceptual stability, and it seems unlikely that all such constraints could be provided by the perceptual system. How would, say, mutual exclusivity be perceptually represented?

At this point, the no-core view, although important for reminding us of the variability in concepts, seems particularly ill-suited to provide a portrait of stability, because it denies its very existence. Although we do not propose to solve the problem of stability, a couple of points are worth noting. First, the nature of conceptual stability may be quite abstract, at the level of ontological commitments ("X is an animal") rather than particular features. Ontological status appears to be remarkably stable and unchanging across uses of a word or variations of a concept (Keil, 1989). Ontologies are implicitly built into our grammar (e.g., with classifier systems; see Silverstein, 1986). Even when concepts are variable, ontological commitments tend not to change. For example, although prototypes change with context (Barsalou, 1991), such changes typically leave ontological kind unaffected (e.g., although typicality ratings of birds vary depending on whether one adopts a "U.S." vs. "Chinese" point of view, across both contexts, birds are presumed to be animate, egg-laying creatures). Psychological essentialism may be one kind of ontological commitment.

The other point is that there is more stability when task is kept constant than when averaging across tasks. Task effects are clearly systematic. Similarity judgments, categorization, and inductive inferences all yield different patterns of responses (Carey, 1985; Deák & Bauer, 1995; S. A. Gelman, Collman, & Maccoby, 1986; Rips & Collins, 1993; Taylor & Gelman, 1993). Subjects who are expert in a domain classify differently from novices (Chi, Hutchinson, & Robin, 1989). Under time pressure, subjects are more likely to use global similarity than dimensional similarity (Ward, 1983) and more likely to use perceptual salience than formal category structure (Lamberts, 1995). As noted earlier, use of language has implications for classification (Markman & Hutchinson, 1984; Waxman, 1991). The general pattern is that tasks reflecting the accumulation of expertise and deep analysis are the tasks for which subjects more consistently use information that can be characterized as nonobvious. There seems to be a distinction between rough-and-ready information, used when we need to be quick, versus more time-consuming, less obvious information, used when we need to be thoughtful. The "quick" information is what we find salient; the "thoughtful" information is what we believe the world is like. Although the two are highly correlated, nonobvious properties are privileged on tasks requiring expertise and lexicalization.

Nevertheless, perceptual information is not developmentally earlier than theoretical information (Bruner, 1973; Piaget, 1951). There is no perceptual-to-conceptual shift in ontogenesis (S. A. Gelman, 1996; Jones & Smith, 1993; Simons & Keil, 1995). Young children are sensitive to the task effects described previously. Thus, given the appropriate task (e.g., induction), even 2-year-olds give essentialist responses (S. A. Gelman & Coley, 1990). Moreover, even on "quick" identification tasks, detection and use of subtle ontological information may be immediate and may allow children to identify an instance as a real animal versus a statue, for example (Massey

& Gelman, 1988). Similarly, 2-year-olds attend to eyes; 3-year-olds attend more to tiny self-initiated movements than to large other-initiated movements, when explaining animal movement (S. A. Gelman & Gottfried, 1996); and 4-year-olds attend to subtle details of a drawing to detect the category membership of an item (e.g., the antennae on a leaf insect; Gelman & Markman, 1987). L. B. Smith and Heise (1992) have suggested that these sorts of subtle perceptual cues make perception smart and have argued against the need to posit theories or essentialism; we suggest instead that these cues provide evidence that perception is constrained by and imbued with theories.

WHAT'S IN A CONCEPT? THE QUESTION
OF REPRESENTATION

Our review points out that concepts pose a puzzle for the study of representations: They are context sensitive, leading some to question what (if anything) is stable in their representation. The skeptic might insist that nothing is stable and so nothing is represented. We have been arguing that much is represented, but it is of skeletal form and varies depending on the kind of concept and kind of conceptual task under consideration. The argument for skeletal structures is akin to R. Gelman's (1990) suggestion about skeletal principles underlying children's acquisition of fundamental concepts such as number and animacy. It differs, however, in that R. Gelman's skeletal principles are domain-specific, contentful prototheories that are extended in domain-specific ways, whereas our notion of essentialist concept may span domains (cf. Carey, 1995; Hirschfeld, 1996; Wellman & Gelman, 1997). Here we sketch what might be represented in a basic-level natural kind concept.

Three components seem to be central: an ontology, a notion of essence or kind, and a perceptually based prototype. The evidence for early representation of ontology is too vast to review here, but is supported by developmental evidence (Mandler, 1993) and neuropsychological evidence (e.g., Caramazza, Hillis, Leek, & Miozzo, 1994). Once again, we stress that the notion of essence or kind is skeletal: What is stored is not *what* the essence is, but *that* it is there. We suggest either essence or kind as two related versions, the former stronger than the latter (S. A. Gelman, 1995). The notion of *kind* suggests that the category is treated as real and entails rich commonalities; the notion of *essence* includes the notion of kind plus the additional element of some entity or force that is causally responsible. Finally, the linking of the first two components with a perceptually based prototype accounts for how reasoners (naturally) link theories with evidence and accounts for the information used during rapid identification of instances.

We conclude with the observation that essentialism does not make the problem of representation easier and may even complicate it considerably. Because the essence itself is typically not represented in full, it does not solve the problem of what specifically is stored in memory. Moreover, knowledge—especially causal knowledge, or what we have been calling *theories*—becomes an important part of the concept. This conclusion should not be surprising, however, when we consider that one of the primary functions of concepts is to work with our theory-rich understandings of the world.

ACKNOWLEDGMENTS

The research in this chapter was supported by a National Science Foundation grant (BNS-9100348) and a J. S. Guggenheim fellowship to Gelman. We are very grateful to Ellin Scholnick and Katherine Nelson for their thoughtful comments on an earlier draft.

REFERENCES

Ahn, W.-K., Kalish, C. W., Medin, D. L., & Gelman, S. A. (1995). The role of covariation versus mechanism information in causal attribution. *Cognition, 54*, 299–352.

Ahn, W.-K., & Lassaline, M. E. (1996). *Causal structure in categorization.* Unpublished manuscript.

Atran, S. (1990). *Cognitive foundations of natural history.* New York: Cambridge University Press.

Atran, S. (1995). Causal constraints on categories and categorical constraints on biological reasoning across cultures. In D. Sperber, D. Premack, & A. Premack (Eds.), *Causal cognition: A multidisciplinary debate* (pp. 205–233). Oxford, England: Oxford University Press.

Atran, S., Estin, P., Coley, J., & Medin, D. (1996). *Generic species and basic levels: Essence and appearance in folk biology.* Unpublished ms.

Backscheider, A. B., Shatz, M., & Gelman, S. A. (1993). Preschoolers' ability to distinguish living kinds as a function of regrowth. *Child Development, 64*, 1242–1257.

Baldwin, D. A. (1992). Clarifying the role of shape in children's taxonomic assumption. *Journal of Experimental Child Psychology, 54*, 392–416.

Barsalou, L. W. (1991). Deriving categories to achieve goals. In G. H. Bower (Ed.), *The psychology of learning and motivation* (pp. 1–64). New York: Academic Press.

Barsalou, L. W. (1993). Flexibility, structure, and linguistic vagary in concepts: Manifestations of a compositional system of perceptual symbols. In A. C. Collins, S. E. Gathercole, & P. E. M. Morris (Eds.), *Theories of memory* (pp. 29–101). Hillsdale, NJ: Lawrence Erlbaum Associates.

Benelli, B. (1988). If it is a dog, can it be an animal? The role of metalinguistic knowledge in the acquisition of linguistic superordination. *Journal of Psycholinguistic Research, 17*, 227–243.

Braisby, N., Franks, B., & Hampton, J. (1996). Essentialism, word use, and concepts. *Cognition, 59*, 247–274.

Brook, J. S. (1970). A test of Piaget's theory of "nominal realism." *Journal of Genetic Psychology,* *116,* 165–175.

Bruner, J. S. (1973). *Beyond the information given.* New York: Norton.

Caramazza, A., Hillis, A., Leek, E. C., & Miozzo, M. (1994). The organization of lexical knowledge in the brain: Evidence from category- and modality-specific deficits. In L. A. Hirschfeld & S. A. Gelman (Eds.), *Mapping the mind: Domain specificity in cognition and culture* (pp. 68–84). Cambridge, England: Cambridge University Press.

Carey, S. (1985). *Conceptual change in childhood.* Cambridge, MA: MIT Press.

Carey, S. (1995). On the origins of causal understanding. In D. Sperber, D. Premack, & A. Premack (Eds.), *Causal cognition: A multidisciplinary debate* (pp. 268–302). Oxford, England: Oxford University Press.

Chi, M., Hutchinson, J., & Robin, A. (1989). How inferences about novel domain-related concepts can be constrained by structured knowledge. *Merrill-Palmer Quarterly, 35,* 27–62.

Clark, E. V. (1973). What's in a word? On the child's acquisition of semantics in his first language. In T. E. Moore (Ed.), *Cognitive development and the acquisition of language* (pp. 65–110). New York: Academic Press.

Coley, J. D. (1993). *Emerging differentiation of folkbiology and folkpsychology: Similarity judgments and property attributions.* Unpublished doctoral dissertation, University of Michigan.

Daniel, V. (1985). *Fluid signs.* Los Angeles: University of California Press.

Davidson, N. S., & Gelman, S. A. (1990). Inductions from novel categories: The role of language and conceptual structure. *Cognitive Development, 5,* 151–176.

Deák, G., & Bauer, P. J. (1995). The effects of task comprehension on preschoolers' and adults' categorization choices. *Journal of Experimental Child Psychology, 60,* 393–427.

Diesendruck, G. (1997). *Essentialism and word learning: A cross-cultural investigation.* Manuscript submitted for publication.

Diesendruck, G., Gelman, S. A., & Lebowitz, K. (1998). Conceptual and linguistic biases in children's word learning. *Developmental Psychology, 34,* 823–839.

Dupré, J. (1993). *The disorder of things: Metaphysical foundations of the disunity of science.* Cambridge, MA: Harvard University Press.

Eimas, P. D. (1994). Categorization in early infancy and the continuity of development. *Cognition, 50,* 83–93.

Gelman, R. (1990). First principles organize attention to and learning about relevant data: Number and the animate-inanimate distinction as examples. *Cognitive Science, 14,* 79–106.

Gelman, R., & Baillargeon, R. (1983). A review of some Piagetian concepts. In J. H. Flavell & E. M. Markman (Eds.), *Handbook of child psychology* (Vol. 3, pp. 167–230). New York: Wiley.

Gelman, R., & Williams, E. M. (1997). Enabling constraints for cognitive development and learning: Domain specificity and epigenesis. In D. Kuhn & R. S. Siegler (Eds.), *Handbook of child psychology, Vol. 2: Cognition, perception, and language* (pp. 575–630). New York: Wiley.

Gelman, S. A. (1988). The development of induction within natural kind and artifact categories. *Cognitive Psychology, 20,* 65–95.

Gelman, S. A. (1995, November). *The development of a concept of "kind."* Paper presented at a workshop on permanence and change in conceptual knowledge, Kazimierz, Poland.

Gelman, S. A. (1996). Concepts and theories. In R. Gelman & T. K. Au (Eds.), *Perceptual and cognitive development* (pp. 117–150). New York: Academic Press.

Gelman, S. A., & Coley, J. D. (1990). The importance of knowing a dodo is a bird: Categories and inferences in two-year-olds. *Developmental Psychology, 26,* 796–804.

Gelman, S. A., Coley, J. D., & Gottfried, G. M. (1994). Essentialist beliefs in children: The acquisition of concepts and theories. In L. A. Hirschfeld & S. A. Gelman (Eds.), *Mapping the mind: Domain specificity in cognition and culture* (pp. 341–365). Cambridge, England: Cambridge University Press.

Gelman, S. A., Collman, P., & Maccoby, E. E. (1986). Inferring properties from categories versus inferring categories from properties: The case of gender. *Child Development, 57*, 396–404.

Gelman, S. A., Croft, W., Fu, P., Clausner, T., & Gottfried, G. (in press). Why is a pomegranate an "apple"? The role of shape, taxonomic relatedness, and prior knowledge in children's overextensions. *Journal of Child Language.*

Gelman, S. A., & Ebeling, K. S. (1998). Shape and representational status in children's early naming. *Cognition, 66*, B35–B47.

Gelman, S. A., & Gottfried, G. M. (1996). Children's causal explanations of animate and inanimate motion. *Child Development, 67*, 1970–1987.

Gelman, S. A., & Markman, E. M. (1986). Categories and induction in young children. *Cognition, 23*, 183–209.

Gelman, S. A., & Markman, E. M. (1987). Young children's inductions from natural kinds: The role of categories and appearances. *Child Development, 8*, 157–167.

Gelman, S. A., & Medin, D. L. (1993). What's so essential about essentialism? A different perspective on the interaction of perception, language, and conceptual knowledge. *Cognitive Development, 8*, 157–167.

Gelman, S. A., Wilcox, S. A., & Clark, E. V. (1989). Conceptual and lexical hierarchies in young children. *Cognitive Development, 4*, 309–326.

Golinkoff, R. M., Shuff-Bailey, M., Olguin, R., & Ruan, W. (1995). Young children extend novel words at the basic level: Evidence for the principle of categorical scope. *Developmental Psychology, 31*, 494–507.

Goodman, N. (1972). Seven strictures on similarity. In N. Goodman (Ed.), *Problems and projects* (pp. 437–447). Indianapolis, IN: Bobbs-Merrill.

Greenberg, J. H. (1966). *Language universals.* The Hague, Netherlands: Mouton.

Hampton, J. A. (1982). A demonstration of intransitivity in natural categories. *Cognition, 12*, 151–164.

Heit, E., & Rubinstein, J. (1994). Similarity and property effects in inductive reasoning. *Journal of Experimental Psychology: Learning, Memory, and Cognition, 20*, 411–422.

Hickling, A. K., & Gelman, S. A. (1995). How does your garden grow? Early conceptualization of seeds and their place in the plant growth cycle. *Child Development, 66*, 856–876.

Hirschfeld, L. A. (1996). *Race in the making.* Cambridge, MA: MIT Press.

Imai, M., Gentner, D., & Uchida, N. (1994). Children's theories of word meaning: The role of shape similarity in early acquisition. *Cognitive Development, 9*, 45–75.

Inhelder, B., & Piaget, J. (1964). *The early growth of logic in the child.* New York: Norton.

Johnson, K., Mervis, C., & Boster, J. (1992). Developmental changes within the structure of the mammal domain. *Developmental Psychology, 28*, 74–83.

Johnson-Laird, P. N., & Wason, P. C. (1977). *Thinking: Readings in cognitive science.* Cambridge, England: Cambridge University Press.

Jones, S. S., & Smith, L. B. (1993). The place of perception in children's concepts. *Cognitive Development, 8*, 113–139.

Kalish, C. (1995). Essentialism and graded membership in animal and artifact categories. *Memory and Cognition, 23*, 335–353.

Keil, F. C. (1989). *Concepts, kinds, and cognitive development.* Cambridge, MA: MIT Press.

Keil, F. C. (1995). *The growth of causal understandings of natural kinds.* In D. Sperber, D. Premack, & A. Premack (Eds.), *Causal cognition: A multidisciplinary debate* (pp. 234–262). Oxford, England: Oxford University Press.

Kolstad, V., & Baillargeon, R. (1996). *Appearance- and knowledge-based responses of 10.5-month-old infants to containers.* Unpublished manuscript.

Lamberts, K. (1995). Categorization under time pressure. *Journal of Experimental Psychology: General, 124*, 161–180.

Landau, B., Jones, S. S., & Smith, L. B (1992). Perception, ontology, and naming in young children: Commentary on Soja, Carey, and Spelke. *Cognition, 43,* 85–91.

Landau, B., Smith, L. B., & Jones, S. S. (1988). The importance of shape in early lexical learning. *Cognitive Development, 3,* 299–321.

Locke, J. (1959). *An essay concerning human understanding, Vol. 2.* New York: Dover. (Original work published 1894)

Malt, B. C. (1990). Features and beliefs in the mental representation of categories. *Journal of Memory and Language, 29,* 289–315.

Malt, B. C. (1994). Water is not H₂O. *Cognitive Psychology, 27,* 41–70.

Mandler, J. M. (1993). On concepts. *Cognitive Development, 8,* 141–148.

Mandler, J. M., & McDonough, L. (1993). Concept formation in infancy. *Cognitive Development, 8,* 291–318.

Markman, E. M. (1976). Children's difficulty with word-referent differentiation. *Child Development, 47,* 742–749.

Markman, E. M. (1989). *Categorization and naming in children: Problems of induction.* Cambridge, MA: MIT Press.

Markman, E. M., & Callanan, M. A. (1984). An analysis of hierarchical classification. In R. J. Sternberg (Ed.), *Advances in the psychology of human intelligence* (Vol. 2, pp. 325–365). Hillsdale, NJ: Lawrence Erlbaum Associates.

Markman, E. M., & Hutchinson, J. E. (1984). Children's sensitivity to constraints on word meaning: Taxonomic versus thematic relations. *Cognitive Psychology, 16,* 1–27.

Massey, C., & Gelman, R. (1988). Preschoolers' ability to decide whether a photographed unfamiliar object can move itself. *Developmental Psychology, 24,* 307–317.

Mayr, E. (1991). *One long argument: Charles Darwin and the genesis of modern evolutionary thought.* Cambridge, MA: Harvard University Press.

McCloskey, M. E., & Glucksberg, S. (1978). Natural categories: Well defined or fuzzy sets? *Memory and Cognition, 6,* 462–472.

Medin, D. L. (1989). Concepts and conceptual structure. *American Psychologist, 44,* 1469–1481.

Medin, D. L., & Ortony, A. (1989). Psychological essentialism. In S. Vosniadou & A. Ortony (Eds.), *Similarity and analogical reasoning* (pp. 179–195). Cambridge, England: Cambridge University Press.

Medin, D. L., & Shoben, E. J. (1988). Context and structure in conceptual combination. *Cognitive Psychology, 20,* 158–190.

Merriman, W. E., & Bowman, L. L. (1989). The mutual exclusivity bias in children's word learning. *Monographs of the Society for Research in Child Development, 54* (No. 3–4).

Mervis, C. B., Johnson, K. E., & Scott, P. (1993). Perceptual knowledge, conceptual knowledge, and expertise: Comment on Jones and Smith. *Cognitive Development, 8,* 149–155.

Murphy, G. L. (1993). Theories and concept formation. In I. Van Mechelen, J. Hampton, R. Michalski, & P. Theuns (Eds.), *Categories and concepts: Theoretical views and inductive data analysis* (pp. 173–200). New York: Academic Press.

Murphy, G. L., & Medin, D. L. (1985). The role of theories in conceptual coherence. *Psychological Review, 92,* 289–316.

Nelson, K. (1974). Concept, word, and sentence: Interrelations in acquisition and development. *Psychological Review, 81,* 267–285.

Olseth, K. L., & Barsalou, L. W. (1995). The spontaneous use of perceptual representations during conceptual processing. In *Proceedings of the 17th annual meeting of the Cognitive Science Society* (pp. 310–315). Hillsdale, NJ: Lawrence Erlbaum Associates.

Piaget, J. (1929). *The child's conception of the world.* New York: Harcourt, Brace.

Piaget, J. (1951). *Play, dreams, and imitation in childhood.* New York: Norton.

Rips, L. J., & Collins, A. (1993). Categories and resemblance. *Journal of Experimental Psychology: General, 122,* 468–486.

Rosch, E. (1978). Principles of categorization. In E. Rosch & B. B. Lloyd (Eds.), *Cognition and categorization* (pp. 27–48). Hillsdale, NJ: Lawrence Erlbaum Associates.

Rosenblum, T., & Pinker, S. A. (1983). Word magic revisited: Monolingual and bilingual children's understanding of the word–object relationship. *Child Development, 54,* 773–780.

Ross, G. S. (1980). Categorization in 1- to 2-year-olds. *Developmental Psychology, 16,* 391–396.

Schwartz, S. P. (Ed.). (1977). *Naming, necessity, and natural kinds.* Ithaca, NY: Cornell University Press.

Silverstein, M. (1986). Cognitive implications of a referential hierarchy. In M. Hickmann (Ed.), *Social and functional approaches to language and thought* (pp. 125–164). New York: Academic Press.

Simons, D. J., & Keil, F. C. (1995). An abstract to concrete shift in the development of biological thought: The insides story. *Cognition, 56,* 129–163.

Smith, E. E., & Medin, D. L. (1981). *Categories and concepts.* Cambridge, MA: Harvard University Press.

Smith, L. B., & Heise, D. (1992). Perceptual similarity and conceptual structure. In B. Burns (Ed.), *Percepts, concepts and categories* (pp. 233–272). Amsterdam: North-Holland.

Sober, E. (1994). *From a biological point of view.* Cambridge, England: Cambridge University Press.

Soja, N. N., Carey, S., & Spelke, E. S. (1991). Ontological categories guide young children's inductions of word meaning: Object terms and substance terms. *Cognition, 38,* 179–211.

Soja, N. N., Carey, S., & Spelke, E. S. (1992). Perception, ontology, and word meaning. *Cognition, 45,* 101–107.

Taylor, M. G., & Gelman, S. A. (1993). Children's gender- and age-based categorization in similarity judgments and induction tasks. *Social Development, 2,* 104–121.

Ward, T. B. (1983). Response tempo and separable-integral responding: Evidence for an integral-to-separable processing sequence in visual perception. *Journal of Experimental Psychology: Human Perception and Performance, 9,* 103–112.

Waxman, S. R. (1991). Convergences between semantic and conceptual organization in the preschool years. In S. A. Gelman & J. P. Byrnes (Eds.), *Perspectives on language and thought* (pp. 107–145). Cambridge, England: Cambridge University Press.

Waxman, S. R., & Braig, B. (1996, April). *Stars and starfish: How far can shape take us?* Paper presented at the 10th biennial International Conference on Infant Studies, Providence, RI.

Waxman, S. R., & Markow, D. B. (1995, April). *Object properties and object kind: 21-month-old infants' extension of novel adjectives.* Poster presented at the biennial meeting of the Society for Research in Child Development, Indianapolis, IN.

Wellman, H. M., & Gelman, S. A. (1992). Cognitive development: Foundational theories of core domains. *Annual Review of Psychology, 43,* 337–375.

Wellman, H. M., & Gelman, S. A. (1997). Knowledge acquisition. In D. Kuhn & R. Siegler (Eds.), *Handbook of child psychology, 5th ed., Cognitive development* (pp. 523–573). New York: Wiley.

White, P. A. (1995). *The understanding of causation and the production of action: From infancy to adulthood.* Hove, England: Lawrence Erlbaum Associates.

Williams, R. (1977). Nominal realism in the child of the seventies? A replication. *Journal of Genetic Psychology, 130,* 161–162.

Chapter 5

Explanatory Understanding in Conceptual Development

Frank C. Keil
Kristi L. Lockhart
Yale University, New Haven, CT

This book commemorates the 100th anniversary of Jean Piaget's birth. This chapter explores how some Piagetian themes relate to recent studies of conceptual structure and use. It is especially appropriate that Piaget should be central to such a discussion, because much of his work on conceptual change and understanding resonates more strongly with recent work on concepts than with work 1 or 2 decades earlier. Piaget, for example, was clearly aware that concepts must be studied not as isolated entities or islands of thought but as parts of much larger knowledge structures. Moreover, Piaget often stressed the importance of children's understanding of cause and mechanism in his accounts of their conceptual development. Finally, most of Piaget's studies were of conceptual understanding and development in naturalistic settings, in which children were asked about naturally occurring categories and relations and about real causal mechanisms. Such a naturalistic emphasis is a good approach, not simply because it reflects current enthusiasm for ecological validity, but also because it provides unique and powerful insights into how explanation, cause, and mechanism are central to understanding conceptual development. In the end, we draw quite different conclusions from Piaget about the nature of conceptual development and the roles of cause, explanation, and mechanism in understanding such patterns of development; but in true Piagetian tradition, it is powerfully evident that his ideas seem to have formed an almost necessary scaffold for current notions.

THREE CLAIMS

Three patterns emerging from recent research suggest a particular account of how conceptual knowledge emerges in development. This chapter focuses on these three patterns and the effects of their working together. The patterns can be summarized as follows:

1. Concepts are represented and linked to each other and to other aspects of knowledge in ways that require heterogeneous knowledge structures.

2. These heterogeneous structures have often led to claims of qualitative developmental change, that is, from one facet of a heterogeneous structure to another or from an incomplete, immature structure containing only one facet to a complete, multifaceted adult system.

3. These claims of qualitative change are often wrong because they are based on incorrect models of adult concepts and on a mischaracterization of developmental change. There can be dramatic developmental change, to be sure, but under any reasonable sense of qualitative representational change, qualitative changes are much less common than might appear. (See also S. A. Gelman, 1996, for extensive discussion of the corruption of developmental models by adoption of incorrect adult models.)

This chapter considers each of these claims in turn and then considers a different account of how conceptual knowledge might change with development.

HETEROGENEITY OF CONCEPT STRUCTURE

A recurrently popular model of concepts, especially when concepts are assumed to be the mental entities that represent object categories like *dog*, *robin*, and *chair*, assumes that concepts are built up from probabilistic renderings of feature sets. Thus, a concept of *dog* might consist of a set of features or properties with probabilities attached to each feature. Alternatively, the concept could be a set of dog exemplars, each stored as a set of features. Some probabilistic assessment of the exemplar space then builds the concept, one that weights more frequent features more heavily. Several other variants are also possible (see Reisberg, 1997, for a recent summary), but the common assumption in all these models is that frequencies of instances, their properties, or both, as well as higher order statistical operations on the properties, such as correlation computations, are all that are needed to provide a full account of concept structure. Such models usually refer to the *similarity* space for concepts, with the implication that the space is structured solely by frequencies and correlations. Thus, the typicality of features and feature–feature correlations forms the basis for similarity and concept structure.

This model of concepts is hardly new. Associationist models of mind favored such a view for centuries. Interestingly, however, not all empiricists thought that the end state of adult knowledge was merely associative. Locke (1964/1690), for example, in his *Essay Concerning Human Understanding*, saw a developmental change occurring as children acquired the ability to reflect on their own minds and ideas. Their concepts changed to include conscious rules or principles arising from such reflections, ending ultimately in what Locke called "sublime" thoughts, those concepts that gave us understanding and explanatory insight. There is far more here than the usual empiricist slogan that all knowledge comes from the senses; there is also the idea that later ideas and concepts changed in their nature to be more precise, abstract, and propositional, and all the while, never lost their sense-based component of raw similarity.

The raw similarity component of concepts seems to have found a natural home in some connectionist accounts of learning and knowledge. A hallmark of some simple connectionist systems is their relentless tracking of the frequencies and correlations of features and microfeatures in the environment. It is therefore tempting to assume that concepts and knowledge are simply built from large records of such frequencies, whether in feature summaries or in exemplar-based models (e.g., Krushke, 1992). Connectionist architectures are certainly not obligated to model concepts in this way (e.g., Clark, 1993; Elman et al., 1996), but there is little doubt that some versions are ideal for capturing the basic tenets of associationism.

Despite the appeals of associationist accounts and their resonance with connectionism, one of the most popular movements in cognitive science today, it has long been recognized that the classic associationist approaches have severe limitations. Indeed, Piaget, was acutely aware of the limits of associationist models of mind when he proposed that children come to have powerful logical structures governing their concepts and knowledge (Piaget, 1970). Modern connectionist models can simulate at least some aspects of logical reasoning (Elman et al., 1996) but, especially in Piaget's time, it was clear that older associationist models could not. The logical, rulelike nature to human thought seems sharply distinct from its associationist aspects (Neisser, 1963; Sloman, 1996).

It is tempting to see the rulelike versus associative contrast in terms of mental representations embedded in language versus those common in prelinguistic and nonlinguistic minds, but such capacities are unlikely to be launched ex nihilo by the emergence of language. Instead, the capacity to represent and think about the world in a manner that resembles propositional thought may be part of the original competences of some species, most notably of humans. Today, sufficiently powerful connectionist systems might be able to model much of propositional thought and other rulelike aspects of cognition, but even then the intuition of a powerful duality of cognition remains such that two different complementary systems become organized and function in different ways regardless of how they might have originated (Sloman, 1996). Indeed, there have been claims that different neural systems may come to subserve the associative and rulelike components (Smith, Patalano, Jonides, & Koeppe, 1996).

Bare rules, however, may not be enough. There is also the impression that many concepts must include a strong sense of explanation, often of a causal nature. We not only store information about feature frequencies and correlations; we also have a sense of why those correlations and frequencies are the way they are (see also Ahn, Kalish, Medin & Gelman, 1995; Medin, 1989). Rules may help to organize and predict some correlations, but they do not on their own guarantee a sense of explanation. Thus, for many, a rule like "red sky at night, sailor's delight, red sky at morning, sailor's warning," offers no explanatory insight unless we understood something about directions of prevailing winds, the rotation of the earth, and causal interactions between these factors and the scattering of light in different atmospheric conditions. The explanatory sense may be partly illusory, as we shall see, but it is intuitively strong and captures part of how we grasp reality. We constantly invoke notions of causes and mechanisms in our spontaneous drive to explain the statistical patterns around us. Thus, concepts seem to have a facet that includes explanation and understanding of the probabilistic information associated with categories and their members. This situation is, of course, not universally the case. Regularities in mathematics and logic may be explainable in some sense, but not in a causal sense. This discussion of concepts is restricted to regularities that are presumed to arise from causal interactions.

This view of concepts is often called the *concepts-as-theories* view, because it entails a drive for achieving conceptual coherence through systems of explanation in which concepts are embedded (Keil, 1989; Murphy & Medin, 1985; Wellman & Gelman, 1997). Moreover, attempts to model conceptual change in childhood must take into account the theory-based part of concepts or else seem hopelessly ad hoc (e.g., Keil, 1987). Thus, developmental shifts in how children identify instances of categories and reason about them make little sense when understood merely as changing typicality distributions. Seven-year-olds who no longer think of a whale as a fish but accept a manta ray as a fish do so not because of a changing fish prototype or a dramatically different exemplar space; they do so because they have acquired more theoretical principles about fish in contrast to mammals (Carey, 1985). We could attempt to describe the shift as changing representations of what features are most typical, but such attempts are either false in view of the relatively equal frequency of salient features across ages or become empty when we make up arbitrarily complex features to model the data. When researchers have carefully modeled conceptual change in a particular domain, they seemed to invariably uncover changes in deeper theory-like relations and not changes in what appears to be a relatively constant associative structure (e.g., Chi, 1992; Keil & Batterman, 1984).

The concepts-as-theories view is now well entrenched in the literature, and there are several demonstrations of how the causal explanatory aspects of concepts can lead to illusory correlations, distorted frequency estimates, shifts in conceptual combinations, and a host of other concept-related phenomena (e.g., Medin, 1989). It is therefore nothing new to argue that concepts must have a theory-like part; indeed this argument seems to lead to a view of adult concepts as hybrid in nature, an interdependent mix of an associationist component and a theory-based component (Keil, 1995). Other might still try to model concepts solely in terms of feature frequencies and correlational structures (Cheng & Novick, 1992; Glymour, 1998) or conversely solely in nonassociative forms (Fodor, 1994), but in this chapter we assume that there is a hybrid structure or heterogeneity to concepts. This assumption is common and has a long history in developmental theory; by assuming it here, we may seem to ally ourselves with those who favor qualitative changes in concept structure with development. The challenge here is to show why such an inference is wrong. To anticipate, this chapter argues that hybrid structure is intrinsic to concepts, not just in adults but at any point in human development, and that it could not be any other way.

In some views of heterogeneous structure, certain problems can arise for models of concept acquisition and use. If the components are seen as relatively autonomous alternatives for conceptualizing reality, questions naturally occur as to the circumstances in which one sort of component is expected to dominate; that is, principles are needed to account for patterns of usage. It has been often suggested that the associative aspect of concepts appears first in processing and that rulelike and explanatory components take over after more considered reflection (e.g., Sloman, Love, & Ahn, in press). Such accounts seem to fit with views of the associative as being developmentally primitive, under the assumption that what is quick is usually easier and simpler to learn. Such an assumption, however, is not at all clear-cut. Moreover, it presumes a hybrid of relatively autonomous components that represent different "takes" on reality. The hybrid view here assumes a functional complementarity of components, such that all components are brought to bear in concept learning and use and in such a manner that they mutually support each other. This functional interdependence is illustrated in models of conceptual development.

HETEROGENEOUSLY STRUCTURED ADULT CONCEPTS DO NOT ENTAIL QUALITATIVE CHANGES IN DEVELOPMENT

If concepts are mixes of associative and explanatory-rulelike components that are qualitatively different from each other, it is natural to wonder whether one component is psychologically more primitive and therefore developmentally more basic. Perhaps children or infants are initially able to represent the world only in terms of one such component and then with time acquire the second component either through maturation or through its emergence from the first. Any such account gravitates toward the associative component as developmentally more primitive. After all, associative learning principles have been invoked across a wide range of species, and even the simplest neural net with just a handful of units at the input, hidden, and output layers can nicely model many aspects of associative learning (see Roitblat & Meyer, 1995).

Perhaps young human infants are purely associative beasts as well, and perhaps this associative component continues to dominate through much of early childhood. This conjecture seems to agree with many developmental phenomena. Inhelder and Piaget (1958), for example, talked of a conceptual shift from accidental to essential features, a view implying that early knowledge and reasoning might be based on tabulations of the most salient and typical information and later knowledge on deeper, more logical and causal relational information. Vygotsky (1986/1934) offered a similar proposal of children's concepts moving from instance-bound forms to rule-governed ones (in his case, mediated by the internalization of language). Werner (1948) proposed a holistic-to-analytic shift with a similar theme, one that was resurrected by Kemler and Smith (1978), using Garner's (1974) integral and separable dimensions, arguing that integral (read *holistic*) dimensions were developmentally more primitive. Finally, an apparent characteristic-to-defining shift in the acquisition of word meaning seems to further support such a claim (Keil, 1989; Keil & Batterman, 1984).

One of the most eloquent and dramatic accounts of such change was offered by Quine (1977) in his essay on natural kinds. He described children shifting from an "animal sense of similarity," which is an associative one driven by behaviorist contingencies, to a theory-laden one. Quine's "doctrine of original sim" (Keil, 1989), is therefore a highly appealing account of conceptual change, one that has resonated with many major developmental theorists of the century, including Piaget at times; to his credit, however, there was always an unwillingness in Piaget's mind to make even the youngest infant purely an associative beast (e.g., Piaget, 1952). There is a problem with this general account of concept development: Quine left unspecified, as has everyone else, how we make the transition from correlation to causation, from frequencies to explanation, or from contingencies to mechanism. The extreme difficulty of explaining such transitions leads to an understandable, but misguided, impulse to brand such notions of explanatory beliefs and sense of cause as illusory and epiphenomenal and bound to be eliminated by the eventually "true" theory of mind (Churchland, 1995). Fortunately, most researchers in cognitive development have been reluctant to abandon those aspects of mind that concern beliefs, and they have assumed that somehow theoretical beliefs do emerge from an earlier atheoretic state. This assumption may well be wrong, but the preservation of a level of cognition with explanatory beliefs is surely right.

The purported shifts from raw similarity to theory could happen in two ways: as a global reorganization of the ways in which we represent and use knowledge, a mental metamorphosis that has consequences across all aspects and contents of cognition, or as a domain-specific journey wherein not only children but adults who are novice in some area undergo a shift in that bounded area of knowledge from a largely associative way of rendering reality to a more theory-driven, analytic one (e.g., Chi, Feltovich, & Glaser, 1981). One casualty of the last 2 decades has been domain-general models of conceptual change. It has become increasingly difficult to document that some general aspect of our representational capacity changes in childhood, such that younger children are unable to represent reality in a mental format that is available to older children. In this sense, an idea that was central to Piaget's theory (i.e., qualitative changes in domain-general mental structures) has encountered great difficulty. Because of these difficulties, recent researchers sympathetic with Piaget's perspective have attempted to define sophisticated ways in which domain-general cognitive changes still occur and have consequences for thinking and reasoning in childhood. Several other chapters in this book present arguments for such patterns of developmental change (e.g., chap. 2). But these arguments, even in the very compelling forms offered here, are not so obviously relevant to claims about children's inability to have certain kinds of concepts that are available to older children and adults.

In short, the heterogeneity of concepts suggests to many that one qualitatively distinct aspect of the heterogeneous structure is developmentally primitive and perhaps spawns the emergence of later facets. In a domain-general form, this notion is difficult to sustain, but it might be more viable in a domain-specific way, in which, for each kind of knowledge, there is a natural trajectory from association to rules and explanation. Perhaps in that sense, ontogeny does recapitulate phylogeny, if animals have the associationist "animal sense of similarity" described by Quine. Contrary to Quine, however, a close look at animal cognition raises questions about whether even animals all have the so-called animal sense of similarity. Many different species show patterns of learning and categorization apparently at odds with simple associative tabulations of features (Thompson, 1995). In most cases, there is a strong sense that something beyond the associative is needed, but the nature of these nonassociative components often remains underspecified. This underspecification is particularly vivid in the different senses of explanation in the literature. Part of the problem seems to lie in the earlier-mentioned assumption that explanation and association are separable and perhaps even mutually exclusive ways of organizing the world. Once this assumption is discarded and the two are seen to work in concert, an association to explanation shift in development is much less compelling. A closer look at explanation helps illustrate this different perspective.

HOW A DIFFERENT VIEW OF CONCEPTS
REQUIRES A DIFFERENT ACCOUNT
OF CONCEPTUAL DEVELOPMENT

Even as researchers have mostly embraced the concepts-as-theories idea, different senses of theory and explanation and the role of cause in both may confuse the picture of what develops. It is therefore useful to consider some things that theories can and cannot do.

Most important, theories cannot exhaustively specify concrete mechanisms in the domains they cover, except in the most circumscribed and artificial cases. Theories of the natural world, especially lay theories, but usually scientific theories as well, give necessarily incomplete explanations that we are somehow usually satisfied with as bona fide. Apparently, we develop partial explanations that give us enough insight into the workings of the world to be of value and to have relatively low probabilities of later being undermined.

Across almost all natural phenomena, whether explanations of photosynthesis, of the phenomenal properties of elements as a function of their position in the periodic table, or of how DNA sequences ultimately result in three-dimensional physiological organs, almost everyone has some idea of the most relevant properties and often of relevant families of mechanisms, but no one knows the full story. In most cases, we critically rely on an "epistemic dependence" (Hardwig, 1985) on others who we believe are legitimate experts in various domains. Our confidence in these experts (perhaps often misplaced) may be critical to our being content with partial and incomplete explanations.

Laypeople as well as individual scientists have therefore often operated not as if they had a precise concrete mechanism in mind, but rather as if they had a framework explanation that told them what properties are likely to be causally important in a domain, perhaps what causal relations are involved, and perhaps something about their general patternings (see also

Wellman, 1990, on framework theories). We can think of these frameworks as "modes of construal" that guide us in our attempts to construe a pattern in terms of causal relations (Keil, 1995). It was supposed for a time that experienced scientists developed explanations and predictions in a "deductive-nomological" manner (Hempel, 1965), in which they took certain natural laws as axioms, proposed a few more laws or principles, and then looked at their deductive consequences in the set of axioms. This was surely the ultimate version of explanation as a formal set of abstract rules in propositional form. Individual scientists, however, have almost never worked in that manner, and rarely has science as a whole, except in some idealized historical reconstructions (Salmon, 1989). Instead, scientists have constructed explanatory hypotheses in a haphazard and incomplete manner. They developed families of explanations and then chose among them by using not just their conformity with data but also their conformity with intuitive modes of construal (Dunbar, 1994).

Our explanatory knowledge, however, is much more than broad framework expectations about how things act and interact in specific realms. We also have at least some concrete mechanisms in mind. In addition, our explanatory understanding is linked to the associative, atheoretical tabulations of feature frequencies and correlations. Probabilistic information is needed as a raw database for theory building; yet such databases are hopeless even to construct if they are not constrained by the framework theoretical biases. The number of possible features, frequencies, and correlations to notice is indefinitely large and beyond not just the human mind's capacity but that of any system with finite storage capacity (Keil, 1981; Murphy & Medin, 1985). The methods of limiting what goes into the frequency tables differ depending on the realm in question. For example, in trying to understand the causal interactions in a classical physical mechanical system, we tend to exclude correlated events that occur in different spatial locations and with no intervening solid physical connections. For causal interactions in a social psychological system, such events with action at a distance can be absolutely central.

We can therefore discount correlations when they do not agree with a reasonable explanatory schema for a domain. Sometimes, however, strong and salient correlations can powerfully compel a search for mechanisms even when none seems initially plausible. We have all experienced powerful temporal contiguities accompanied by a compelling sense of cause without clear mechanism. A character in a old movie being shown on television presses a doorbell just as the doorbell in our house rings. Most of us cannot help having an eerie feeling that the character is causally connected to our own doorbell even as we know the idea to be patently absurd. In such cases, our explanatory schema helps us quickly curtail our search for mechanisms, and we conclude that the coincidence is just that. Certain patterns of concidence and contiguity may prompt searches for mechanism, but when these patterns do not fit with any available explanatory schema, we find it easy to dismiss them (see also Ahn & Kalish, in press).

Specific mechanism knowledge is also part of the explanatory component. It may radically reduce which correlations and frequencies seem relevant. A highly specific mental model of how a system functions can take us far beyond the interpretive guidelines offered by a general explanatory schema. Specific mechanisms may also increase confidence in the particular mode of construal applied to a set of probabilistic patterns. We might, for example, have tentatively adopted an essentialist bias in developing explanations of some insect's behavior, such as a spider's web spinning, but we are much more confident of that stance when we learn about specific mechanisms that reveal genetic pathways governing specific functional subcomponents in the web-building process (Dawkins, 1996). Finally, further details about mechanism might suddenly render highly implausible a previous mapping between a mode of construal and a set of probabilistic patterns.

Most adult theories, especially of natural phenomena, have the two facets of explanation, the framework modes of construal and some fragmentary sense of local mechanisms, as well as tabulations of feature frequencies and correlations that are linked to these two facets of explanation. Even a vague preliminary understanding must have an explanatory framework that both interprets and constrains relevant associative information, and thereby also depends on that information, and fragments of more specific mechanistic insights that serve to sharpen and focus understanding. One of the most complex problems in the current philosophy of science is knowing how to fit all these components together in one system (Wilson & Keil, 1998).

We do not yet know precisely how these components fit together, but they do seem to be intertwined throughout the course of development, albeit in different degrees of elaboration. To demonstrate this point, we consider the case of biological thought.

THE CASE WITH SOME CONCEPTS IN BIOLOGY

We have suggested that concepts have three components: the associative component, and a two-part explanatory component consisting of skeletal modes of construal and an incompletely populated set of concrete mechanisms. It might then seem that, even if there is not an initial state in human development in which early concepts are merely associative, there could at least be early concepts in which the explanatory component is only concrete local mechanisms, with the abstracted modes of construal developing much later from related sets of such concrete mechanisms.

This notion seems intuitively correct and fits the the developmental idea of changes in thought from the concrete to the abstract. It is very common to think of young children as trapped in a world of concrete interpretations, unable to abstract higher order regularities and principles that are distanced from the here and now. In the same vein, these concrete mechanisms might be seen as forming a patchwork, inchoate set that only later becomes integrated by higher order abstract rules and principles. Piaget certainly had views along these lines (Piaget, 1952).

It is not so easy to define *concrete* and *abstract*, but however we try to do so, the suspected developmental shift does not appear to be the dominant pattern. In biology, there are several clear counterexamples: ignorance about the appearance of insides while understanding general functional properties (Simons & Keil, 1995); not understanding any details about germs as mediating agents of contagious diseases, yet having strong expectations about disease and contagion (Kalish, in press; Keil, Levin, Gutheil, & Richman, in press; Springer & Keil, 1989); and knowing little about mechanisms of inheritance of properties and the relations to reproduction and physiology, yet having broad beliefs about how properties are inherited (Hirschfeld, 1996; Springer & Keil, 1989). In each of these cases, it appears possible to have some relevant causal knowledge without many concrete details. To illustrate this point, consider the cases of insides and disease.

It can be quite surprising how clueless young children often are about the appearance of the inside parts of living things. Thus, when shown drawings of the insides of stereotypical machines and mammals and asked to indicate which drawing represents the insides of a sheep or a car, many preschoolers respond at chance levels (Simons & Keil, 1995). They are equally poor with photographs of animal and machine interiors and with matching these to exteriors. These failures are surprising: A simple strategy could be to assume that there is some global similarity between outsides and insides, such as more rounded edges with inside parts of animals. Most dramatic, however, are cases in which jars of actual animal and machine insides were shown to children, many of whom, even at age 4, were unable to match such insides to photographs of the real animals and machines. These reponse patterns seem to be a failure in concrete knowledge in the sense that a simple image of what insides look like would enable children to succeed on these tasks. Such imagelike representations have often been presumed to be a hallmark of childlike concrete thought (e.g., Bruner et al., 1966).

In view of such surprising difficulties in knowing the concrete appearances of inside parts, we might assume that children at such an age must also be ignorant about other less concrete knowledge about insides; such knowledge would be built out of knowledge of concrete particulars. Most versions of a concrete to abstract shift in cognitive development consider young children as having something like iconic images of entities, stored mentally until higher symbolic processes can operate on them. Children are assumed to be excellent at storing perceptual information about instances, in which *perceptual* tends to mean properties of static images. This information is then supposed to be the database for higher order cognitions.

In reality, however, preschoolers can have intuitions about principled differences between the insides of animals and machines even as they have little or no idea what those insides look like in any concrete manner. We have yet to fully exhaust what preschoolers know, but at the least they seem to know that animal insides tend to be more invariant across members of the same animal kind than across the same kind of machine (e.g., different pickup trucks might have quite different engine types and still all be pickup trucks, but different Labrador retrievers do not have equivalent differences in organs (Keil, Smith, Simons, & Levin, in press). They know that animal essences are different from and more important than those of artifacts (S. A. Gelman & Hirschfeld, in press), that animal insides are necessary for animal identity and functioning (S. A. Gelman & Wellman, 1991), and that animal insides are also connected to a vital force responsible for many specifically biological processes and governed by different cause–effect relations than are those for nonliving kinds (Hatano & Inagaki, in press). Preschoolers seem to have a sense of all these distinctions, and probably several others, yet they can be terrible on the details. At least in the case of concepts of insides, we concluded that development went from the abstract to concrete rather than the other direction (Simons & Keil, 1995).

For theories of contagious disease, a similar pattern arises. Most young children have little idea of what germs look like or even that they are microscopic. Some are not even familiar with the word. Similarly, young children have almost no concrete understanding of human physiology or anatomy. If all understanding of disease had to spring from such concrete particulars as a clockwork mechanistic visualization of the process of infection by an agent and its proliferation and subsequent causing of damage, then surely preschoolers should have no notions of disease whatsoever. We have some inkling that this account for disease might not work; the germ theory of disease is very recent in human history, and it is surprising to think that people's beliefs about disease had no grains of truth, no partially correct or greater than chance capturings of reality, during the last several millennia.

The discrepancy between the germ theory approach and general understandings about disease was vividly apparent to us in a series of studies of the ways that children differentiated psychological from physiological afflictions and the most likely ways in which each could be transmitted from person to person (Keil, Levin et al., in press). For example, in one study, children heard stories describing people with either a biological or a mental ailment, such as having large blue spots appear all over their skin or developing the belief that Big Bird was following them around and talking to them. Two events were then described in which the afflicted individual came into contact with a potential receiver of the illness. In one of the situations, the contact was exclusively physical, not social (e.g., mistakenly drinking an afflicted person's soda and eating popcorn in a darkened movie theater without either party knowing); in the other, it was exclusively social, not physical (e.g., talking with an afflicted individual in another town by videophone). Each of the stories was accompanied by a series of drawings depicting the social and physical interactions. Children ranging from 3 to 12 years and college students were asked who would catch the main character's illness: the individual who engaged only in the social interaction or the one who had only the physical interaction. They were also asked to justify their responses.

Even the youngest group of children seemed able to match each kind of illness with the most likely method of transmission. For both story types, their performance was significantly above chance. Accuracy for the biological stories showed a relatively smooth progression of improvement throughout development, but at the cost of overgeneralization as seen in below-chance performance in the mental illness stories in the three older groups of children. Surprisingly, older children seem to have thought that physical contact was necessary to catch both biological and mental afflictions. In their justifications, the older children used their understanding of biological illnesses to explain the mental afflictions by invoking germs as an explanation for transmission. (The youngest children rarely invoked germs, and the few that did resembled the older children.) There was a U-shaped developmental curve for responses on the mental anomalies, with a drop during a middle period of development. The dip seemed to be caused by a move from an abstract understanding of biological and mental disorders to a more concrete model and mechanism. The new mechanism, *germs*, when first incorporated, was incorrectly construed in such a manner as to cause an overgeneralization of their mediating power to mental contents. Children who first learned about germs seemed to use a rule roughly of the sort that germs mediate physical transmission of anomalies (not social transmission) and that they can transmit all anomalies. The children were correct in limiting the method of transmission of germs to physical contact, but their conceptions of germs themselves and what they can transmit seemed to be much less constrained; germs were seen as universal carriers of all contents. As children grew older, they started to limit what germs could transmit to biological illness.

The youngest children did better on the mental items because they had not yet incorporated a germ model and relied on a more abstract and vaguer sense that mental and biological anomalies are fundamentally different and that the mental is more associated with social contexts and the biological more with physical contexts. The same pattern appeared in follow-up studies, and the results support the idea that concrete mechanisms can sometimes disrupt a schematic mode of understanding.

Two patterns emerge: First, there is a major developmental change occurring as children come to learn many of the details about the mechanisms underlying disease (cf. Au & Romo, in press; Kalish, in press), an understanding that can continue to grow into a postgraduate career in medicine. Second, there is a schematic mode of understanding with much earlier origins, which guides distinct intuitions about biological and behavioral sets of relations throughout early and middle childhood. The acquisition of specific mechanism knowledge is not always instantly and smoothly integrated into the schematic knowledge.

HOW CAN SCHEMATIC MODES OF UNDERSTANDING BE STRUCTURED AND WHAT CAUSE CAN BE PRESENT WITHOUT VIVID MECHANISM?

We have described several instances in which young children seem to segregate natural phenomena into reasonable and conceptually coherent groups that obey common laws and principles, but do so in ways that suggest little or no understanding of detailed principles, mechanisms, or other vivid, imagelike depictions. What representations capture these schematic understandings such that they differentiate domains of phenomena? The term *schematic* is used here instead of *theoretic* to indicate that children's understanding might be quite different from explicit, well-developed theories and yet to recognize that it might be compatible with a framework sense of theory. There are several ways in which schematic modes of understanding might arise and be represented without involving richly detailed theories of a propositional nature.

Causal Potency of Properties

Certain properties seem to figure much more prominently in understandings in some domains as opposed to others. In general, color looms large in importance in discussions of the properties of substances like gold, water, or coal. If a natural substance has a different color throughout, such as a substance that is purported to be gold but is bright blue, we wonder what kind of stuff it really is. (This is not to say that each substance must have a unique color, but that there is thought to be a very tight causal path between essence and color for substances even if the color for something like carbon can vary from black in coal to transparent in a diamond.) Color is not so important in understandings of most artifacts. Even if an object is a highly atypical color throughout, such as a purple refrigerator, we tend to retain high confidence that it is a refrigerator. Living kinds, such as plants and animals, seem somewhere in between: Color is seen as important because of the adaptive roles it often plays for an animal or plant, but such roles do not seem as close to the core understanding of a kind as in the case of substances. (The case is actually a bit more complicated because any color seems fine for most artifacts, whereas for living kinds, although they may vary more in colors than do substances, some colors (or absence thereof) seem highly disruptive of their integrity [e.g., a transparent redwood or a bright pink crow]). By contrast, overall shape or number of discrete external parts matters little for substances but greatly for the integrity of living kinds. We could, therefore, have a knowledge about what properties are likely to be causally potent in a domain, and, over enough types of properties, this knowledge might constitute one sort of causal schematic knowledge about a domain that was devoid of specific mechanisms.

To what extent are such notions of potency truly causal in nature as opposed to a neutral sense of centrality, perhaps arising from very high property–kind correlations and patterns of property × property correlations? Complex, multilayered patterns of covariation may indeed be strongly linked to what almost everyone regards as causal relations (e.g., Glymour, 1998), but the sense of causal potency is stronger than these patterns. It implies a distinct sense of causal efficacy as opposed to mere importance. At present, no systematic findings contrast general notions of centrality or potency with those of causal potency, but in several of our studies, adults and children of all ages showed justifications indicating a causal interpretation of potency. They talked about how properties enabled or allowed certain events to occur, about how a property embodied a functional or adaptive relation, and about how a property made other things happen. This causal sense is also revealed by people of all ages who have intuitions that, once a counterfactual is granted for a property (which is harder for younger children than for older to grant), it is very likely to affect other properties, not an inference that follows from intuitions based solely on simple patterns of covariation. There is a clear need to better delineate the extent of intuitions of causal potency as opposed to mere centrality and to chart the developmental progress of those delineations. Such a task is difficult because younger children simply give fewer and sparser justifications in general than do older children.

Causal Powers

Causal potency is related to, but importantly different from, the notion of causal powers, which can be another way of developing causal schemata for kinds (Shoemaker, 1984; Wilson, 1995). Causal powers are ways of individuating properties in terms of their roles in causal events. Thus, the property *fragile*, when applied to *x*, means that *x* is disposed to lose its structural integrity when put in a range of events that subject it to sufficient mechanical forces. An entity or phenomenon may be understood in terms of its causal powers to the extent that its properties are understood in such terms. Thus, a magnet may be understood in terms of being metallic, attractive to ferrous compounds, and hard. Each of these properties is then understood as the full range of events in which the dispositions of things with such properties are apparent. Such understandings may be extremely causally rich and connected to a vast array of knowledge, yet nowhere is there any sense of the mechanisms that explain why something is magnetic or how magnetism works.

In a sense, knowing causal powers is understanding a thing simply as the set of properties that correlate with it; but importantly, it is also understanding a thing in terms of a rich array of causal events in which it is disposed to behave in specific ways. Presumably, different domains of things have different causal powers that are similar in a category. Moreover, we can understand members of a kind in terms of a list of properties and the causal powers of each of these properties for members of the kind without really integrating all of them into a coherently structured theory. Hence, even a very rich knowledge of causal powers does not entail theory and explanation. In contrast to causal potency, however, causal powers offer the possibility of much more specificity, and highly distinctive powers can be associated with low-level categories, ranging from subspecies of dogs (the causal powers of Dobermans and Pekingese are quite different) to subtypes of vehicles (the causal powers of a limousine and a pickup truck are also quite different). At the levels of causal potency profiles, these categories are all pretty much the same.

Kinds of Agencies and Kinds of Causes

Domains can differ in terms of the kinds of cause normally assumed to be at work in a domain or at work in well-specified situations (such as forces that initially motivate action or forces that guide changes of surface properties over time). One way to think of such contrasts is in terms of different agencies, with the three most sharply contrasting being mechanical agency (billiard ball collisions of the sort studied by Michotte, 1963), intentional agency (belief–desire causal sequences leading to actions) and nonintentional goal seeking (deterministic behaviors that are goal directed). These three can be seen as the principal agencies that distinguish Dennett's three stances: mechanical, intentional, and design (Dennett, 1987). From a related point of view, we can consider Aristotle's four causes: efficient, material, formal, and final. Different things can be understood in terms of which causes dominate explanations of their behaviors even if the explanations themselves are not known in advance. The relations are intricate: One kind of thing, such as people, can have different aspects of behaviors explained in terms of all three kinds of agency; the special configuration of how these agencies interact may allow us to understand a distinctive form of explanation for humans. All this can be done without detailed mechanisms. Interestingly, one way of understanding animacy (Piaget, 1954) is to see it as an excessive bias to understand most causal relations in terms of intentional agency.

Causal Patternings

A host of distinctive causal patterns apparently associated with domains can set them off as distinct without specifying detailed mechanisms. The possible patterns are too extensive to list exhaustively here, but a range of examples suffices to illustrate the point.

Purposes Directed Inward Versus Outward (Contrasting Living Kinds vs. Artifacts). In general, most properties of living kinds, such as having thorns or sharp teeth, are present to serve some need of that living kind, such as protection or procuring food. For artifacts, properties are likely to be present to serve the needs of an external agent, either directly (such as a handle that affords a good grip) or through a short series of causal steps (such as the cooling fan that keeps the central processing unit from overheating and allows a user to have a powerful processor for substantial periods).

Action at a Distance Versus Not (Social vs. Mechanical Interactions). Social objects often act on other social objects at a distance and over substantial time delays. Such patterns are much less common for simple mechanical interactions (cf. R. Gelman & Spelke, 1981; Gergely, Nadasdy, Csibra, & Biro, 1995).

Homeostatic Versus Property Clusters (Full Homeostasis Is More Common in Natural Kinds). We tend to think of most properties of natural kinds as supporting the presence of other properties in a causally homeostatic manner. Each property may be involved in supporting the presence of at least one other property. For artifacts, we are more likely to allow accidental properties that have no real purpose. Even if most mattresses made in the United States are made by a company whose name begins with the letter *S*, no one assumes that *S* is anything more than an accidental property associated with mattresses. This assumption of a causal role of every property of a living kind may at times be a faulty cognitive bias (e.g., Gould & Lewontin, 1978), but we believe it is a preponderant pattern for all natural kinds, not just living ones. Thus, even for various elements, we tend to see fewer of their properties as accidental and unrelated to their essential nature than we do for artifacts.

Purpose of Whole Versus Parts (Artifacts vs. Living Kinds). We tend to think it more natural to ask what an artifact as a whole is for rather than what an animal or plant is for, unless the animal or plant is domesticated, in which case it is partly an artifact.

Unique Paths of Origin for Each Kind (Living Kinds vs. Artifacts). Living kinds tend to reach their final mature form in one way, or else they are different kinds. The path of creation is an essential part of their identity. Not so for artifacts, which can reach the same final form through many different routes and still be the same thing at the end. Even cloning of animals is not an exception if we consider the path of origin as starting with the very early stages of embryology and not with the act of conception.

Dispositional Versus Situational Factors Explain Behavior (Social vs. Inanimate). We have a bias to explain the actions of other agents in dispositional terms rather than in situational factors that affect them. By contrast, we easily see many inanimate systems as swayed by situational factors. Although such biases differ across cultures (Peng & Nisbett, in press), here the focus is on difference across domains with the suggestion that, above and beyond cultural differences, there is a stronger dispositional attribution than to inanimate systems.

In short, the four factors of causal potency, causal powers, kinds of agency, and causal patternings illustrate that schematic modes of understanding can perhaps sharply constrain explanations in domains or sharply guide searches for the best explanation without in themselves embodying precise, mechanistic beliefs. There may be other patterns beyond these four, such as typical durations of effects and general order of complexity of causal patterns, but these four cases make the point. These patterns presumably reflect structural regularities in the world, regularities that humans are particularly adept at noticing and using to help construct and constrain explanations in a domain.

ILLUSTRATING SCHEMATIC MODES OF CONSTRUAL

Our argument has been that the schematic modes of construal may play a far more powerful role in development than we normally envision and that it should be possible to find evidence for such modes in relatively young children. To explore this possibility, we have conducted several studies in the realm of biological thought and have contrasted it with other modes of thought. Many of the different causal patternings just described seem to be in the ken of preschoolers although they clearly cannot articulate them directly. Children can adopt design, intentional, and mechanical stances and can apply them with some discrimination to different things (see Keil, 1995; Kelleman, 1996, for different views on how specifically these stances are applied early on to different domains). They can know that essences are more different for living kinds than they are for other things (Gelman & Hirschfeld, in press), and they can see a vitalistic force in living kinds (Hatano & Inagaki, in press). The challenge is to pin down in detail how each of the four schematic understandings described earlier unfolds in development. Here, we briefly describe recent work on the first notion, causal potency, as a way of documenting in detail how a schematic causal understanding emerges without understanding mechanisms.

With adults, it is possible to construct causal potency profiles in which properties are differentially important across different things. For example, in our first explorations in this area, we took familiar things, such as a lion or a refrigerator, and asked participants to judge whether other entities that had specific properties counterfactualized were still legitimate members of that kind (Keil, 1994). If I asked whether something could still be a lion but be magnetic, you tend to evaluate that question by thinking about the causal consequences of being magnetic on other lion properties. You might think about how that entity would still function as a lion and whether the counterfactual property would causally impact on function. You might ask whether the counterfactual property affects other properties. Does being magnetic affect its physiology or anatomy or both? Counterfactualization can also affect questions about origins. Can that entity still come into being in such a way that it possesses all the other properties of normal entities? Thus, does being magnetic render implausible the normal causal chain of events that end up making something a lion?

When such counterfactual questions have been asked of a category like lions, they generated a characteristic profile in which some properties are clearly more causally potent or central than are others. We do not yet know whether all such central properties are always potent for causal reasons. This issue needs to be addressed directly; in some cases in the literature, causal role does not easily correlate with centrality (Sloman et al., in press). In the studies described here, however, it is likely that the measures are indeed indications of casual potency, and, with adults at least, there are strong demonstrations of links between patterns of centrality and causal roles of features (Ahn & Lassaline, 1998).

At what level of categorization are such profiles distinct across things? We might think they are maximally distinct at what is known as the basic level of categorization, that level at which things seem to be most distinct from each other in terms of typical feature clusters (Rosch, Mervis, Gray, Johnson, & Boyes-Braem, 1976). Dogs and birds are at the basic level for most of us because that is the highest level of categorization at which members of the same category share a large number of features and the lowest level at which the features across categories are maximally different (dogs have many more features contrasting with birds than retrievers do with terriers). The causal potency task, however, is probing a different intuition, not how typical a feature is, but what is the causal impact of changing a feature from its typical value to one that is unambiguously false for all known members of the category (see also Medin & Shoben, 1988).

The most typical color for one animal can be radically different from that for another animal. In addition, colors vary much more widely for some animals, such as subspecies of dogs, than they do for others, such as subspecies of camels. Both typicality and variability can contrast greatly across animals, even in related groups, such as mammals. Perhaps, in contrast, the impact of a clearly counterfactual property is more uniform at lower than at higher levels. This possibility was examined by comparing the profiles for things such as ants with other insects, then for insects with mammals, for mammals with plants, and so on along the hierarchic tree of kinds. Almost all animal profiles turned out to be nearly superimposable. Thus, having a deviant material composition (e.g., being corrugated) tends to have roughly the same major destabilizing impact whether the animal is an insect or a mammal whereas having a deviant size tends to have the same, less powerful impact across mammals and insects. Even animals and plants were quite similar in terms of causal potency profiles, with the major contrasts occurring when animals as a whole were compared to artifacts or nonliving natural kinds. (See Keil & Smith, 1996; Keil, Smith et al., 1998, for more details on these and related studies.)

The counterfactuals task apparently taps knowledge about the relative causal importance of properties, a knowledge that works only at high levels of categorization. This seemingly abstract level of knowledge could powerfully shape the nature of preferred explanations in such domains as animals. It is possible to obtain similar patterns of profiles in adults by using induction tasks and tasks in which novel subcategories of mammals and insects and machines and hand tools are taught to participants. In such cases, there are no a priori typicality patterns for such novel categories, and causal potency profiles are assessed purely. In these cases as well, calling something a novel insect versus a novel mammal has almost no differential impact on causal potency of taught properties, but it has a dramatic impact on animals versus artifacts (Keil & Smith, 1996).

We can therefore see causal potency profiles as one way of assessing the schematic modes of construal that may help set up skeletal frameworks of explanation. The critical question is how such profiles emerge in children. To explore this question, we have been conducting a series of studies with children from ages 5 to 10. Perhaps potency profiles slowly migrate from the basic level as more and more abstract insights are obtained. Perhaps they differentiate downward from very superordinate categories as children learn more and more ways in which subordinates of the most global categories are different. Perhaps even quite young children notice causal patterns and potency profiles in much the same way as adults do; this common sensitivity may form a shared framework for development. One study taught children novel animals and artifacts and looked at the profiles across ages. By teaching novel animals and then introducing a new set with one different feature, we were able to avoid giving children direct counterfactuals about known categories, a task that is interesting in its own right, but that forces subjects to think about cases that directly contradict what they know to be true. Instead, in this novel kinds method, the children were able to evaluate a new class of things and to judge whether they were likely to be members of a just-learned category.

We conducted such a study with children in kindergarten, second, and fourth grades (Keil, Smith et al., 1998). Teaching new kinds takes some time; only a few novel categories can be taught across all subjects, and very simple property descriptions were needed. Nonetheless, a clear pattern emerged across all ages. Animals had one distinct profile that sharply contrasted with artifacts. More important, the profile contrasts were essentially the same at all ages, with no real variations. Thus, from 5 to 10 years, a period of enormous conceptual change on many fronts, the basic causal potency profiles remained the same and sharply distinguished animals from artifacts in the same way for the entire period. This knowledge is largely implicit; even few adults are directly aware that such profile contrasts exist. Yet such knowledge might guide how we choose the best explanation in a domain and how we construct and elaborate explanations.

Three studies are now exploring causal potency more closely and asking how it interacts with other information in conceptual development. One study is examining how judgments of causal power interact with familiar cases for which there are many well-known, highly typical features. With adults, we know that counterfactuals about familiar entities tend to yield profile contrasts similar to those for novel entities when no low-level typicality structure is present. Thus, our judgments about the extent to which a counterfactualized property affects a category do not seem much influenced by the extent to which that property is normally distinctive (how rare it is for entities in general to have such a property) or typical (how frequently members have that property). Black might be the most typical color for car tires and cameras, but it might be more typical for tires. If degree of typicality and distinctiveness reliably interacted with intuitions of causal potency, we would expect potency to seem stronger for tires than for cameras. In such a case, counterfactualizing that property in a way that was not true for either tires or cameras (e.g., could something be bright white and still be a tire or camera?) should cause more disruption for tires. In practice, such effects were rarely noticed. Adults seemed to have strong intuitions about the causal potency of properties that are largely independent of their typicality structure (cf. Medin & Shoben, 1988).

With children, the intuitions may be different. Pilot work for our first study suggested that young children can be swayed by typicality and distinctiveness as indicative of causal potency. Kindergarteners may show a good deal of variation in judgments across members of categories and thus yield noisy profiles that do not contrast systematically across category types. Indeed, if we looked only at intuitions about familiar kinds, we might conclude that there is a powerful developmental shift in which young children have only a weak sense of the abstract causal potency profiles for different kinds. The findings of very reliable contrasts at all ages with novel kinds, however, suggests that a clear knowledge of causal potency is present by age 5 but may be obscured when real objects are queried. Thus, even though young children might assume that color is largely irrelevant for artifacts in general, they may infer a strong relevance when a particular artifact has a highly typical and distinctive color, such as videocasettes being black, a pattern that repeatedly happened in our pilot studies. Young children may therefore adopt a strategy of assuming that degree of typicality and distinctiveness is indicative of causal potency. This strategy should generally work at greater than chance levels because a highly typical feature is less variable and because low variability is often related to more causally potent features. As with cases in which the characteristic features of a category can overwhelm defining features, the most characteristic features can suggest greater causal potency than do the less characteristic ones. As children get older, however, they come to segregate causal relational information more strictly from mere distinctiveness and typicality.

A second follow-up study is further documenting that young children do indeed generate clearly distinct causal potency profiles when thinking about novel entities that cannot be influenced by known patterns of feature frequencies and correlations. Using a version of the induction paradigm we used with adults, we are asking whether kindergartners create different profiles based on the differential inductive strength of properties across kinds. It is too early to tell whether kindergartners are essentially the same as older children or whether they honor the distinctions between kinds but at a rougher level. If they do show profiles in these induction tasks, such framework knowledge could provide powerful support in learning about the likely properties of most members of novel categories.

Finally, we have begun to explore ways in which specific concrete understandings about properties might undergo dramatic developmental changes during the same periods in which the skeletal frameworks remain relatively invariant. Even if a sense of the causal potency of colors for living kinds remains roughly constant from ages 5 to 10, a wide variety of intuitions about color and its causal manifestations might change dramatically. Five-year-olds are likely to know less about the chemical makeup of animal versus artifact colors, or about how color might be removed from part of the surfaces of the two kinds, than are ten-year-olds. The relative importance of adhesion in most surface colorants on artifacts as opposed to animals might take some time to understand. Similarly, there are dramatic developmental changes for children coming to understand the specific causal mechanisms through which a property is important for a kind. A child might assume that being yellow is very important to being a daffodil, but it might take years before that color's role in attracting pollinating insects is understood. Some general sense of functional importance may well precede any understandings of specific functions or mechanisms. Similarly, the general importance of electrical power to a computer may be easily understood, but it might take many years to understand how electrical currents are used in a computer to give rise to most of its properties.

The same developmental patterns surely occur for all other properties as well. There are thousands of details to learn as well as local causal mechanisms for each property; this kind of learning can continue for a lifetime, as we all come to accumulate more and more of this explicit knowledge. The research program here is to lay out systematically how mechanisms become known for different properties in different domains.

It is also critical to ask about the extent to which intuitions about what we call causal potency are really causal as opposed to being acausal notions about centrality. It is possible that causality gradually emerges from notions of centrality over the childhood years. We doubt this possibility because many studies show clear evidence for causal thought by at least the end of the 1st year of life and possibly much earlier (e.g., several chaps. in Sperber, Premack, & Premack, 1995). Moreover, children spontaneously use rich causal language in the early preschool school years (Callanan & Oakes, 1992; S. A. Gelman & Kremer, 1991; Hickling, 1996). It is, however, important to try to find ways of directly demonstrating that intuitions about properties' key roles in counterfactuals involve causal notions. We already know that children in our studies conducted so far do occasionally use causal language in judgments about why a property change might or might not undermine membership in a category. Such spontaneous comments are not particularly frequent, however. Converging methods are needed to directly assess the extent to which such notions are explicitly causal.

BEYOND POTENCY

As described earlier, notions of what properties are most potent in a domain are only a small part of the understandings that might form skeletal explanatory schemata at levels far above those of concrete mechanisms.

Such profiles are of interest because they can depict in easily visualizable ways how part of this knowledge does help frame explanations for different kinds. What remain are studies to explore how the sense of different agencies, causal patternings, and causal powers might also be represented early in development and then come to guide concept acquisition and development. Early on, children may have several modes of construal that use all these different causal relational patterns. There may be considerable development in such explanatory schemata as well, but the primary development may not occur either at the associative level or at the level of general explanatory patterns. Instead, inchoate fragments of local mechanisms may come to gradually cohere into larger and larger bodies of explicitly statable mechanisms and often rules and principles that can be shared socially. Much of that level of specific mechanism is distributed socially, just because it can be explicitly accessed and shared. Part of our explanatory understanding is coming to know how knowledge is connected to distinct areas of specialization in different subgroups of a large community. We have raised this practice to a high art in the modern university, but informally, it is has been the norm of social communities since the earliest ages when people chose to specialize in distinct areas of value to the community. Some notion of cognitive specialization is intrinsic to virtually any characterization of civilization and culture. There remains a clear need to better characterize what we need to know to be able to navigate the sociocultural pathways that provide access to particular sources of explanatory understanding. This understanding is far more than simply knowing that ther are experts in different domains with different knowledge. It requires some sense of the domains themselves, a sense both at the level of explanatory schemata and at the level of association.

As for the general themes of this book and Piaget's legacy for current research in cognitive development, it is obvious that, in many respects, his ideas are still very much on the mark. The notion of global metamorphoses in the structure of thought remains highly controversial, but Piaget also suggested many different ways in which explanation, understanding, and concepts might be structured, from associative-like mechanisms to concrete mechanistic notions to abstract principles. He also illustrated that individual concepts are connected in large systems of understanding and that each depends on the other for characterizations of its structures. Here, we have suggested that all these facets to concepts and understanding are present throughout much of human development and that the area of most pronounced development may not be in either the tabulations of lower level frequencies or the apprehension of abstract causal patterns, potencies, and kinds. Instead, the explicit level of understanding precise mechanisms and rules may be the area in which much of the most dramatic change in childhood occurs. In many ways, this level was the one in which Piaget made many of his most striking discoveries of developmental change.

ACKNOWLEDGMENTS

Much of the research described in this chapter was supported by a National Institutes of Health grant (R01-HD23922). Many thanks to Joy Beck, Katherine Nelson, Ellin Scholnick, and especially Susan Gelman, for helpful comments on earlier drafts of this chapter.

REFERENCES

Ahn, W. K., & Kalish, C. W. (in press). In F. Keil & R. Wilson (Eds.), *Cognition and explanation*. Cambridge, MA: MIT Press.

Ahn, W. K., Kalish, C. W., Medin, D. L., & Gelman, S. A. (1995). The role of covariation versus mechanism information in causal attribution. *Cognition, 54,* 299–352.

Ahn, W. K., & Lassaline, M. (1998). *The role of causal knowledge in natural kinds, artifacts, and nominal kinds: A test of causal status hypothesis (Part 2).* Manuscript submitted for publication.

Au, T., & Romo, L. (in press). Building a conception of HIV transmission: A new approach to AIDS education. In D. Medin (Ed.), *The psychology of learning and motivation.* New York: Academic Press.

Bruner, J. S., Olver, R. R., Greenfield, P. M., & et al. (1966). *Studies in cognitive growth.* New York: Wiley.

Callanan, M. A., & Oakes, L. M. (1992). Preschoolers' questions and parents' explanations: Causal thinking in everyday activity. *Cognitive Development, 7,* 213–233.

Carey, S. (1985). *Conceptual change in childhood.* Cambridge, MA: MIT Press.

Cheng, P., & Novick, L. (1992). Covariation in natural causal induction. *Psychological Review, 99*(2), 365–382.

Chi, M. T. H. (1992). Conceptual change within and across ontological categories: Examples from learning and discovery in science. In R. Giere (Ed.), *Cognitive models of science: Minnesota studies in the philosophy of science* (pp. 129–186). Minneapolis: University of Minnesota Press.

Chi, M., Feltovich, P. J., & Glaser, R. (1981). Categorization and representation of physics problems by experts and novices. *Cognitive Science, 5,* 121–152.

Churchland, P. (1995). *The engine of reason, the seat of the soul: A philosophical journey into the brain.* Cambridge, MA: MIT Press.

Clark, A. (1993). *Associative engines: Connectionism, concepts, and representational change.* Cambridge, MA: MIT Press.

Dawkins, R. (1996). *Climbing Mount Improbable.* New York: Norton.

Dennett, D. C. (1987). *The intentional stance.* Cambridge, MA: MIT Press.

Dunbar, K. (1994). How scientists really reason: Scientific reasoning in real-world laboratories. In R. J. Sternberg & J. Davidson (Eds.), *Mechanisms of insight* (pp. 365–395). Cambridge, MA: MIT Press.

Elman, J. L., Bates, E. A., Johnson, M. H., Karmiloff-Smith, A., Parisi, D., & Plunkett, K. (1996). *Rethinking innateness.* Cambridge, MA: MIT Press.

Fodor, J. (1994). Concepts: A potboiler. *Cognition, 50*, 95–113.

Garner, W. R. (1974). *The processing of information and structure.* Potomac, MD: Lawrence Erlbaum Associates.

Gelman, R., & Spelke, E. (1981). The development of thoughts about animate and inanimate objects: Implications for research on social cognition. In J. H. Flavell & L. Ross (Eds.), *Social cognitive development: Frontiers and possible futures* (pp. 43–66). New York: Cambridge University Press.

Gelman, S. A. (1996). Concepts and theories. In R. Gelman & T. K. Au (Eds.), *Handbook of perception and cognition, Vol. 13: Perceptual and cognitive development* (pp. 117–150). New York: Academic Press.

Gelman, S. A., & Hirschfeld, L. (in press). How biological is essentialism? In D. Medin & S. Atran (Eds.), *Folkbiology.* Cambridge, MA: MIT Press.

Gelman, S. A., & Kremer, K. E. (1991). Understanding natural cause: Children's explanations of how objects and their properties originate. *Child Development, 62*, 396–414.

Gelman, S. A., & Wellman, H. M. (1991). Insides and essences: Early understandings of the non-obvious. *Cognition, 38*, 213–244.

Gergely, G., Nadasdy, Z., Csibra, G., & Biro, S. (1995). Taking the intentional stance at 12 months of age. *Cognition, 56*, 165–193.

Gould, S. J., & Lewontin, R. C. (1978). The spandrels of San Marco and the Panglossian paradigm. *Proceedings of the Royal Society, London, 205*, 581–598.

Glymour, C. (1998). Learning causes. *Minds and Machines, 8*, 41–64.

Hardwig, J. (1985). Epistemic dependence. *Journal of Philosophy, 85*, 335–349.

Hatano, G., & Inagaki, K. (in press). A developmental perspective on informal biology. In D. Medin & S. Atran (Eds.), *Folkbiology.* Cambridge, MA: MIT Press.

Hempel, C. G. (1965). *Aspects of explanation and other essays in the philosphy of science.* New York: Macmillan.

Hickling, A. K. (1996). *The emergence of causal explanation in everyday thought: Evidence from ordinary conversation.* (Doctoral dissertation, University of Michigan, 1996). *Dissertation Abstracts International, 57*, 07B, pp. 4745– .

Hirschfeld, L. (1996). *Race in the making: Cognition, culture, and the child's construction of human kinds.* Cambridge, MA: MIT Press.

Inhelder, B., & Piaget, J. (1958). *The growth of logical thinking from childhood to adolescence.* New York: Basic Books.

Kalish, C. (in press). What young children know about contamination and contagion and what that tells us about their concepts of illness. In M. Siegal & L. Peterson (Eds.), *Children's understanding of biology and health.* Cambridge, England: Cambridge University Press.

Keil, F. C. (1981). Constraints on knowledge and cognitive development. *Psychological Review, 88*, 197–227.

Keil, F. C. (1987). Conceptual development and category structure. In U. Neisser (Ed.), *Concepts and conceptual development: Ecological and intellectual factors in categorization* (pp. 175–200). New York: Cambridge University Press.

Keil, F. C. (1989). *Concepts, kinds, and cognitive development.* Cambridge, MA: MIT Press.

Keil, F. C. (1994). Explanation based constraints on the acquisition of word meaning. *Lingua, 92*, 169–196.

Keil, F. C. (1995). The growth of causal understandings of natural kinds. In D. Sperber, D. Premack, & A. Premack (Eds.), *Causal cognition: A multidisciplinary debate* (pp. 234–262). Oxford, England: Oxford University Press.

Keil, F. C., & Batterman, N. (1984). A characteristic-to-defining shift in the development of word meaning. *Journal of Verbal Learning and Verbal Behavior, 23*, 221–236.

Keil, F. C., Levin, D., Gutheil, G., & Richman, B. (in press). Explanation, cause and mechanism: The case of contagion. In D. Medin & S. Atran (Eds.), *Folkbiology*. Cambridge, MA: MIT Press.

Keil, F. C., & Smith, W. C. (1996, November). *Is there a different "basic" level for cause?* Paper presented at the annual meeting of the Psychonomics Society, Chicago, IL.

Keil, F. C, Smith, W. C., Simons, D., & Levin, D. (1998). Two dogmas of conceptual empircism. *Cognition, 66*, 103–135.

Kelleman, D. (1996). *The nature and development of the teleological stance*. Unpublished doctoral dissertation, University of Arizona, Tucson.

Kemler, D. G., & Smith, L. B. (1978). Is there a developmental trend from integrality to separability in perception? *Journal of Experimental Child Psychology, 26*, 498–507.

Krushke, J. K. (1992). ALCOVE: An exemplar-based connectionist model of category learning. *Psychological Review, 99*, 22–44.

Locke, J. (1964). *An essay concerning human understanding* (A. D. Woozley, Ed.). New York: New American Library. (Original work published 1690)

Medin, D. (1989). Concepts and conceptual structure. *American Psychologist, 44*, 1469–1481.

Medin, D. L., & Shoben, E. J. (1988). Context and structure in conceptual combination. *Cognitive Psychology, 20*, 158–190.

Michotte, A. (1963). *The perception of causality* (T. R. Miles & E. Miles, Trans.). London: Methuen.

Murphy, G. L., & Medin, D. (1985). The role of theories in conceptual coherence. *Psychological Review, 92*, 289–316.

Neisser, U. (1963). The multiplicity of thought. *British Journal of Psychology, 54*, 1–14.

Peng, K., & Nisbett, R. E. (in press). Cross-cultural similarity and difference in understanding physical causality. In M. Shale (Ed.), *Culture and science*. Frankfort: Kentucky State University Press.

Piaget, J. (1952). *The origins of intelligence in children*. New York: Norton.

Piaget, J. (1954). *The construction of reality in the child*. New York: Basic Books.

Piaget, J. (1970). Piaget's theory. In P. H. Mussen (Ed.), *Carmichael's manual of child psychology* (3rd ed., pp. 703–732). New York: Wiley.

Quine, W. V. O. (1977). Natural kinds. In S. P. Schwartz (Ed.), *Naming, necessity, and natural kinds* (pp. 155–175). Ithaca, NY: Cornell University Press.

Reisberg, D. (1997). *Cognition: Exploring the science of the mind*. New York: W.W. Norton & Company.

Roitblat, H. L., & Meyer, J. A. (Eds.). (1995). *Comparative approaches to cognitive science*. Cambridge, MA: MIT Press.

Rosch, E., Mervis, C. B., Gray, W. D., Johnson, D., & Boyes-Braem, P. (1976). Basic objects in natural categories. *Cognitive Psychology, 8*, 382–439.

Salmon, W. C. (1989). *Four decades of scientific explanation*. Minneapolis: University of Minnesota Press.

Shoemaker, S. (1984). *Identity, cause, and mind: Philosophical essays*. New York: Cambridge University Press.

Simons, D., & Keil, F. C. (1995). An abstract to concrete shift in cognitive development: The insides story. *Cognition, 56*, 129–163.

Sloman, S. A. (1996). The empirical case for two systems of reasoning. *Psychological Bulliten, 119*(1), 3–22.

Sloman, S. A., Love, B. C., & Ahn, W. (in press). Feature centrality and conceptual coherence. *Cognitive Science*.

Smith, E. E., Patalano, A. L., Jonides, J., & Koeppe, R. A. (1996, November). *PET evidence for different categorization mechanisms*. Paper presented at the annual meeting of the Psychonomics Society, Chicago, IL.

Sperber, D., Premack, A. L., & Premack, D. (Eds.). (1995). *Causal cognition: A multi-disciplinary debate.* New York: Oxford University Press.

Springer, K., & Keil, F. C. (1989). On the development of biologically specific beliefs: The case of inheritance. *Child Development, 60,* 637–648.

Thompson, R. K. R. (1995). Natural and relational concepts in animals. In H. L. Roitblat & J. A. Meyer (Eds.), *Comparative approaches cognitive science* (pp. 175–214). Cambridge, MA: MIT Press.

Vygotsky, L. S. (1986). *Thought and language.* Cambridge, MA: MIT Press. (Original work published 1934)

Wellman, H. (1990). *The child's theory of mind.* Cambridge, MA: MIT Press.

Wellman, H. M., & Gelman, S. (1997). Knowledge acquisition in foundational domains. In D. Kuhn & R. Siegler (Eds.), *Cognition, perception and language, Vol 2: Handbook of Child Psychology* (5th ed., pp. 332–386). New York: Wiley.

Werner, H. (1948). *Comparative psychology of mental development* (2nd ed.). New York: International Universities Press.

Wilson, R. A. (1995). *Cartesian psychology and physical minds: Individualism and the sciences of the mind.* Cambridge, England: Cambridge University Press.

Wilson, R. A., & Keil, F. C. (1998).

Chapter 6

The Conceptual Habitat: In What Kind of System Can Concepts Develop?

David Klahr
Carnegie Mellon University, Pittsburgh, PA

Some theories of conceptual development focus on the content of domain-specific conceptual acquisitions (e.g., Carey, 1985), while other theories emphasize domain-general processes that support the various acquisitions (e.g., Halford, 1993). A few offer balanced accounts of content and process, but in limited domains such as arithmetic (e.g., Siegler, 1996; Siegler & Shipley, 1995). In this chapter, I focus on a third aspect of conceptual development by addressing the following question: In what kind of system can conceptual development occur? This question differs from questions about the content or process of conceptual development because it addresses the nature of the *underlying system* that represents content and executes processes.

This difference can best be understood in terms of the following analogy. Consider the situation you find yourself in when you purchase a new piece of software. You know that the compact disk (CD) contains all the data and programs required to function properly, but something else is necessary before the programs and data can become operational. They can work only if you have a computer with both a minimal hardware capacity (i.e., disk space, random-access memory capacity, monitor specifications) and a minimal level of operating system. If any of these constraints is not met, you cannot use the CD. Now imagine that your CD contains a "universal conceptual development kit." (See Fig. 6.1.) Do you have a system that can handle it? Analogously, given any particular theoretical statement about the mechanisms of conceptual development, we can ask: What kind of

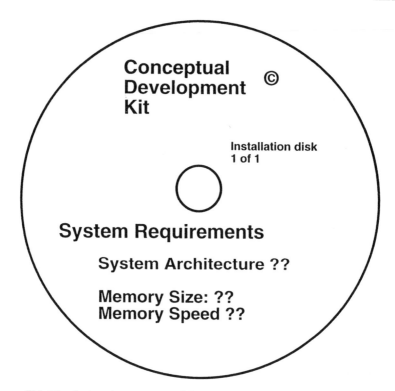

FIG. 6.1.   An imaginary compact disk containing a conceptual development
system.

mental architecture is necessary to support the concepts and processes
proposed by that theory?

Just as ecologists find it necessary to characterize the ecological niche
of their focal species in order to fully understand their evolution and
survival, psychologists need to ask about the nature of the system in which
conceptual development takes place. In other words, they need to ask:
"What is the conceptual habitat?"

In this chapter, I suggest that self-modifying computational models provide a means of answering this fundamental question. They do so not only
by providing detailed accounts of a variety of phenomena associated with
conceptual development, but also, and more important, by providing theories of the human cognitive architecture.

Newell (1990) defined a cognitive architecture as "the fixed (or slowly
varying) structure that forms the framework for the immediate processes
of cognitive performance and learning" (p. 12). What is the nature of this
cognitive architecture? How is it organized? What are the computational
principles and constraints under which it operates? Such questions define

the research frontiers for those formulating computational models of thought.

Two relatively distinct approaches to computational modeling of developmental phenomena have emerged along these frontiers: production systems and connectionist systems. Production systems have tended to focus on symbolically based, rule-oriented, higher cognitive processes, whereas connectionist systems have focused on the subsymbolic (or nonsymbolic), neurally analogous, microstructure of cognition (see T. J. Simon & Halford, 1995; Klahr & MacWhinney, 1997, for extensive descriptions and comparisons of these approaches).

PIAGET'S ATTEMPTS TO CHARACTERIZE THE SYSTEM

Before describing these computational approaches, I start with a bit of history. The effort to characterize the system in which concepts develop is not a new endeavor: Piaget's legacy is his lifelong inquiry about the dynamic system in which conceptual development occurs. Piaget characterized this system in terms of the formalisms available to him at the time. From logic and mathematics, he constructed a representational system. From biology, he borrowed the notion of assimilation and accommodation (cf. Case, 1997). However, Piaget's initial characterization of these processes was at a highly abstract level, and no one has yet figured out how to translate his ideas into an unambiguous operational system.

Even Piaget was dissatisfied with his early formulation of the equilibration process, and he continually reconceptualized and refined it. Thus, as late as 1975, he was using representations like the one in Fig. 6.2 to describe assimilation and accommodation. Although the notation gives the appearance of a more precisely conceptualized account of equilibration, the accompanying text makes it clear that the mechanisms it depicts remain obscure. "Before sufficiently precise models are achieved, therefore, one witnesses a succession of states indicating progressive equilibration. The initial states of this progression achieve unstable forms of equilibrium only because of lacunae, because of perturbations, and above all, because of real or potential contradictions" (Piaget, 1985/1975, p. 47).

COMPUTATIONAL MODELS OF COGNITIVE DEVELOPMENT

About 30 years ago, at the same time that U.S. psychologists began to wrestle with Piaget's ideas, there emerged in this country what has been called "the cognitive revolution" and with it the information-processing

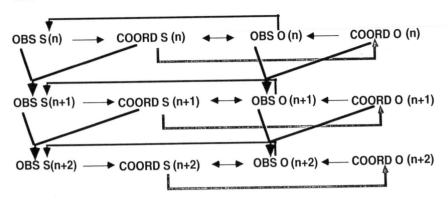

FIG. 6.2. A depiction of part of Piaget's model of assimilation and accommodation. OBS S—"observables relative to the subject's action"; OBS O—"observables relative to objects"; COORD S—"inferential coordinations of the subject's actions or operations"; COORD O—"inferential coordinations among objects." From *The Equilibration of Cognitive Structures* (p. 44), by J. Piaget, 1985, Chicago: University of Chicago Press. Copyright 1985 by the University of Chicago Press. Reprinted with permission.

approach to cognitive development (R. Brown, 1970; Klahr, 1992; H. A. Simon, 1962). Fig. 6.3 presents a concise depiction of its essential ideas. The most important of these is that cognitive theories can be stated as computer programs. This idea is not only fundamentally important but also widely misunderstood. Many people have argued that computational modelers equate the human mind to a digital computer (A. L. Brown, 1982; Miller, 1983). As Mark Antony said of Julius Caesar's ambition: "If it were so, it were a grievous fault." But it is *not* so.

Perhaps the misconception can be corrected by considering an example from another field in which computational models play a central role. Meteorologists who run computer simulations of hurricanes do not believe that the atmosphere works like a computer or that their models generate fog, rain, snow, or sunshine. They *do* believe that their characterizations of the atmosphere are so complex that only a computer can draw out their implications. It is the equations, the models, that are supposed to work like the atmosphere, not the computer on which the models run. They are also aware that their current models are only that: models. As such, they fail to capture many complexities, subtleties, and local anomalies of meteorological processes. So too for computational models of conceptual development: Such models assume neither that the underlying silicon bears any relation to neural tissue nor that any single model captures all of cognition.

Another idea, and the one that is important for developmentalists, is that children's knowledge at different states or levels can be described by different computational models. A third idea follows from the first two: If different states of cognitive development can be accounted for by computational models (i.e., by performance models), then so too can the developmental process that produced those states (i.e., adaptation models). Such programs would have the capacity to alter and extend their own processes and structures. That is, they would be self-modifying computational models, and the model building enterprise would have two steps. First, build the sequence of state models and then build the transition model.

The earliest computational models of developmental phenomena addressed states but not transitions (Baylor & Gascon, 1974; Klahr & Wallace, 1976). The plan was that the adaptive transition models could come later, after the performance models for successive states were developed and evaluated. This two-step approach has gradually given way to models in which performance and adaptation occur simultaneously (indicated by 3′ in Fig. 6.3).

It is difficult to achieve an appropriate balance between performance and adaptation. The two primary approaches to computational modeling mentioned earlier—production systems and connectionist systems—have tended to emphasize different aspects of this delicate balance: Production systems tend to emphasize performance over adaptation, whereas connectionist systems tend to emphasize adaptation over performance. Descriptions and examples of both approaches are provided later in this chapter, and it will become evident that there are important distinctions as well as some fundamental commonalties.

1. Cognitive theory can be stated as a computer program

(But: mind is **NOT** a computer!)

2. Distinct program for each knowledge level

3. Transition program to modify from one level to the next

3′. Performance and adaptation intermingled

FIG. 6.3.   Basic assumptions in computation models of cognitive development.

One of the most important commonalties is the feature that distinguishes computational models from all other types of theoretical statements: *They independently execute the mental processes that they represent.* That is, rather than leaving it to readers to interpret a verbal description or a diagram of such processes as searching a problem space, redescribing a representation, or coordinating an inference, computational models actually *do* the searching, redescribing, and coordinating. This similarity, in my mind, outweighs all the real and apparent differences between symbolic and subsymbolic computational models. In fact, as I suggest later, the distinctions between the two approaches are diminishing as both devote more effort to addressing developmental issues. In the next two sections, I briefly describe each approach.

PRODUCTION SYSTEMS

The important properties of production system architectures are listed in Table 6.1. This list describes only *current* properties, which will certainly change as we learn more about how to build adaptive production systems that capture important developmental phenomena. I review the basics of production systems and then focus on some interesting issues in the field.

Declarative ("Working") Memory

A production system consists of two primary structures: declarative memory and production memory. Declarative memory is used to represent objects, features, and goals. It is usually called working memory, but it is more accurate to call it declarative memory. It contains both long-term knowledge and aspects of the immediate situation such as goals and subgoals. An important design feature of different production-system architectures is the way that they resolve several related questions about the dynamics and complexity of declarative memory elements. How permanent are the declarative memory elements? Are they erased after the task is complete, or do they remain indefinitely? The basic problem is that the more infor-

TABLE 6.1
Current Properties of Production Systems

Declarative memory ("working memory") represents objects, features, and goals.
Procedural knowledge is stored as if–then rules ("productions").
Executing ("firing," "satisfying") a production is the fundamental unit of thought.
Adaptation takes place through the acquisition and modification of productions.
The results of computation are stored in a (temporary?) declarative memory.
Knowledge is (mostly) modular.

mation there is in declarative memory, the more likely it is that many productions are satisfied simultaneously. This situation complicates the conflict resolution process.

These questions have been answered in several different ways by production system designers. At one extreme are systems in which items *do* stay around forever. At the other extreme are systems in which items are deleted once the system moves on to the next task. Intermediate between these two extremes are systems in which the elements vary in activation (which in turn determines how available or easily retrieved they are). The activation increases each time the represented facts or items are encountered and decays with time after each encounter.

Production Memory

The second basic structure consists of a set of if–then rules or *productions* that represent skills or procedures for interacting with the world. In these productions, the *if* side is called the *condition* and the *then* side is called the *action*. The condition side of a production is a list of entities that must appear in declarative memory. When the conditions of a production are true of the current state of declarative memory, then the production is said to *fire* or *match* (or to *be satisfied*). The action side of a production can refer to either behavioral actions or new declarative memory elements representing a new piece of knowledge or a new goal. Because all productions are matched in parallel, these systems have the power to be reactive to changes in the environment and to consider large numbers of responses simultaneously.

How does the system decide what to do when more than one production's conditions are satisfied? The process by which a production system chooses among satisfied productions is called *conflict resolution*. These decisions are viewed as an integral part of the cognitive architecture. A number of conflict resolution schemes have been used over the past 25 years. These schemes include:

1. *Recency:* favoring productions whose conditions refer to declarative memory elements that have been most recently added or changed.
2. *Specificity:* favoring productions with many conditions (i.e., more specific productions) over productions with few conditions.
3. *Importance:* setting a rank ordering among productions according to a predetermined scheme.
4. *Frequency:* giving preference to productions that have been used most often and most successfully. In this way, production order can be adapted to different experience. (I return to this issue later when I discuss learning in production systems.)

A more radical approach to deciding which production to fire is to just "do it," to fire all the satisfied productions. In one such scheme, the productions make suggestions only about what to do (applying knowledge from past experiences), and then another conflict resolution scheme must decide among these suggestions (Newell, 1990). In another scheme, all productions fire, but they must compete for a limited pool of activation resources (Just & Carpenter, 1992). The full implications of these different schemes are still being determined. This problem is one of the research frontiers in the production system world.

Self-Modification in Production Systems

How can a production system adapt, learn, and develop? At present, there are two primary mechanisms for self-modification: One set of mechanisms creates new productions, and the other modifies or tunes existing productions.

Creating New Productions. One way in which new productions can be created is via *compilation,* in which a new production is produced; this production does, in one step, the action of several productions. An important variant of compilation is the chunking algorithm used in the Soar production system (Newell, 1990). The *chunking* algorithm determines which pieces of declarative knowledge were used by a recently successful sequence of productions and then creates a new production that looks for these declarative memory elements and directly produces the desired conclusion without going through the intermediate steps. This mechanism is used by T. J. Simon and Klahr (1995) to account for children's learning in one of Rochel Gelman's conservation training studies (Gelman, 1982).

Another mechanism is *analogy.* This mechanism, used in Anderson's (1993) ACT-R production system, converts examples in declarative memory into productions. When no production works in the current context, the system tries to make an analogy between the current goal and the corresponding goal in an example and creates productions that achieve the current goal by using steps analogous to the ones used to achieve the source goal.

Modifying Existing Productions. Other production-learning mechanisms create productions by *combining* or *mutating* existing productions. For example, adding or deleting conditions to a production thereby makes it more or less situation specific. Classifiers are a special case of this process (Holland, 1975). They consist of a set of rules for classifying instances into different categories. New rules are created by randomly mutating some conditions of existing rules. The rules that do a good job of classifying the instances are kept, whereas new rules that do a poor job are discarded.

In many domains, performance improves gradually, not abruptly. How might a production system achieve this gradualism if learning new productions creates discrete jumps in performance? One way to do this is to formulate productions at a very fine-grained level of detail such that many productions are required to produce each external action. In such a scheme, the addition of each production produces only a minor improvement in performance. Another solution is to associate with each production parameters that cause productions to perform slowly, suboptimally, or infrequently when they are first created and then gradually to become faster, more efficient, or more frequent. Productions can be strengthened according to their record of successful and unsuccessful use. Production strength can then determine the likelihood that the production is selected during the conflict resolution phase.

Other Self-Modification Mechanisms? One of the fundamental research questions in this area is just how many of the major phenomena of cognitive development can be explained by the self-modification processes described thus far. For example, it is not yet clear whether basic production modification processes such as generalization, discrimination, composition, proceduralization, and chunking can account for the apparent reorganization necessary to get from novice to expert level (Hunter, 1968; Larkin, 1981; Lewis, 1978; D. P. Simon & Simon, 1978). Such reorganization may involve much more than refinements in the productions governing *when* suboperations are performed. These refinements could be produced by generalization and discrimination mechanisms, but producing a new procedure requires the introduction of new operators that, in turn, may require the introduction of novel elements or goals—something that generalization, discrimination, composition, and chunking are not clearly able to do.

Some additional mechanisms and processes have been suggested, but they remain to be implemented in computational models. For example, Wallace, Klahr, and Bluff (1987) proposed a production system architecture that included a hierarchically organized set of nodes, each of which is a semiautonomous production system, communicating via a shared working memory. Each of these nodes can be simultaneously activated. The basic developmental process involves the construction of new nodes by processing a representation of episodic sequences for the system's previous behavior (the time line). Another example of a plausible concept that remains to be computationally implemented is Karmiloff-Smith's (1992) "representational redescription"—a process in which the underlying engine of cognitive development involves increasingly efficient reorganizations of knowledge structures and the processes that operate on them. Spensley

(1995) has proposed an interesting integration and extension of both Wallace et al.'s and Karmiloff-Smith's proposals.

Such soft-core notions present challenges to the hard-core approach[1] described in this chapter: Either implement these ideas or show that they are theoretically unnecessary or create a computational alternative that accomplishes the same thing.

Knowledge Is (Mostly) Modular

How does knowledge interact, and how does learning generalize? Production systems provide strong answers to these fundamental questions: Learning occurs at the unit of productions; transfer from one situation to another occurs to the extent that the same productions are applicable in both situations.

Because of their modularity, production systems scale up well to complex tasks. That is, production systems function well not only on small, simple tasks but also in realistic environments involving many subtasks and tens of thousands of knowledge elements. This modularity is not perfect, and some productions may not be entirely independent of all other productions. This situation can be particularly troublesome in *adaptive* production systems because new productions can interfere with the previously smooth functioning of an earlier series of productions. This problem is one of the most difficult aspects of building production system models.

CONNECTIONIST SYSTEMS—A BRIEF OVERVIEW

All connectionist models share a set of assumptions about the nature of neural computation: its connectivity, its representation of knowledge, and the rules that govern learning.[2] Connectionist systems use neither symbols nor rules to represent knowledge. The only sense in which they embody a cognitive architecture is their strong commitment to distributed knowledge and a loose commitment to the notion that the models are connected somewhat analogous to the way that the brain is wired.

Connectionist systems consist of elementary nodes or units, each of which has some degree of activation. Nodes are connected to each other in such a way that active units can either excite or inhibit other units. Connectionist networks are dynamic systems that propagate activation among units until a stable state is reached. Information or knowledge is

---

[1]See Klahr (1992) for a discussion of the distinction between hard-core and soft-core information-processing approaches in developmental psychology.

[2]This section is adapted from Klahr and MacWhinney (1997).

represented in the system not by any particular unit, but rather by the *pattern of activation* over a large set of units, any one of which may participate to some degree in representing any particular piece of knowledge. McClelland (1995) succinctly characterized the essence of these models:

> On this approach—also sometimes called the parallel-distributed processing or PDP approach—information processing takes place through the interactions of large numbers of simple, neuron-like processing units, arranged into modules. An active representation—such as the representation one may have of a current perceptual situation, for example, or of an appropriate overt response—is a distributed pattern of activation, over several modules, representing different aspects of the event or experience, perhaps at many levels of description. Processing in such systems occurs through the propagation of activation among the units, through weighted excitatory and inhibitory connections.
>
> As already suggested, the knowledge in a connectionist system is stored in the connection weights: it is they that determine what representations we form when we perceive the world and what responses these representations will lead us to execute. Such knowledge has several essential characteristics: First it is inchoate, implicit, completely opaque to verbal description. Second, even in its implicit form it is not necessarily accessible to all tasks; rather it can be used only when the units it connects are actively involved in performing the task. Third, it can approximate symbolic knowledge arbitrarily closely, but it may not; it admits of states that are cumbersome at best to describe by rules; and fourth, its acquisition can proceed gradually, through a simple, experience-driven process. (p. 158)

Because connectionist systems are inherently learning systems, the two-step approach to modeling conceptual development described earlier (first performance models, then transition models) has not been used. Instead, designers of connectionist models have focused on models that learn continuously, and they have attempted to illustrate that different distributions of connectivity among the nodes of their networks correspond to different knowledge levels in children. The earliest applications were in the area of language acquisition (e.g., Rumelhart & McClelland, 1986), but more recent models—some of which I describe next—have begun to examine conceptual development and problem solving.

Basic Principles of Neural Networks

Connectionist models are implemented in terms of artificial neural networks. Neural networks that are able to learn from input are known as adaptive neural networks. Such networks can be specified in terms of eight design features:

1. *Units.* The basic components of the network are a number of simple elements called variously neurons, units, cells, or nodes. In Fig. 6.4, the units are labeled with letters such as x1.

2. *Connections.* Units or pools of units are connected by a set of pathways variously called connections, links, pathways, or arcs. In most models, these connections are unidirectional and go from a sending unit to a receiving unit. This unidirectionality assumption corresponds to the fact that neural connections also operate in only one direction. The only information conveyed across connections is activation information. No signals or codes are passed. In Fig. 6.4, the connection between units x1 and y1 is marked with a thick line.

3. *Patterns of connectivity.* Units are typically grouped into pools or layers. Connections can operate in or between layers. In some models (such as the one shown in Fig. 6.4), there are no in-layer connections; in others, all units in a given layer are interconnected. Units or layers can be further divided into three classes:

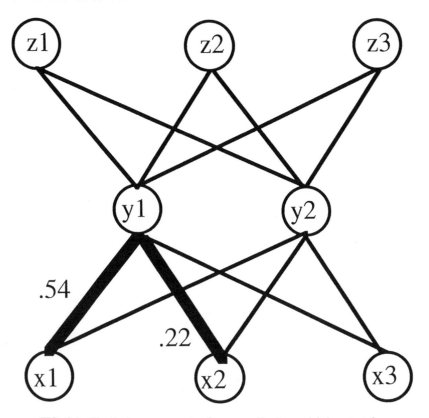

FIG. 6.4. The basic components of a connectionist model (see text for explanation).

Input units, which represent signals from earlier networks. These units are marked x in Fig. 6.4.

Output units, which represent the choices or decisions made by the network. These units are marked z in Fig. 6.4.

Hidden units, which represent additional units juxtaposed between input and output for the purposes of computing more complex, nonlinear relations. These units are marked y in Fig. 6.4.

4. *Weights.* Each connection has a numerical weight that is designed to represent the degree to which it can convey activation from the sending unit to the receiving unit. Learning is achieved by changing the weights on connections. For example, the weight on the connection between x1 and y1 is given as .54 in Fig. 6.4.

5. *Net inputs.* The total amount of input from a sending unit to a receiving unit is determined by multiplying the weights on each connection to the receiving unit by the activation of the sending unit. This net input to the receiving unit is the sum of all such inputs from sending units. In Fig. 6.4, the net input to y1 is .76, if we assume that the activations of x1 and x2 are both 1 and the x1y1 weight is .54 and the x2y1 weight is .22.

6. *Activation functions.* Each unit has a level of activation. These activation levels can vary continuously between 0 and 1. To determine a new activation level, activation functions are applied to the net input. Functions that "squash" high values can be used to make sure that all new activations stay in the range of 0 to 1.

7. *Thresholds and biases.* Although activations can take on any value between 0 and 1, often thresholds and bias functions are used to force units to be either fully on or fully off.

8. *A learning rule.* The basic goal of training is to bring the neural net into a state in which it can take a given input and produce the correct output. To do this, a learning rule is used to change the weights on the connections.

The most common approach—called *back propagation*—is to present the network with an input pattern and to compare the output pattern it produces with the one that is desired (i.e., the thing to be learned). The system then computes the difference between these two and adjusts the weights so as to approach the desired pattern in an optimal way. The basic idea is to adjust each parameter in the network in proportion to the effect that the adjustment has on the overall fit to the desired output. Once the adjustments are made, another comparison is done, and the system reiterates this process for many cycles.

Another approach—called *cascade correlation*—has been used by Shultz, Schmidt, Buckingham, and Mareschal (1995) to model several developmental domains, including causal reasoning, seriation, integration of distance, time, and velocity, and personal pronouns. Cascade correlation models start with a network that has no hidden units. Such units are added—as part of the training–learning process—when the system decides that its rate of learning has reached a plateau.

All connectionist networks share this common language of units, connections, weights, and learning rules, but models differ markedly both in their detailed patterns of connectivity and in the specific rules used for activation and learning.[3]

TWO COMPUTATIONAL APPROACHES TO THE SAME DOMAIN: THE BALANCE SCALE

In general, the domains in which production system models and connectionist models have been proposed have been nonoverlapping. Production systems have been used mainly to model higher order problem-solving domains, whereas connectionist models have tended to focus on perceptual and language development. In one domain, familiar to all developmentalists, however, both types of models have been formulated: Piaget's balance scale prediction task.

Production Systems for the Balance Scale

Siegler (1978, 1976) proposed an elegant analysis of rule sequences characterizing how children (from 3 years to 17 years old) make predictions on this task (as well as in several other domains having a similar formal structure). This work has provided the basis for many subsequent empirical and theoretical analyses, including computational theories cast as both production systems and connectionist networks.

The basic physical concept that underlies the operation of the balance scale is torque: The scale rotates in the direction of the greater of the two torques acting on its arms. Because the pegs are at equal intervals from the fulcrum and the weights are all equal, a simple torque calculation is possible. It is the sum of the products of the number of weights on a peg times the ordinal position of the peg from the fulcrum. This calculation is done for each side, and the side with the greater sum of products is the side that goes down. (If they are equal, the scale balances.)

Siegler (1976) demonstrated that children's different levels of knowledge about this task can be represented in the form of a sequence of four increasingly mature rules or models. A child using Model I considers only

---

[3]For excellent, readable introductions to the theory and practice of neural network modeling, readers may wish to consult Bechtel and Abrahamsen (1991) or Fausett (1994). For a mathematically advanced treatment, see Hertz, Krogh, and Palmer (1991).

the number of weights on each side: If they are the same, the child predicts balance; otherwise he or she predicts that the side with the greater weight will go down. For a child using Model II, a difference in weight still dominates, but if weight is equal, then a difference in distance is sought. If it exists, the greater distance determines which side goes down; otherwise the prediction is balance.

A child using Model III tests both weight and distance in all cases. If both are equal, the child predicts balance; if only one is equal, then the other one determines the outcome; if they are both unequal but on the same side with respect to their inequality, then that side is predicted to go down. In a situation in which one side has greater weight and the other has greater distance, the child, although recognizing the conflict, does not have a consistent way to resolve it but simply muddles through by making a random prediction.

A child using Model IV represents mature knowledge of the task: Because it includes the sum-of-products calculation, children using it always make the correct prediction, but if they can base their prediction on simpler tests, they do so. The components of this knowledge are acquired over a remarkably long span of experience and education. Although children as young as 5 years old usually know that balances such as teeter-totters tend to fall toward the side with more weight, most college students are unable to solve balance scale problems consistently.

Siegler represented these different levels of knowledge in the form of binary decision trees that could make clear predictions about the responses made by a child using one of these rules for any specific configuration of weights. Such decision trees are silent on the dynamics of the decision process, however, and they do not make a clear distinction between encoding processes and decision processes. By recasting the rules as production systems, Klahr and Siegler (1978) were able to make a more precise characterization of what develops than was afforded by the decision-tree representation.

Their production system is listed in Table 6.2. For example, Model II in Table 6.2 is a production system consisting of three productions. The condition elements in this system are all tests for sameness or difference in weight or distance. The actions all refer to behavioral responses. None of the models in Table 6.2 contains a representation for any finer grain knowledge, such as the actual amount of weight or distance or the means used to encode that information. There is no explicit representation of how the system produces the final verbal output. It is simply assumed that the system has processes or operators that produce encoded representations of the relational information stated in the conditions.

On any recognize-act cycle, only one of these productions fires, depending on the type of knowledge that the encoding processes have placed in working memory. If the weights are unequal, then P2 fires; if the weights

TABLE 6.2
Production System Representations for Balance Scale Models I–IV

Model I	P1: [(Same W) → (Say "Balance")]
	P2: [(Side X more W) → (Say "X down")]
Model II	P1: [(Same W) → (Say "Balance")]
	P2: [(Side X more W) → (Say "X down")]
	P3: [(Same W) (Side X more D) → (Say "X down")]
Model III	P1: [(Same W) → (Say "Balance")]
	P2: [(Side X more W) → (Say "X down")]
	P3: [(Same W) (Side X more D) → (Say "X down")]
	P4: [(Side X more W) (Side X less D) → muddle through]
	P5: [(Side X more W) (Side X more D) → (Say "X down")]
Model IV	P1: [(Same W) → (Say "Balance")]
	P2: [(Side X more W) → (Say "X down")]
	P3: [(Same W) (Side X more D) → (Say "X down")]
	P4': [(Side X more W) (Side X less D) → (get torque)]
	P5: [(Side X more W) (Side X more D) → (Say "X down")]
	P6: [(Same torque) → (Say "Balance")]
	P7: [(Side X more torque) → (Say "X down")]

Transitional Requirements

Transitions	Production Modifications	New Operators
I → II	Add P3	Add distance encoding and comparison.
II → III	Add P4, P5	None.
III → IV	Modify P4; add P6, P7	Add torque computation and comparison.

Note. D = Distance; W = Weight.

are equal and the distances are not, then both P1 and P3 are satisfied, and this conflict must be resolved by the production system architecture. For the production system that Klahr and Siegler proposed, the conflict is resolved by a specificity principle that always selects the more specific of two productions when one is a special case of the other. Finally, if both weights and distances are equal, then only P1 is satisfied, and it fires. The task facing a transition model is indicated at the bottom of Table 6.2. At the level of productions, the requisite modifications are straightforward: Transition from Model I to Model II requires the addition of P3; from Model II to III, the addition of P4 and P5; and from model III to IV, the addition of P6 and P7 and the modification of P4 to P4'.

Thus far I have compared the models at the level of productions, but productions need information provided by the operators that encode the external configuration. Consequently, it is informative to compare the four models at a finer level of analysis by looking at the implicit requirements for encoding and comparing the important qualities in the environment. The production system for Model I tests for sameness or difference in weight. It requires an encoding process that either directly encodes relative weight or encodes an absolute amount of each and then inputs these representations into a comparison process. Whatever the form of the comparison process, it must be able to produce not only a same-or-different symbol, but if there is a difference, it must be able to keep track of which side is greater. The production system for Model II requires the additional capacity to make these decisions about distance as well as weight. This might constitute a completely separate encoding and comparison system for distance representations, or it might be the same system except for the interface with the environment.

Model III's production system needs no additional operators at this level, and it differs from Model II only in the way it utilizes information that is already accessible to Model II. The Model IV production system requires a much more powerful set of quantitative operators than does any of the preceding models. To determine relative torque, it must first determine the absolute torque on each side of the scale, and this calculation requires exact numerical representation of weight and distance. In addition, the torque computation requires access to the necessary arithmetic production systems to actually do the sum of products calculations.

Although I have compared the four models at two distinct levels—productions and operators—the levels are not that easily separated. Missing from these models is a set of productions that indicates the interdependence: productions that explicitly determine which encoding the system makes. In these models, there are almost no productions of the form: (want to compare weights) $\rightarrow$ (attend to stimulus and notice weight). The sole exception to this occurs in P4' in Model IV. When this model is confronted with a nonconflict problem, either P1, P2, P3, or P5 fires on the first recognize cycle. For a conflict problem, P4' fires, and the system attempts to "get torques." The result of this unmodeled action, as described previously, produces a knowledge element that could satisfy either P6 or P7 on the next cycle.

Representing the Immediate Task Context. One advantage of a production system formulation is that it facilitates the extension of a basic model of the *logical* properties of a task to include the processing of verbal instructions, encoding of the stimulus, keeping track of where the child is in the overall task, and so on. For example, in their analysis of *individual* subject protocols on the balance scale, Klahr and Siegler proposed several distinct models to account for some children's idiosyncratic but consistent response patterns. Some of these models included not only the basic productions for a variant of one of Siegler's four models for balance scale predictions, but also knowledge about the instantaneous task context.

These models are too detailed to present here, but it is instructive to consider the way in which such detailed models could characterize how much more than balance scale knowledge, as such, is required by a child performing this task. For example, one of Klahr and Siegler's subjects tended to encode both weight and distances as either big or small. Their model for that subject dealt with the way in which the child maintained declarative memory elements representing the following pieces of information: Which side has *more* weight or distance, which side has a *big* weight or distance, what the current criterion value is (for big weights or distances), what the scale is expected to do, what the scale actually did, whether the prediction is yet to be made or has been made, and whether it is correct or incorrect.

Thus, their model makes a strong claim about how much encoded knowledge must be available at any one moment and hence about the dynamics of declarative memory mentioned earlier. Although production system models do not generally impose any clear constraints on the size of working memory, they provide the potential for such an analysis. One of the relatively unexplored areas for future computational modelers is to attempt to integrate the theoretical constructs and empirical results described by working memory capacity theorists, such as Case (1986) and Bidell and Fischer (1994), with the added formalisms and precision of production system models. Promising steps in this direction are represented by work by Halford and his colleagues (Halford, 1993; Halford et al., 1995).

The balance scale production systems exemplify the sequence-of-stages approach used in the early days of production system modeling. The primary goal was to explore the nature of the system that could display the different levels of performance observed in children's responses to these tasks. Although, as noted earlier, adaptive production systems exist in other domains, as yet there is no such adaptive production system for the balance scale domain. This area is one of the few involved in higher order conceptual development in which connectionist models *have* been constructed. I turn to these next.

Connectionist Models for the Balance Scale

McClelland (1989, 1995) noted that, although the production system models for the balance scale provided a good description of the four rules discussed earlier, they tell us little about the forces that drive children from one rule system to the next. In addition, none of the existing rule-based models can account for the torque-difference effect; thus children do better when the discrepancy between the torques on each side of the balance scale is increased (Ferretti & Butterfield, 1986; Wilkening & Anderson, 1982). McClelland constructed a back propagation model of the balance beam problem with 20 input units. One positional unit was devoted to each of the 10 pegs (5 to the left and 5 to the right of the fulcrum). Ten weight units represented the numbers of weights stacked up at a position, with 5 units for the possible number of weights on the left and 5 units for the possible weights on the right. Every possible problem could be encoded with only 4 units turned on. For example, in a problem with 4 weights on the third peg from the right and 5 weights on the second peg from left, the units turned on would then be 4-right-weight, 5-left-weight, 3-right-distance, and 2-left-distance. To capture the common assumption that children have more exposure to weight as a cause of going-down effects, McClelland biased the network toward reliance on the weight cue over the distance cue by including a large number of cases in which the distance cue was neutralized. (This kind of hand-wired bias is justifiably used to put the model in the same initial state as the children studied in Siegler's original studies. It makes no attempt to account for how children reach this initial state.)

Using this type of representation, McClelland was able to model many aspects of the learning of this task. The network began with performance that relied on Model I and moved on to learn Model II and then Model III. It never acquired full use of Model IV, because, McClelland argued, some aspects of the use of Model IV by adults involved the application of full mathematical analysis. The network was, however, able to capture aspects of the torque distance effect mentioned previously. Torque distance effects indicate that subjects did not simply apply an all-or-none rule, but performed a cue weighting that is much like that conducted inside a neural network.

Shultz et al. (1995) extended McClelland's model by using the cascade correlation procedure described earlier. Shultz et al. argued that static back propagation networks with only a few hidden units can succeed at modeling the first stages of development but are unable to reach higher levels of performance, because their weights become too closely tuned to solving the basic levels of the problem. This was true for McClelland's balance beam model, which learned Models I, II, and aspects of III, but was unable to learn Model IV. Using the cascade correlation framework, however, Shultz et al. were able to model successful learning of all four rules.

These models make two important points. First, both the McClelland and the Shultz et al. models showed that connectionist models can provide good accounts of perceptual aspects of learning such as the torque distance effect. Second, as Mareschal and Shultz (1996) pointed out, cascade correlation models are inherently generative and thus provide a strong existence proof for the plausibility of a constructivist approach to cognitive development.

COMPUTATIONAL MODELS OF OTHER
DEVELOPMENTAL PHENOMENA

I have focused on the balance scale in order to compare the two approaches to computational modeling, but many other computational models now address a variety of other domains and the issue of relevance to cognitive development. The domains include classic Piagetian tasks (conservation, seriation, object permanence) as well as arithmetic and language acquisition. The developmental issues include rule learning, stages, strategy change, generalization, and efficiency (see Table 6.3). Of particular interest is Shultz's (1997) recent cascade correlation model of number conservation, which captures an impressive array of conservation phenomena and proposes a novel explanation for some of them.

CONCLUSION

In concluding, I want to make three points. First, the two computational approaches are not as distinct as their practitioners have often claimed (MacWhinney, 1993, makes a similar point). Second, for all of their accomplishments, both approaches must solve some very difficult remaining problems, but these problems are fairly well defined, so that progress (or failure) can be measured. Third, I suggest how to relate these new ideas to earlier Piagetian notions.

TABLE 6.3
Recent Computational Models of Developmental Relevance

Model Type Domain	Issues Addressed	Authors
Connectionist		
Seriation	Rule learning, stages, perceptual effects	Shultz et al. (1995)
Distance, time		
Causal reasoning		
Pronoun acquisition		
Language acquisition	Learning gender of definite articles in German	MacWhinney et al. (1989)
Object permanence	Graded representations of knowledge and strategies	Munakata, McClelland, Johnson, & Siegler (1997)
Number conservation	Problem size effect, length bias effect, screening effect	Shultz (1997)
Production System		
Transitivity	Strategy change, capacity, complexity Analogical reasoning in skill acquisition	Halford et al. (1995)
Number conservation	Durability and robustness of learning, generalization, operational level and structural change, speed of learning	T. J. Simon & Klahr (1995)
Arithmetic	Development of increasingly efficient procedures for single-digit addition	Neches (1987)
Concept learning and language acquisition	First language acquisition	Langley (1987)

Comparing Production Systems and Connectionist Systems

What are the fundamental differences between production system and connectionist approaches? Here are some candidates:

1. *Parallelism*. The inherent parallelism of connectionist models is often contrasted with the serial recognize-act cycle of production systems. Production systems, however, also have a high degree of parallelism because during the *match* or *recognize* phase of a production system's recognize-act cycle, the condition side of all productions is matched in parallel with all the active declarative memory elements.

2. *Distributed knowledge*. The extent to which knowledge is distributed or modularized in a production system depends entirely on the grain size that elements or productions are supposed to capture. A single production might represent a very explicit and verbalizable rule; it might represent a small piece of processing for a complex, implicit piece of knowledge; or it might represent a complex pattern of cue associations much like those found in connectionist models. Similarly, in parallel distributed processing (PDP) models, the individual element can represent knowledge at any grain size from an individual neuron to an assembly of neurons to the word *neuron*. Nothing inherent in either formulation specifies what this grain should be until additional constraints are imposed on the model.

3. *Continuity*. Another purported difference between PDP models and production system models is the *gradualism* of the former and the *abruptness* of the latter. We can, however, create a production system architecture with continuously varying strengths of productions. Hence production systems can exhibit gradualism. Because of the appropriate grain size on a performance window, connectionist models could appear to be undergoing discontinuous changes.

Of course, there *are* important pragmatic and theoretical differences here,[4] but I believe that the internecine battle between the symbolic and subsymbolic camps has overstated the differences and ignored the fact that the two approaches share many important properties. Indeed, it should not be surprising that there are many points of convergence, because both approaches pursue common goals and face a common constraint: the real behavior of real children. As I noted earlier, perhaps the most important

---

[4]Perhaps the difference in these approaches is in the rhetoric. Although production system descriptions are burdened with a pedestrian terminology of "matching," "recognizing," "acting," "conflict resolution," and "chunking," connectionist models enjoy the lyrical characterizations of such things as "cascade correlation," "graceful degradation," "optimal harmony," "victory," and "epochs." It's hard to beat that!

common feature is the conviction that computational models provide a very precise language in which to describe the conceptual habitat.

Problems to Be Solved

The area of unsolved problems is exciting, productive, and cumulative because the discipline of creating computational models forces our ignorance to the forefront. The unresolved questions are sufficiently specific that it is possible to assess theoretical progress (see Mareschal & Shultz, 1996, for a cogent example). A recent compendium of computational models of cognitive development (T. J. Simon & Halford, 1995) contains several illuminating disagreements among people who have modeled the same domain, but from different approaches.

It is clear that the ultimate understanding of transition mechanisms requires insights from both connectionist and production system perspectives. Claims for the superiority of one approach over the other are premature, and both approaches still face some difficult challenges. Here are a few of the issues on the research frontier for computational models of conceptual development.

Scalability. To date, both symbolic and subsymbolic models of cognitive development have focused on highly circumscribed domains, and in those domains, on small-scale exemplars of the domain. For all the work on connectionist models of language, no one has yet been able to construct a complete connectionist model of language acquisition. For example, developmental neural networks are often constrained to well-defined topics such as the acquisition of the English past tense (Cottrell & Plunkett, 1991) or learning German gender (MacWhinney, Leinbach, Taraban, & McDonald, 1989). The toy model approach often reduces large problems such as question answering (St. John, 1992) or word sense disambiguation (Harris, 1994) to small problems by using only a few dozen sentences or words in the input corpus. In fact, there is not even a reasonably complete account for smaller skill domains such as word learning or syntactic development. For all the work on Piagetian and other types of problem solving, no one has constructed a production system or a neural net that performs the full range of tasks encountered by a normal 5-year-old child. In essence, all the work so far has been on toy versions of larger domains.

Computational modelers have argued, either explicitly or implicitly, that in principle, such models can be expanded substantially with no major theoretical modifications. But can they? The plausibility of these claims varies according to the approach, and the symbolic models have the better track record. Although there are no large-scale developmental production systems, there do exist several very large production systems that start with a few hundred initial hand-coded productions and go on to learn over 100,000 productions. Domains include both artificial-intelligence–type tasks and cognitive models (see Doorenbos, 1995, for a review and evaluation of several such large-scale production systems).

With respect to scaling up connectionist systems, there are grounds for skepticism. For example, in the language-learning domain, when one attempts to add additional words or sentences to many connectionist language models, their performance begins to degenerate. One of the major challenges for computational modelers, then, is a direct attack on this scalability problem.

Ad Hoc Assumptions About the Environment. Another problem facing both connectionist and production system models is the lack of a principled, data-constrained theory of the *effective* environment in which such models operate. For many models, the training to which they are exposed is based on arbitrary, unprincipled, ecologically ungrounded assumptions about the environmental inputs that children receive. Until we have better ways of measuring the actual properties of patterns in the effective environment, we cannot really claim that our models are being properly constrained by real empirical data.

Fortunately, there are two promising research avenues that may soon begin to alleviate this problem. The first avenue is the development of rich computerized databases. In the area of language development, the Child Language Data Exchange System (CHILDES) database (MacWhinney, 1995) has collected transcript data from dozens of major empirical projects. These transcripts document both the language input to children and children's developing conversational competence. These data are now being supplemented by digitized audio and video records that give researchers access to the full richness of the original interactions. Because this database is computerized according to a standardized format, it is possible to use a wide variety of computer programs for search and analysis of patterns in both the input and children's productions. Increasingly, simulations of language learning are being based on properties of input as computed from the CHILDES database and similar computerized sources.

A second promising development is the growth of microgenetic studies. This research is designed to capture developmental processes as they occur by looking at fine-grained moment-to-moment changes in cognition and behavior. Kuhn (1995) has applied microgenetic techniques to the study of scientific reasoning, and Siegler and Crowley (1991) and Alibali (1993) have applied this methodology to the study of strategy development in mathematics. The technique can be used equally well with basic behaviors such as walking (Adolph, 1995) or reaching (Thelen & Smith, 1994). Because microgenetic methods have such a fine-grained level of analysis, they collect quantities of data that are rich enough to support interesting tests of connectionist (MacWhinney & Leinbach, 1991), symbolic (Marcus et al., 1992), and dynamic systems (van der Maas & Molenaar, 1992) approaches to cognitive development.

Cabbages and Kings

Finally, I want to move to a metatheoretical issue, which concerns the way in which workers in our field have viewed theoretical progress. In particular, how are the questions addressed here related to Piaget's efforts to characterize the developmental process?

The message I have attempted to convey is twofold: Questions about the conceptual habitat can be answered in terms of computational models, and an active field of research in cognitive science is exploring the capacity and limits of different cognitive architectures. The field is lively, somewhat contentious, and highly technical. I have tried to indicate its current contributions and its potential for our area, as well as some of its knottiest problems. I am concerned, however, that, as psychologists interested in cognitive development, we have been unnecessarily burdened by the shadow of the massive theoretical edifices of the past. The problem, as depicted in Fig. 6.5, is that the earlier constructs of assimilation and accommodation may impose an unnecessary and potentially unproductive constraint on both new empirical work and new theoretical concepts. Indeed, developmentalists of all stripes—including computational modelers—seem to feel obliged to comment on the extent to which their theories can be placed in correspondence with the Piagetian notions of assimilation and accommodation. For example, consider the mapping by Shultz et al. (1995):

> Using Piaget's terms, one can conceptualize three general types of cognitive encounters in cascade-correlation nets: (1) assimilation, (2) assimilative learning, and (3) accommodation. Pure assimilation occurs without learning. It is represented in cascade-correlation by correct generalization to novel problems without either weight changes or hidden unit recruitment. Assimilative learning occurs by weight adjustment, but without hidden unit recruitment. Here the network learns new patterns that do not require non-linear changes in representational power. Accommodation occurs via hidden unit recruitment when new patterns cannot be learned without non-linear increases in computational power. (p. 53)

Shultz et al. go on to discuss other types of computational models in relation to the processes of assimilation and accommodation:

> Adaptation through assimilation and accommodation can also be re-interpreted through rule-based and back-propagation perspectives, but with less

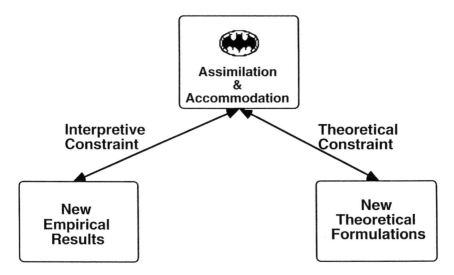

FIG. 6.5.   Current neo-Piagetian paradigm.

satisfactory results. In a rule-based learning system like Soar, assimilation could be construed as rule-firing and accommodation could be construed as chunking new rules through impasse-driven search. In back-propagation learning, accommodation could be viewed in terms of weight adjustment and assimilation as the absence of such adjustment. (p. 54)

These attempts to map the new computational constructs to precomputational theoretical constructs have been widespread among connectionists. The following from Bechtel and Abrahamsen's (1991) introductory text on the topic illustrates the genre:

Connectionism could be viewed as a modern mechanism for achieving stage-like states by means of the heretofore somewhat mysterious processes of accommodation and assimilation. Specifically, assimilation can be interpreted in terms of the tendency of an interactive network to settle into the most appropriate of its stable (attractor) states . . . when input is presented to it; in Piaget's language, this is the schema to which the experience has been assimilated. Accommodation can be interpreted as the changes in activations as well as weights that occur in order to assimilate the experience. (That is, transient state changes and learning are highly interrelated both in connectionist networks and in Piaget's notion of accommodation. The assimilation of any experience involves both of these aspects of accommodation.) (p. 271)

The proclivity to look over one's theoretical shoulder for evidence of "equilibratory correctness" is not limited to computational modelers. For example, in summarizing the current state of theory-theory, Gopnik (1996) made the mapping as follows: "Thus, the interpretive effects of theories seem much like assimilation, and the processes of falsification and counter evidence, which lead to theory change, are reminiscent of accommodation" (p. 221).

It strikes me that the search for assimilation and accommodation in modern computational theories of development represents a curiously non-Piagetian approach to conceptual development. Let me make the point by starting with a quotation from Piaget, who put it this way: "A rabbit that eats a cabbage doesn't become a cabbage; it's a cabbage that becomes rabbit—that's assimilation" (Piaget, quoted in Bringuier, 1980, p. 42). Let me make an analogy to this rabbit–cabbage relation. In this analogy, the cabbage is Piaget's theory of equilibration, and the rabbit—the entity doing the assimilation and accommodation—is us: the collective understanding of our field about the nature of cognitive development.

If our field's conceptual development followed the Piagetian model, then, as the rabbit did to the cabbage, we would assimilate and accommodate his theory. The field would, at first, accommodate its earlier theoretical constructs such that it could come to grips with new ideas. Simultaneously, the assimilation process would exercise its function, and the theoretical insights would be dissolved, decomposed, extracted, and intermingled with our existing conceptual structures. Moreover, new data, new questions, and new theoretical languages would, in their turn, be assimilated and accommodated into the conceptual structure of the field. In other words, we rabbits would digest this theoretical cabbage, would eat other cabbages and other vegetables, but would remain rabbits.

But I think something else has happened, at least in part of our field. The accommodation process is all that ever got started. To take apart the theory, to extract its essential nutrients, and pass on the rest is sometimes viewed as a misguided mixture of heresy and ignorance. But such a view, however, minimizes assimilation, and if there is no assimilation, then instead of the cabbage becoming a rabbit, the rabbit becomes a cabbage.

However, this is quite unnecessary. There is no burden of responsibility for computational modelers—or any other contemporary theorists—to scrutinize their models to identify the parts that are doing accommodation and the parts that are doing assimilation. It is hard to see how such efforts can be productive in view of the inherent ambiguity of the initial constructs. This point has been noted repeatedly in the literature:

> Piaget's particular models of equilibration represent his efforts to [produce a theory of self-organization], but they fall somewhat short because of their excessive abstractness. So the task of producing a concrete theory of cognitive development as a self-organizing process remains, and that theory may or may not resemble Piaget's own models very closely. (Chapman, 1992, p. 47)

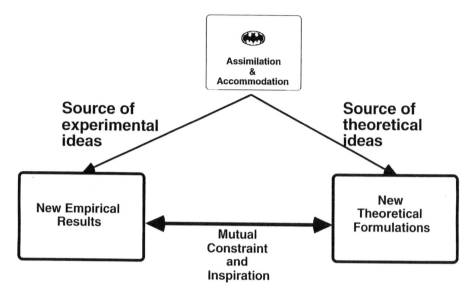

FIG. 6.6. Proposed neo-neo-Piagetian paradigm.

Theoretical development could be greatly stimulated if less effort were devoted to testing Piaget's theory and more were devoted to testing contemporary theories. This is analogous to what is done in other research areas.
For example, memory researchers do not devote most of their efforts to
testing theories by James (1890) or Bartlett (1932) but to contemporary
theories such as those of Craik and Lockhart (1972) or Murdock (1982).
Reference is still made to earlier works, but as a source of insight and ideas
rather than as explicit theory. (Halford, 1989, p. 351)

This perspective suggests that it is more productive to use the old constructs as inspiration rather than as constraints (see Fig. 6.6). Our only
constraints need then be between our developing theories and our developing, emerging results. Moreover, I believe that such an approach is
entirely consistent with Inhelder's advice: "Instead of praising Piaget for
what he accomplished, the best tribute we can pay to his memory is to go
forward" (Inhelder, 1992, p. xiii).

ACKNOWLEDGMENTS

Thanks to my colleagues Martha Alibali, Zhe Chen, and Bethany Rittle
Johnson for comments on an earlier draft of this chapter. Its preparation
was supported in part by a grant from the National Institute of Child
Health and Human Development (R01-HD25211). Sections of this chapter

are partly based on chapters with Christian Schunn (Schunn & Klahr, 1997) and Brian MacWhinney (Klahr & MacWhinney, 1997), but I am solely responsible for the views expressed here.

REFERENCES

Adolph, K. (1995). Psychophysical assessment of toddlers' ability to cope with slopes. *Journal of Experimental Psychology, 21,* 734–750.

Alibali, M. (1993). Gesture–speech mismatch and mechanisms of learning: What the hands reveal about a child's state of mind. *Cognitive Psychology, 25,* 468–523.

Anderson, J. (1993). *Rules of the mind.* Hillsdale, NJ: Lawrence Erlbaum Associates.

Bartlett, F. C. (1932). *Remembering: A study in experimental and social psychology.* Cambridge, England: Cambridge University Press.

Baylor, G. W., & Gascon, J. (1974). An information processing theory of aspects of the development of weight seriation in children. *Cognitive Psychology, 6,* 1–40.

Bechtel, W., & Abrahamsen, A. (1991). *Connectionism and the mind: An introduction to parallel processing in networks.* Cambridge, MA: Basil Blackwell.

Bidell, T. R., & Fischer, K. W. (1994). Developmental transitions in children's early on-line planning. In M. M. Haith, J. B. Benson, R. J. Roberts, & B. F. Pennington (Eds.), *The development of future-oriented processes* (pp. 141–176). Chicago: University of Chicago Press.

Bringuier, J. (1980). *Conversations With Jean Piaget.* Chicago: University of Chicago Press.

Brown, A. L. (1982). Learning and development: The problem of compatibility, access and induction. *Human Development, 25,* 89–115.

Brown, R. (1970). Introduction. In Society for Research in Child Development (Ed.), *Cognitive development in children* (pp. ix–xii). Chicago: University of Chicago Press.

Carey, S. (1985). *Conceptual change in childhood.* Cambridge, MA: Bradford Books/MIT Press.

Case, R. (1985). *Intellectual development: A systematic reinterpretation.* New York: Academic Press.

Case, R. (1986). The new stage theories in intellectual development: Why we need them; what they assert. In M. Perlmutter (Ed.), *Perspectives for intellectual development* (pp. 57–91). Hillsdale, NJ: Lawrence Erlbaum Associates.

Case, R. (1997). The development of conceptual structures. In D. Kuhn and R. S. Siegler (Eds.), *Handbook of child psychology* (5th ed.), *Vol. 2: Cognition, perception, and language* (pp. 745–800). New York: Wiley.

Chapman, M. (1992). Equilibration and the dialectics of organization In H. Beilin, & P. Pufall (Eds.), *Piaget's theory, prospects and possibilities* (pp. 135–176). Hillsdale, NJ: Lawrence Erlbaum Associates.

Cottrell, G., & Plunkett, K. (1991). Learning the past tense in a recurrent network: Acquiring the mapping from meaning to sounds. In *Proceedings of the 13th annual conference of the Cognitive Science Society.* Hillsdale, NJ: Lawrence Erlbaum Associates.

Craik, F. I. M., & Lockhart, R. S. (1972). Levels of processing: A framework for memory research. *Journal of Verbal Learning and Verbal Behavior, 11,* 671–684.

Doorenbos, R. B. (1995). *Production matching for large learning systems.* Unpublished doctoral dissertation, Carnegie Mellon University, Pittsburgh, PA.

Fausett, L. (1994). *Fundamentals of neural networks.* Englewood Cliffs, NJ: Prentice-Hall.

Ferretti, R. P., & Butterfield, E. C. (1986). Are children's rule assessment classifications invariant across instances of problem types? *Child Development, 57,* 1419–1428.

Gelman, R. (1982). Accessing one-to-one correspondence: Still another paper about conservation. *British Journal of Psychology, 73,* 209–220.

Gopnik, A. (1996). The post-Piaget era. *Psychological Science, 7,* 221–225.

Halford, G. S. (1989). Reflections of 25 years of Piagetian cognitive developmental psychology, 1963–1988. *Human Development, 32,* 325–357.

Halford, G. S. (1993). *Children's understanding: The development of mental models.* Hillsdale, NJ: Lawrence Erlbaum Associates.

Halford, G. S., Smith, S. B., Dickson, J. C., Mayberry, M. T., Kelly, M. E., Bain, J. D., & Stewart, J. E. M. (1995). Modeling the development of reasoning strategies: The roles of analogy, knowledge, and capacity. In T. Simon & G. Halford (Eds.), *Developing cognitive competence: New approaches to process modeling* (pp. 77–156). Hillsdale, NJ: Lawrence Erlbaum Associates.

Harris, C. (1994). Coarse coding and the lexicon. In C. Fuchs & B. Victorri (Eds.), *Continuity in linguistic semantics* (pp. 205–229). Amsterdam, The Netherlands: John Benjamins.

Hertz, J., Krogh, A., & Palmer, R. (1991). *Introduction to the theory of neural computation.* New York: Addison-Wesley.

Holland, J. H. (1975). *Adaptation in natural and artificial systems.* Ann Arbor: University of Michigan Press.

Hunter, I. M. L. (1968). Mental calculation. In P. C. Wason & P. N. Johnson-Laird (Eds.), *Thinking and reasoning* (pp. 341–351). Baltimore: Penguin Books.

Inhelder, B. (1992). Foreword. In H. Beilin & P. Pufall (Eds.), *Piaget's theory: Prospects and possibilities* (pp. iv–x). Hillsdale, NJ: Lawrence Erlbaum Associates.

James, W. (1890). *The principles of psychology.* New York: Holt.

Just, M. A., & Carpenter, P. A. (1992). A capacity theory of comprehension: Individual differences in working memory. *Psychological Review, 99,* 122–149.

Karmiloff-Smith, A. (1992). *Beyond modularity: A developmental perspective on cognitive science.* Cambridge, MA: MIT Press.

Klahr, D. (1992). Information processing approaches to cognitive development. In M. H. Bornstein & M. E. Lamb (Eds.), *Developmental psychology: An advanced textbook* (3rd ed., pp. 273–336). Hillsdale, NJ: Lawrence Erlbaum Associates.

Klahr, D., & MacWhinney, B. (1997). Information processing. In D. Kuhn & R. S. Siegler (Eds.), W. Damon (Series Ed.), *Handbook of child psychology (5th ed.), Vol. 2: Cognition, perception, and language* (pp. 631–678). New York: Wiley.

Klahr, D., & Siegler, R. S. (1978). The representation of children's knowledge. In H. W. Reese & L. P. Lipsitt (Eds.), *Advances in child development and behavior* (Vol. 12, pp. 61–116). New York: Academic Press.

Klahr, D., & Wallace, J. G. (1976). *Cognitive development: An information-processing view.* Hillsdale, NJ: Lawrence Erlbaum Associates.

Kuhn, D. (1995). Microgenetic study of change: What has it told us? *Psychological Science, 6,* 133–139.

Kuhn, D., Garcia-Mila, M., Zohar, A., & Andersen, C. (1995). Strategies of knowledge acquisition. *Monographs of the Society for Research in Child Development.* Vol. 60 (3, Serial no. 245).

Langley, P. (1987). A general theory of discrimination learning. In D. Klahr, P. Langley & R. Neches (Eds.), *Production system models of learning and development* (pp. 99–162). Cambridge, MA: MIT Press.

Larkin, J. H. (1981). Enriching formal knowledge: A model for learning to solve textbook physics problems. In J. R. Anderson (Ed.), *Cognitive skills and their acquisition* (pp. 311–334). Hillsdale, NJ: Lawrence Erlbaum Associates.

Lewis, C. (1978). *Production system models of practice effects.* Ann Arbor: University of Michigan Press.

MacWhinney, B. (1993). Connections and symbols: Closing the gap. *Cognition, 49,* 291–296.

MacWhinney, B. (1995). *The CHILDES project: Tools for analyzing talk* (2nd ed.). Hillsdale, NJ: Lawrence Erlbaum Associates.

MacWhinney, B., & Leinbach, J. (1991). Implementations are not conceptualizations: Revising the verb learning model. *Cognition, 29,* 121–157.

MacWhinney, B. J., Leinbach, J., Taraban, R., & McDonald, J. L. (1989). Language learning: Cues or rules? *Journal of Memory and Language, 28*, 255–277.

Marcus, G., Ullman, M., Pinker, S., Hollander, M., Rosen, T., & Xu, F. (1992). Overregularization in language acquisition. *Monographs of the Society for Research in Child Development, 57*(4).

Mareschal, D., & Shultz, T. R. (1996). Generative connectionist networks and constructivist cognitive development. *Cognitive Development, 11*, 571–603.

McClelland, J. L. (1989). Parallel distributed processing: Implications for cognition and development. In R. G. M. Morris (Ed.), *Parallel distributed processing: Implications for psychology and neurobiology.* Oxford, England: Oxford University Press.

McClelland, J. L. (1995). A connectionist perspective on knowledge and development. In T. J. Simon & G. S. Halford (Eds.), *Developing cognitive competence: New approaches to process modeling* (pp. 157–204). Hillsdale, NJ: Lawrence Erlbaum Associates.

Miller, P. H. (1983). *Theories of developmental psychology.* San Francisco: Freeman.

Munakata, Y., McClelland, J. L., Johnson, M. J., & Siegler, R. S. (1997). Rethinking infant knowledge: Toward an adaptive process account of successes and failures in object permanence tasks. *Psychological Review, 104*, 686–713.

Murdock, B. B., Jr. (1982). A theory for the storage and retrieval of item and associative information. *Psychological Review, 89*, 609–626.

Neches, R. (1987). Learning through incremental refinement of procedures. In D. Klahr, P. Langley, & R. Neches (Eds.), *Production system models of learning and development* (pp. 163–220). Cambridge, MA: MIT Press.

Newell, A. (1990). *A unified theory of cognition.* Cambridge, MA.: Harvard University Press.

Piaget, J. (1985). *The equilibration of cognitive structures* (Trans. T. Brown & J. Thampy). Chicago: University of Chicago Press. (Original work published 1975)

Rumelhart, D. E., & McClelland, J. L. (1986). On learning the past tenses of English verbs. In *Parallel distributed processing, Vol. 2: Psychological and biological models* (pp. 216–271). Cambridge, MA: MIT Press.

Schunn, C. D., & Klahr, D. (1998). Production systems: Views on intelligent behavior. In W. Bechtel & G. Graham (Eds.), *A companion to cognitive science.* Oxford, England: Blackwell.

Shultz, T. R. (1997). *A computational analysis of conservation.* Working paper, Department of Psychology, McGill University, Montreal, Canada.

Shultz, T. R., Schmidt, W. C., Buckingham, D., & Mareschal, D. (1995). Modeling cognitive development with a generative connectionist algorithm. In T. J. Simon & G. S. Halford (Eds.), *Developing cognitive competence: New approaches to process modeling* (pp. 205–262). Hillsdale, NJ: Lawrence Erlbaum Associates.

Siegler, R. S. (1976). Three aspects of cognitive development. *Cognitive Psychology, 8*, 481–520.

Siegler, R. S. (Ed.). (1978). *Children's thinking: What develops?* Hillsdale, NJ: Lawrence Erlbaum Associates.

Siegler, R. S. (1996). *Emerging minds.* New York: Oxford University Press.

Siegler, R. S., & Crowley, K. (1991). The microgenetic method: A direct means for studying cognitive development. *American Psychologist, 46*, 606–620.

Siegler, R. S., & Shipley, C. (1995). Variation, selection, and cognitive change. In G. Halford & T. Simon (Eds.), *Developing cognitive competence: New approaches to process modeling* (pp. 31–76). Hillsdale, NJ: Lawrence Erlbaum Associates.

Simon, D. P., & Simon, H. A. (1978). Individual differences in solving physics problems. In R. Siegler (Ed.), *Children's thinking: What develops?* (pp. 325–348). Hillsdale, NJ: Lawrence Erlbaum Associates.

Simon, H. A. (1962). An information processing theory of intellectual development. *Monographs of the Society for Research in Child Development, 27* (Serial No. 82).

Simon, T. J., & Halford, G. (Eds.). (1995). *Developing cognitive competence: New approaches to process modeling.* Hillsdale, NJ: Lawrence Erlbaum Associates.

Simon, T. J., & Klahr, D. (1995). A theory of children's learning about number conservation. In T. J. Simon & G. Halford (Eds.), *Developing cognitive competence: New approaches to process modeling* (pp. 315–354). Hillsdale, NJ: Lawrence Erlbaum Associates.

Spensley, M. F. (1995). *Representational redescription and the development of cognitive flexibility.* Unpublished doctoral dissertation, The Open University, London, England.

St. John, M. (1992). The story gestalt: A model of knowledge-intensive processes in text comprehension. *Cognitive Science, 16*, 271–306.

Thelen, E., & Smith, L. (1994). *A dynamic systems approach to the development of cognition and action.* Cambridge, MA: MIT Press.

van der Maas, H., & Molenaar, P. (1992). Stagewise cognitive development: An application of catastrophe theory. *Psychological Review, 99*, 395–417.

Wallace, J. G., Klahr, D., & Bluff, K. (1987). A self-modifying production system for conservation acquisition. In D. Klahr, P. Langley, & R. Neches (Eds.), *Production system models of learning and development* (pp. 359–435). Cambridge, MA: MIT Press.

Wilkening, F., & Anderson, N. H. (1982). Representation and diagnosis of knowledge structures in developmental psychology. In N. H. Anderson (Ed.), *Contributions to integration theory, Vol. 3: Developmental.* Hillsdale, NJ: Lawrence Erlbaum Associates.

Part II

HOW DOES THE CHILD CONSTRUCT A MENTAL MODEL DURING THE COURSE OF DEVELOPMENT? WHAT IS THE DEVELOPMENTAL ORIGIN OF THIS MODEL?

Chapter 7

A Systemic Interpretation
of Piaget's Theory of Knowledge

Rolando García
Center for Research and Advanced Studies, Mexico City

EPISTEMOLOGY AND THE FOUNDATION OF SCIENCE

The history of the development of thought in the individual—which genetic psychology attempts to systematize—and the history of the development of knowledge accumulated by society over time—systematized by the historicocritical analysis of science—have the objective of achieving a coherent conceptualization of the type of activity that leads us to known reality.

But what is reality? The immediate response obtained when this question is asked is that what we call *reality* is the set of observables that correspond to our perceptions. One of the artificers of the scientific revolution brought about by quantum mechanics expressed this concept in the following terms: "The set of invariants of our sense impressions is the physical reality which our minds construct in a perfectly unconscious way." He added: "Science is nothing else than the endeavour to construct these invariants where they are not obvious" (Born, 1948, p. 104). According to this formulation, reality is *what is there*, directly *given* in our experience. The table on which I work, the lamp that gives me light, the people I speak to, myself, *we are reality*. And what is it that we observe when *we observe reality?*

"There is no pure reading of experience,"[1] said Piaget. "Every observable is theory laden,"[2] repeated the teachers of philosophy of science after Russell Hanson.

---

[1]This idea is developed in Jonckheer, Mandelbrot, and Piaget (1958) and Bruner, Bresson, Morf, and Piaget (1958).

[2]This sentence is the leitmotiv of Russell Hanson (1965).

I see the table, I touch it, I lean on it. What is the basis of the statement that there are no pure readings of experience? Where is the theory that these observables are laden with?

Although it would appear that they made similar statements, the responses of Piaget and of Russell Hanson are fundamentally different.

Hanson's dictum is based on the analysis of numerous examples, which he used to show that what appears as a direct observation already contains an interpretation belonging to the observer and varying from one observer to another *depending on the previous knowledge of each.* Quine responded to this statement by indicating: "What counts as an *observation sentence* varies with the width of community considered. But we can also get an absolute standard by taking in all speakers of the language, or most" (Quine, 1969, p. 88).

Quine was right insofar as the statement in question is concerned. However, what is important for us is that Russell Hanson did not touch at all the basic epistemological problem that is involved in Piaget's dictum, as we shall see. Curiously enough, Quine did not mention the epistemological problem in his remark to Hanson although he was quite aware of it, and he said so emphatically: "The notion of observation as the impartial and objective source of evidence for science is bankrupt" (Quine, 1969, p. 88).

Quine was, without doubt, the empiricist who most throughly analyzed the presuppositions of empiricism. These analyses led him to profound revision of the epistemological creed that he had proclaimed for a long period and that led Putnam to describe him as "The Greatest Logical Positivist."[3]

I submit that the radical change of Quine's epistemological position may be considered one of the most transcendental events in the philosophy of science. It deserves a profound analysis that goes far beyond the limits of this presentation. For our purposes, it suffices to quote a few statements in which the transit to a *new* epistemology was registered with his characteristic sharpness: "[W]e gave up trying to justify our knowledge of the external world by rational reconstruction . . . we have stopped dreaming of deducing science from sense data" (Quine, 1969, p. 84).

Quite right. But what did Quine offer in its place? Let us follow his line of thought:

The only information that can reach our sensory surfaces from external objects must be limited to two dimensional optical projections and various impacts from air waves on the ear drums and some gaseous reactions in the nasal passages and a few kindred odds and ends. How could one hope to find about the external world from such meager traces? In short, if our science were true, how could we know it? Clearly, in confronting this challenge,

---

[3]The expression quoted is the title of chap. 20 in Putnam (1990).

the epistemologist may make free use of all scientific theory. His problem is that of finding ways, in keeping with natural sciences, whereby the human mind can have projected this same science, from the sensory information that could reach him, according to this science. (Quine, 1973, p. 2)

From here onward, Quine was to concern himself with demonstrating that although circular, his proposal does not contain a vicious circle. It is *in making free use of all scientific theory* that he located the point of transition between what he called "the old epistemology" and the new formulation of the problem. Where did Quine break the circle so that is not a vicious one? I do not repeat his journey here. I just state his surprising conclusion: "Our liberated epistemologist ends up as an empirical psychologist, scientifically investigating man's acquisition of science" (Quine, 1973, p. 3).

In his famous essay *Epistemology Naturalized* (1969), already cited, Quine was even more explicit: "The old epistemology aspired to contain, in a sense, natural science; it would construct it somehow from sense data. Epistemology in its new setting, conversely, is contained in natural science, as a chapter of psychology" (p. 83). And again another surprising statement: "In the old anti-psychologist days the question of epistemological priority was moot. . . . Now that we are permitted to appeal to physical stimulation, the problem dissolves" (pp. 84–85).

The greatest logical positivist, recognizing his "old anti-psychologist days," made considerable progress with respect to the old empiricist epistemology, but the end of his road remained dramatically in the shadow because the psychology he turned to ended up being purely speculative.[4]

Why have the century's great empiricists reached a dead end and stayed there without exploring other paths? Let us remember that only in the last paragraph of the last chapter of his last book on philosophy, did the great Bertrand Russell confess: "It must be admitted, empiricism as a theory of knowledge has proven inadequate, though less so than any other previous theory of knowledge" (Russell, 1948, p. 507).

Why did they not try what appears an obvious alternative to many of us, that is, constructivism?

Let us return to Piaget and Russell Hanson. In my view, Quine's comment with regard to Hanson was sufficiently conclusive and showed that, contrary to what is usually argued, Hanson's dictum fit in a wide conception of empiricism, but he did not go beyond.

Thus, there remains only Piaget's position with respect to the reading experience. What was this position based on? Genetic psychology has given us the verdict: The reconstruction of the development of knowledge of an

---

[4]See for example, Quine, 1973, and especially the section Psychogenesis Summed Up (p. 123).

individual shows that to reach his or her conception of the world with objects and properties distributed in a space and participating in a process of a certain duration, the individual must pass through a long process that takes place throughout childhood and that culminates in adolescence.

An empiricist à la Quine would say: Very good! But finally everyone recognizes that there are tables, lamps, and people. What is the fuss about? Is this not a process of learning? Once a child learns to distinguish between a table and a lamp and between a real dog and a stuffed dog, where is the theory? Why do we say that the reading of experience is not pure? Is it not on the basis of this shared experience that science begins?

Strangely enough, Quine's position has some points of contact with constructivism. For Quine, the problem faced by the epistemologist was to understand how to move from observations to science, *once we have renounced the deduction of science from sense data.* To this end, Quine considered the use of knowledge acquired through science as legitimate. He then looked for *the* science that links observations with conceptualizations and arrived at psychology. At this point, his impeccable logic ceased, and his empiricist ideology took over: Quine's psychology can be none other than behaviorism. His argument remained at the level of how, in behavioral terms, the child *learns the language* of objects and of space and time. In this respect, Quine seemed to take the psychology prevalent at a certain time and in a certain geographical area as being *the* psychology and could not find a way out of empiricism.

What did Quine do to epistemology? Did he kill, it or did he let it escape? This area was Quine's Achilles' heel and the Achilles' heel of those contemporary philosophers who recognized the collapse of empiricism and tried to save it. To put it briefly, they had no epistemology left! By turning, in extremis, to behavioral psychology, they showed that they found themselves at a dead end. From this point, I return empty-handed to my original question: What is *reality*? How do we know?

I maintain that in renouncing the answers to these questions, philosophers of science resigned their main function (to account for the foundation of scientific knowledge), turned to sociology of science, and left out the theory of knowledge.

Piaget entered the scene of this discussion with a complete reformulation of the problem and took the only direction left after the collapse of empiricism: *constructivism.*

A very condensed formulation of Piagetian answers to the previous questions may be reduced (with great risk of oversimplifications) to a few basic tenets of genetic epistemology:

- *Experience* starts from actions and their coordinations in action schemes. The organization of experience data begins with rudimentary relations of implications between actions.

- The framework of relations, based on inferences, which are constructed by the subject, arrives at the constitution of logic and logicomathematical structures, which are the necessary forms of all knowledge.

- The interdependence of subject's constructions and the experience data is shown at the most elementary levels by the common indistinguishable origin of logic and causal relations. Such interdependence is the foundation of a conception of causality leading to a new conceptualization of the traditional problem of scientific explanation.

- There is an implicit ontology in the organization of experience data, which assumes that the qualitative changes, the displacements, the changes of movements are none other than external manifestations of relations between inferred objects. The relations themselves run over the frontiers of the observable. They are *reconstructed* by the subject on the basis of inferences and *attributed* to the inferred objects. The resulting ontology is what we call *reality*.

These four points have a heavy content of epistemological theory. Their justification and validation cannot be meaningfully made statement by statement out of the context of the whole theory. In these respects, I adhere strongly to the well-known Duhem–Quine thesis according to which a theory confronts the tribunal of experience as an organized totality, not piecemeal (Quine, 1951). It is this thesis I refer to when I find myself faced with the surprisingly superficial opinion that dismisses Piaget's theory of knowledge as *dépassé* on the basis of some new findings in developmental psychology.[5]

It must be admitted, however that the application of the Duhem–Quine thesis in this case is confronted with a serious obstacle. We find in the monumental production left by Piaget all the elements of his theory of knowledge. However, it must be admitted that Piaget did not present a totally integrated *theory* (when I say *integrated*, I do not mean a closed and finished theory, because the characteristic of his scientific epistemology is precisely that of being subject to modifications and extensions, like any scientific theory). The integration of his theory is the task left to those of us who feel that we are disciples of his school and who do not have the psychoanalytic inclination "to kill the father."

As a contribution to this task, I am working toward an integrative proposal that includes the plurality of elements found in the Piagetian conception of epistemology: the psychogenetic, biological, and social components; the logical and empirical components; the historical, cultural, and scientific components. In my view, the only conceptual methodological analysis capable of carrying out this integration must be based on a theory of development of knowledge as a *complex system*. To this end, I consider it

---

[5]See the later section The Stratified Universe.

necessary to show how we conceive of the analysis of complex systems today. I am going to argue, against the majority of his critics, that Piaget was a brilliant precursor of ideas that have arisen in contemporary science in recent decades.

CONSTRUCTIVISM AND CONTEMPORARY DEVELOPMENTS IN SCIENCE

Much has happened and much is happening in the science of the second half of the century and thus much is offered for epistemological reflection. The profound changes that have taken place in the conception of the universe in this period have led to the conviction that we are witnessing a new scientific revolution. I refer to only three conceptual changes that are closely linked to our interpretation of Piagetian conceptions of the construction of knowledge. Such interpretation is based on a general theory of complex systems, a theory that I have developed in connection with other studies.[6]

The Stratified Universe

As a starting point, I take a statement made by Einstein at the beginning of this century enunciating a belief that he maintained throughout his life: "The supreme object of the physicist is to arrive at those universal elementary laws from which the cosmos can be built by pure deduction." Today we know that this ideal cannot be achieved, because such conception implies a universe in which the same laws, the same forms of organization, the same dynamics of development rule in all domains and for all scales of phenomena. One of the surprising facts in the recent history of science is that *in* physics itself—the discipline par excellence in which Einstein's conception had become most rooted—the demonstration that the universe cannot be conceived of in this way has arisen. I can reduce this part of the new conceptions to two points:

1. The physical world presents itself as constituted by semiautonomous levels of organizations, with different structures. They are semi-autonomous in the sense of having different *dynamics*, but interact in such a way that they integrate *totalities*.
2. Different levels can be *decoupled* in the sense that the theory developed at one of the levels can have sufficient stability so that it is not perturbed by discoveries or developments at another level.

---

[6]My publications in this area are in Spanish, with the exceptions of García 1984 and 1993.

This second point is most important, and I would like to illustrate it with an example contributed by an incisive physicist and historian of science:

> High energy physics and condensed matter physics have become essentially decoupled in the sense that the existence of a top quark or any new heavy particle is irrelevant to the concerns of condensed matter physicists—no matter how great their intellectual interest in it may be. (Schweber, 1993)

This organization by levels, and this *decoupling* of the levels, had already been shown in other domains before this conclusion from microphysics. If I go back to my years of research on atmospheric dynamics, I can state that meteorology had already found that atmospheric movements, which apparently cover a continuous spectrum of frequencies, are distributed in levels of organization with characteristic dynamics in each level.

On the other hand, Herbert Simon, who has explored science in many directions, has frequently insisted on the hierarchic organization adopted by what he called "the organization of complex systems" (Simon, 1977, sect. 4.4). The typical example given by Simon is the hierarchic structure of biological systems: "If we look at the cell as if it were building brick, we find cells organized in tissue, tissues in organs, organs in systems."

Simon's hierarchic systems are similar to the Chinese boxes that fit inside each other so that each box contains another, which in turn is contained in a larger one (except perhaps the first and the last). I should point out that my conception of stratified systems does not correspond to Chinese boxes. Likewise, Simon gives the name *subsystems* to the structures that correspond to each of the levels of organization in the hierarchy, whereas I use such terms with a different meaning.

The terminology of *hierarchic systems* and of the corresponding subsystems is very widely encountered—in view of the authority of Simon—and corresponds to the notions that have points of contact with other systemic conceptions of development. But I must warn of the possibility of confusion in the case of the same term used with meanings that can be markedly different.

The Nonlinear Universe

In recent decades, a vast literature on what is usually called—to my mind, erroneously—the sciences of complexity has accumulated. As is known, the explosive growth of this literature was to a large extent due to the introduction of extraordinarily fast computers, which allowed the solution of problems that were previously beyond the possibilities of mathematical methods. On this basis, what is more appropriately called *nonlinear science* was developed.

The problems that were taken on in very diverse disciplines and the quantity of spectacular results obtained led to statements that I consider to be illegitimate mathematical extrapolations.

Those who presented themselves as participants in this revolution tended to invoke methods of analysis of complex phenomena, which, it is said, "are capable of breaking down the barriers between disciplines." Quite a number of authors have made assertions of this type (Prigogine, 1994; Thom, 1993, among them). These statements may lead us to think that we are faced with a new attempt to unify the sciences.

In the past, the "breaking down of the barriers between disciplines" was invoked by those with reductionist positions. The most characteristic historical examples are the mechanistic thinking of the 18th century and the program of the *Encyclopedia of Unified Science* launched by logical empiricism. Are we now faced with a new form of reductionism?

The current situation is different. We are not dealing with the ontological and nomological unification of the ultimate constituent of reality—as mechanistic thinking attempted—or the logicolinguistic unity of all sciences, proclaimed by the school of Vienna. The focus of attention has changed and is now centered on what I might call "the dynamics of the change." Here there has effectively been very clear progress, which I can sum up in the following statement: Phenomena of very diverse natures, which belong to the domain of different disciplines and which from the point of view of a purely phenomenological description appear to have nothing in common, present, however, similar characteristics in their temporal evolution.

From this perspective, which goes far beyond the models of dynamic systems, it can be legitimately stated that the developments that have occurred around the problems of complexity not only contribute to a better understanding of a large number of phenomena from multiple disciplines, but also allow the establishment of a conceptual framework for the interdisciplinary study of complex systems.

I think is necessary to say, however, that there has been frequent abuse of the new concepts and methods. There is a sort of imperialism of computers in this trying to apply mathematical modeling with systems of nonlinear differential equations to all types of phenomena. On the other hand, the fact that similar dynamic equations are applied to problems of physics, biology, demography does not *break down barriers* between disciplines or initiate a *new dialogue* between them.

What I would like to recover from all the work carried out in this domain is the fact that much has been learned about the dynamics of change of complex systems. In particular, I refer to what appears to be the most general law: nonlinear and structurally discontinuous evolution that proceeds by successive reorganizations.

The principle of stratification and the nonlinearity of evolutionary processes fall into line with the tenets of genetic epistemology. The so much criticized *stages* in the construction of knowledge (often referred to as the myth of stages) and the assertion that the development of the cognitive system is neither a continuous growth nor a linear process but proceeds by successive reorganizations turned out to be special cases of quite general laws governing processes in all domains.

Complexity

The third conceptual development that is relevant to my study comes under the somewhat misleading title of complexity and requires a more detailed analysis.

COMPLEXITY AND COMPLEX SYSTEMS

First, I am going to make a declaration of faith: I do not believe it is possible to give a satisfactory definition of the noun *complexity*. What *can* be defined is the adjective *complex*. More precisely, I believe there are phenomena, situations, behaviors, models that may be described as complex, but in each case, the word has a different meaning. This does not mean that the term *complexity* cannot be used meaningfully. It implies withdrawing legitimacy from the question "What is complexity?" and it implies also calling into question the expression *theories of complexity*, which is, more often than not, restricted to the applications of dynamic systems.

The use and abuse of *dynamic systems*, as well as the fetishism of the computer, had led many writers, some of them well-known, to formulate problems of complexity in such a way that implies that phenomena or situations not admitting some form of mathematization are relegated to the level of vague intuitive ideas. This proposition leaves aside the possibility of rationally studying, among others, the great social, economic, and political themes that profoundly concern the contemporary world. Is not environmental deterioration at a global level, for example, a problem of great complexity? Which notion of complexity applies to it? Dynamic equations, information theory, deterministic chaos, neuronal networks could hardly have direct application here (except in the modeling of very partial aspects, the results of which may be used as inputs for the study of the general problem). I am going to argue, however, that we have sufficiently solid bases today to approach the study of these themes in such a way that a high degree of rigor and precision can be achieved even though the work is not based on a mathematical model. The systemic conception of Piagetian constructivism falls in these considerations.

Systems and Complex Systems: Some Definitions

I use the term *system* in a specific sense, applied to the representation of a set of situations, phenomena, processes, *cut out* from reality, which can be modeled as an organized totality with a characteristic form of functioning. Here the term *functioning* designates the set of activities that the system can carry out (or allows to be carried out) as a result of the coordination of the *functions* fulfilled by its parts.[7]

Two major categories are contained in this general concept:

1. *Decomposable systems.* Their parts can be isolated and modified independently of each other. A house is an example of a system that can be decomposed. As a system, a house has properties and functioning characteristic of a totality, but its elements (electrical systems, water supply, floors, windows) can be modified without the modifications of the other elements. Systems of this sort can be called complicated but not complex.

2. *Complex systems.* Here the adjective *complex* acquires a very specific meaning qualifying a kind of system in which the processes that determine their functioning are the result of the confluence of multiple factors interacting in such a way that they cannot be isolated. Consequently, the system cannot be described by merely adding together partial perspectives from independent studies of each of its components (i.e., they are not decomposable).

The study of a complex system thus defined presents serious difficulties, but a systematic study can be carried out by taking into account the considerations made previously. The extension and application of these considerations to complex systems can be condensed in the following principles.

Principles of Organization

Stratification. The factors that directly or indirectly determine the functioning of a complex system are distributed in structurally differentiated levels with their own dynamics. The levels are not interdefinable, but the interactions between levels are such that each level determines the boundary conditions of the adjacent levels in a precise sense that I specify later.

Internal Articulation. The study of a complex system generally starts with a particular situation or a set of phenomena, which occur at a given level of organization that I call *base level*. The intervening factors correspond to certain scales of phenomena and certain processes, which can be grouped in *subsystems* constituted by elements between which there is a greater degree of interconnection that with the other elements of the system. These subsystems function as *subtotalities*, which are articulated by relations that together constitute the structure of the system.

---

[7]The distinction between the *functioning* of a system and the *functions* of its parts was introduced by Piaget (1975).

Boundary Conditions. The phenomena that occur at the base level are not independent of the other processes located at different levels, although as I have said, each level has its own dynamics. They interact, sometimes weakly, but, in other cases, in such a way that one level may condition the evolution of the next level. The interactions take place by means of fluxes (of matter, energy, information, policies, etc.). The set of fluxes at one level, with respect to the others, constitutes the *boundary conditions* of the system defined at that level.

Because it is a matter of ingoing and outgoing fluxes, that is, interactions in a strong sense, the boundary conditions are not rigid conditions imposing on the system; they are not direct or unidirectional. Their role in the structuring of the system is fundamental in that they condition the development of the internal structure of the system *but do not determine it.*[8]

Principles of Evolution

As I indicated at the outset, the developments that have taken place in a wide diversity of themes and disciplines and that are usually grouped under the generic heading of *complexity* converge on the fact that the evolution of very dissimilar phenomena and processes presents common characteristics.

The complex systems I am considering suffer transformations across time, which are peculiar to *open systems.* The evolution of such systems does not take place by means of processes that modify gradually and continuously, but proceeds by a succession of processes of disequilibration. Each restructuring leads to a period of relative dynamic equilibrium during which the system maintains these structures with fluctuations in certain limits.

THE COGNITIVE SYSTEM AS A COMPLEX SYSTEM

The overall range of studies involved in the Piagetian researches about knowledge may be organized in three levels of analysis:[9]

The *first level* includes the material provided by empirical research in two distinct areas: the psychogenesis of concepts from childhood to adolescence (which gave rise to a new discipline: genetic psychology) and the historical development of scientific ideas, concepts, and theories.

---

[8]This distinction is clarified in the section on internal dynamics of the cognitive system.

[9]Unfortunately, the term *level* is used in the literature with a variety of meanings. I use it in three different contexts: level of analysis (as defined here); level of organization (referring to the structure of a system); developmental level (such as a stage in psychogenesis).

At the *second level* is the formulation of the theory of knowledge that accounts for the findings at the first level. This is the domain of genetic epistemology in a strict sense.

The *third level* of analysis is concerned with the applications of the theory as a tool for the analysis and interpretation of foundational problems in the theory of science.

My proposal of a systemic approach to the cognitive system refers to the second level of analysis (genetic epistemology).

I define the cognitive system in a wide sense as the set of interrelated activities pertaining to three different domains: biological, psychological (mental), and social. The activities in each domain have their own specific organizations defining levels of organization of the overall system. With this terminology, I consider the cognitive system in a wide sense, as a complex system having components from three levels of organization: the biological level, the psychological level (mental), and the social level. I call these components, taken together, system Σ.

System Σ is therefore a complex system with three semiautonomous levels of organization, each of which has its own dynamics and is in permanent interaction with the others. The psychological or mental level by itself constitutes a system (subsystem of Σ), which I call cognitive system in a strict sense or System C. To start with, I center my analysis on System C, which thus is the base level defined earlier.

To establish the characteristics that qualify System C as a complex system, it is necessary to define its elements (or subsystems that are subsubsystems of Σ) with their interactions and to identify the boundary conditions through which the biological and social levels of System Σ interact with System C.

System C presents specific problems not found in other fields. In dealing with physical, biological, and social systems, we may focus attention on the elements (chemical elements, solid bodies, biological organisms, people, institutions), or on the structure (the set of relations among the elements or the functioning of the system as a whole). In the case of cognition, the system, the elements, and the relations are all sets of interrelated structures. This composition of C increases the difficulties of the analysis and makes unavoidable a constructionistic approach. There are therefore two kinds of problems to be considered: the organization of the system at one given level (stage) and the structuring processes in the succession of developmental levels. (The second is point b dealt with later.)

Here I consider the organization of the system only at the psychogenetic levels.[10]

---

[10] The organization of the system at the prescientific and scientific levels cannot be treated in the limits of this chapter.

The Components of C at the Elementary Levels

At the elementary levels of cognitive development, a convenient way of defining the elements of C is found in Piaget's well-known diagram of equilibration (introduced in Piaget, 1975, p. 59). The four elements of the system are:[11]

Obs O: Observables related to the objects.

Obs S: Observables related to the subject's actions.

Coord S: Coordinations inferred from the subject's actions.

Coord O: Coordinations inferred between objects.

The interdefinibility of the elements or subsystems—an essential part of the definition of a complex system—is clearly illustrated in the cyclic sequence of the arrows and their merging in the progression from level to level.[12]

The Boundary Conditions[13] of the Cognitive System in Strict Sense (C)

The knowing subject whose mental activities are the elements of System C is, at the same time, a biological organism and a social protagonist. The definition of C as a subsystem of Σ implies that it interacts with the other subsystems: the biological (B) and the social (S). Thus, there are two interfaces in the System Σ: C/B and C/S. There are therefore two types of boundary conditions to be considered.

The Boundary Conditions at the Interface C/B

In his extended studies on the interrelations between psychogenetic and biological development, Piaget anticipated some findings that the development of neurobiology was to demonstrate, particularly in regard to the interactions between neuronal development and perceptive activity in newborn infants. I take the following reference from the seminar on biology and knowledge held in Mexico during the celebration of the centennial anniversary of Jean Piaget in April 1996 (Aréchiga, 1997):

---

[11]There are no ultimate *elements* of the system. Depending on the purpose of the analysis, I can consider Obs S as a subsystem whose elements are action schemes.

[12]Piaget (1975), diagram, p. 62.

[13]I use the term *boundary* for want of a better word and know the risk of misunderstanding. It should be clear that I am not referring to any *entity*, physical or otherwise. The term is just a convenient way of talking about interactions between subsystems of different natures.

It is known that in some neuronal circuits, spontaneous activity while intrinsic to the neuronal system can be modulated by external influences. Since 1962, Torsten Wiesel and David Hubel had demonstrated that in experimental animals (cats), the suppression of visual information from one eye prevented the maturation of the connections in the visual cortex of the eye, leaving the animal without visual neurons with binocular entry, essential for the integration of stereoscopic vision. Deprivation of visual binocular entry has to take place during a fixed period of time in order to produce this difference, a little after birth, which is precisely when the interneuronal connections of the visual system mature. These experiments led to the discovery of the explanation of a fact observed from many years in medicine. In case of strabismus in children, there is full recovery of the binocular function when it is corrected surgically at an early age, whereas when a surgery is delayed, recovery does not occur. It is also possible to explain why the late recovery of visual sensibility in those blind from birth does not allow them to develop normal vision.

I want to emphasize the distinction made by Aréchiga between the activity intrinsic to a system and its modulation by external influences. This example is a typical and clear formulation of the way that the effects of boundary conditions are exerted. This example may also illustrate and clarify the distinction made earlier between *to determine* and *to condition* when I referred in the section on complexity to the action of boundary conditions on the structuring process in a system.

THE INTERNAL DYNAMICS OF THE COGNITIVE SYSTEM

The systemic character of genetic epistemology becomes evident when we analyze Piaget's discovery of the stages in psychogenesis as well as his theory of equilibration. The controversies about the very concept of stage and the supposed refutations by prominent logicians[14] cannot be sustained anymore: The nonlinear character of evolution by successive reorganizations is a common feature in quite different domains (physical, biological, social).

Nevertheless, evolution by successive reorganizations in the case of the cognitive system has very distinctive characteristics.

My definition of a complex system involves the concept of an open system (the reciprocal is not true!). It is well known today (particularly because of the work of Prigogine's school) that open systems are far from equilibrium conditions, that they can be kept stationary by the action of

---

[14]See in particular Apostel (1992/1982) and my answer in Piaget and García (1991/1987), chap. 10).

boundary conditions, and that they evolve by reorganizations *fed by exchanges with the environment*.[15] However, it should be kept in mind that the classic models of open systems found in the literature are not complex systems in my sense and therefore the conclusions of such studies should be applied to my cognitive system with caution.

In the analysis of the development of Cognitive System C, it is necessary to make a clear distinction between the internal development processes of C, which I call its internal dynamics, and the role played by the boundary conditions.

As for the internal dynamics at the most elementary levels, the two predominant processes are the coordination of actions, leading to the generation of logic, and the coordination of observables, leading to causality. Here I must introduce two important specifications.

First, it should be noticed that coordinations of actions and coordinations of observables were referred to previously as elements of System C. Now I refer to them as dynamic processes. This dual utilization of these terms is connected with my remark that the special nature of the cognitive system consists of the fact that the system, the elements, the relations, and the internal processes are all structures (or structuring processes). At a given level of organization, the already *structured* coordinations are elements of the system, whereas the *coordinations among them are structuring processes.*

Action schemes are primitive structures. Such structures are forms depending very much on their contents. The logic starts at a gradual process of development that goes from coordinations of actions to inferential anticipation of results and to coordination of inferences. This process was shown in detail in various chapters of Piaget and García (1991/1987) and García (1992b). The important fact, with reference to my present analysis, is that "from the beginning, *forms* partially depend upon contents while remaining necessary for assimilating them" (Piaget & García, 1991/1987, p. 29).

This fact leads to the second specification. The interaction between *forms* and *content* is the raw material with which we proceed to the organization of experience data leading to the knowledge of the empirical world. *Knowledge* means here, in short, the capacity of providing causal explanations. The common sources of logic and causality[16] as well as the role of logic and logicomathematical structures in causal explanations (Piaget & García, 1974/1971) are, I submit, the core of Piaget's epistemological theory.

---

[15]I have dealt with the application of the concept of self-organizing system to the cognitive system (García, 1992a, 1992b).

[16]As explained by Piaget in a number of his books and articles. See in particular Piaget & García (1991/1987) and Piaget (1980).

An important aspect (often overlooked) of Piaget's theory of knowledge is the clear distinction, in the analysis of the development of cognition, between the logic (deductivistic) phases of the stabilized system and the dialectic character of the developmental processes (Piaget, 1980). The latter led the heterodox Marxist Lucien Goldman to assert that Piagetian theory was "the only existing dialectic epistemology."[17]

The Role of Boundary Conditions at C/S Interface

When applied to the specific case of cognition, the theory of complex systems outlined here leads to a consideration of the social subsystem of System Σ, as a boundary condition of System C, that may be summarized as follows:

1. System C possesses an activity generated by the inner dynamics, referred to earlier.

2. This dynamics determines possible paths of development, which can take multiple directions.

3. The boundary conditions that interact with System C in the total System Σ perform functions that act either to favor or inhibit the realization of one of these possible directions and at the same time to contribute to the content that such direction takes. In this sense the interactions S/C *condition* the structure adopted by the system, but do not *determine* the structure as such.

4. The specific way in which the social subsystem of Σ operates in establishing boundary conditions of C has characteristic features at different levels of development. In Piaget and García, 1983), this problem was taken up in connection with the history of science without any reference to systemic analysis. The concepts of epistemic frame and changes in epistemic frames—introduced to explain profound conceptual differences in different cultures and in different historical periods[18]—are embedded in my present conception of boundary conditions.

5. System C is not a passive recipient of ingoing fluxes but interacts with them and modifies their action.

It should be clear that the five preceding points refer *only* to the mechanisms through which the Interactions C/S intervene in the construction of knowledge. I have not touched here the problem of the sociogenesis of concepts and theories treated in Piaget (1980).

---

[17]Mentioned by Piaget in his obituary to Goldman.
[18]See in particular Piaget and García (1983), chap. 9.

CONCLUDING REMARKS

The kind of system analysis I have presented here, although in a very sketchy form, is meant to show the way for a comprehensive interpretation of genetic epistemology taking into account the multiplicity of factors that intervene in the construction of knowledge. These factors have been studied by Piaget throughout his monumental production, but he never put them together into an integrated theory.

There is, of course, *L'Équilibration des structures cognitives* (Piaget, 1975) and also the three epistemological syntheses referred to by Bärbel Inhelder in the preface of *Psychogenesis and History of Science* (Piaget & García, 1983). What is lacking, in my opinion, is the formulation of a constructivistic theory of knowledge as an organized totality, in the sense of the Duhem–Quine thesis, detached from the description of the experimental case studies that the theory is supposed to explain. My proposal for the study of the cognitive system as a complex system that was outlined here goes in that direction.

However, my aim goes beyond the theoretical requirement of having a well-formulated theory that could provide a solid basis for the analysis of its foundations and its scope. My aim points in another direction. Piaget's conception of the construction of knowledge has been subjected to much criticism. The analysis of much of what I have heard and read by way of criticism and dismissal seems to me to be based on misinterpretations and deformations. Nevertheless, and without lack of respect to the master, I must admit that Piaget was partially guilty. Like any true scientist, he was always exploring ideas and was not afraid to venture into new territories and to advance interpretations that were left floating in the air and that in some cases he himself would have to reject.

My contention is that genetic epistemology, built by him through a monumental effort of interpretation of an immense amount of psychogenetic and historical material, has all the elements of a consistent and self-contained theory of knowledge. I further venture to say that there is at present no alternative theory of knowledge having the same degree of consistency and empirical support with which it can be confronted.

Let us go back to the misunderstandings that have served as the basis to discredit Piagetian constructivism. What is needed is a formulation of the theory through which the sources of such misinterpretations become evident. The systemic interpretation outlined earlier (on which I am now working) has such an objective. Its elaboration exceeds the scope of this presentation. Here I only point out very briefly three areas in which much of the misunderstanding has been concentrated.

The first two have to do with the assumed *biologism* of the theory and the supposed consequent neglect of the role of social and cultural factors in the construction of knowledge. From the perspective of the systemic approach to both problems, it becomes clear that the total System Σ involves three levels of organization with different dynamics but interacting at the inter-faces B/C and C/S. These interactions neither overemphasize the action of Subsystem B nor neglect or diminish the role of Subsystem S. The analysis of the overall System Σ brings up the peculiarity of the interactions in both cases (B/C and S/C) because they take place between subsystems that differ in their own organization insofar as they pertain to different domains of phenomena. There is no question that the subsystems interact. The problem is what the mechanisms of interaction are. As an example, I previously summarized a way of operating at the interactions S/C.

The third area of misunderstanding has to do with the structuralism (*tout court*, without qualification) attributed to Piaget. The polemic on structuralism versus historicism culminating in France toward the middle of the 20th century was surpassed by Piaget with his *genetic structuralism* that he condensed in his well-known formula: neither structure without history, nor history without structure. Such structuralism is an unavoidable consequence of constructivism.

Piaget concentrated his efforts on the clarification of the internal dynam-ics of System C, which is an absolute requirement for the functioning of the overall System Σ. The interactions between the subsystems cannot be properly analyzed without taking into account the way in which System C performs its functions. In short, what C does is to incorporate the raw material of experience into an organizational frame. The cognitive activity of C becomes an exploration in the *organizability* of experience. And organization implies structure.

REFERENCES

Apostel, L. (1992). The future of Piagetian logic. In L. Smith (Ed.), *Critical assessments* (pp. –). London: Routledge. (Original work published 1982)

Aréchiga, H. (1997). Los fundamentos neurobiológicos de la teoría de Piaget sobre la génesis del conocimiento. In R. García (Ed.), *Epistemología genética y la ciencia contemporanea.* Buenos Aires, Argentina: Gedisa.

Born, M. (1948). *Natural philosophy of cause and chance.* Oxford, England: Clarendon Press.

Bruner, J. S., Bresson, F., Morf, A., & Piaget, J. (1958). *Logique et perception* [Logic and perception]: *Études d'épistémologie génétique*, Vol. 6. Paris: Press Universitaires de France.

García, R. (1984). *Food systems and society. A conceptual and methodological challenge.* Geneva, Switzerland: United Nations Research Institute for Social Development.

García, R. (1992a). Cambiamenti strutturali nei sistemi aperti: Il caso della cognizione. In M. Ceruti (Ed.), *Evoluzione e conoscenza: L'Epistemologie genetica di Jean Piaget e le prospettive del costruttivismo.* Bergamo, Italy: Pierluigi Lubrina Editore.

García, R. (1992b). The structures of knowledge and the knowledge of structures. In H. Beilin & P. B. Pufall (Eds), *Piaget's theory: Prospects and possibilitie.* Hillsdale, NJ: Lawrence Erlbaum Associates.

García, R. (1993). *From planning to evaluation: A systems approach to sustainable development.* Rome: International Fund for Agricultural Development.

Jonckheere, A., Mandelbrot, B., & Piaget, J. (1958). *La Lecture de l'expérience* [The reading of experience]: *Études d'épistémologie génétique,* Vol. 5. Paris: Press Universitaires de France.

Piaget, J. (1975). *L'Équilibration des structures cognitives: Problème central du dévelopement* [Equilibration of cognitive structures: The central problem of development]. Paris: Press Universitaires de France.

Piaget, J. (1980). *Les Formes élémentaires de la dialectique* [The elementary forms of dialectic]. Paris: Gallimard.

Piaget, J., & García, R. (1974). *Understanding causality.* New York: Norton. (Original work published 1971)

Piaget, R., & García, R. (1983). *Psychogenèse et histoire des sciences* [Psychogenesis and history of science]. Paris: Flammarion.

Piaget, J., & García, R. (1991). *Toward a logic of meanings.* Hillsdale, NJ: Lawrence Erlbaum Associates. (Original work published 1987)

Prigogine, I. (1994). *Les Lois du chaos* [The laws of chaos]. Paris: Flammarion.

Putnam, H. (1990). *Realism with a human face.* Cambridge, MA: Harvard University Press.

Quine, W. V. (1951). Two dogmas of empiricism. *Philosophical Review, 60,* 20–43.

Quine, W. V. (1969). *Ontological relativity and other essays.* New York: Columbia University Press.

Quine, W. V. (1973). *The roots of reference.* Chicago: Open Court.

Russell, B. (1948). *Human knowledge: Its scope and limits.* New York: Simon & Schuster.

Russell Hanson, N. (1965). *Patterns of discovery.* Cambridge, England: Cambridge University Press.

Schweber, S. S. (1993, November). Physics, community and the crisis in physical theory. *Physics Today,* 34–40.

Simon, H., A. (1977). *Models of discovery.* Boston: Reidel.

Thom, R. (1993). *Prédire n'est pas expliquer* [To predict is not to explain]. Paris: Flammarion.

Chapter 8

Locating Development: Locating Developmental Systems

Susan Oyama
*City University of New York Graduate School
and John Jay College, City University of New York*

In pursuing a parallel between inside–outside relations in evolution on the one hand and classical epistemological questions about the knower and the known on the other, Jean Piaget found prevailing evolutionary thinking inadequate. Admirably committed to overcoming certain troublesome dualities and to giving the development and activity of organisms their proper role in biology, he nevertheless remained bound in certain respects to a framework in which an external force of natural selection was constrained by internal developmental factors (Oyama, 1992b). In this he was like many others who have sought to locate the topic of development in evolutionary theory. Some of these theorists are discussed here, and although Piaget is not the focus of the comments that follow, I address some of the inside–outside polarities with which he struggled and that he did much to overcome.

In this chapter, I consider three more recent critical approaches in evolutionary theory. All three have addressed the endlessly difficult internal-external dimension and its relations with the issues of organismic activity and formative causation in biology, and like Piaget, they have done so with the language of process and complex systems. One approach is that of developmental systems (DST),[1] in which I work (P. Bateson 1988;

---

[1]Developmental systems theory, or DST appears in the literature, and I shall also use these terms for convenience, without wishing to imply that the scheme discussed here fits everyone's notion of a theory.

Gottlieb, 1992; Gray, 1992; Griffiths & Gray, 1994; Johnston & Gottlieb, 1990; Oyama, 1979, 1989, in press-b), and which I believe has much to offer to both evolutionists and developmentalists, including, perhaps, psychologists interested in cognitive development. In DST, the emphasis is on interactive processes at various scales, organized not by genetic programs, representations, or instructions but by the dynamics of the processes themselves. Organisms and their environments are considered to constitute a single system, and there are smaller and larger systems as well, often nested. In this approach, various dualities, including those of nature and nurture in development and constraints and selection in evolution, are undone; form and function are seen to emerge in process.

The other two critical positions are the process structuralism primarily identified with Brian Goodwin, Gerry Webster (Goodwin, 1982; Webster & Goodwin, 1982), Mae-Wan Ho (1984), and Peter Saunders (Ho & Saunders, 1979), and the theory of autopoiesis promulgated by Humberto Maturana and Francisco Varela (1987; Varela, 1979, 1987). Only process structuralism explicitly invokes a structuralist lineage to which Piaget might be considered to belong. Like Piaget, the structuralist theorists have treated development as an internal constraint on evolutionary change. They have tended to emphasize physical necessity and have spoken of laws of form and generic morphologies that recur and persist in evolution despite the historical uncertainties of natural selection. Theorists of autopoiesis have also emphasized the importance of internal processes and have used the self-defining and self-producing properties of the cell as a model for biological processes.

By placing these three approaches in the wider landscape of evolutionary thinking, I also locate them with respect to each other. Psychologists have sometimes had an overly restrictive idea of what it means to adopt an evolutionary perspective, and the first section of this paper is meant to enlarge their sense of possibilities. In the second section, I look at the notions of internalization, symbolic representations, and context that have been so central to studies of cognitive development and show that a DST-inflected treatment converges on some connectionist critiques of classical cognitivism. This encounter between DST and models of cognition does not magically produce a theory of conceptual development, but it does, I think, point rather more firmly toward some current approaches than others. If the approaches indicated are not the ones most commonly presented as having an "evolutionary perspective," it is in part because these latter often rely on dubious assumptions about the nature of development (indeed, even about its importance) and about its relation to evolution.

I thus intend to survey a peculiar, rather abstract terrain, between disciplines and between the practical level of theory-building activity and the broader conceptual and research environments in which it occurs. The wish to extend psychologists' range of possibilities is also a wish to render the landscape of evolutionary theory more easily navigable, by indicating a few of its fault lines: recalcitrant but unstable oppositions that help account for some frequently observed conceptual moves and positions. Standard neo-Darwinian thought has embodied certain ways of dealing with these issues, as the less orthodox alternatives have done. Theoretical paths diverge in some places and run parallel or overlap in others, as scholars with diverse backgrounds seek to chart the relations among the processes of developing, evolving, and knowing. Piaget might not have approved of all that follows (and his work predated most of it), but perhaps the general aim of placing cognition in its developmental and evolutionary contexts would have won his blessing.

Although I cannot pretend to do justice to the difficult and contentious topics on which I touch, I hope that seeing cognitive development as an instance of biological processes contextualizes it in an illuminating manner. The problem is how biological processes are to be conceived, and here my movement among the levels of theory and metatheory is important: These can also be levels of context.

Any act of knowing occurs in a world and is part of a history of interaction with that world. Knowing, including that of scientists, implies a certain configuration of the physical, social, and conceptual environment; to follow the discussion in the second section of this chapter, it helps to be familiar with the large arena of evolutionary thinking. Cognition is, after all, an aspect of more general relations between organisms and their surroundings and involves the same kinds of questions that arise in any biological investigation: the relations between the interior and exterior worlds (as well as the utility of concepts of externalization and internalization in linking them) and the sources of regularity and order (as well as the utility of storage metaphors in explaining them). We can ask of any model or theoretical statement: What kinds of world does it assume? What kinds of developmental and evolutionary processes, what kinds of theoretical alliances and explanatory means?

CRITICAL VOICES

The three streams of critical thought to be discussed arose more or less separately, and none is monolithic. They all express dissatisfaction with certain aspects of the neo-Darwinian evolutionary synthesis: a sometimes narrow, gene-centered focus, the resulting neglect of active, developing organisms, and the notion of adaptation as the solving of pre-existing environmental problems (Lewontin, 1980/1984). Each also has quarrels with standard neo-Darwinism's treatment of inside–outside relations, in which the developmental formation of organisms is controlled from the inside (often by genetic programs) and in which evolution is largely a matter of shaping by the external environment (Oyama, 1992a).

Because of these shared discomforts, the developmental systems framework has occasionally been compared with both process structuralism and autopoiesis, and this first section is in part a response to queries about DST's precise relations with the others. In briefly characterizing structuralism and autopoiesis in terms of their stance toward standard neo-Darwinian evolutionary theory, then, I also contrast them with developmental systems views. The comparisons can also serve as an introduction to DST for those not already familiar with it. Some details of the treatment that follows will probably be most meaningful for readers who have some familiarity with the ideas, but I hope that the kinship between the conceptual problems that these theorists are struggling with and the ones that dominate cognitive studies is evident to all.

A schematic analysis of neo-Darwinism, process structuralism, and DST by Cor van der Weele (in press) provides a useful starting point. She distinguished each position from the other two by a single feature. Although she did not discuss autopoiesis in detail, her set of distinctive features can be redeployed when we turn to the work of Maturana and Varela. As a first approximation, these two biologists, who have often written collaboratively, can be placed with the process structuralists; Goodwin himself (1994, p. 162) has likened autopoiesis to his own vision of biological autonomy. There are nevertheless some differences, considered later, that may be relevant to the project of understanding cognition.

For van der Weele, neo-Darwinism's genecentrism contrasts with the more systemic, relational view of developmental causality embraced by process structuralism and developmental systems theory. The structuralists emphasize ahistorical laws of form, whereas historical contingency is more important in DST and in neo-Darwinism. Finally, DST, with its constructivist interactionism, rejects the largely internalist view of development found in both process structuralism and neo-Darwinism. A developmental system is not bounded by the organism's skin but includes developmentally relevant aspects of the environment as well.

Van der Weele's comparison was admirably concise. It is important to note, though, that terms like *internalism* and *contingency* change their meanings when embedded in a different theoretical context. Structuralists' internalism stems from the autonomous dynamics of self-organization, whereas neo-Darwinists' indicates their reliance on one-way genetic causation (hence their frequent recourse to program metaphors). For both traditions, in fact, development must be seen as internally regulated precisely because, for them as for most people (including Piaget, to whom I return later), contingency connotes unpredictability, arbitrariness, or accident. This is true whether it is ontogenetic or phylogenetic processes that are at issue. Thus neo-Darwinists, relying heavily on the power of natural selection in evolution and wishing to emphasize the undirectedness of evolutionary change, tend to speak of it in distinctly *externalist* terms. The environment is seen as varying capriciously, shaping organisms by setting them one adaptive challenge after another and eliminating the unfit by selection. Then, to explain the regularity and apparent goal directedness of ontogeny, neo-Darwinists invoke *internal* causes, hence, genetic programs or instructions. Following this logic, those who, like the process structuralists, are impressed by the *non*randomness of evolutionary change, see lawlike internal factors as curbing the power of natural selection: hence the literature on developmental constraints.[2]

Developmental systems theory, however, contests just these assumptions about capriciously varying outsides and fixed insides. Instead, we speak of more or less reliably recurring cascades of developmental contingencies: interactions in organism–environment systems that singly may not be universal or necessary, but that can nevertheless produce very reliable sequences because of their interrelations (Gray, 1987, 1988, 1992; Griffiths & Gray, 1994; Oyama, 1988, 1992a, 1995). Because developmental and evolutionary processes are ecologically embedded, causal contingencies lose the air of randomness that they have in many treatments. Neither internal nor external factors are given a priori privilege for developmental *or* evolutionary formation, although investigation of specific questions may focus on variables on one side of the skin or the other.

The concept of inheritance, for instance, is expanded to include the whole system of entities and processes that are available to a life cycle. Some of these are tightly interlocked and exceedingly regular, but not all are: *System* implies interdependent influences, but not the infallible regularity that this term indicates to some, just as the inclusion of extraorganismic influences does not entail the unlimited malleability that is sometimes inferred from an invocation of the environment. Developmental and evolutionary stability, when they they are found, are explained by investigating the relevant processes themselves.

---

[2]This large literature does not all align with the views of the process structuralists treated here, but it addresses many of the same issues. See Maynard Smith et al. (1985) for a valiant attempt at summary and Gilbert, Opitz, and Raff (1996) for a more recent contribution. See also Stuart Kauffman on "ahistorical universals" (1985) and on development as an internal constraint in evolution (1983); more recent elaboration of these and related themes is found in his (1993) book. Kauffman's kinship to the workers discussed here is sometimes missed because of his emphasis on genetic networks, but many of the same internalist and universalist themes run through his writings.

All the traditions discussed in this section are considerably simplified, and each is identified with only a few figures. I believe this reduction of variety and complexity is permissible in the interests of presenting a brief comparison concentrated on a few salient issues.

Process Structuralism

Goodwin's frequent use of the idea of a morphogenetic field signals the process structuralists' holism (1994; see also Ho, 1988). These theorists, who trace their preoccupation with the laws of form back to the pre-Darwinian rational morphologists (Webster, 1984; Webster & Goodwin, 1982), tend to place considerable reliance on chemistry and physics in their explorations of regularities in the development of form. In their allegiance to internally directed self-forming and to a rational, mathematically describable order underlying the vagaries of the historical record, they differ from developmental systems theorists, who stress the emergence of causal complexes over both ontogenetic and evolutionary time.

For process structuralists, the weakness of neo-Darwinian explanation is that filtering by natural selection assumes, but does not explain, the origin of biological form. The transformational sets produced by the laws of organic form, asserted Webster and Goodwin (1982, pp. 17, 44), refer to "internal relations." They wrote, "[L]et us now choose to leave history behind" (p. 46). In a similar spirit, Ho and Saunders stated that science should concentrate on "the delimitation of the necessities which underlie the process of evolution, *without recourse to contingencies*" (1979, p. 590).

This desire to tame chance with internal factors, found in some of Piaget's work as well, is evident in Goodwin's (1982) "cognitive" view of biology: Organisms increase their independence from the environment by internalizing models of it. These internalizations "transform randomness and contingency . . . into appropriate order" (p. 537). He spoke of circadian rhythms as internal models of external periodicities and of the shapes of sea creatures as an internalization of the properties of the aquatic environment (p. 542).

In DST, by contrast, where the integral role of contexts is stressed and the inside–outside boundary is less prominent, the idea of independence from the environment finds no place, although an organism may become less responsive to some *variations* through *change* in relations with its environment. Nor does the notion of forming models or representations by internalization seem useful; I return to this complicated issue later.

Compare Goodwin's description of mastery through internalization with Piaget's definition of phenocopying as the replacement of an "exogenous" adaptation by an "endogenously"—that is, genetically—reconstructed one (1975/1977; 1976/1978).[3] Put these together with psychologists' reliance

---

[3]Ho (1984, 1988) has also written on phenocopying and the internalization of environments. Piaget's definition of phenocopying, which involved the replacement of an environmentally caused variant by a genetically caused one, was idiosyncratic (Oyama, 1992b), but in general phenocopying refers to the possibility of producing the same phenotypic character either from the normal genotype in an atypical environment or from an unusual genotype in the usual environment (Oyama, 1981).

on internalized representations, and we have a particularly striking point of contact between evolutionary theorizing and the problems addressed by students of cognitive development.

It is important to recognize that despite similarities in argument and despite Goodwin's reference to "cognitive biology," the object of explanation in these two accounts of internalization is a bit different. Goodwin, like other process structuralists and theorists of developmental constraints (see footnote 2), is primarily interested in *morphology*; an organism's shape (or, in the case of circadian rhythms, its physiology) is treated as an internalized representation of environmental features. Although Piaget's writings on phenocopying included discussions of the shapes of snail shells and plants and although he sought to ground his accounts of cognition in general notions of biological adaptation, his ultimate quarry was not morphology per se but abstract representational *knowledge* (hence his "genetic epistemology").[4] Piaget's mistrust of the historical contingencies preserved in the evolutionary record stemmed in part from his conviction that a series of accidents could not produce the objective, necessary knowledge he wished to explain. After all, different creatures "know" all sorts of things instinctively, but for Piaget this kind of knowing, being the product of selection, is irredeemably contaminated by its contingent past. It must be transcended if true knowledge is to be attained.

Still, the structuralist affinities are robust. Webster and Goodwin (1982) cited Piaget (1971) when they defined that tradition by an emphasis on wholeness, transformation, and self-regulation. They also cited Chomsky's generative grammars, which specify possible utterances in a language. It is in their preoccupation with internal necessity, organisms' essential natures (Webster, 1984), transformational sets, and timeless law, that these theorists' structuralist connections are probably clearest, and where they differ most from people working in developmental systems.

The structuralist notion of a transformational set can be likened in some ways to the *norm of reaction* in genetics. The range of phenotypes that can develop from a given genotype is commonly said to be defined by the genes. Just as genes specify or circumscribe potential in the usual account of ontogeny, laws of form define evolutionary possibility for the process structuralists. In the first case, environmental contingencies specify which phenotype develops, whereas in structuralism, genes and other accidental "hereditary particulars" (Goodwin, 1984) stabilize one or the other solution from a "logically closed set" of evolutionary transformations (Webster & Goodwin, 1982, p. 41).

---

[4]Amundson (1994) observed that the debates over developmental constraints on evolution often fail to distinguish between constraints on *form* and on *adaptation*. Process structuralists have focused on the first. Neo-Darwinians have been more interested in the second, which is probably more relevant to epistemological issues.

In DST, by contrast, potential is seen as an emergent *developmental* phenomenon, formed in ontogenetic interactions and changing over time. The point of Waddington's (1975) famous epigenetic landscape, in fact, was that some things *become* possible as an organism moves along a developmental trajectory whereas other possibilities recede. A developmentally useful concept of potential refers to the ways in which the array of possible next steps changes with the changing organism in a changing surround. (Hendriks-Jansen, 1996, p. 30, pointed out the importance of interactive emergence in altering behavioral possibilities.) Power to define the field of possibilities is not attributed in DST to inner factors, with external ones merely selecting the result. Instead, interactants of many types and at many scales, both inside the skin and outside it, contribute to stability, and many interactants can make the difference between one result and another, thus "specifying" a particular one. DST treats system dynamics as not only being *perturbable* by these particulars but as *identical to their interactions* (see also Thelen & Smith, 1994, p. 216, on the inseparability of "global order" and "local variability").

Before moving on, we should note the considerable common ground between process structuralists and DST. When, in fact, they emphasize the continuity of process across generations (Ho, 1988) and the integration of organisms with their surrounds (Goodwin, 1984), when they accord greater importance to historical change in developmental dynamics (Ho, in press) or criticize the neo-Darwinian depiction of the genes as program or "central directing agency" (Ho & Saunders, 1979; Webster & Goodwin, 1982), the distance between us can seem minimal. I have long been sympathetic to many of their concerns, including those about the "disappearance of the organism" from a biology increasingly fixed on molecular plans (Webster & Goodwin, 1982, p. 42) and abstract gene pools.

Overall, I think that for developmental psychologists the importance of this position lies primarily in the way its structuralist bent is played out in evolutionary critique and developmental biology—in its general approach to problems of form, regularity, and internal-external relations (and so to the intelligibility of the natural world *to scientists*). DST and autopoiesis, to be discussed next, both have a rather more direct concern with the processes of knowing.

Autopoiesis

Autopoiesis refers to the autonomous character of some entities, including living ones—to their ability to define and produce themselves by their own dynamics. Such a system is not causally *independent* of its environment but becomes differentiated from it by its operation. It simultaneously specifies its surroundings and determines their impact on itself. In this view, we do not acquire knowledge by taking facts from the outside and storing them in our heads; the appearance of the world is tied to the operation of the cognizing entity (Maturana & Varela, 1987, pp. 25–26). Thus, these theorists of autopoiesis have treated all biological processes as cognitive: "All doing is knowing and all knowing is doing," they said. Each act of knowing "brings forth a world" (Maturana & Varela, 1987, p. 27). Cognition is effective action (p. 29), and like adaptation (p. 114), it is coextensive with life itself.

Biologists Humberto Maturana and Francisco Varela opposed what they saw as an excessive externalism in usual presentations of natural selection, in which the environment poses challenges to organisms and then selects them on the basis of their ability to meet those challenges. We have often heard, for instance, how selection shapes or molds living beings, as though organisms were inert and pliable protoplasmic putty. As noted previously, van der Weele placed Maturana and Varela with the process structuralists in her comparative scheme. In many ways, this organization is apt, for although they joined both process structuralism and DST in taking a critical stance with respect to neo-Darwinians' evolutionary externalism, they played out their opposition by largely *internalist* moves (in Godfrey-Smith's sense of explaining some internal features by others, 1996). In DST, by contrast, this very choice is called into question. Neither insides nor outsides are given explanatory priority in evolutionary or developmental formation; form and causal control emerge interactively, by reciprocal selection and influence.

Descriptions of autopoietic systems are, on the other hand, quite emphatic in their privileging of internal dynamics over external perturbations. Maturana and Varela wrote, "[I]t is the structure of the unity [biological entity] that determines its interaction in the environment and the world it lives in"; outside influences "trigger," but do not "instruct" changes in an autopoietic system (1987, pp. 86, 97). Sharing with the structuralists a vocabulary of autonomy and self-regulation, they described as autonomous a system that "can specify its own laws, what is proper to it" (Maturana & Varela, 1987, p. 48). According to them (p. 10), Maturana embarked in the 1960s on the project of describing "living systems in terms of the processes that realized them, and not in terms of the relationship with an environment."

This internalist predilection most evident in passages on operational independence and the self-defining, self-producing qualities of the paradigmatic autopoietic system, the cell, is not shared by DST, where this kind of argument by reversed polarity is viewed with considerable suspicion. In fact, when Maturana and Varela stress the internal definition of the set of possible changes that an entity may undergo (structural changes are *triggered* by the perturbing environment but not *specified* by it), they bring to

mind the insides-define-the-possibilities-and-outsides-select-the-result reasoning criticized earlier. (See Oyama, 1989, 1992a, in press-b for critiques
of such explanations.)

Possibly mitigating this last interpretation is these authors' emphasis on
the role of the observer, both in picking out entities (by making distinctions
that bring an object out from its background) and in viewing interactions
between these entities and their surroundings. The observer's attention
can shift from the entity to its medium, and presumably a similar description can then be given of *it*—its perturbations triggered from the outside
but specified from the inside. Maturana and Varela asserted that scientific
treatment requires *any* entity, not just living ones, to be treated as "structurally determined," as defining its own possibilities. Two entities may
perturb each other, but each specifies for itself the changes of state it may
undergo, including destructive ones. This mutual perturbation or triggering is called "structural coupling" (1987, pp. 95–99). "So in the interaction
of a living system and its medium, although what happens to the system
is determined by its structure, and what happens to the medium is determined by its structure, the coincidence of these two selects which changes
of state will occur" (Maturana, 1987, p. 75).

I still question the distinction between triggering on the one hand and
specifying or "instructing" on the other. Triggers are usually seen as merely
setting off trains of events that are in some sense already organized or
prepared; triggering releases a structured response but does not contribute
to it in any substantive way (van der Weele, in press). Varela (1979, chap.
16) wrote that one speaks of triggering or instructing relations depending
on one's perspective, so that the distinction seems to emphasize the asym-
metry between insides and outsides when the organism is being viewed
either as an autonomous, self-specifying (autopoietic) system or as an input–output device. In view of the pragmatic shifting of both perspective
and question that characterizes the writings on autopoiesis, there may be
room here for some mutual accommodation with DST. Moss (1995) and
Thompson and Varela (1998) both considered such a possibility. Certainly,
when Maturana and Varela discussed organism–environment and organism–organism mutuality in structural coupling, or embeddedness and
densely interrelated processes changing over time, they made common
cause with DST.

There is an interesting contrast between Maturana and Varela's non-
representationist approach to cognition/life and Goodwin's notion of internalized representations of the environment. Far from being grudging
about the significance of history, furthermore, theorists of autopoiesis see
it as fundamental to life and knowledge. In this acceptance of histories of
mutual engagement, of both developmental and evolutionary contingency,
they resemble developmental systems theorists. All this makes me feel that

the gap that separates us might be bridgeable without serious deformation to either view.[5]

By sketching the overlapping concerns and explanatory preferences of neo-Darwinism and three critical traditions, this section is meant to highlight the persistence with which certain very general conceptual problems confront theorists of life processes, as well as some recurrent responses to these problems. The benefit of shifting disciplines and operating at a quite abstract level is that commonalities and differences that are invisible in finer grained analyses can be glimpsed; such are the virtues of an aerial view. We now descend a bit, to an elevation from which some ground activity can be discerned.

CONCEPTUAL DEVELOPMENT IN CONTEXT

The panel at which this chapter was first presented was entitled Origins of Conceptual Development, but so far I have had rather more to say about the concept of development than the development of concepts. Cognition can be viewed, though, from diverse perspectives. In one reading of the heading of this section, the study of conceptual development is necessarily conducted in some larger theoretical context. A psychologist taking an "evolutionary approach to cognition" would want to reflect on just what implications follow from such a move, and my admittedly partisan sketch of evolutionary heterodoxies is meant to prompt such reflection. Theoretical context can also be more general: Even in the absence of a specific interest in evolution, beliefs about biological bases figure at least tacitly in any psychologist's theoretical background. At the same time, the computer revolution has infused biology, psychology, and even anthropology with the computational language of cognitivism, so that all sorts of processes are now explained by symbolic representations, programs, and plans.

This unholy alliance of traditional biology and computer science suggests another meaning of "conceptual development in context." At a time when taking a biological turn often means packing the head with more and more hermetically sealed modules and when countering that turn often means finding ways to *get society in there too*, perhaps we should pause, not only to wonder how much our poor skulls can accommodate, but to

---

[5]In their book *The Embodied Mind* (1991, p. 197), Varela, philosopher Evan Thompson, and cognitive psychologist Eleanor Rosch replaced the opposition between internal and external causes with mutual specification of organism and environment. This stance is less internalist than that taken earlier by Maturana and Varela (1987) and articulates well with DST.

consider again the endlessly fraught boundary between inside and outside and the attention given to the ill-defined external world. The context, psychology's stand-in for what is outside the head, plays a variety of roles in treatments of cognition. In DST, not only does development occur in particular settings and not only is it modulated by these settings, it is *constituted* by changing interactions with settings at many scales. Some of these settings are themselves generated in development, so that the context is not just a locality or modifier but part of the formative processes themselves. As Fentress (1989, p. 67) wrote, "*[O]nce contextual factors are taken appropriately into account,* developmental events in physical systems can be characterized as self-organizing. Thus, sensitivity to environmental context and self-organization are not mutually exclusive alternatives." (See also Hendriks-Jansen, 1996, especially chap. 7, on the ways this patterned activity both emerges in context and generates its own context.)

Application of these principles to cognition moves us from mind as text to mind as process (Clark, 1993, p. 8), from storage and persistence to dynamic, recurrent construction. In this latter view, the organism and its environment are (changing) participants in, and (changing) products of, these (changing) processes, at once cause and effect, process and product. This, of course, is the view of multileveled constructive interactions that characterizes DST. The vision is of an integrated account in which individual and social, body and mind, biology and culture are unified in a developmental and evolutionary process. Even though precise predictions about cognitive development do not flow automatically from a developmental systems framework, certain approaches are bound to be more compatible with it than are others.

Earlier I characterized cognition as an aspect of more general relations between organisms and their surroundings and tried to show that notions like representation, internalization, and externalization, so commonly used by cognitive psychologists, are employed by evolutionary theorists in very similar ways. In the following discussion, I occasionally draw on Andy Clark's (1993) book on connectionist models of the mind. Although such models arguably do not provide satisfactory explanations for mental processes (depending on what one accepts as an explanation; see Hendriks-Jansen, 1996, on models, redescription, and explanation), they can call attention to certain problems with existing conceptions of cognition while suggesting other ways of thinking. I neither endorse the particular technical features of these models nor make a general argument about connectionism and the mind, although I do offer some brief comments on the latter toward the end of this section. As noted earlier, there appears to be an intriguing convergence between DST analyses and certain connectionist critiques of classical cognitive science, and it is these critical points I wish to highlight here.

Internalization

By blurring the distinction between structure and process (Thelen & Smith, 1994, p. 38), connectionist approaches can call into question assumptions of localizable data structures. Clark (1993, pp. 3, 29) lamented classical cognitive science's antidevelopmental reliance on static, context-free symbols. He mentioned the "hallucination of a stable and manipulable symbol or data object where none exists." Analysts attribute to their learning networks just the knowledge of features and categories they themselves use (p. 69), even though a network may be able to distinguish between, say, nouns and verbs without these categories being "available" to the net itself (p. 71). This idea is reminiscent of the widespread (in standard neo-Darwinism and elsewhere) habit of describing dynamic developmental processes by invoking stores of genetic information or plans: Compare cognitivists' combinatorial schemes of autonomous meaning-bearing mental atoms and biologists' "genes for" or "instructions for" traits (Varela et al., 1993, p. 101). In fact, investigators often project the fruits of their analyses back into the organism and then construe them as causal mechanisms. A developmental process that can be simulated by a program is said to have been produced by a macromolecular program; a phenotype that can be described as a set of structures is said to have been constructed on the basis of a blueprint for those structures (Moss, 1992; Nijhout, 1990; Oyama, in press-b; Smith, in press).[6]

Bringing the environment or, more restrictedly, culture, into the picture frequently means positing a body of externally stored information, which must somehow be brought into the organism. Gene–culture coevolution schemes, although they are often devised to rectify an overemphasis on biology, have tended to perpetuate the larger set of assumptions that spawns the narrowly biological treatments in the first place: The two channels of information flow, genetic and cultural, support the developmental dualism of the nature–nurture opposition. Internalized representations are often part of this complex.

Internalization is usually the means whereby a culture enters and controls its members,[7] but, interestingly enough, its appearance in a theory

---

[6]Thelen and Smith (1994, p. 7) made a similar point about explaining movement by central pattern generators in the nervous system, and in a discussion of internalization, Maturana and Varela (1987, p. 172) said that scientists may act "as though something useful to us for communication between observers were an operational element of the nervous system." Hendriks-Jansen (1996) gave many other examples. For a history of the computer metaphor of mind and some provocative thoughts on the the relation between research tools and theory, see Gigerenzer and Goldstein (1996).

[7]Geertz (1973/1966, pp. 44–45) declared that culture is best conceptualized as programs or control mechanisms, and Sampson (1991, pp. 29–30, 48) spoke of the "social world that creates the various programs that people learn." See Donald (1991) for a dual-channel model

can signal an insistence on a real contribution of the organism to its own development or evolution. Consider Goodwin's (1982) concern, noted earlier, that organisms not be seen as mere "sediments of contingencies which have passed the survival test" of natural selection. He reminded us that the organism is "the generator of biological order in accordance with universal generative laws of form" (pp. 536–537). His view of internalization as the making of inner models of the world is also a view of organisms as imparters of order: A kind of biological agency appears to be at stake.

Valsiner's review (1991) of a book by Rogoff revealed, I think, a similar desire to retain some idea of individuals with *interiors* and sometimes contrary desires in the face of what he deemed an excessively externalist sociogenetic model. Valsiner worried that Rogoff slighted "intramental psychological functions" (p. 311) so that these individual processes became "subservient to settings" (p. 312). He argued for an "*inclusive* separation" of individuals from culture, which, he said, avoids the dualism of "exclusive separation," but allows us to recognize that persons are "biologically emerged structure[s]" whereas cultures are "socially created" (p. 314). Internalization and externalization, Valsiner continued, allow these interdependent entities to function.

We seem to have a complementary pair: internalizations of environmental structure and externalizations or expressions of internal forms. This notion is explicit in Lawrence and Valsiner's (1993) article, in which "transmission" and "transformation" models of importation by internalization are discussed. Ingold (1996a), too, referred to the ways that anthropologists theorize about cultures that must be internalized, then expressed back into the world. The assumption seems to be that "a system acts on the basis of internal representations," as Varela and colleagues put it (1991, p. 134), and representation tends to be taken "in its strong sense as the re-presentation of a pregiven world" (p. 148).

I am unconvinced that Valsiner's solution eliminates the problems of the dualism of the individual and the culture, and I find his notions of inclusive and exclusive separation hard to grasp.[8] Still, he did not treat internalization as simple importation or re-presentation; rather, he stressed

less focused on control mechanisms. Costall (1993) aired misgivings about Donald's scheme, whereas Nelson (1996) was more appreciative.

Valsiner's treatment of culture in terms of adoption, recombination, and transformation of elements (1991, p. 311) recalls the computational processes of classical cognitivism, and when Spiro (1984, p. 323) called culture a propositional, cognitive system, he exemplified what Casson (1994) called the "cognitive turn" in the human sciences. See Ingold (1995, 1996a), and Oyama (1989, 1992b, 1994, in press) for discussion.

[8]In Lawrence and Valsiner (1993, p. 151), the link of internalization and externalization to "the basic duality between person and society" is affirmed. See also Wertsch's 1993 commentary. Certainly the variegated nuances of "dualism," like those of internalization itself, present a dense interpretational thicket that can only be alluded to here.

people's ability to alter and refuse what is offered from the outside (see also Valsiner, 1992). Shotter (1993a, 1993b) offered an interpretation of Vygotskian internalization departing even more from direct importation, and Hendriks-Jansen's critical treatment (1996, chap. 17) stretched the concept to the breaking point. This is the point at which I do not think it fits even an elastic interpretation of the term, and, not coincidentally, at which it becomes compatible with DST. That is, it is the point at which we can no longer speak of forms or information moving in and out across cell or organism boundaries but must refer instead to the generation of form and function in constructive interactions in which internal and external structure cospecify the continuously emerging outcome. Children and their developmental environments are parts of the same system, so we can recognize the constitutive importance of the sociocultural without minimizing children's part in their own development and without having to contrast the social with the biologically given.

Representations: Fixed Symbols, Emergent Patterns

Representation, like *internalization*, has a multitude of meanings, and the concept is altered in suggestive ways in some connectionist work. Some of the authors cited here (Thelen & Smith, 1994, pp. 42–43; Varela et al., 1991) share both Clark's (1993) dissatisfaction with classical cognitivism, partly because of its reliance on symbolic representations, and his appreciation of connectionists' explorations of emergent, dynamic patterns. In Elman's category-forming network (cited in Clark, 1993, pp. 26–27), the "representation" of a word always incorporates a temporal aspect, and there is no separate stage in which isolated words are retrieved. Clark (pp. 93, 204) also discussed Barsalou's work, in which dynamic states "representing" concepts are constructed on the spot. No two states are identical; conceptual regularity is captured by more-or-less reliably recurring patterns, rather than enduring (or even precisely recurring) structures. It is not just that context affects the use of information, Clark noted, but rather that the incorporation of context into the process calls into question the very existence of persistent structures underlying concepts. As was the case in the discussion of internalization, the emphasis on contexts that enter constitutively into processes, rather than serving as mere backgrounds or modulators, articulates well with trends both inside and outside developmental psychology, trends toward seeing minds as enmeshed with social worlds in such a way that neither can be characterized alone (Costall, 1993, 1995; Fogel, 1993; Gellatly, Rogers, & Sloboda, 1989; Hendriks-Jansen, 1996; Ingold, 1995, 1996a, 1996b; Lave, 1986; Mercer, 1993; Richards & Light, 1986; Thelen & Smith, 1994; Thompson & Varela, 1998; Turvey, 1980; Varela et al., 1991).

Although the concept of information has generally escaped the critical scrutiny to which the cognitivists' symbolic representations have been subjected, it is recruited to perform many of the same tasks. Because the changing phenotype is constantly reframing its developmental resources, however, so that a given difference does not always make the same difference (to use Gregory Bateson's 1972 definition of information), the idea of fixed bits of developmental significance becomes quite unintelligible. Clark (1993, chap. 2) included a section called Why Context Sensitivity Does Not Have to "Bottom Out." Although he usually wrote of information without comment, it seems to me that a situationally embedded, organism- and level-relative notion is consistent with his allover approach.

There can be a substantial difference between referring to a reliable relation between input and output and giving an adequate account of the events and entities that support that relation. This difference is not just a matter of remembering that the machine's- or organism's-eye view is not necessarily the same as the investigator's; it also entails recognizing that the organism at one moment or at one level of analysis is different from that organism at other times or other levels. What counts as relevant input (or indeed, what it is input *to*) is by no means transparent. Because of DST's refusal of a context-independent concept of information, it seems likely that a usable notion of representation must be closer to the "construal" that Varela et al. considered unobjectionable than to the cognitivist "re-presentation of pregiven world" that they contested (1991, p. 134).

Repeated Construction in Context: Recurrent Resources

There is a final area in which innovations in connectionism parallel some thinking in DST. It is precisely the problem that, according to Ingold (1996b), has remained untouched even by theorists of society and culture who decry mind–body dualities while emphasizing experience, activity, and embodiment: the very distinction between biology and culture (recall Valsiner's insistence on distinguishing persons produced by biology from socially created cultures). Biological inheritance, usually discussed in terms of a store of information passed to the next generation in the genes (a kind of species memory that, as pointed out earlier, must be supplemented by cultural programs or representations) is conceptualized in DST as reliably available means or resources that include aspects of the environment. Resources need not be continuously present to be efficacious at a particular developmental moment, as long as they are recurrently constructed, supplied, or encountered at the proper time. We could treat the entire repeating organism–environment system, including its social aspects, as distributed memory—that is, as providing what is needed to produce the next cycle. This treatment works only if we consider memory in terms of repeatedly arising patterns of activity rather than as storage of static representations (Moss, 1996; Rosenfield, 1988) and if we recall that nothing is a resource or interactant except with respect to a particular system. This view has a number of implications for theories of development and evolution, but what is pertinent here is that it definitively eliminates the dual-inheritance (dual transmission channel, dual information storage) scheme that has supported, and depended on, the mind–body dichotomy.

One of the modelers discussed by Clark (1993, p. 123) is Kirsh, who argued that although explicit, fixed, textlike structures are often assumed in cognitive science, another way of understanding explicitness is as "usability" or easy availability. Clark continued that once structure and explicitness are defined relative to the processor, the notion of processing device can be expanded to include the environment, "for it is not clear why the skin should constitute the boundary of the processing environment relative to which such questions are to be decided" (pp. 127–28). Neither the content of a state nor its explicitness can be specified independently of the context.

Clark's subhead for this section, fittingly enough, was All the World's a Processor. He concluded his discussion with this comment: "[B]oth the nature and ultimately the content . . . of our inner states are always joint functions of their intrinsic natures and the broader environment in which they exist" (p. 128). In DST, it goes without saying that what counts as "environment" depends on organismic state, and consistency requires us to extend this reasoning to "intrinsic natures" as well.

These analyses show that an apparently impoverished (or, in some cases, overly complex) environment, or even an unchanging one, can play a substantive role in the emergence of quite intricate, flexible, and discerning networks. Clark's discussions (1993, especially chap. 7, on scaffolded learning) of the difference between "gross" and "effective" input included a heterogeneous mix of factors, both inside and outside a developing child, that can constrain, direct, filter, or otherwise affect the impact of "the environment." Nelson (1996, pp. 137–140) also wrote of the importance of the child's "cognitive context" at a particular moment in determining what is relevant about the language that may be heard. This context includes shared understanding and again helps make the difference between *gross* and *effective* input. According to Nelson, it also helps explain the difference between the level of mastery suggested by children's language production in context and that shown in comprehension tests lacking in comparable interpretive support. Working with an earlier developmental period, Turkewitz and Kenny (1982) showed how the organization of development can regulate effective sensory stimulation. These accounts demonstrate the impressive degree of mobile and historically inflected specificity and complexity from which cognitive functions may develop.

CONCLUSION

Although I did not set myself the task of evaluating connectionist models of cognitive development *as models*, it may be that even as they contribute to a rethinking of cognition and context, they run up against their own limitations as well. Some theorists who have found connectionism heuristically useful have had reservations about its ultimate adequacy. Their doubts tended to center on connectionism's continued reliance on a representational relation between internal and external domains (despite some reconceptualization of representation) and the implication of a world whose features and qualities are already defined, ready to be picked up by organisms (as Hendriks-Jansen, 1996, p. 55, said, "preregistered"), as well as the disembodied nature of the networks. Ingold (1996a, p. 109) declared that connectionism, like cognitive science in general, continues to rely on a "Cartesian ontology . . . that divorces the activity of the mind from that of the body in the world."

I share these reservations. Hendriks-Jansen (1996) presented an incisive discussion of the limitations of connectionism, along with a wide-ranging and meticulously detailed critique of cognitive science's attempts to ground its internal representations in natural selection. He concluded that the attempts are misguided. His "interactive emergence" fits nicely with the developmental systems emphasis on active organisms' worlds as being definable only by reference to them, as arising *with* them.[9] The same, I think, can be said of Varela and colleagues' "enactment." Rather than assuming the features of the world to be given beforehand and thus considering "information to be a prespecified quantity, one that exists independently in the world and can act as the input to a cognitive system" (1991, p. 139), they described the embodied "*bringing forth* of meaning" (or "a world of relevance for a system," p. 156). In an ongoing engagement or coupling that "selects or enacts . . . a domain of distinctions" (p. 155), what counts as a difference (distinction) that makes a difference is a system- (and question-) relative phenomenon. Explicitly contextualized, process and activity based, this difference-making emerges in a history of environmentally embedded interaction.

For those who value the boundary-stretching qualities of the connectionist work to which I have alluded but harbor doubts about the depth

---

[9]The denial of a prelabeled world, a world with properties already defined, should not be taken to be a denial of *the world* but an insistence that what constitutes a characteristic or a relevant aspect of the world (a cue, an opportunity or resource, etc.) is organism defined, just as the aspects of the organism relevant to the encounter depend on the organism's state and the rest of the situation. It is also an error to associate these ideas with the belief that we can "make" just any kind of world, either by imagining it or by pushing it about; one of the points of multiple embeddings and historically continuous engagement is that possible interactions and consequences are neither arbitrary nor unlimited.

of understanding that these simulations can finally offer, I have adverted to an independent tradition of thought that has produced many of the same insights without being tied to the image of a disembodied net in a world already carved into categories. The point on effective input, for instance, is made in DST by saying that the characteristics and effects of an "effective stimulus" or, more generally, the "developmentally relevant environment," are determinable only with respect to the rest of the system, so that a setting that is not changing from an observer's perspective can be shifting in developmental significance for the organism. We make the same point, this time moving from the inside out, by showing that the developmental information "contained" in a bit of DNA—that is, its import, if any, for ongoing ontogenetic processes—is also context dependent (Moss, 1992; Neumann-Held, in press).

A developmental system is composed of a host of interrelated interactants and resources, from the microscopic to the social and ecological. Perhaps I can do no better in explaining what "causes" development than to point to the entire organism–environment system, moving through time and space. Similarly I cannot identify its beginnings (even if I am assigned the topic, Origins of Conceptual Development). In this case, it is not stacked turtles, but nested developmental systems all the way down and all the way back, not just to the beginning of a life cycle, but beyond, to the previous organism–environment complexes that produced the present one.[10] Causation is not finally traceable to a single source or even to a discrete set of sources, although particular factors operative in particular arrays can be identified by the usual methods of manipulating, controlling, and ignoring variables. Hendriks-Jansen (1996) has argued forcefully for the indispensablity of *historical* explanation in accounting for developmental and evolutionary emergence, rather than the task description, functional decomposition, and conceptual analysis commonly used in cognitive science and evolutionary accounts of mind (see also Griffiths, 1997; Griffiths & Gray, 1994).

Some theories explicitly advertised as biological have not been discussed here, not because of any antibiological attitude on my part, but rather because of a discomfort with common ways of invoking biology. Evolutionary psychology's attention to the psychological level is an improvement on the older sociobiological tradition, which had a dismaying tendency to bypass it altogether. But much evolutionary psychology is minimally devel-

---

[10]Bonner (1974) wrote persuasively about the life cycle and the continuities that are carried through the reproductive bottleneck of the one-celled stage in many organisms. The life cycle in DST is much more extensive. It is not restricted to the fertilized cell, but includes the highly ramified and indefinitely extended environments whose layered complexity is precisely what makes possible that drastic narrowing of cellular continuity. For a developmental systems account of the life cycle, see Griffiths and Gray (1994).

opmental, characterized as it is by a sometimes unreflective adaptationism coupled with heavy reliance on modularity and programmed universals (Tooby & Cosmides, 1992, p. 39).[11] Varela (1987, p. 57) has observed that representationism in cognitive science is the equivalent of evolutionary adaptationism. Both involve a notion of correspondence or fit (between reality and some representation of it) and a pronounced organism–environment boundary, and the characteristics of the environment or object are considered to exist independently of, and before, the adapting organism or knowing subject.

Psychologists are under increasing pressure to adopt an evolutionary perspective, but traditional conceptions of evolution and inheritance militate against a satisfying account of development. Developmental systems theory offers the possibility of an integrated, fully ecologically embedded view of both ontogeny and phylogeny. Evolutionary change is not reckoned in terms of disembodied gene pools but rather of the constitution and distribution of organism–environment systems. These systems are delineated in different ways for different purposes; boundary drawing in DST is a pragmatic matter, having to do with the investigatory focus (Oyama, in press-a). Indeed, to insist on a single way of picking out systems (which variables and assumptions, how much and what kinds of associations, etc.) independently of research context would be at least stylistically incongruent. Hence, to speak as I do of a system's being composed of "developmentally relevant" influences leaves the particular relevance to be specified in the course of research.

Although the developmental systems approach is neither paleo- nor neo-Piagetian, it does share Piaget's desire for a genetic—that is, a developmental—epistemology, as well as certain of his conceptual preferences. Its aim is a biology, not as pre-existing base, and not as set of fixed, context-free givens, but as a framework within which all vital processes may be seen, from the most automatic-seeming aspects of embryogenesis to the knowledgable activity of persons in their changing social worlds.

ACKNOWLEDGMENTS

I am grateful for comments from Richard Francis, Peter Godfrey-Smith, Horst Hendriks-Jansen, Katherine Nelson, Patricia Miller, and members of the CUNY Graduate School Developmental Psychology Brown-Bag Seminar, at which part of this material was also presented.

---

[11]See their list of modules, p. 113. Thelen and Smith (1994, p. 38) commented on the "Balkanization of developmental phenomena" in such treatments, and Clark (1993) and Karmiloff-Smith (1992) gave developmental accounts of modularization. For reviews of *The Adapted Mind*, see Sterelny (1996) and especially Griffiths (1997, chap. 5).

REFERENCES

Amundson, R. (1994). Two concepts of constraint: Adaptationism and the challenge from developmental biology. *Philosophy of Science, 61*, 556–578.

Bateson, G. (1972). *Steps to an ecology of mind.* New York: Ballantine Books.

Bateson, P. [P. G.] (1988). The active role of behaviour in evolution. In M.-W. Ho & S. W. Fox (Eds.), *Evolutionary processes and metaphors* (pp. 191–207). London: Wiley.

Bonner, J. T. (1974). *On development.* Cambridge, MA: Harvard University Press.

Casson, R. W. (1994). Cognitive anthropology. In P. Bock (Ed.), *Handbook of psychological anthropology* (pp. 61–96). Westport, CT: Greenwood Press.

Clark, A. (1993). *Associative engines: Connectionism, concepts, and representational change.* Cambridge, MA: MIT Press/Bradford.

Costall, A. (1993). The place of cognition in human evolution. *Behavioral and Brain Sciences, 16*, 755.

Costall, A. (1995). Socializing affordances. *Theory and Psychology, 5*, 467–482.

Donald, M. (1991). *Origins of the modern mind.* Cambridge, MA: Harvard University Press.

Fentress, J. C. (1989). Developmental roots of behavioral order: Systemic approaches to the examination of core developmental issues. In M. Gunnar & E. Thelen (Eds.), *Systems and development: Minnesota symposia on child psychology, Vol. 22* (pp. 35–76). Hillsdale, NJ: Lawrence Erlbaum Associates.

Fogel, A. (1993). *Developing through relationships.* Chicago: University of Chicago Press.

Geertz, C. (1973). The impact of the concept of culture on the concept of man. In C. Geertz, *The interpretation of cultures* (pp. 33–54). New York: Basic Books. (Original work published 1966 in J. Platt (Ed.), *New views of the nature of man* [pp. 93–118]. Chicago: University of Chicago Press)

Gellatly, A., Rogers, D., & Sloboda, J. A. (Eds.). (1989). *Cognition and social worlds.* Oxford, England: Clarendon Press.

Gigerenzer, G., & Goldstein, D. G. (1996). *Mind as computer: The birth of a metaphor.* Unpublished manuscript.

Gilbert, S. F., Opitz, J. M., & Raff, R. A. (1996). Resynthesizing evolutionary and developmental biology. *Developmental Biology, 173*, 357–372.

Godfrey-Smith, P. (1996). *Complexity and the function of mind in nature.* Cambridge, England: Cambridge University Press.

Goodwin, B. C. (1982). Genetic epistemology and constructionist biology. *Revue Internationale de Philosophie, 142–143*, 527–548.

Goodwin, B. C. (1984). A relational or field theory of reproduction and its evolutionary implications. In In M.-W. Ho & P. T. Saunders (Eds.), *Beyond neo-Darwinism: An introduction to the new evolutionary paradigm* (pp. 219–241). London: Academic Press.

Goodwin, B. C. (1994). *How the leopard changed its spots.* New York: Scribner's.

Gottlieb, G. (1992). *Individual development and evolution.* Oxford, England: Oxford University Press.

Gray, R. D. (1987). Beyond labels and binary oppositions: What can be learnt from the nature/nurture dispute? *Rivista di Biologia/Biological Forum, 80*, 192–196.

Gray, R. D. (1988). Metaphors and methods: Behavioural ecology, panbiogeography and the evolving synthesis. In M.-W. Ho & S. W. Fox (Eds.), *Evolutionary processes and metaphors* (pp. 209–242). London: Wiley.

Gray, R. D. (1992). Death of the gene: Developmental systems strike back. In P. Griffiths (Ed.), *Trees of life: Essays in philosophy of biology* (pp. 165–209). Boston: Kluwer.

Griffths, P. E. (1997). *What emotions really are: The problem of psychological categories.* Chicago: University of Chicago Press.

Griffths, P. E., & Gray, R. D. (1994). Developmental systems and evolutionary explanation. *Journal of Philosophy, 91,* 277–304.

Hendriks-Jansen, H. (1996). *Catching ourselves in the act.* Cambridge, MA: MIT Press/Bradford Books.

Ho, M.-W. (1984). Environment and heredity in development and evolution. In M.-W. Ho & P. T. Saunders (Eds.), *Beyond neo-Darwinism: An introduction to the new evolutionary paradigm* (pp. 267–289). London: Academic Press.

Ho, M.-W. (1988). On not holding nature still: Evolution by process, not by consequence. In M.-W. Ho & S. W. Fox (Eds.), *Evolutionary processes and metaphors* (pp. 117–144). Chichester, England: Wiley.

Ho, M.-W. (in press). Evolution. In G. Greenberg & M. Haraway (Eds.), *Encyclopedia of comparative psychology.* New York: Garland.

Ho, M.-W., & Saunders, P. T. (1979). Beyond neo-Darwinism—An epigenetic approach to evolution. *Journal of Theoretical Biology, 78,* 573–591.

Ingold, T. (1995). "People like us": The concept of the anatomically modern human. *Cultural Dynamics, 7,* 187–214.

Ingold, T. (1996a). Culture, perception and cognition. In J. Haworth (Ed.), *Psychological research: Innovative methods and strategies* (pp. 99–119). London: Routledge.

Ingold, T. (1996b). Life beyond the edge of nature? or, the mirage of society. In J. D. Greenwood (Ed.), *The mark of the social* (pp. 231–252). Latham, MD: Rowman & Littlefield.

Johnston, T. D., & Gottlieb, G. (1990). Neophenogenesis: A developmental theory of phenotypic evolution. *Journal of Theoretical Biology, 147,* 471–495.

Karmiloff-Smith, A. (1992). *Beyond modularity: A developmental perspective on cognitive science.* Cambridge, MA: MIT Press.

Kauffman, S. A. (1983). Developmental constraints: Internal factors in evolution. In B. C. Goodwin, N. Holder, & C. G. Wylie (Eds.), *Development and evolution* (pp. 195–226). Cambridge, England: Cambridge University Press.

Kauffman, S. A. (1985). Self organization, selective adaptation, and its limits: A new pattern of inference in evolution and development. In D. J. Depew & B. H. Weber (Eds.), *Evolutionary theory at the crossroads: The new biology and the new philosophy of science* (pp. 169–207). Cambridge, MA: Bradford Books/MIT Press.

Kauffman, S. A. (1993). *The origins of order.* New York & Oxford, England: Oxford University Press.

Lave, J. (1986). The values of quantification. In J. Law (Ed.), *Power, action and belief: A new sociology of knowledge?* (pp. 88–111). (Sociological Review Monograph 32). London: Routledge & Kegan Paul.

Lawrence, J. A., & Valsiner, J. (1993). Conceptual roots of internalization: From transmission to transformation. *Human Development 36,* 150–167.

Lewontin, R. C. (1984). Adaptation. In E. Sober (Ed.), *Conceptual issues in evolutionary biology: An anthology* (pp. 235–251). Cambridge, MA: MIT Press/Bradford Books. (Original work published in 1980 in *Encyclopedia Einaudi,* Milan)

Maturana, H. (1987). Everything is said by an observer. In W. I. Thompson (Ed.), *Gaia: A way of knowing. Political implications of the new biology* (pp. 65–82). Great Barrington, MA: Linisfarne Press.

Maturana, H. R., & Varela, F. J. (1987). *The tree of knowledge.* Boston, MA: New Science Library.

Maynard Smith, J., Burian, R., Kauffman, S., Alberch, P., Campbell, H., Goodwin, B., Lande, R., Raup, D., & Wolpert, L. (1985). Developmental constraints and evolution. *Quarterly Review of Biology, 60,* 265–287.

Mercer, N. (1993). Culture, context and the construction of knowledge in the classroom. In P. Light & G. Butterworth (Eds.), *Context and cognition: Ways of learning and knowing* (pp. 28–46). Hillsdale, NJ: Lawrence Erlbaum Associates.

Moss, L. (1992). A kernel of truth? On the reality of the genetic program. In D. L. Hull, M. Forbes, & K. Okruhlik (Eds.), *Philosophy of Science Association Proceedings, 1*, 335–348.

Moss, L. (1995). *What's selecting what?* Unpublished manuscript.

Moss, L. (1996). *Relations of memory.* Unpublished manuscript.

Nelson, K. (1996). *Language in cognitive development.* Cambridge, MA: Harvard University Press.

Neumann-Held, E. (in press). The gene is dead—Long live the gene. In P. Koslowski (Ed.), *Sociobiology and bioeconomics. The theory of evolution in biological and economic theory* (pp. 105–137). Berlin, Germany: Springer-Verlag.

Nijhout, H. F. (1990). Metaphors and the role of genes in development. *BioEssays, 12*, 441–446.

Oyama, S. (1979). The concept of the sensitive period in developmental studies. *Merrill-Palmer Quarterly, 25*, 83–103.

Oyama, S. (1981). What does the phenocopy copy? *Psychological Reports, 48*, 571–581.

Oyama, S. (1988). Stasis, development and heredity. In M.-W. Ho & S. W. Fox (Eds.), *Evolutionary processes and metaphors* (pp. 255–274). London: Wiley.

Oyama, S. (1989). Ontogeny and the central dogma. In M. Gunnar & E. Thelen (Eds.), *Systems and development: Minnesota symposia on child psychology* (Vol. 22, pp. 1–34). Hillsdale, NJ: Lawrence Erlbaum Associates.

Oyama, S. (1992a). Ontogeny and phylogeny: A case of metarecapitulation? In P. E. Griffiths (Ed.), *Trees of life: Essays in philosophy of biology* (pp. 211–239). Dordrecht, Netherlands: Kluwer Academic.

Oyama, S. (1992b). Pensare d'evoluzione. L'integrazione del contesto nell'ontogenesi, nella filogenesi, nella cognizione [Thinking about evolution: Integrating the context in ontogeny, phylogeny and cognition]. In M. Ceruti (Ed.), *Evoluzione e cognizione. L'epistemologia genetica di Jean Piaget e le prospettive del costruttivismo* (pp. 47–60). Bergamo, Italy: Lubrina Editore.

Oyama, S. (1994). Rethinking development. In P. Bock (Ed.), *Handbook of psychological anthropology* (pp. 185–196). Westport, CT: Greenwood.

Oyama, S. (1995). The accidental chordate: Contingency in developmental systems. *South Atlantic Quarterly, 94*(2), 509–526.

Oyama, S. (in press-a). Developmental and evolutionary formation: Politics of the boundary. In P. Koslowski (Ed.), *Sociobiology and bioeconomics. The theory of evolution in biological and economic theory* (pp. 79–104). Berlin, Germany: Springer-Verlag.

Oyama, S. (in press-b). *The ontogeny of information* (Rev. ed.). Durham, NC: Duke University Press.

Piaget, J. (1971). *Structuralism.* London: Routledge & Kegan Paul.

Piaget, J. (1977). Phenocopy in biology and the psychological development of knowledge (H. E. Gruber & J. J. Vonéche, Trans.) In H. E. Gruber & J. J. Vonéche (Eds.), *The essential Piaget* (pp. 803–813). New York: Basic Books. (Original work published in 1975 in *The Urban Review, 8*, 209–218.)

Piaget, J. (1978). *Behavior and evolution* (D. Nicholson-Smith, Trans.). New York: Pantheon. (Originally work published 1976)

Richards, M., & Light, P. (Eds.). (1986). *Children of social worlds.* Cambridge, MA: Harvard University Press.

Rosenfield, I. (1988). *The invention of memory.* New York: Basic Books.

Sampson, E. E. (1991). *Social worlds, personal lives.* San Diego, CA: Harcourt Brace Jovanovich.

Shotter, J. (1993a). Bakhtin and Vygotsky: Internalization as a boundary phenomenon. *New Ideas in Psychology, 3*, 379–390.

Shotter, J. (1993b). Harré, Vygotsky, Bakhtin, Vico, Wittgenstein: Academic discourses and conversational realities. *Journal for the Theory of Social Behaviour, 23*, 459–482.

Smith, K. C. (in press). What is a genetic trait? In D. Magnus (Ed.), *Contemporary genetic technology: Ethical, legal and social challenges.* Melbourne, FL: Krieger Publishing.

Spiro, M. E. (1984). Some reflections on cultural determinism and relativism with special reference to emotion and reason. In R. A. Shweder & R. A. LeVine (Eds.), *Culture theory: Essays on mind, self, and emotion* (pp. 323–346). Cambridge, England: Cambridge University Press.

Sterelny, K. (1996). [Review of the book *The adapted mind*]. *Biology and Philosophy, 10*, 365–380.

Thelen, E., & Smith, L. B. (1994). *A dynamic systems approach to the development of cognition and action.* Cambridge, MA: MIT Press/Bradford Books.

Thompson, E., & Varela, F. J. (1998). *Why the mind isn't in the head.* Manuscript in preparation.

Tooby, J., & Cosmides, L. (1992). The psychological foundations of culture. In J. H. Barkow, L. Cosmides, & J. Tooby (Eds.), *The adapted mind* (pp. 19–136). Oxford, England: Oxford University Press.

Turkewitz, G., & Kenny, P. A. (1982). Limitation on input as a basis for neural organization and perceptual development: A preliminary theoretical statement. *Developmental Psychobiology, 15*, 357–368.

Turvey, M. T. (1980). Clues from the organization of motor systems. In U. Bellugi & M. Studdert-Kennedy (Eds.), *Signed and spoken language: Biological constraints on linguistic form* (pp. 41–56). Weinheim, Germany: Verlag Chemie GmbH.

Valsiner, J. (1991). Building theoretical bridges over a lagoon of everyday events. [Review of the book *Apprenticeship in thinking: Cognitive development in social context*]. *Human Development, 34*, 307–315.

Valsiner, J. (1992). Social organization of cognitive development: Internalization and externalization of constraint systems. In A. Demetriou, M. Shayer, & A. Efklides (Eds.), *Neo-Piagetian theories of cognitive development* (pp. 65–78). London & New York: Routledge.

van der Weele, C. (in press). *Images of development: Environmental causes in ontogeny.* Albany, NY: SUNY Press.

Varela, F. J. (1979). *Principles of biological autonomy.* New York: Elsevier North-Holland.

Varela, F. J. (1987). Laying down a path in walking. In W. I. Thompson (Ed.), *Gaia: A way of knowing. Political implications of the new biology* (pp. 48–64). Great Barrington, MA: Lindisfarne Press.

Varela, F. J., Thompson, E., & Rosch, E. (1991). *The embodied mind.* Cambridge, MA: MIT Press.

Waddington, C. H. (1975). Canalization and the development of quantitative characters. In C. H. Waddington (Ed.), *The evolution of an evolutionist* (pp. 98–103). Ithaca, NY: Cornell University Press.

Webster, G. (1984). The relations of natural forms. In M.-W. Ho & P. T. Saunders (Eds.), *Beyond neo-Darwinism: An introduction to the new evolutionary paradigm* (pp. 193–217). London: Academic Press.

Webster, G., & Goodwin, B. C. (1982). The origin of species: A structuralist approach. *Journal of Social and Biological Structures, 5*, 15–47.

Wertsch, J. V. (1993). Commentary. *Human Development 36*, 168–171.

Chapter 9

Developmental Change: Lessons From Microgenesis

Patricia H. Miller
Thomas R. Coyle
University of Florida, Gainesville

Both Piaget and others have seen the process of change as central to the study of development. Developmentalists have addressed issues such as what causes change and whether change is quantitative or qualitative, but change has turned out to be quite difficult to conceptualize, observe, and quantify. In particular, in cross-sectional studies, we see the *products* of change, not the *process*. One promising approach is the focus on microgenesis: moment-by-moment change during a short time, usually changes throughout an experimental session for a number of sessions over weeks or months. Vygotsky (1978) and Werner (1948) described this approach years ago, but recently several researchers (e.g., Bjorklund, Coyle, & Gaultney, 1992; Kuhn, Garcia-Mila, Zohar, & Andersen, 1995; Kuhn & Phelps, 1982; Siegler, 1996; Siegler & Crowley, 1991) have revitalized the microgenetic approach and stimulated its widespread use by showing that it reveals interesting phenomena about children's thinking.

The present chapter differs from these influential publications in that it places the microgenetic approach in a broader context of long-standing issues about developmental change and of other theoretical approaches. We focus on the most systematic, recent, and provocative microgenetic studies. First, we describe the microgenetic method, as currently used by most researchers, and present its advantages and limitations. We then describe several exciting new findings about processes and sources of change revealed by microgenetic approaches. Finally, we suggest new directions for research.

DESCRIPTION OF THE MICROGENETIC METHOD

In a prototypic microgenetic study, children receive multiple trials of a problem, or several versions of a type of problem, over several testing sessions. Researchers attempt, by densely sampling behavior during periods of rapid change, to describe accurately, and to begin to understand, change. They examine patterns of changes in behavior over time in and between testing sessions in an effort to detect the processes underlying both quantitative and qualitative change. Traditional designs and analyses that do not carefully examine trial-by-trial change may mask these intricate patterns of change. Ideally, observations span the entire period of rapid change, from its beginning to a period of relative stability. With this method, researchers can examine not only spontaneous changes but also accelerated change when the experimenter provides a high concentration of the experiences thought to cause changes in performance in the natural environment.

Microgenetic studies vary a great deal in the extent to which they involve these principles. For example, studies that could be considered microgenetic range from a relatively brief 30-minute session (Bjorklund et al., 1992; Miller & Aloise-Young, 1996) to multiple sessions spanning several months (e.g., Kuhn et al., 1995; Siegler & Jenkins, 1989). Although strictly speaking a microgenetic study involves multiple sessions, the spirit (and most advantages) of the approach can be found in carefully constructed single-session studies, which are also included in this chapter. Specifically, these studies can, with adequate pilot testing, appropriate choice of ages of subjects, and good luck, encompass the entire period of change, although they are less likely to do so than are multisession studies. These shorter studies emphasize dense sampling during rapid change and intense analysis of change over trials. Thus, some, but not all, multitrial single session studies are microgenetic. Microgenetic studies are still relatively uncommon—about 40 to 50, depending on how strict a criterion one uses for defining microgenetic studies (see Catan, 1986, for historical issues surrounding the appropriate use of the term *microgenesis*).

ADVANTAGES OF THE MICROGENETIC METHOD
FOR STUDYING CHANGE

As a way of studying mechanisms of change, the microgenetic method possesses four strengths (Kuhn, 1995; Siegler & Crowley, 1991). First, *change is observed directly, while it is occurring*. Most researchers have used cross-sectional and, occasionally, longitudinal methods to examine changes in children's thinking. These methods have yielded valuable information about children's abilities at different ages but have revealed little about how thinking changes from one age to the next because researchers can infer the process of change only by comparing behavior before and after the change. Children become a collection of cross-sectional or longitudinal slices on a developmental timetable. Even in longitudinal studies, often considered the choice for studying developmental change, the time between observations is usually too great to infer the processes that gave rise to the change. Important brief periods of rapid change, such as short-term transitional strategies (e.g., the short-cut sum strategy identified by Siegler and Jenkins, 1989, in their study of single-digit arithmetic) may be missed altogether. In contrast, the microgenetic method is ideally suited for capturing and examining change.

Second, *the method can examine various aspects of change.* Siegler (1996) has noted five important dimensions of change that can be detected by microgenetic designs: path, rate, breadth, variability, and sources of change. *Path* refers to the sequence of behaviors or understanding over trials. *Rate* refers to how fast the changes occur. Siegler and Crowley (1991) pointed out that what appears from group data to be gradual developmental change may actually be very rapid change at different times in different individuals (Shimojo, Bauer, O'Connell, & Held, 1986; Siegler, 1987). Thus, group data can mask the rate of change (as well as the presence of qualitative change). *Breadth* involves the degree of generalization to related concepts or skills. *Variability* refers to individual differences in the three previous dimensions. Finally, *sources of change* refer to causes. A main contribution of the microgenetic method is that it can identify specifically the conditions under which change is most likely to occur (e.g., providing feedback), the probable causes (i.e., what happened just before the change), and the way in which causes have their effects (e.g., qualitative or quantitative change). Because these five aspects may vary across individuals, tasks, and situations (Siegler & Stern, in press), the microgenetic method can capture the complexity of change. The very process of change may be influenced by variables such as age, capacity demands of the task, degree of instruction, extent of familiarity with the task, and a child's interest in the task.

Third, *the method can detect variability in behavior.* Cross-sectional designs and group analyses draw researchers' attention to the typical behavior of children at each age. Investigators have described children as "having" a certain mental structure, processing limit, rule, or strategy, which is eventually *replaced* by another such cognitive attribute. In contrast, microgenetic research also considers the performance of individual children on individual trials. This characteristic is important because group performance can mask between-child diversity in performance (e.g., Kuhn et al., 1995; Siegler, 1987) and collapsing data across trials can mask variability in a child.

Fourth, *the method is flexible; it can be used to study a variety of concepts and is congenial to a variety of theoretical perspectives.* Piagetian (e.g., Chletsos & DeLisi, 1991), neo-Piagetian (e.g., Bidell, 1990), Vygotskian (e.g., Duncan & Pratt, 1997; Wertsch & Stone, 1978), theory-change (e.g., Kuhn et al., 1995; Schauble, 1996), and information-processing (e.g., Siegler & Jenkins, 1989) researchers have fruitfully used the method.

A CRITIQUE OF THE MICROGENETIC METHOD FOR STUDYING CHANGE

Although the microgenetic method reveals how behavior *can* change, it is less clear whether behavior typically *does* change in this way in natural settings. The microgenetic laboratory experience is artificial in several ways. In everyday life, relevant experiences are not usually condensed into a very brief period and repeated as they are in microgenetic sessions. In addition, naturally occurring feedback typically is not consistent and immediate, as in some microgenetic studies. This issue is reminiscent of the controversy in the late 1960s and 1970s about whether studies demonstrating that children could be trained to understand Piagetian concepts revealed anything about the natural development of these concepts.

This criticism is more valid for some studies than for others. Some experiences provided in microgenetic studies do mimic those outside the laboratory fairly well. Repeated experience with mathematics problems (e.g., Siegler) is one example. In school, children are often asked to solve a series of such problems over several days, weeks, and months (although if immediate feedback is given after each problem in the laboratory, this distinction remains). Other examples of real-life activities of a microgenetic nature are the repeated playing of computer games at home and the repeated reading exercises at school. Memorizing a series of word lists, however, is more distant from everyday life than are these activities. Kuhn (1995, p. 105) addressed this issue and concluded that the form and direction of change look very similar when she compared her microgenetic and cross-sectional data.

A second issue is whether the processes of change are the same for short-term and long-term change—microgenesis and ontogenesis. This question may not be fruitful, however, because these two kinds of change are tightly interwoven and may be impossible to disentangle (Siegler & Crowley, 1991). And even if microgenetic change turns out to differ from ontogenetic change, it is still important to examine microgenetic change because it relates to learning, readiness, and ontogenetic constraints (see later discussion).

These two criticisms pertain to both the description of change and the processes of change. Perhaps, for example, microgenetic analyses accurately describe ontogenetic sequences, but fare less well in identifying the processes of change, or vice versa.

Third, microgenetic designs have several methodological limitations. They are resource demanding (e.g., labor intensive) and place demands on children's motivation (e.g., numerous trials and, often, multiple sessions). Moreover, the effects of repeated experience with the tasks are not always assessed. Although multiple trials provide a rich picture of changes in behavior, early trials introduce experience (e.g., practice with the task, repeated questioning, feedback) that may affect behavior on later trials (Pressley, 1992). In a sense, this experience is desirable in that it can be examined for causes of the later change and one can assess a child's potential to learn (Vygotsky's "zone of proximal development"). Assessment and training, however, become confused. Only the first trial permits a clean assessment of a child's typical, current level of functioning. When children produce a new strategy on a later trial, is it because this strategy has been in their repertoire all along but simply has not emerged or is it because it is acquired as a result of experience with other strategies on previous trials? This issue is particularly pertinent when children are asked to provide explanations for their behavior after each trial, a practice that may encourage them to think about their choices of behaviors. One way to partially address this issue is to include a control group that receives only a pre- and post-test—a design used in only a few microgenetic studies (e.g., Kuhn & Ho, 1980) or to include two or more groups with several degrees of experience or types of training (e.g., Siegler, 1995; Siegler & Stern, in press). (For another critique of the microgenetic method, see Pressley, 1992.)

WHAT MICROGENETIC STUDIES HAVE REVEALED ABOUT CHANGE

Variability in Behavior

Cognitive developmental researchers, especially stage theorists, have tended to emphasize the typical behavior of children at each age. In contrast, using a microgenetic design, Siegler and his colleagues (e.g., Siegler & Jenkins, 1989) have found a surprising degree of variability during the process of change, both between children (so-called individual differences) and within a child. In between-children variability, children of the same age use different patterns of strategies when solving a given problem. More interesting is within-child variability, in which a single child uses several strategies within a problem-solving session or across sessions. Siegler and Jenkins (1989) found that preschoolers used at least five adding strategies, for example, adding 4 and 5 by counting from 1 to 9 on their fingers, by counting from 5 to 9, or guessing. A child cannot be said to be "in the _____ stage" or to fit into some other typology according to what he or she *is* or *has*. More and less advanced strategies coexist side by side, often for a long time. One strategy may be most dominant, and the optimal strategy may win in the end, but variability is the rule rather than the exception. Remarkably, a single child sometimes uses different strategies on different trials *on the very same problem*. Conventional designs that do not examine multiple trials and problems probably would not have detected these intrachild types of variability.

These types of variability measure variability in terms of the number of different strategies used. A more recent measure of variability refers to the number of trial-by-trial *changes* in strategy use—additions or deletions of strategies on consecutive trials. This measure is somewhat independent of the number of strategies, which focuses on the sheer number of strategies used irrespective of additions and deletions. Coyle and Bjorklund (1997) gave second- through fourth-grade children five sort–recall trials with different words and categories. They assessed four strategies on each trial: sorting, physically moving the stimulus items; rehearsal, saying out loud the words; category naming, saying the category name of a group of items; and clustering, recalling words by category. In addition to using several strategies, often on a single problem-solving trial, all children showed considerable trial-by-trial switching of strategies.

Cognitive variability appears to operate continually throughout development, rather than only at particular stress points (Kuhn et al., 1995; Siegler, 1996) such as brief periods of disequilibrium. However, intrachild variability appears to increase during transitional periods (Goldin-Meadow & Alibali, 1995) and to be at its highest when children have moderate experience (Siegler, 1996). Indeed, cognitive variability appears to hasten cognitive change (e.g., Graham & Perry, 1993; Siegler, 1995) and thus can be used as an indicator of impending change. Variability is clearly a theoretically interesting phenomenon rather than an uninteresting nuisance to be eliminated by pretraining or practice trials. Based on his microgenetic studies, Siegler (1996) constructed a model of development as a series of overlapping waves. Children of a given age use several strategies, and their frequency of using these strategies changes during development. This model contrasts with stage models, which give little attention to variability. Variability may be adaptive because it offers a cognitive arsenal from which to choose and permits flexibility in coping with the demands of a particular situation (Siegler, 1996). Also, variability prevents knowledge from being stuck at a given level, in a particular perspective (Granott, 1996).

Children may use multiple strategies or rules partly because of conflict between their pre-existing beliefs and reality. Kuhn, Schauble, and Garcia-

Mila (1992) gave fourth graders two sessions of scientific reasoning problems per week for 10 weeks. For example, in one problem, children tried to identify the set of features (color of car, muffler, engine size, tail fin, wheel size) that affect the speed of a racing car. Children rarely displayed a single approach to the problems. Their problem-solving repertoire included both valid strategies, such as comparing outcomes on two trials in which only one feature differed, and invalid strategies, such as staying with erroneous pre-existing notions about cars or interpreting covariation as causality without examining the effect of other covariates. If a prediction based on a child's false pre-existing theory was not confirmed, the child often simply ignored this outcome and switched to other variables to examine. Valid and invalid strategies coexisted and competed for dominance, often for many sessions. The ratio between the two did change over trials, with the more valid one typically becoming more prevalent.

Variability seems to be an inherent part of change not only in strategies of addition and scientific reasoning but also in strategies of attention (Miller & Aloise-Young, 1996), word organization or rehearsal during memorizing (Bjorklund et al., 1992; Bjorklund, Schneider, Cassel, & Ashley, 1994; Coyle & Bjorklund, 1997; McGilly & Siegler, 1989; Siegler & McGilly, 1989), problem solving about a robot's behavior (Granott, 1996), conservation (Siegler, 1995), social problem solving (Kuhn et al., 1995; Wertsch & Hickmann, 1987), multiplication (Cooney, Swanson, & Ladd, 1988), practical mathematical thinking during play (Cohen, 1996), measurement (Van Voorhis & Ellis, 1997), and tick tack toe (Crowley & Siegler, 1993), among others. Importantly, variability appears even for logical concepts, such as conservation, which are assumed to undergo qualitative change. Siegler (1995) found that even after children learned conservation of number on a microgenetic training study they still continued to use several bases for making judgments about number on later trials.

In summary, a satisfactory account of the processes of cognitive change must address the fact that variability seems to be a general characteristic of human behavior, not only a symptom of children in transitional states. Adults also show considerable variability in their cognitive strategies (Kuhn et al., 1995).

In addition to revealing considerable variability in strategy use, microgenetic studies have revealed relations between strategy variability and performance. In the sort–recall study by Coyle and Bjorklund (1997) described earlier in which second- through fourth-grade children showed both multiple strategies and frequent trial-by-trial changes in strategies, variability was related to levels of recall. Relatively high levels of recall were associated with the stable use of several different strategies (i.e., few trial-by-trial changes), although such relations generally were significant for older children only. Such a finding probably would not have been revealed without the intense trial-by-trial analyses of strategy use associated with microgenetic methods.

Processes of Change

Discovery of New Solutions. Siegler and Jenkins (1989) used the microgenetic method to reveal the processes that contribute to the discovery of a new strategy. Immediately before the discovery, children took twice as long to solve problems as they did in general (medians of 18 vs. 9 seconds) and showed long pauses, expressions of affect, and strange statements that resisted interpretation. These behaviors suggest that the children were experiencing a great deal of cognitive activity, which culminated in the discovery of a new strategy. Similarly, in a very different type of problem—the three-disk version of the Tower of Hanoi problem—children go through a phase of inefficient moves, hesitations, and pauses before successfully solving the problem (Bidell, 1990).

Perhaps most interesting is Siegler and Jenkins' finding that, in contrast to a common view that discoveries generally occur after an impasse—when a difficult problem cannot be solved with available procedures—children sometimes discovered a new strategy on an easy problem, including one that earlier had been solved easily using a different strategy. Relatedly, a new strategy sometimes emerged when the most recently used strategy was successful. Miller and Aloise-Young (1996) reported that children had correct judgments 71% of the time on the trial *preceding* the trial on which they first switched to the best attentional strategy. Moreover, children showed many routes to this best strategy; no one type of strategy tended to be used on the trial immediately preceding the emergence of the best strategy.

Generalization to Other Domains. Most microgenetic studies use a single type of problem. Thus, it is not clear whether the acquisition of a given concept or skill shows the same pattern of microgenetic change in different content domains and whether a new skill acquired during microgenesis generalizes to a different domain. To examine these issues, Kuhn et al. (1995) studied changes in both knowledge and strategies of knowledge acquisition in fourth graders and college students solving two social problems (e.g., inferring causes of school failure from school records) and two physical problems (e.g., determining which variables affect the speed of a toy boat being pulled). Subjects worked on one physical problem and one social problem once each week for 5 weeks. For both domains, the two age groups showed the same microgenetic pattern: multiple-strategy use with more accurate strategies gradually becoming more prevalent. Moreover, new strategies emerged at about the same time in the two domains, even though performance in the social domain lagged behind that in the physical domain overall. In the 6th week, new content was substituted in both domains, and problem solving continued through Week 10. The accuracy of inferences temporarily declined until the new content was mastered, but the level of reasoning strategies did not decline. Thus, microgenetic changes may be somewhat general across domains, and advances in one domain may generalize to new content in that domain. Change has been less general (i.e., narrower transfer), however, in some studies (e.g., certain concepts and strategies regarding quantity in Siegler, 1995), particularly when children were unaware of using the new strategy (Siegler, 1996). The microgenetic transfer design nicely complements the traditional transfer-of-training designs.

Surprising Principles of Strategy Choice. Microgenetic studies are ideal for examining the process of competition among the various strategies in a child's repertoire during a problem-solving session. Models of changes in problem solving have tended to view children as rational problem solvers. Perhaps because of the historical influence of learning theory, many researchers have assumed that children keep successful strategies and discard unsuccessful strategies. In support of this assumption, a microgenetic study by Coyle (1997) showed that children continue to use strategies that yield optimal performance. Second and fourth graders received seven sort–recall trials with different sets of categorizable words on each trial. Children in both grades tended to continue a particular strategy when it had resulted in perfect recall on the immediately preceding trial. In contrast, children tended to switch to a different strategy when a strategy resulted in less than perfect recall. Children, however, do not always behave in this rational way in other studies. Although children may favor the most successful strategy by the end of the session, earlier they typically do not follow the win–stay, lose–shift principle. Children often drop successful strategies and return to unsuccessful ones. This halting and uneven use of newly discovered competencies has been found in many areas, such as scientific reasoning (Kuhn et al., 1995; Kuhn & Phelps, 1982), language development (Karmiloff-Smith, 1984, 1986), attentional strategies (Miller & Aloise-Young, 1996), pictorial representation (Karmiloff-Smith, 1984, 1986), problem solving (Wertsch & Hickmann, 1987), mathematical calculations (Siegler & Jenkins, 1989), and memory strategies (Siegler & Jenkins, 1989). Letting go of older ways of thinking seems to be as much a part of cognitive development as the acquisition of new ways of thinking.

The willingness to discard, at least temporarily, successful (and often superior) strategies is apparent even when these strategies are quite conscious. Kuhn et al. (1992) found that even after children articulated a new, high-level principle of scientific reasoning they often later fell back on explanations expressing their earlier faulty strategies.

Initial Level of Competence Affects Change. Does a learner's starting point determine how far he or she can progress microgenetically? That is, do older, brighter, or more knowledgeable learners progress more quickly? In the Kuhn et al. (1995) transfer-of-learning study discussed earlier, fourth graders and college students did not vary greatly in their initial levels of strategic performance, but the latter showed a more rapid evolution of strategies. In a study of noncollege adults and sixth graders who conducted experiments over six half-hour sessions, Schauble (1996, p. 118) found that adults "proceeded more systematically, both in the way that each new trial built on the previous one and in the overall structure of their experimentation." Adults devoted more time to figuring out variables that they originally did not understand, whereas children wasted their time by drawing conclusions about variables that they already understood.

Bright children resemble adults (Johnson & Mervis, 1994). Brighter 5-year-olds both learned more about shorebirds and organized that information better than did less bright children of the same age, despite starting at the same novice level. Children with initial high levels of knowledge about shorebirds showed the same advantage.

The Development of Knowledge: Acquiring Expertise. Nearly all nonmicrogenetic studies of change in expertise have compared experts and novices and thus cannot detect the steps between the two. Microgenetic designs are well suited for studying how children develop from novice to expert levels. For example, as predicted by Vygotsky, as young children become more familiar with a problem over trials, they decrease their private speech (Duncan & Pratt, 1997), presumably because problem solving becomes more internalized. Cross-sectional research could not have mapped this process of change so carefully. Moreover, using several sessions increased the chances that virtually all the children produced private speech at least once.

Johnson and Mervis (1994) traced the microgenetic development of expertise by examining 5-year-olds who were novices about shorebirds. During four sessions over 17 days, children learned a label for each shorebird as well as a physical and a behavioral attribute. The children acquired a great deal of knowledge about shorebirds and showed at least some generalization to unfamiliar shorebirds. In an interesting transitional phase, children knew the attributes of the birds, but did not yet use these attributes consistently to categorize the birds. Thus, a certain amount of quantitative change in expertise may be required before qualitative shifts in the organization of this knowledge can occur. This phase could be observed because of the microgenetic nature of the design, with the high density of measurements.

One finding is relevant to an issue raised earlier: whether microgenetic change pertains to longer term developmental change. Johnson and Mervis

(1994) pointed out that, in both their microgenetic and cross-sectional studies of expertise, knowledge about physical, directly observable attributes precedes knowledge about less directly observed behavioral attributes. Similarities between microgenetic and ontogenetic change are addressed next.

Microgenesis Recapitulates Ontogenesis. Granott (1994) has noted a curious pattern of change in her own work and that of several others. Namely, older children and adults often regress to the strategies of younger children at the beginning of an unfamiliar task. In her research, adults tried to solve complex and unfamiliar problems involving the functioning of robots. The robots differed in that they responded to light, sound, and touch with different patterns of movement. For example, one robot might move toward shadows. Adults typically began to explore this task in a primitive, sensory-motor way. They played with the robots and observed their patterns of movements, which gave the adults a "practical understanding" of the robots. They "let the robot move on the floor, put hands above and around it, flashed lights on it, or put it in the shadow . . . they clapped, whistled, snapped fingers, and sometimes, jokingly, shouted at the robot" (Granott, 1994, p. 17). As they continued to notice that variability in their actions related to variability in the robot's movements, they formed representations about the task. They continued to proceed through steps of increasingly abstract reasoning described by Fischer's (1980) skill theory, although they went back and forth among their various levels of strategies. Thus, they began at an early developmental level and then progressed through an ontogenetic sequence.

When Granott's subjects tried to skip part of the sequence and prematurely jump to a higher level, they discovered that such a move was not productive and returned to the skipped level. In addition, they sometimes went through the developmental sequence several times in a session. This repetition sometimes happened when solving one aspect of the robot's functioning revealed a novel characteristic to be explored further through the same developmental sequence.

Granott's work is relevant to our critique about the similarity between adult microgenetic, child microgenetic, and child ontogenetic change. She argued that micro- and ontogenesis are parallel processes because they have sequences of cognitive structures and mechanisms of change in common. In both cases, these hypothesized mechanisms are the differentiation, coordination, and integration of knowledge structures (Fischer, 1980; Werner, 1948; and see Granott, 1994, for a discussion of parallel mechanisms proposed by others). Relevant to our earlier discussion of the importance of the learner's initial level, however, is the fact that this parallelism does not mean that adults and children behave identically during microgenesis. Adults bring to the task general scientific-inquiry skills, such as knowing how to generate hypotheses, isolate variables, and test hypotheses, but they have to determine the specific relevant variables and their effects in a novel specific context. Adults can transfer knowledge to unfamiliar situations by rapidly reconstructing this knowledge.

One interesting implication of Granott's findings is that just as various strategies coexist in the strategy research discussed previously, so do knowledge structures at different levels coexist; newer structures do not replace older ones during ontogenetic development. The old ones remain available for microgenetic change, as when adults use sensory-motor procedures.

Regressions and Progressions. Granott's microgenetic analysis detected temporary regressions that most likely would have gone unnoticed in traditional designs (see also Karmiloff-Smith, 1984). Similarly, Siegler (1995) noted that children who gave a logical explanation on a conservation pretest did so less than half the time when that item was presented again later. By seeing regressions in the context of subsequent progress over trials, however, the positive, rather than negative, aspect of regressions becomes apparent (see also Duncker, 1945; Werner, 1948). For example, some children briefly regress in their recall, as a result of producing a more mature strategy, before they can progress (Miller & Seier, 1994). Moreover, the return to less mature strategies after constructing new strategies, as described earlier in the context of work by Siegler and others, could be interpreted as positive regression. Children may need to strengthen or automatize these components that converge in the more advanced strategy, or they may need to make certain that these earlier strategies are in fact less useful. In any case, the regression is in the service of progression.

Models of Strategy Change. Several investigators have developed models of strategy change during microgenesis. Kuhn et al. (1995) have proposed that strategic competence, metastrategic competence, and metacognitive competence contribute to microgenetic changes in knowledge-acquisition strategies. *Strategic competence* refers to the ability to execute correct strategies. Children strengthen new strategies as a result of practice, which eventually enables these strategies to win out over older strategies during microgenesis. *Metastrategic processes* refer to knowing how, when, and why a strategy should be used. Both strategies and tasks must be understood. Processes include evaluating strategies in one's repertoire, selecting strategies, and monitoring strategy effectiveness. *Metacognitive competence* involves thinking about one's theories in light of the evidence. People sometimes do not fully understand that evidence and theories are separate; they have trouble acknowledging that evidence is discrepant with their theory and subsequently revising their theory. Such biases towards pre-existing beliefs are especially likely when the evidence is ambiguous, involves small effects, or both. In one such study, adults and fifth and sixth graders rarely considered the possibility of measurement error unless they could use it to preserve their favored theory (Schauble, 1996).

Microgenetic analyses reveal the course of change of all three competencies—strategic, metastrategic, metacognitive—and suggest hypotheses about their developmental relation. Moreover, microgenetic changes in conceptual knowledge about a domain and in strategic behaviors can interact to produce change, as they support, or bootstrap, each other (Schauble, 1996).

Siegler (1996) views strategy development as proceeding via competition among strategies and eventual survival of the "fittest" strategy, as well as "competitive negotiation" between associative and metacognitive mechanisms. Certain strategies become stronger over trials, but goals, motivations, values, metacognitive knowledge, and beliefs also guide strategy selection. For example, "goal sketches" (Siegler & Jenkins, 1989) refer to children's knowledge of the goals that legitimate strategies must meet in a particular domain. Children can sense that they are on the right track in selecting a particular strategy even if it does not yet pay off; that is, strategy choice is constrained, not random. Because of these goal sketches, children may be able to discover new strategies without engaging in trial and error with inappropriate strategies. A desire for novelty or an "aesthetic sense" of what constitutes a good strategy may guide strategy selection as well. This realization that associative strength, perceived effectiveness, values, and metacognitive understanding all contribute to strategy change was stimulated by tracking microgenetic changes in strategy choice, explanations, and events and behaviors before and after strategy change. In particular, self-modification through problem-solving experience appears to be important (Siegler & Shipley, 1995).

Kuhn and Ho (1980) addressed the role of self-directed activities by presenting experimental and yoked-control fourth and fifth graders with the same set of task-relevant information (i.e., antecedent–outcome chemical events). The control group lacked the free choice of information-seeking activities permitted in the experimental group. The controls showed less change over the 11 sessions. Thus, the active, planned, participatory aspects of a child's behavior are important for change, but the beliefs that people bring to a problem-solving task often constrain this process of information seeking. Children and adults often use their initial *theory* of underlying causes to selectively gather and interpret evidence (Kuhn et al., 1995). This confirmatory bias protects beliefs.

Karmiloff-Smith's microgenetic analyses (1992) suggest a different, multiphase microgenetic process. Knowledge is at first implicit and nonrepresentational, but gradually becomes more explicit. It is redescribed in a representational code and later, after another redescription, becomes conscious knowledge. Still later, explicit redescription permits the translation from one representational code into another. Other researchers have proposed other mechanisms of microgenetic change as well, such as the coordination of lower level skills into a higher level skill (e.g., Fischer, 1980; Granott, 1995; Werner, 1948).

Utilization Deficiency

Another phenomenon of developmental change addressed by researchers using microgenetic approaches is a strategy utilization deficiency—a temporary period in strategy development when children spontaneously produce a strategy but gain little or no benefit from it (Miller, 1990; Miller & Harris, 1988; for reviews, see Bjorklund & Coyle, 1995; Bjorklund, Miller, Coyle, & Slawinski, 1997; Miller & Seier, 1994). That is, developmental change is sometimes characterized by a gap between acquisition of and effectiveness of a new skill. In contrast, strategies traditionally have been defined as goal-directed procedures that facilitate task performance (e.g., Harnishfeger & Bjorklund, 1990).

In a review of research on strategy development from 1974 to the present, Miller and Seier (1994) found evidence for utilization deficiencies in more than 10 different strategies over an age range of 3 to 14 years on a variety of tasks. In most of these experiments, utilization deficiencies were inferred from group analyses and designs that were not microgenetic. For example, correlations between strategy use and performance were higher for older children than for younger, and, among equally strategic children, older children recalled significantly more than did younger ones.

Because these studies do not focus on individuals' change over trials, they cannot identify particular children as utilization deficient. One microgenetic design, however, examined individual children's acquisition and maintenance of an organizational strategy (Bjorklund et al., 1992). Kindergartners, third, and eighth graders received five free-recall trials with different lists of words and categories on each trial. Two sorts of microgenetic analyses revealed utilization deficiencies. Over-trial analyses of groups showed that third graders had increased clustering over trials not accompanied by an increase in recall over trials. Thus, at this age, increased strategic behavior did not appear to be beneficial. (Both recall and clustering over trials generally decreased for the kindergartners and increased for the eighth graders.)

A second microgenetic analysis classified individual children as utilization deficient or not, according to their patterns of recall and clustering over the five trials. To be classified as utilization deficient, children had to show a significant increase in clustering from Trial n to Trial $n + 1$ and had to maintain this increase for at least one subsequent trial (i.e., $n + 2$) in the absence of any significant increase in recall. Moreover, clustering scores had to change from below-chance values on Trial n to above-chance values on Trials $n + 1$ and $n + 2$. With these criteria, a number of third graders (38%) were classified as utilization deficient. Kindergartners were not utilization deficient because they rarely even produced the strategy. Eighth graders were not utilization deficient because they were proficient at producing the strategy, probably with little effort (Miller, Seier, Probert, & Aloise, 1991), and could benefit from the strategy. Thus, the group and individual microgenetic analyses of patterns of recall and clustering over trials yielded converging, and complementary, evidence for utilization deficiencies in third graders.

Interestingly, different children showed different patterns in the relation between clustering and recall. In addition to the increased clustering without increased recall in the utilization-deficient children, some children showed increased recall preceding, or in the absence of, increased clustering, and others showed increases in both or no systematic change.

Another microgenetic study (Coyle & Bjorklund, 1996) revealed that a utilization deficiency has different meaning in the case of younger and older children. Utilization-deficient second graders were *ahead* of their peers in strategy production, so may have produced the strategy before they were ready to utilize it fully. Utilization-deficient fourth graders were *behind* their peers in both strategy production and utilization.

Because utilization deficiencies represent a phase in strategy acquisition rather than a characteristic of a particular age, they appear not only in elementary school children using a relatively complex (organizational) strategy but also in younger children using relatively simple strategies. In a microgenetic experiment (Miller & Aloise-Young, 1996), preschoolers examined 12 drawings of toys concealed by two rows of six doors on the surface of a rectangular box. Over six trials, children had to determine whether the top and bottom rows contained the same drawings in the same order. The most efficient strategy—a "vertical pairs" strategy—was to open each vertically adjacent set of doors and determine whether the two drawings in the box in each column were the same or different. Strategy production and effectiveness were inferred from children's patterns of door openings and same-different judgments over the six trials. Nonmicrogenetic analyses (correlations and analyses of variance) provided mixed evidence for utilization deficiencies. Microgenetic analyses clarified this inconsistency by identifying exactly where strategy production and same-different judgments were or were not in synchrony. Overall, changes in strategy use over trials were not accompanied by parallel changes in correct judgments, a finding suggesting a utilization deficiency. For example, the largest increase in strategy production—from Trial 4 to Trial 5—was accompanied by a slight decrease in judgments, and the largest decline in judgments—from Trial 1 to Trial 2—was accompanied by a slight increase in strategic behavior. A trial-by-trial analysis comparing the judgments of strategic and nonstrategic children on each trial, however, showed that *on some trials* the strategy helped. Thus, the microgenetic analyses revealed some of the subtleties of strategy effectiveness that had appeared as simply inconsistencies in the traditional analyses. Also, the group *between-trial* variability in strategy *effectiveness* emerging in this study complements the *between-subject* variability in the relation between strategy production and recall in the Bjorklund et al. (1992) study described earlier. Moreover, this study provided another example that not attending to individual trials can distort the results. An overall significant correlation between strategy production and accuracy of judgments, which suggests strategy effectiveness, masked a lack of strategy effectiveness on certain trials.

A pattern of changes over trials in strategy effectiveness, which suggested the overcoming of a utilization deficiency, emerged in the microgenetic study by Coyle and Bjorklund (1997) described previously. They examined trial-by-trial changes of strategy additions and deletions on each trial transition (Trials 1 to 2, 2 to 3, 3 to 4, and 4 to 5). The relation between strategy variability (increases or decreases in the number of strategies used) and recall (increases or decreases) was significant on none of the four trial transitions for second graders (utilization deficiency), on the last two trials transitions for third graders, and on all trial transitions for fourth graders (no utilization deficiency). The third graders apparently overcame a utilization deficiency on the later trials.

These studies of variability and changes in strategy *effectiveness* complement the previously described studies that demonstrate variability in strategy *production*. They also show that a design that combines microgenetic and cross-sectional designs can be more powerful than either one alone for studying change.

Conclusions

The microgenetic, up-close nature of these studies resulted in certain outcomes that probably would have been much less apparent with other methods. These outcomes about change suggest that a new model of developmental change in problem solving is in order. This model would consider the following: Development is uneven and halting because old and new, good and poor, strategies, knowledge structures, or both coexist for a considerable time. Striking intra- and interchild individual variability characterizes problem solving. The success of a strategy does not necessarily lead to its retention, and failure of a strategy does not necessarily lead to its abandonment. Children sometimes move away from the goal temporarily in order to move closer to it later, as when they regress to less advanced strategies or sensory-motor forms of problem solving or retain an ultimately useful strategy that temporarily is not helping or is even hindering them. Strategies change microgenetically in both their frequency and their effectiveness. Quantitative and qualitative changes intertwine during the acquisition of expertise. Certain sequences, such as the shift from sensory-motor or physical to conceptual representations and problem solving, may characterize both ontogenesis and microgenesis, although the two may differ in other ways. A learner's initial level of competence affects microgenetic change.

MECHANISMS OF CHANGE RECONSIDERED

We now return to one question that stimulated this chapter: Do microgenetic studies identify mechanisms of change? Microgenetic studies clearly can provide a more detailed *description* of change in their trial-by-trial account of online verbal and nonverbal behaviors than can most other methods. It is much more difficult (for any method) to identify *mechanisms* of change, but the microgenetic method is quite promising in this respect because it can focus on the periods just before and during the time of rapid change. For example, researchers can see the effect of success or failure of a strategy on subsequent behavior and can note unusual behaviors such as a long silence, expressions of emotion, or changes in attention just before a change. Although this procedure may not directly reveal mechanisms of change, the procedure at least suggests plausible hypotheses about underlying mechanisms. For example, data on addition strategies from Siegler and Jenkins' (1989) study constrained the mechanisms in a later simulation model (Shrager & Siegler, 1998).

This issue of mechanisms of change, however, involves subtleties that have not yet been addressed satisfactorily by microgenetic researchers. In particular, microgenetic research still needs to identify similarities and differences in how various aspects of change (path, rate, breadth, variability, sources; Siegler, 1996) are involved in various types of acquisitions (e.g., strategy, behavior, belief, knowledge, skill). In addition, researchers have not clearly differentiated the causes of three types of microgenetic change: the emergence of a new skill or new conceptual understanding of a domain, the eventual production of a pre-existing skill during problem solving, and the increased prevalence over trials or sessions of this new or pre-existing skill. The underlying mechanisms may be quite different in the three cases. For example, the three, respectively, may involve the integration of subskills, a change in how the task is represented, or redescription (see the earlier discussion of Karmiloff-Smith's work); metacognitive judgments affecting strategy choice, goal sketches, an aesthetic sense about strategies, or a desire for novelty; and the strengthening of a skill through practice, or the scaffolding of one skill by another, metacognitive monitoring of strategy effectiveness, competition among strategies, or inhibition of less effective strategies or previous beliefs. All three types of microgenetic change may be affected by increased automaticity of certain skills over trials with a resulting increase in available capacity or an increased understanding of the goal of the task. A promising advance is a recent computer simulation that includes both metacognitive and associative learning mechanisms that successfully generate behavior paralleling both children's discovery of new strategies and their selection among alternative strategies (Shrager & Siegler, 1998).

Finally, do the same mechanisms of microgenetic change characterize children of different developmental levels, of different levels of expertise on a particular task, or both? For example, does competition among old and new strategies direct strategy development among 3-year-olds as well as 10-year-olds? Do contradictory behaviors (e.g., saying one thing and doing another) signal imminent change at both ages? Because most mechanisms of change, such as capacity and inhibition, are undergoing development themselves, their role in microgenesis may differ from one age to another.

NEW DIRECTIONS FOR MICROGENETIC RESEARCH ON CHANGE

The purpose of this section is to place the microgenetic approach into the context of theoretical issues of current interest about change and to suggest new applications and implications of the approach.

Fruitful Integrations With Other Theoretical Approaches

Dynamic Systems Theory. The microgenetic method could productively be combined with an area of current interest that also focuses on change: dynamic systems theory (e.g., Thelen & Smith, 1994; van Geert, 1994). Dynamic systems theory addresses change over time in complex systems, especially self-organizing ones. In this view, new complex forms or skills emerge from the relations among parts; they fall out of the current status of the system in context. Thus, strategic behavior may "self-organize in response to information specifying the task and the physical environment" (Thelen, 1992, p. 190). The theory acknowledges variability, but also a preferred state in which the system tends to reside. Multiple levels of causation underlie change. Thus, dynamic systems theory appears to describe well many of the microgenetic phenomena discussed here: dynamic changes, emerging skills, variability as well as stability, and quantitative change leading to qualitative change. Both the dynamic systems and microgenetic approaches attempt to locate the point of most rapid and significant change and to intensively study moment-to-moment change during that time. In dynamic systems, when a system becomes unstable, underlying mechanisms and processes can be revealed and examined intensely.

Dynamic systems theory places microgenetic phenomena into a broad theoretical perspective—nonlinear, emergent, self-organizing changes characteristic of many kinds of systems. Moreover, the theory suggests new directions for the microgenetic approach. For example, a central concept of dynamic systems models is that a small initial difference or effect can have reverberations that culminate in large, dramatic differences or effects later. This notion suggests that an appropriate microgenetic analysis requires examining behavior and individual differences not only in the trials immediately preceding observable change but also in trials, or perhaps even sessions, much earlier. Similarly, because a small change causes changes throughout the system, microgenetic experiments should broaden the set of behaviors that are examined after a change. In addition, the dynamic systems approach directs microgenetic investigations toward the organism in context: "Development proceeds as a series of continual matches between the current dynamics of the individual—the preferred states—and his or her intentions, the demands of the task, and the affordances of the environment" (Thelen, 1992, p. 191). Microgenetic changes in strategy production may be seen as an attempt to achieve a match between a child's current competencies and motivations, and the demands of the task.

In the opposite direction, microgenetic work can contribute to dynamic systems theory. Certainly, as a method, the microgenetic approach permits the careful documentation of moment-to-moment change over trials and sessions and of individual variation in behavior. Empirical findings already discussed about principles of strategy choice, adults' temporary regressions in new situations, and the roles of goal-relevant processes such as goal sketches, motivation, and metacognition can also enrich dynamic systems work. In one attempt to use a microgenetic method in a dynamic systems framework (Thelen, Fisher, & Ridley-Johnson, 1984), infants' stepping was accelerated by changing the weight on their legs—a condensation of normal development. Also, Granott (1996) has described the microgenetic process of problem solving about robots' behavior with a dynamic systems model.

Indexing Transitional Knowledge States. In another approach of current interest, investigators propose that contradictions in a child's behavior on a single problem—especially gesture–speech mismatches—indicate imminent cognitive change (Goldin-Meadow, Alibali, & Church, 1993). Church and Goldin-Meadow (1986), for example, found that on conservation tasks some children referred to beaker height in their explanations but beaker width with their hands. Children with discordant behaviors such as these progressed more after training than did children with concordant speech and gestures (see also Perry, Church, & Goldin-Meadow, 1988). The typical assessments of knowledge relying on correctness of answers do not differentiate between children who give an incorrect answer but do or do not have more than one basis for their judgments. The former are more ready to benefit from training. Gesture–speech mismatches have been observed in various ages and problem domains, such as preschoolers counting (Graham, 1994), middle schoolers reasoning about seasonal change (Crowder & Newman, 1993), and adults reasoning about gears (Perry & Elder, 1997).

Goldin-Meadow, Alibali, and Church (1993) argued that during a transitional state two beliefs, or representations, are *simultaneously* expressed—one in gesture (implicit knowledge) and one in speech (explicit knowledge), with the gestural representation usually the more advanced. There is a cost, however, to being in transition. These children work under increased cognitive demands (Goldin-Meadow, Nusbaum, Garber, & Church, 1993) and thus are vulnerable to regressing to a more stable state in which only one belief—an incorrect one—is produced, if training is not provided (Church, 1990).

Another harbinger of change is lack of clarity in explanations. Children in transition give vague, less specific explanations (Alibali & Perrott, 1996) and benefit from instruction more than do children who give explicit, specific explanations (Graham & Perry, 1993). The latter may have stable knowledge and so are unreceptive to suggestion. As Siegler and Jenkins (1989) observed, children become less articulate just before and during the discovery of a new strategy.

The microgenetic method is well suited for examining the emergence and disappearance of such discordances, for assessing both progress and regression, and for testing whether discordances index a readiness to learn. By tracing discordant and concordant individuals' responses to training over trials, researchers can obtain a more precise account of readiness and mechanisms of development. In one such study, Alibali and Goldin-Meadow (1993) found that most 9- and 10-year-olds who improved their understanding of mathematical equivalence over a number of trials and several sessions fit into the following sequence: concordant incorrect, discordant, concordant correct. In another microgenetic study, Alibali (1994) gave children mild instruction in mathematical equivalence and found several patterns over trials: remain concordant incorrect, progress from concordant incorrect to discordant, regress from discordant to concordant incorrect, and remain discordant. Interestingly, the children who remained discordant and thus appeared to make no progress in fact revamped their repertoires. That is, they kept some old procedures, abandoned others, and generated some new procedures, although the total number of procedures remained the same. This evidence that children had been working on the task probably would not have been detected without a detailed microscopic microgenetic analysis.

More generally, the microgenetic method can assess, and thereby clarify, the nature of transitional states. A transitional phase can involve a state of readiness to learn, a state in which guidance improves performance (the zone of proximal development), a state of partial knowledge, or a state in which multiple hypotheses are considered sequentially or simultaneously (Goldin-Meadow, Alibali, & Church, 1993). Only by examining, microgenetically, trial-by-trial changes before, during, and after training can one decide among these hypotheses.

In the other direction, gesture–speech discordant studies have implications for microgenetic studies. First, one should examine a variety of simultaneously occurring verbal and nonverbal behaviors to adequately assess knowledge. It may be particularly important to assess concepts, procedures, or strategies expressed in gestures, because such new acquisitions during a transitional state appear to be expressed in gesture and not in speech. Second, an additional type of intrachild variability to be examined is the use of more than one strategy, procedure, or concept *within* a single trial (Siegler, 1996), particularly when these behaviors are contradictory.

Clarification of Relations Among Microgenesis, Ontogenesis, and Phylogenesis

What are the causal relations among the three time frames of change: microgenesis, ontogenesis, and phylogenesis? Children's phylogenetic inheritance and current developmental level (ontogenesis) surely affect the nature and speed of microgenetic change. As for ontogenesis, when adults and 9-year-olds begin at the same level of strategic functioning, they show similar patterns of microgenetic change, for example, the coexistence of more and less adequate strategies (Kuhn et al., 1995). Still, adults progress more rapidly and reach a higher final level. In Granott's (1994) work, adults could solve robot problems by rapidly running through an ontogenetic sequence. Similar age differences have emerged in other domains as well (e.g., Bidell, 1990; Karmiloff-Smith & Inhelder, 1974; Metz, 1985; Wertsch & Stone, 1978). Developmental changes, such as an increase in cognitive capacity or the movement from one rule, cognitive stage, or theory of reality to another, create new microgenetic possibilities.

Just as ontogenesis and phylogenesis influence microgenesis, the latter also influences the former two. An accumulation of specific microgenetic change could lead to pervasive ontogenetic change and even, in certain environments and reproductive situations, phylogenetic change. In short, microgenetic, ontogenetic, and phylogenetic changes form an interrelated network, with each level making its own unique contribution to the process of change. Little attention has been given to these linkages.

Implications for Central Issues of Developmental Change

Qualitative Versus Quantitative Change. The microgenetic method has identified both types of change (e.g., Kuhn et al., 1995; Schauble, 1996). For example, strategy use changes quantitatively in terms of completeness, frequency, and degree of benefit to recall, and qualitatively in terms of the type of strategy or set of strategies selected. Children show qualitative change as they fine-tune their strategy by moving, for example, from a partial vertical-pairs strategy to a full vertical-pairs strategy when making same-different judgments and show qualitative change when changing from attending along a horizontal plane to attending to vertically aligned pairs (Miller & Aloise-Young, 1996). The microgenetic method can examine whether different mechanisms underlie quantitative and qualitative change. This pattern would be suggested if different events and behaviors predict the two types of change.

One tenacious issue has been how quantitative change can lead to qualitative change. The microgenetic method is fruitful for addressing this issue. Coyle and Bjorklund (1997) assessed quantitative change (the number of trial-by-trial changes in strategy use) and qualitative change (type of strategy combinations used). The number of trial-by-trial changes in strategy use decreased with age, with older children showing greater stability in strategy use than did younger children. This stability could be attributed to a corresponding age-related increase in the consistent use of the four-strategy combination of sorting, rehearsal, category naming, and clustering. Thus, a quantitative decrease in strategy change was accompanied by a qualitative change in the configuration of strategies used over trials. Such a pattern would not have been revealed without a detailed microgenetic analysis of both quantitative and qualitative aspects of strategy use.

As another example, using a Tower of Hanoi task, Bidell (1990) found that children aged 6 to 11 spent a period making nonoptimal moves before they coordinated components of their problem-solving skills and showed a sudden, qualitative shift to an optimal strategy (see also a microgenetic analysis of this task by Fireman, 1996). In addition, the study of expertise about shorebirds (Johnson & Mervis, 1994) described previously showed ways in which quantitative change can lead to qualitative change.

Developmental Sequences and Concurrences. Microgenetic studies can test for hypothesized sequences of acquiring skills during development by assessing when the skills emerge in a session or over several multitrial sessions.

Piagetian logical concepts, in particular, are believed to develop in a particular sequence. Microgenetic studies have revealed both sequences and variable orders of acquisition (e.g., Granott, 1994; Johnson & Mervis, 1994; Siegler, 1995; Siegler & Jenkins, 1989; Siegler & Stern, in press) of concepts or strategies. A second promising line of future microgenetic research would clarify the developmental relations among the identified skills in a sequence, which sometimes provides clues about developmental processes. Such research can test for various hypothesized relations (Flavell, 1972; Goldin-Meadow, Alibali, & Church, 1993). For example, does Skill 2 join, replace, subsume, or emerge as a modification of Skill 1? In one microgenetic study (Van Voorhis & Ellis, 1997), after receiving measurement problems weekly for 6 weeks, some kindergartners joined and integrated two strategies, for example, by using informal measurement tools such as fingers, hands, or arms in measurement in conjunction with the use of a formal measurement tool such as a ruler.

Concurrences could also be fruitfully examined microgenetically. An investigator can assess the time of emergence of skills hypothesized to be related, for example, by reflecting the same stage. Their simultaneous emergence would support this claim. It often is asserted that longitudinal studies are necessary for adequately testing sequences and concurrences. Yet microgenetic studies also can fulfill this function and can do so over a shorter time and with less danger of missing the emergence of one or both the competencies.

Accessing and Perfecting Skills or Knowledge Already in the Repertoire. Researchers have increased the accessibility of a child's skill, and thus revealed the child's highest, albeit fragile, level of functioning, in several ways. These usually include simplifying instructions or materials, increasing the salience of the relevant dimension, decreasing verbal demands, or adding a familiar or interesting story context (see Flavell, Miller, & Miller, 1993, chap. 8, for references and a discussion of issues of assessment). The microgenetic method provides an alternative way to make a relatively inaccessible skill accessible. Providing multiple trials increases the chances that the skill eventually emerges. Moreover, perhaps more important, the method has the potential to assess developmental or individual differences in the accessibility of the skill. Some children access the skill on the first trial or two, others on later trials of that session, and still others in later sessions or perhaps not even by the end of testing.

Children also perfect their skills, as when they change from partially producing a strategy to fully producing it. For example, they may study items somewhat selectively on a selective memory task before they do so in a completely selective way (Miller, 1990). Or a strategy may be beneficial on some trials but not others before it produces consistent benefit (Bjorklund et al., 1992; Miller & Aloise-Young, 1996). The refined analysis of change provided by the microgenetic method is a promising tool for addressing this issue because it addresses how to conceptualize the levels of competence ranging from the first fragile, rudimentary version of a skill to its final stable, generalized, abstract version during natural development. Does the same basic skill become stronger or does the very nature of the skill undergo a series of qualitative changes, for example, from a perceptual, concrete, sensory-motor version to a conceptual, abstract, cognitive operational version or from an isolated skill to one that is fully integrated into the conceptual system?

Change Involving Social Processes and Behaviors

In Vygotsky's (1978) conceptualization of microgenesis, change occurred primarily in a social-collaborative context. He focused on how a supportive adult or more competent peer helps a child progress cognitively through leading questions, examples, and demonstrations during the microgenetic procedure. He used the microgenetic method as a dynamic assessment of children's abilities by uncovering what they can do (or learn) with support: "It is only in movement that a body shows what it is" (Vygotsky, 1978, p. 65). Interpersonal interaction during problem solving is essential to Vygotsky's view of development because he thought that children internalize their dialogic exchanges with people. The intermental becomes intramental; the social creates the psychological. The issue for current microgenetic research, then, is whether change during joint problem solving mirrors change during individual problem solving. Social processes may affect microgenetic change in unique ways.

The assimilation of Werner and Vygotsky's microgenetic method into contemporary research on cognitive development, particularly into the information-processing approach, nicely illustrates how a scientific procedure from one theoretical and historical context is selectively assimilated into another. In particular, most microgenetic researchers have replaced Vygotsky's emphasis on culture and the context of social support with a focus on an individual child solving problems on his or her own.

Extending microgenetic approaches to social situations may direct researchers' attention to change mechanisms that differ from those during solitary activity. Examples are the gradual shift in responsibility in problem solving from the adult or more competent peer to the child, internalization of verbal or nonverbal interaction with the other person, modeling, and changing one's perspective (see also chap. 11, this volume). Researchers have documented the value of adults' scaffolding a child's attempts to learn in mother–child or experimenter–child interaction over time during problem solving in a single session (e.g., Chletsos & DeLisi, 1991; Saxe,

Guberman, & Gearhart, 1987; Wertsch & Hickmann, 1987). A microgenetic design is useful for documenting in a specific way a child's gradually taking on more responsibility for problem solving (e.g., Wertsch & Hickmann, 1987). Such a design tracks, and correlates, specific moment-to-moment changes in the nature of the social interaction and specific changes in cognitive performance. Moreover, even simply embedding individual problem-solving activity in a social context may elicit different microgenetic processes. For example, preschoolers who participated in a mathematical-oriented activity while trying to fill customers' requests for orders of vegetables in a play-store setting across three sessions became increasingly efficient at choosing the best strategies (Cohen, 1996).

As for perspective changes, Siegler (1995) found that microgenetic training of conservation of number was more effective when 5-year-olds were asked to explain the reasoning behind an adult's feedback (i.e., the correct answer) than when only feedback or feedback and explanations were requested. Thus, when the social context requires children to consider the reasoning of others, change is encouraged.

In addition to these studies of adult scaffolding or other intervention, a few microgenetic studies of peer dyads or small groups have begun to appear. Small groups may co-construct more advanced knowledge structures during problem solving by considering each other's statements, actions, and gestures (Fischer & Granott, 1995). Ellis, Klahr, and Siegler (1993) showed that peer collaboration can cause change. They examined microgenetic changes in solving decimal problems (e.g., "Which is bigger, 0.239 or 0.47?") during peer collaborations. Fifth-grade dyads solved 12 problems in a single session. On each problem, the two children first gave their answers independently and then compared their answers and explained their own answers. Two other groups solved problems either alone or "alone with explanation" (i.e., explained their answers to the experimenter). Some children received feedback (i.e., the correct answer) on each problem, and others did not. The opportunity to work with a peer facilitated performance over working alone, but only when accuracy feedback was provided. Interestingly, the most successful dyads were those in which one child reacted with interest and enthusiasm to the other child's correct explanation. Notably, dyads who generated the correct solution together, rather than one child before the other or one child not at all, gave the clearest explanations. In a negative direction, a partner offering vague or confusing explanations did not bring about consistently correct performance in the dyad. Moreover, unsuccessful dyads tended to shift the discussion from solutions to problems. Thus, microgenetic changes during collaborative problem solving differs from those of independent problem solving in important ways. Social collaborative processes, including motivation, influence whether a new solution to a problem emerges, solidifies, and survives. For example, a child who generates a correct strategy during microgenesis may abandon it if the partner does not respond positively. By tracking trial-by-trial changes in the performance of each child in a dyad and temporally linking specific types of social changes and specific cognitive events (Ellis, 1995), researchers can provide a much more precise picture of socially embedded change than did previous nonmicrogenetic studies.

One largely unexplored application of the microgenetic method is a careful examination of the effects of various types or degrees of help from other people. There may, for example, be different patterns of change following adults' prompts and direct interventions. Studies of adult instruction assess the degree of progress in a child, but typically do not conduct a detailed analysis of the trial-by-trial changes during and after the intervention.

Our final comment about the social realm is that social behavior is not only an influence on behavior but also a phenomenon that itself can be studied microgenetically. To our knowledge, there are no multitrial, multisession studies focusing on social cognition, social strategies (e.g., help seeking, persuasion), or social behavior. Microgenetic changes in social behavior may be rapid during key events, such as starting school (Siegler, 1996). The few "social" microgenetic studies already discussed have involved two people working together to solve a nonsocial problem.

Change in Other Populations

The microgenetic method could fruitfully be extended to studying change in diverse populations. For example, this method could reveal the specific ways in which children with low IQs, high IQs, or learning disabilities specifically diverge from their peers in one or more of the aspects of change described earlier—path, rate, breadth, variability, and sources of change. For example, high IQ children show more stable strategy use (i.e., fewer adding or removing of strategies) across trials and greater recall than do nongifted children (Coyle, Colbert, & Read, 1997). Thus, gifted children consistently used successful strategies. Moreover, although infants seem to be ideal subjects for a microgenetic analysis because they are developing so rapidly, little such research exists.

CONCLUSIONS

The microgenetic approach offers a useful lens through which to view change. This approach addresses some of the same issues as did Piaget's assimilation–accommodation model of change, such as the emergence of new knowledge, the interplay of old and new knowledge, and the relations between quantitative and qualitative change. The microgenetic approach, however, offers a different methodology for examining these issues and thus has produced a new set of findings about change in strategies, reasoning, and problem solving: Change is characterized by within-child and between-child variability, and old and new concepts or strategies coexist for quite a while. New acquisitions or selection among current skills cannot be predicted by simple models based on previous success or failure. Both a child's initial level of competence and the specific learning, social, or task environment affect the course of change. Change can be halting and uneven and even involve a temporary regression or period of ineffectiveness of a new, advanced skill. Quantitative and qualitative changes are intertwined.

Microgenetic concepts and methods can be fruitfully integrated with other approaches to produce a powerful account of change. By providing badly needed tools for identifying and understanding mechanisms of development, the microgenetic approach advances our understanding of cognitive development. The suggested extensions of the approach can further fulfill its promise as a way to identify sources of developmental change.

ACKNOWLEDGMENTS

The authors thank Robert Siegler, Shari Ellis, and this volume's editors for their comments on an earlier draft of this chapter.

REFERENCES

Alibali, M. W. (1994). *Processes of cognitive change revealed in gesture and speech.* Unpublished doctoral dissertation, University of Chicago, Chicago, IL.

Alibali, M. W., & Goldin-Meadow, S. (1993). Gesture–speech mismatch and mechanisms of learning: What the hands reveal about a child's state of mind. *Cognitive Psychology, 25,* 468–573.

Alibali, M. W., & Perrott, M. A. (1996, June). *The structure of children's verbal explanations reveals the stability of their knowledge.* Paper presented at the meeting of the Jean Piaget Society, Philadelphia, PA.

Bidell, T. R. (1990). *Mechanisms of cognitive development in problem solving: A structural integration approach.* Unpublished doctoral dissertation, Harvard University, Cambridge, MA.

Bjorklund, D. F., & Coyle, T. R. (1995). Utilization deficiencies in the development of memory strategies. In F. E. Weinert and W. Schneider (Eds.), *Memory performance and competencies: Issues in growth and development* (pp. 161–180). Mahwah, NJ: Lawrence Erlbaum Associates.

Bjorklund, D. F., Coyle, T. R., & Gaultney, J. F. (1992). Developmental differences in the acquisition and maintenance of an organizational strategy: Evidence for the utilization deficiency hypothesis. *Journal of Experimental Child Psychology, 54,* 434–438.

Bjorklund, D. F., Miller, P. H., Coyle, T. R., & Slawinski, J. L. (1997). Instructing children to use memory strategies: Evidence of utilization deficiencies in memory training studies. *Developmental Review, 17,* 411–441.

Bjorklund, D. F., Schneider, W., Cassel, W. S., & Ashley, E. (1994). Training and extension of a memory strategy: Evidence for utilization deficiencies in the acquisition of an organizational strategy in high- and low-IQ children. *Child Development, 65,* 951–965.

Catan, L. (1986). The dynamic display of process: Historical development and contemporary uses of the microgenetic method. *Human Development, 29,* 252–263.

Chletsos, P. N., & DeLisi, R. (1991). A microgenetic study of proportional reasoning using balance scale problems. *Journal of Applied Developmental Psychology, 12,* 307–330.

Church, R. B. (1990, May). *Equilibration: Using gesture and speech to monitor cognitive change.* Paper presented at the meeting of the Jean Piaget Society, Philadelphia, PA.

Church, R. B., & Goldin-Meadow, S. (1986). The mismatch between gesture and speech as an index of transitional knowledge. *Cognition, 23,* 43–71.

Cohen, M. (1996). Preschoolers' practical thinking and problem solving: The acquisition of an optimal solution strategy. *Cognitive Development, 11,* 357–373.

Cooney, J. B., Swanson, H. L., & Ladd, S. F. (1988). Acquisition of mental multiplication skill: Evidence for the transition between counting and retrieval strategies. *Cognition and Instruction, 5,* 323–345.

Coyle, T. R. (1997). *Variability and utilization deficiencies in children's memory strategies: A developmental study.* Unpublished doctoral dissertation, University of Florida, Gainesville.

Coyle, T. R., & Bjorklund, D. F. (1996). The development of strategic memory: A modified microgenetic assessment of utilization deficiencies. *Cognitive Development, 11,* 295–314.

Coyle, T. R., & Bjorklund, D. F. (1997). Age differences in, and consequences of, multiple- and variable-strategy use on a multitrial sort–recall task. *Developmental Psychology, 33,* 372–380.

Coyle, T. R., Colbert, C. T., & Read, L. E. (1997, March). *Strategy variability and memory performance in average-and high-IQ children.* Paper presented at the meeting of the Society for Research in Child Development, Washington, DC.

Crowder, E. M., & Newman, D. (1993). Telling what they know: The role of gesture and language in children's science explanations. *Pragmatics and Cognition, 1,* 341–376.

Crowley, K., & Siegler, R. S. (1993). Flexible strategy use in young children's tic-tac-toe. *Cognitive Science, 17,* 531–561.

Duncan, R. M., & Pratt, M. W. (1997). Microgenetic change in the quantity and quality of preschoolers' private speech. *International Journal of Behavioral Development, 20,* 367–383.

Duncker, K. (1945). On problem solving. *Psychological Monographs, 58* (Whole no. 270).

Ellis, S. (1995, April). *Social influences on strategy choice.* Paper presented at the meeting of the Society for Research in Child Development, Indianapolis, IN.

Ellis, S., Klahr, D., & Siegler, R. S. (1993, March). *Effects of feedback and collaboration on changes in children's use of mathematical rules.* Paper presented at the meeting of the Society for Research in Child Development, New Orleans, LA.

Fireman, G. (1996). Developing a plan for solving a problem: A representational shift. *Cognitive Development, 11,* 107–122.

Fischer, K. W. (1980). A theory of cognitive development: The control and construction of hierarchies of skills. *Psychological Review, 87,* 477–531.

Fischer, K. W., & Granott, N. (1995). Beyond one-dimensional change: Multiple, concurrent, socially distributed processes in learning and development. *Human Development, 38,* 302–314.

Flavell, J. H. (1972). An analysis of cognitive-developmental sequences. *Genetic Psychology Monographs, 86,* 279–350.

Flavell, J. H., Miller, P. H., & Miller, S. A. (1993). *Cognitive development* (3rd ed.). Englewood Cliffs, NJ: Prentice-Hall.

Goldin-Meadow, S., & Alibali, M. W. (1995). Mechanisms of transition: Learning with a helping hand. In D. Medin (Ed.), *The psychology of learning and motivation* (Vol. 33, pp. 115–157). New York: Academic Press.

Goldin-Meadow, S., Alibali, M. W., & Church, R. B. (1993). Transitions in concept acquisition: Using the hand to read the mind. *Psychological Review, 100*, 279–297.

Goldin-Meadow, S., Nusbaum, H., Garber, P., & Church, R. B. (1993). Transitions in learning: Evidence for simultaneously activated hypotheses. *Journal of Experimental Psychology: Human Perception and Performance, 19*, 92–107.

Graham, T. (1994, June). *The role of gesture in learning to count*. Paper presented at the meeting of the Jean Piaget Society, Chicago, IL.

Graham, T., & Perry, M. (1993). Indexing transitional knowledge. *Developmental Psychology, 29*, 779–788.

Granott, N. (1994). *From macro to micro and back: An analysis and explanation of microdevelopment.* Unpublished manuscript.

Granott, N. (1995, March). *How is knowledge co-constructed? A microdevelopmental view.* Paper presented at the meeting of the Society for Research in Child Development, Indianapolis, IN.

Granott, N. (1996). *The dynamics of problem solving: Rediscovery, variability, and the complexity of making sense.* Unpublished manuscript.

Harnishfeger, K. K., & Bjorklund, D. F. (1990). Children's strategies: A brief history. In D. F. Bjorklund (Ed.), *Children's strategies: Contemporary views of cognitive development* (pp. 1–22). Hillsdale, NJ: Lawrence Erlbaum Associates.

Johnson, K. E., & Mervis, C. B. (1994). Microgenetic analysis of first steps in children's acquisition of expertise on shorebirds. *Developmental Psychology, 30*, 418–435.

Karmiloff-Smith, A. (1984). Children's problem solving. In M. Lamb, A. L. Brown, & B. Rogoff (Eds.), *Advances in developmental psychology* (Vol. 3, pp. 39–89). Hillsdale, NJ: Lawrence Erlbaum Associates.

Karmiloff-Smith, A. (1986). Stage/structure versus phase/process in modelling linguistic and cognitive development. In I. Levin (Ed.), *Stage and structure: Reopening the debate* (pp. 160–190). Norwood, NJ: Ablex.

Karmiloff-Smith, A. (1992). *Beyond modularity: A developmental perspective on cognitive science.* Cambridge, MA: MIT Press.

Karmiloff-Smith, A., & Inhelder, B. (1974). If you want to get ahead, get a theory. *Cognition, 3*, 195–212.

Kuhn, D. (1995). Microgenetic study of change: What has it told us? *Psychological Science, 6*, 133–139.

Kuhn, D., Garcia-Mila, M., Zohar, A., & Anderson, C. (1995). Strategies of knowledge acquisition. *Monographs of the Society for Research in Child Development, 60* (Serial No. 245).

Kuhn, D., & Ho, V. (1980). Self directed activity and cognitive development. *Journal of Applied Developmental Psychology, 1*, 119–133.

Kuhn, D., & Phelps, E. (1982). The development of problem-solving strategies. In H. Reese (Ed.), *Advances in child development and behavior* (Vol. 17, pp. 1–44). New York: Academic Press.

Kuhn, D., Schauble, L., & Garcia-Mila, M. (1992). Cross-domain development of scientific reasoning. *Cognition and Instruction, 9*, 285–327.

McGilly, K., & Siegler, R. S. (1989). How children choose among serial recall strategies. *Child Development, 60*, 172–182.

Metz, K. (1985). The development of children's problem solving in a gears task: A problem space perspective. *Cognitive Science, 9*, 431–472.

Miller, P. H. (1990). The development of strategies of selective attention. In D. F. Bjorklund (Ed.), *Children's strategies: Contemporary views of cognitive development* (pp. 157–184). Hillsdale, NJ: Lawrence Erlbaum Associates.

Miller, P. H., & Aloise-Young, P. (1996). Preschoolers' strategic behaviors and performance on a same-different task. *Journal of Experimental Child Psychology, 60,* 284–303.

Miller, P. H., & Harris, Y. R. (1988). Preschoolers' strategies of attention on a same-different task. *Developmental Psychology, 24,* 628–633.

Miller, P. H., & Seier, W. S. (1994). Strategy utilization deficiencies in children: When, where and why. In H. W. Reese (Ed.), *Advances in child development and behavior* (Vol. 25, pp. 107–156). New York: Academic Press.

Miller, P. H., Seier, W. S., Probert, J. S., & Aloise, P. A. (1991). Age differences in the capacity demands of a strategy among spontaneously strategic children. *Journal of Experimental Child Psychology, 52,* 149–165.

Perry, M., Church, R. B., & Goldin-Meadow, S. (1988). Transitional knowledge in the acquisition of concepts. *Cognitive Development, 3,* 359–400.

Perry, M., & Elder, A. D. (1997). Knowledge in transition: Adults' developing understanding of a principle of physical causality. *Cognitive Development, 12,* 131–157.

Pressley, M. (1992). How *not* to study strategy discovery. *American Psychologist, 47,* 1240–1241.

Saxe, G. B., Guberman, S. R., & Gearhart, M. (1987). Social processes in early number development. *Monographs of the Society for Research in Child Development, 52* (Serial No. 216).

Schauble, L. (1996). The development of scientific reasoning in knowledge-rich contexts. *Developmental Psychology, 32,* 102–119.

Shimojo, S., Bauer, J., O'Connell, K. M., & Held, R. (1986). Pre-stereoptic binocular vision in infants. *Vision Research, 26,* 501–510.

Shrager, J., & Siegler, R. S. (1998). SCADS: A model of children's strategy choices and strategy discoveries. *Psychological Science, 9,* 405–410.

Siegler, R. S. (1987). The perils of averaging data over strategies: An example from children's addition. *Journal of Experimental Psychology: General, 116,* 250–264.

Siegler, R. S. (1995). How does change occur: A microgenetic study of number conservation. *Cognitive Psychology, 25,* 225–273.

Siegler, R. S. (1996). *Emerging minds: The process of change in children's thinking.* New York: Oxford University Press.

Siegler, R. S., & Crowley, K. (1991). The microgenetic method: A direct means for studying cognitive development. *American Psychologist, 46,* 606–620.

Siegler, R. S., & Jenkins, E. (1989). *How children discover new strategies.* Hillsdale, NJ: Lawrence Erlbaum Associates.

Siegler, R. S., & McGilly, K. (1989). Strategy choices in children's time-telling. In I. Levin & D. Zakay (Eds.), *Time and human cognition: A life span perspective* (pp. 185–218). Amsterdam, The Netherlands: Elsevier.

Siegler, R. S., & Shipley, C. (1995). Variation, selection, and cognitive change. In T. Simon & G. Halford (Eds.), *Developing cognitive competence: New approaches to process modeling* (pp. 31–76). Hillsdale, NJ: Lawrence Erlbaum Associates.

Siegler, R. S., & Stern, E. (in press). Conscious and unconscious strategy discoveries: A microgenetic analysis. *Journal of Experimental Psychology: General.*

Thelen, E. (1992). Development as a dynamic system. *Current Directions in Psychological Science, 1,* 189–193.

Thelen, E., Fisher, D. M., & Ridley-Johnson, R. (1984). Shifting patterns of bilateral coordination and lateral dominance in the leg movements of young infants. *Developmental Psychology, 16,* 29–46.

Thelen, E., & Smith, L. B. (1994). *A dynamic systems approach to the development of cognition and action.* Cambridge, MA: MIT Press/Bradford Books.

van Geert, P. (1994). *Dynamic systems of development: Change between complexity and chaos.* New York: Harvester-Wheatsheaf.

Van Voorhis, F. E., & Ellis, S. (1997, June). *A microgenetic study of the development of iteration in linear measurement.* Paper presented at the meeting of the Jean Piaget Society, Santa Monica, CA.

Vygotsky, L. S. (1978). *Mind and society: The development of higher mental processes.* Cambridge, MA: Harvard University Press.

Werner, H. (1948). *Comparative psychology of mental development.* New York: International Universities Press.

Wertsch, J. V., & Hickmann, M. (1987). Problem solving in social interaction: A microgenetic analysis. In M. Hickmann (Ed.), *Social and functional approaches to language and thought* (pp. 251–266). Orlando, FL: Academic Press.

Wertsch, J. V., & Stone, C. A. (1978). Microgenesis as a tool for developmental analysis. *Laboratory of Comparative Human Cognition, 1,* 8–10.

Part III

WHAT ACCOUNTS FOR THE NOVELTIES THAT ARE THE PRODUCTS AND PRODUCERS OF DEVELOPMENTAL CHANGE?

Chapter 10

The Origin of Piaget's Ideas About Genesis and Development

Jacques Voneche
Archives Jean Piaget, University of Geneva

My aim, in this chapter, is to describe some origins of Piaget's thought and some problems that flow from these origins. I show how Piaget made growing children an instrument for the empirical study of epistemology and used children as evidence for the validity of his own brand of epistemology: genetic epistemology. I do this by tracing the origin of his ideas about genesis and development in other intellectual traditions and describing their subsequent assimilation and transformation by Piaget. Piaget's forging of genetic epistemology in turn raised theoretical and empirical questions for future psychologists to address.

SABATIER

When Piaget started to think over philosophical problems, around the age of 15, he had the good fortune to read Sabatier's (1839–1901) *Esquisse d'une philosophie de la religion d'après la psychologie et l'histoire* (1897), from which he retained the idea that religious dogmas can be reduced to mere symbols evolving over time, as he wrote in his autobiography of 1952. This book was based on the idea that the only way that a young Christian can face and resolve the conflict between science and faith, as it stood at the turn of the century, was by cultivating the feeling of the presence of God in his consciousness, independently of dogmas and institutions. Thus, from then on, Piaget's philosophy was always one of consciousness in the phenomenological tradition of Edmund Husserl (1859–1938), for whom the aim of any consciousness was knowledge. Husserl's transcendental subject is a distant cousin of the future epistemic subject because the latter is also a transcendental abstraction.

BERGSON

The other influence that explains the double concentration on evolution and on knowledge is, of course, Piaget's famous reading of Bergson's (1859–1941) *Creative Evolution* (1911/1907) around 1912, at about the same time as his reading of Sabatier. What Piaget retained from this was the opposition between a science of genera according to Aristotle and a science of laws. The standard science is one of laws, and it leads to a repetitious geometric order allowing mathematical generalization. In opposition to this standard approach, Bergson proposed a revival of the old Aristotelian science of genera based not on a deadly mathematical order but on a living order relying on *élan vital*, a vital impulse springing from life itself and characterized by transformation and change, development, in a word. This vital impulse led, in Bergson's view, to a moral impulse specific to human beings.

BRENTANO

These writers were the recognized influences on Piaget's development, but there were others unrecognized and even denied, such as Darwin's (1809–1882) notion of adaptation and Franz Brentano's (1838–1917) notion of intentional inexistence, psychology, and logic as they appeared in his *Psychology from an Empirical Standpoint* (1995/1874). This book, published in the same year as Wundt's *Grundzüge der physiologischen Psychologie* [Fundamentals of physiological psychology] (1874), represented an entirely different approach to psychology. Whereas Wundt, Fechner, Helmholtz, and Müller believed in "content-psychology" and in rigorous experimental methodology, Brentano was the source of "act-psychology" conforming to the observational methodology of natural sciences as they existed at the time.

This observational methodology is important for understanding Piaget's history and development, because it is the one to which Piaget turned all his life. It is based on an epistemology of the gaze (*épistémologie du regard*), as Michel Foucault put it in *Les Mots et les choses* (1966). The main instrument of observation is the eye: By looking at things, one finds truth. In other words, one reads directly in the great book of Nature. This presupposition explains some archaic aspects of the clinical method "à la Piaget" as well as its difficulties with the U.S. tradition of psychology, which focused on controlled, as opposed to natural, observation.

The influence of Brentano's ideas on his student Sigmund Freud also explains another aspect of the clinical method: its reliance on what children tell as they tell it. The psychoanalytical inspiration for this method has often been pointed out but *not* its origin in Brentano's epistemology and its influence on Husserl. Here, subjectivity is epistemologically valid. In contrast, experimentalists distrust direct self-reports.

At the conceptual level, Piaget was impressed by Brentano's notion of "intentional inexistence," that is, the relation existing between the external object aimed at by consciousness and its internal in-tention (as for a bow in tension) or mental phenomenon. Brentano focused on the nature of meaning and references: An object out there serves as an external referent to an immanent object in the mental sphere (the representation). For instance, a sound is both an external noise and an internal experience of a sound. As we can see, this notion anticipated several ideas of Piaget's, like *le schème*, assimilation, accommodation, or interiorization. It was also based on a combination of ideas taken from both Descartes and British empiricism—No idea, no content—and fit with Piaget's logic of meanings, in which reflective abstraction allowed the mapping of inner knowledge onto various domains of objective knowledge.

BALDWIN

The same synthesis from opposites was made by another whose influence on Piaget has been rarely recognized: James Mark Baldwin (1895). Baldwin unified two opposing currents—the pragmatic current represented by the Puritans (Edwards), natural realism (McCash), eclectic spiritualism (Cousin), scientific realism (Lotze), positivism (Spence), and utilitarianism; and the rationalistic current of anti-Puritanism (Franklin, Johnson, Münsterberg), transcendentalism (Emerson), German idealism, Hegelianism, and absolute idealism (Royce)—into his epistemological evolutionism or pancalism. Baldwin's work influenced Piaget immensely because it suggested that one good way to grasp the nature of mind was through a study of its genesis, or what Baldwin had called genetic epistemology, after Hegel's (1770–1831) *Phenomenology of Mind* (1931/1807). Here again, as in Brentano's psychology, the mind was not a substance fixed, once and for all, but an activity that was "growing and developing" (Baldwin, 1894, p. 2). Psychology was linked with evolution. The very breaking up of phenomena changed radically with Baldwin. Whereas British empiricism practiced a form of genesis by associations of simple sensations, Baldwin wanted to show how psychological processes cut into the relatively undifferentiated form of primitive experience to construct differentiated structures that could be ordered into a developmental sequence.

Contrary to Darwin's or Spencer's organisms, Baldwin's organisms were not neutral with respect to the world. Anatomically and physiologically as well as behaviorally, Baldwinian organisms announced certain tendencies— "hypotheses," "beliefs," and "theories" about the world—that Baldwin called *orthoplasia*. As Baldwin (1894) wrote in *Mental Evolution in the Child and in the Race*:

> We end up with the consideration that evolution from one generation to the next most probably took place under the joint action of natural selection and organic selection in such a way that the direction of racial variations coincided with that of individual adaptations. We arrive at an hypothesis unifying ontogeny with phylogeny in all animal series. All the influences helping animal adaptations and accommodations are combined in one resulting effect to give a determined orientation to the course of evolution. We call these *orienting* influences *orthoplasia*. (chap. 7, sect. 4, p. 41)

This quotation shows the place of psychological research in the economy of Baldwin's genetic epistemology. Psychology should explain the role of individuals in evolution. *Individual accommodations*, as Baldwin called them, were supposed to be momentary substitutes (at the phenotypic level, in today's language) for future "congenital variations" (genotypic variations in post-Mendelian terms) that happen after a certain period of individual behavioral adaptation. Baldwin conceived this distinction as an answer to an objection raised against natural selection when applied to complex entities such as instincts.

In the hypothesis of organic selection proposed by Baldwin, instincts did not need to emerge all mounted and ready to serve. On the contrary, individual accommodations, as conceived by Baldwin, allowed for a more-or-less long period of tinkering with individual, behavioral, local, and cumulative forms of adaptation of natural tendencies to the new situation. The role of these accommodations was to produce an effective complex organ or behavior without having to wait for a mutation (in post-Mendelian terms) to "throw up" just the one gene that was needed, by simply selecting genes already present in low frequencies in a normal population (diploid population in modern biological terms).

In such a perspective, psychology occupied a central place in the system. As the study of behavior, psychology has the task to describe and analyze the unfolding of the transition from one form of natural selection to another. This observation is supposed to provide scientists with the actually missing links in phylogenesis. Contemporary children are the remnants of past-primitive humans. As such, children are living fossils.

HAECKEL, BRUNSCHVICG, CLAPARÈDE, AND DARWIN

This link between ontogeny and phylogeny took very similar forms in Baldwin's biology and in Piaget's phenocopy. The link was influenced in Piaget's thinking by Haeckel's views on recapitulation. Recapitulation has often been considered by psychologists in the simplistic way in which G. Stanley Hall used to view it. In fact, Haeckel was searching, in embryonic development, for the proof for evolution. To him, the evidence in favor of evolution was to be found in the creation of new *forms* of life because every new form is the living memory of a stage of development. To him, the body of the individual was the memory of the species. Every single body preserved the trace of the passage of evolution through itself and could be ordered in a progressive sequence in which every progress in phylogeny was conserved in ontogeny.

The difference between Haeckel's view and Hall's approach is that, when Hall considered contents, Haeckel had processes in mind. Piaget was sensitive to the difference and formed a project similar to Haeckel's. Piaget created a sort of mental embryology to study the mechanisms of evolution and development in the conquest of reality by the growing mind. His theory of knowledge was one of adaptation to reality. But reality, for Piaget, had always a ring of "Bishop Berkeley's idealism," as his mentor, Arnold Reymond (1874–1958), pointed out. So much so that, when Piaget encountered the writings of the French philosopher Léon Brunschvicg (1869–1944), he agreed with Brunschvicg's idea that the assertion of being is based on the determination of being as known and not being as such, as realism has it. This knowledge is attained by a logical analysis of positive science—its history and vicissitudes—which reveals to the mind its unity and infinite spontaneity. Hence, history is the laboratory of the genetic epistemologist. But, if we request from history the secret of the forming mechanisms of knowledge, it should also be able to reconstitute the most elementary cognitive proceedings of prehistoric human beings as well as the very process of humanization. Hence, the unavoidable solution to fill the gaps in our knowledge about this process at the phylogenic level is an appeal to embryogeny and mental ontogeny.

Therefore, genetic epistemology must become a comparative anatomy of the operations of thought and a theory of evolution by mental adaptation to reality. The result is a focus on intelligence and intellectual mechanisms because intelligence, in this pragmatic-idealistic perspective, is nothing but the need for adaptation that arises whenever an individual is faced with an environmental perturbation or disequilibrium between the self and the world. Thus, intelligence becomes a function like breathing or digesting. As Claparède (1873–1940) pointed out, if little children are not reasonable, it is because there is no need or advantage in their present condition to be so, just as the tadpole finds no advantage in having legs and lungs to live in water. This statement presents the functionalist position in all its naked beauty. Piaget drew two conclusions from it: the principle of the immutability of function, which is life itself or the very act of surviving, and the principle of organic and structural transformations that are necessary for development. For instance, the function of the logical principle of noncontradiction remains invariant in the course of mental development, but the structures of logical consistency vary over time during children's growth and the history of humankind.

This central epistemological position about the nature of genesis had immediate consequences in Piaget's thinking. At the biological level, it supposed the rejection of Darwinism for several reasons. At the beginning of Piaget's oeuvre, the rejection was essentially moral: The idea of the struggle for life is an ideology of war, conflict, and death. It favors the bad boys against the good ones, the rich and greedy against the poor and needy. Later, the rejection became factual; Piaget thought that his study of the transplantation of *Limnea lacustris* into lakes with turbulent waters in which they adapted and transmitted this adaptation to their descendants was the demonstration of *phenocopy*. Still later, the rejection became logical. The argument of the survival of the fittest was considered as circular: Who is the fittest? The survivor! Who survives? The fittest. Finally, natural selection made thinking a random process and science very chancy. Life becomes fortuitous, and that is absurd.

KNOWLEDGE AND SOCIETY

At the sociological level, Piaget's position entailed the rejection of the so-called Durkheimian hypothesis of the social genesis of cognition and action, according to which there is a necessary correspondence between social structures, more accurately power structures, and mental structures. This correspondence was thought to be mediated by the structure of symbolic systems such as language, art, religion, and so forth. This rejection came late in Piaget's life. At first, in the 1920s, he thought that social pressure was the source of the passage from egocentrism to social decentration. It was Henri Wallon (1879–1962) who, during a discussion in 1928, at the French Société de Philosophie, changed Piaget's thinking by showing that without the nervous system nothing at all would happen. Piaget remembered this discussion in March 1979 (51 years after), when I interviewed him on Baldwin. He had forgotten Wallon, but he remembered that, because the nervous system is not a social product, the Durkheimian hypothesis must be rejected. Then what? What remained for Piaget, at the social level, was the gradual emergence of cooperation over egocentricism.

Because cooperation could be spelled *co-operation* and because operation is mental, the problem was solved! Here once again the function remained the same, social relation, but it took many successive forms: solipsism, egocentrism, reciprocity in social contract, and co-operation in the sense of logical operation with a co-subject.

GENETIC EPISTEMOLOGY: FUNCTIONAL
CONTINUITY AND STRUCTURAL CHANGE

At the psychological level, the continuity of functions in the discontinuity of structures led to the rejection of both behaviorism and Gestalt psychology, because the former is a genesis without structure and the latter a structure deprived of any genesis. This same line of reasoning can also be applied to various scientific domains. In mathematics, it denies the realism of universals (as being without genesis) as well as of conventionalism (as being solely socially determined) in favor a relativistic form of constructivism. It rejects apriorism and empiricism for the same reasons as for behaviorism and Gestalt psychology. In physics, it shows that all progress is due to a double process of mathematization of physics and physicalization of mathematics.

Thus, children became the living laboratory in which to solve the paradoxes appearing in and among different scientific theories, in the same way that history of science was the laboratory of epistemologists for Brunschvicg. But, if it is relatively easy to know what is meant by history of science, it is much more complicated to know which child is the epistemic subject. After all, childhood, as a separate period of life, is largely dependent on the culture and its particular demands, and, even in Western societies, it is historically dated. Historians have often disagreed about exact dates, but they have agreed on the fact that childhood as a social institution protecting children is extending continuously: Godefroid de Bouillon was a chevalier at 12, Turenne a general at 16 and Napoleon at 20, whereas Schwarzkopf was one at 50. This fact is also apparent in the successive editions of the Wechsler Intelligence Scale, in which the apogee of intellectual competence goes from the age of 16 to 21, reflecting the extension of average schooling over the period that the test was restandardized.

Piaget's children develop according to the history of Western science so much so that non-Westerners show some delay relative to the average development of Westerners; sometimes, in any locale, people regress in their intellectual and moral development. Nevertheless, the sequencing apparently remains the same over the world and over time, and that fact is important from the epistemological standpoint. Of course, it could be argued that this sequencing always goes from the simple to the complex and as such is a truism. But, as Piaget himself pointed out to Fauville in a discussion in Geneva in 1955, this is one more piece of evidence in favor of constructivism, because, if nativism is correct, then there is no reason for gradualism at all, and if empiricism is right, then there is no need for a logical order of development. Thus, the only tenable position is indeed genetic rationalistic constructivism.

Children's spontaneity was fundamental in Piaget's *méthode clinique*. This hypothesis is naturalistic and seems contradictory to that of children as social constructs, which can be historically dated in history and geographically located. Spontaneity goes against the idea of childhood as an institution imagined by the Western world to reproduce its labor forces through an appropriate period of training. Spontaneous development supposes a nature of children absolutely similar to what is called human nature. A spontaneous force (equilibration) pushes development and is inherent in the species.

The corollary of such a spontaneous force is indeed that with the attribution to children of a "nature" goes a universal law of development in the same way that the attribution of human nature entails a universal natural law. But the sorry corollary of this corollary is the possibility of mistaking institutional facts for natural ones and observed facts for norms. When Piaget spoke of an immanent law, he was not far from such a logical error.

NORMS AND NATURE

Normative facts have the privilege of naturalizing institutional phenomena and, by so doing, they legitimize institutional practices and prejudices by ascribing them to biology. A case in point, here, is the status of the concept of maturity. From the descriptive, objective status that the concept has in biology, which is ripeness for something, be it falling off the tree or mating, it acquires, in psychology and social sciences, the status of being impeccable in the eyes of an observer. Maturity is achievement of an organism's essence. The descriptive concept has surreptitiously become prescriptive. Far from being a mere factual observation directly read in the great book of Nature, genesis is a concept by postulation and requires an immanent law to explain it. This law supposes, in turn, a general principle of differentiation and integration of the parts into a whole and thus the logical priority of the whole over the parts as well as the irreducibility of the superior to the inferior. Such a system prevents us from fusing development with passage of time or with accumulation. The oldest forms are not necessarily the most primitive. History is no more the servant of Perfection. Time is not the father of Progress. Recency is not decency. From a logical point of view, these forms are ordered into meaningful sequences. Now, the question is: Is this logic innate or acquired? Is this logic a mere unfolding of neuronal potentialities or is it the result of societal pressures?

Here, again, we feel the strong influence of Lamarckism on Piaget's ideas. Lamarck, in his system of evolution, involved two explanatory factors: one metaphysical in nature, the other environmental. The metaphysical factor was the inalterable scale of living beings that cannot be changed and that form the natural order of species. The environmental factor was called "circumstances" by Lamarck, and it sends readers back to the ideas of the French Revolution. Naturalists of that time had an idea of Nature as being the opposite of the hierarchical Nature imagined by Christian theologians of the Middle Ages. They wanted an egalitarian Nature in which all species were equal but in which some were more active than others. For these naturalists as for Piaget, *behavior* was the motor of evolution. Why behavior and not another candidate, like natural selection, for instance, that fitted so well with the invention of the guillotine? Because behavior was for them at the crossroad between innate organism and environment. Behavior was the way that the body came to grips with the external world. Behavior was action. Action was thus logical; logic was the morality of action, and morality was the logic of action. That conception expressed in these very words by Claparède and Piaget explains a strange aspect of Piaget's thinking by which actions, at the level of concrete operations, suddenly get truth values attached to them. This view is unusual both for action and for logic; logic is more often linked to discourse and argumentation or to language in general. Values, for Piaget, including moral values, found their source in action. Thus, Piaget had no special interest in practical issues, which he conceived of as pure execution of the symbolic functions. Action was not praxis in Piaget's system.

Finally, this genetic approach supposed a certain representation of sciences as unitary and of the history of science as a celebration of genesis. This representation raises the question of the multiplicity of disciplines, whereas Piaget recognized only logic, mathematics, physics, biology, psychology, and sociology. Does mineralogy raise epistemological questions or not? If so, are they specific? Has geography a place in the circle of sciences? All these are open questions.

As far as the history of science is concerned, has not Piaget selected the good examples for his theory as in the case of geometries and Bourbaki's structures? The case is debatable and open to further investigation. Nevertheless, the relation between children's ideas and ancient scientific theories seems striking. Is it superficial? The question can be solved by careful historical studies showing what children thought when adults were thinking like children: a difficult question from many angles. Do we know enough about the modes of thinking of the children of the past? Is the historical passage from childish to adult-thinking-at-a-professional-level authorized scientifically? Doubts can be raised.

In spite of all these open questions, the fact remains that genetic epistemology is an epistemology of the self in which children are taken seriously and can express creativity and personality. This view alone is no small achievement indeed.

REFERENCES

Baldwin, J. M. (1895). *Mental evolution in the child and in the race.* New York: Macmillan.
Bergson, H. (1911). *Creative evolution* (A. Mitchell, Trans.). New York: Holt. (Original work published 1907)
Brentano, F. (1995). *Psychology from an empirical standpoint* (A. C. Rancullo, D. B. Terrell, & L. L. McAlister, Trans.). London & New York: Routledge. (Original work published 1874)
Foucault, M. (1966). *Les mots et les choses.* Paris: Gallimard.
Hegel, G. W. F. (1931). *Phenomenology of mind* (2nd ed.). London & New York: J. B. Baillie. (Original work published 1807)
Sabatier, A. (1897). *Esquisse d'une philosophie de la religion d'après la psychologie et l'histoire.* Paris: Fischbacher.
Wundt, W. M. (1874). *Grundzüge der physiologischen Psychologie* [Fundamentals of physiological psychology]. Leipzig, Germany: Müller.

Chapter 11

Sources of Concepts: A Cultural–Developmental Perspective

Geoffrey B. Saxe
University of California, Berkeley

Piaget's legacy is manifest across a wide range of research endeavors in the behavioral and social sciences. In this chapter, I point to the way that Piaget's theory provides an important basis for my own work on the interplay between culture and cognitive development. In keeping with my charge by the volume's editors, I target sources of development.

INTRODUCTION

Researchers seeking to explain cognitive development have looked to a range of possible social and cultural sources. Some have analyzed social interactional processes, either between adults and children (e.g., Wertsch, 1979; Wood, Bruner, & Ross, 1976) or between peers (e.g., Saxe, Gearhart, Note, & Paduano, 1993; Webb, 1982) as sources of development. Others have identified language and other symbolic or material artifacts as sources of change (Miura, Okamoto, Kim, Steer, & Fayol, 1993). Still others have identified sources in the structures of practices in which children are participants (Berry, 1966; Price-Williams, Gordon, & Ramirez, 1969).

What perhaps best distinguishes Piaget's developmental theory from accounts that locate sources of change in factors *external* to the child is Piaget's strong emphasis on an *internal* locus of causation. Rather than external cultural forces, Piaget's work emphasized processes of self-regulated change as fundamental to the analysis of source. Indeed, in a certain sense, the notion of an external source is a contradiction in terms for Piagetian theory. Although external factors might have implications for change, ultimately the individual, or Piaget's "epistemic subject," had primacy in effecting change and thus was the root source of development (Piaget, 1952, 1977).

In this chapter, I outline an approach for analyzing sources of conceptual development linked to cultural practices. Underlying my remarks is an argument that a systematic treatment of source requires an incorporation of both culture and individual agency in a single analytic framework. Readers knowledgeable in Piagetian theory can find the organizing theme of the volume—Piaget's legacy—well represented. Key Piagetian ideas of epigenesis (that new structures of knowledge have their roots in previous structures) and construction (that individuals are active agents in the epigenetic process) are central to the treatment of source. At the same time, the approach departs from Piagetian thought: Piaget's key focus on cognitive operations that are universal and developed independently of particular cultural practices does not afford a differentiated treatment of history and culture in treatments of cognitive development. Such a concern with historical and cultural processes in a treatment of sources of development is the principal focus here.

The approach that I sketch is *cultural* in that everyday practices—recurrent socially organized activities—are targeted for analysis. I build on research on learning in such practices as games (Fall, 1997; Guberman & Rahm, 1996; Iwanaga, 1997; Nasir, 1997), entrepreneurial activities such as street selling (Carraher, Carraher, & Schliemann, 1985; Saxe, 1991) or weaving (Greenfield, in press; Saxe & Gearhart, 1990), and classroom practices linked to schools (e.g., Ball, 1993; Cobb, Wood, & Yackel, 1993; Gearhart et al., 1997; Lampert, 1990). In the treatment of cognition in practice, individual activity and the social organization of practices are understood *reflexively*: Children's goal-directed activities are in themselves aspects of practices, and at the same time practices give form and social meaning to children's ongoing goal-directed activities. In structuring and accomplishing goals, individuals create novel cognitive developments at once linked to social life and to their own constructive efforts.

The approach is also *developmental.* Cognition in practices (as well as practices themselves) is understood as a process undergoing transformation. The analytic focus is on three related kinds of cognitive change linked to practices: the short-term formation of representations and strategies in individuals' efforts to accomplish goals that emerge in practices (microgenesis); developmental shifts in the structure of individuals' repeated efforts to create and accomplish recurrent goals in practices (ontogenesis); the spread or diffusion of means to accomplish emergent goals in practices in communities (sociogenesis).

THE PRACTICE OF CANDY SELLING

To illustrate the cultural-developmental framework as it bears on questions of sources of development, I draw on observations and analyses of 6- to 15-year-old boys engaged in the practice of candy selling in northeastern Brazil. The children were poor, and many had little or no schooling. My focus is on the unusual mathematics that sellers created as they plied their trade and on what these observations and analyses can tell us about sources of children's mathematics.

In the context of Brazil's long inflationary economic history, the sellers in my study dealt with very large currency values in their street mathematics. The Brazilian unit of currency at the time was the cruzeiro, and tens of thousands of cruzeiros passed through sellers' hands in a day's business. In observations of sellers in their practice and in interviews with them on a range of mathematical tasks, I found that the math that they created in their activities had little resemblance to the mathematics that children learned in school (Saxe, 1991). Indeed, sellers' principal representational system for large numerical values was the currency system. They identified coins and bills from 50 through 50000 cruzeiros, not by the numerals printed on them, but by their figurative characteristics (e.g., color, portraits) and translated these currency units into verbal representations for quantity. Furthermore, they did not use a written arithmetic for performing arithmetical computations, but instead often performed arithmetic computations by using procedures that employed currency: tallying physical quantities of bills or mentally adding and subtracting currency-linked linguistic representations of quantity. They also computed complex markup computations and adjusted for inflation in these computations by using procedures that were widespread in their practice but not known to children in school.

To understand how sellers' mathematics took form in their practice, I focused on sellers' emergent goals as they plied their trade and on developmental transformations in the character of sellers' mathematical problem solving and understandings.

Children's Emergent Goals in the Candy-Selling Practice

Candy sellers created and accomplished a wide variety of goals in their practice. Sometimes, these goals were social and involved issues of self-protection, as when a child tried to affiliate with a group of sellers that traded in one neighborhood to protect himself from "crabs" (sellers who crossed territorial boundaries) or to protect himself from being labeled a crab himself. Other times, goals were economic, as when a seller attempted to bargain with a customer. Still other times, goals involved mathematics, as when a seller was engaged in a markup computation and tried to determine how much he should sell his candy for by units if he paid 12500 cruzeiros in the store and wanted to make a good profit. In the analyses to follow, I show how sellers' mathematical goals emerged and took form in relation to the four parameters depicted in Fig. 11.1: the activity structure of the practice, patterns of social interaction that took form in the practice, artifacts or conventions that were valued in the practice, and the understandings that children brought to bear on practices. As sellers structured and accomplished goals in practices, their developing mathematics became interwoven with their own constructive efforts as well as with social and cultural dimensions of their daily lives.

Activity Structures

Candy selling is an entrepreneurial practice. Typically, children's principal motive for participation is economic. To accomplish their practice, sellers purchased their boxes from wholesale stores during a purchase phase, priced their candy for sale in a prepare-to-sell phase, sold their candy in the street in a sell phase, and then selected new wholesale boxes for purchase in a prepare-to-purchase phase. The cycle then returned to the purchase phase. This economic motive often colored sellers' activities, including their mathematical goals. The inner rectangle of Fig. 11.2 depicts this entrepreneurial structure of activity that takes form in the candy selling practice. To make ends meet in their entrepreneurial activity, sellers had to structure and accomplish various mathematical goals involving the rep-

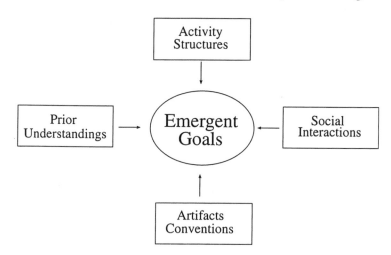

FIG. 11.1. Candy sellers' mathematical goals emerged in relation to the activity structure of the practice, valued artifacts and conventions, social interactions, and sellers' own prior understandings.

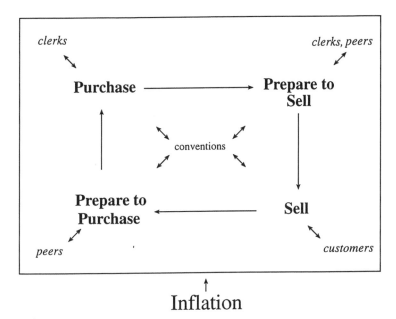

FIG. 11.2. A schematic of the candy selling practice.

resentation of numerical values, the addition and subtraction of values, the comparison of ratios, and goals linked to markup from wholesale to retail price.

Artifacts and Conventions

Various artifacts and conventions that are valued by sellers entered into the mathematical goals that emerged as children plied their trade (represented in the center of Fig. 11.2). Consider both the artifact of currency and a pricing convention that has emerged over the history of the practice.

Because of a long history of inflation, the value of currency in use in selling was quite high. For example, boxes cost thousands of cruzeiros each in wholesale stores, and bills in common use in transactions included notes of Cr$200, Cr$500, Cr$1000, Cr$5000, Cr$10000, and Cr$50000. As a result, when sellers constructed mathematical goals in their practice—whether purchasing a box in a wholesale store or in a transaction with a customer—the goals often involved numbers of great magnitudes.

The price-ratio convention figured centrally into sellers' emergent goals. In selling, virtually all sellers observed offered their candy to customers in the form of a price ratio of units of candy to a particular bill value, generally for some number of units for Cr$1000. Older sellers typically offered their candy to customers for two prices—three packages for Cr$500 or five for Cr$1000. The price ratio became implicated in sellers' mathematical goals in a number of ways. The convention reduced the complexity of arithmetic goals that might emerge in making change. For instance, a seller simply exchanged three bars for a very common unit of currency, the Cr$1000 note, and often no change was required in such transactions. The convention, however, also led sellers to become engaged in ratio comparisons and with other more complex mathematics: In their markup computations, for example, a seller translated a multiunit wholesale box price (e.g., Cr$12000) in terms of a retail price ratio (e.g., X units for Cr$1000) such that he ended with an appropriate profit margin. Whether in face-to-face exchanges with customers or in markup computations, the price-ratio convention was intrinsically linked to the mathematical goals that emerged for sellers.

Finally, another pricing convention was widely used for determining an appropriate profit margin in the selling practice. This convention was called *meio-pelo-meio*. As explained by older sellers, the convention prescribed that one should set a price so that one half the profit goes for the purchase of the next box and one half is kept by the seller as profit. By using this convention, sellers' markup goals took a particular form. One feature of this convention was related to sellers' mathematical goals: Sellers (often unknowingly) adjusted their selling price for inflation when using the convention, because the profit margin always remained 100%, regardless of an increase in wholesale prices for candy boxes.

Social Interactions

At each phase in the structure of the practice, sellers typically interacted with other people, whether clerks, customers, or peers (represented in the inner corners of Fig. 11.2). These social interactions that emerged in a practice simplified the construction and accomplishment of some goals and complicated others. For example, in the prepare-to-sell phase, having purchased a box of candy containing typically 30, 50, or 100 units for which they paid thousands of cruzeiros, sellers had to determine an appropriate price for retail sale. The arithmetic goals that emerged in producing markups differed for sellers of different ages. Particularly with young sellers, clerks or older peers told children an appropriate retail price and accomplished the markup computation for the seller; at other times, sellers marked up their candy in the street, when children provided assistance to and negotiated with each other about appropriate markup. At still other times, sellers marked up prices on their own. Thus, depending on social supports for markup, the mathematical goals that sellers constructed to accomplish markup varied: For the older seller, markup goals and means of achieving them could be quite complex; for a younger child, a markup goal would not involve mathematics.

Bargaining transactions are yet another example of the way that social interactions afforded the emergence of particular goals. In bargaining, a customer indicated that the cost of the candy was too high (or perhaps that the wrapper was sticky owing to the summer's heat). Ensuing negotiations sometimes gave rise to sellers' needs to decide whether a revised price was viable in the context of profit concerns. Like the construction of markup goals, there was evidence in my study that the complexity of goals that emerged in bargaining varied with sellers' ages. Young sellers typically sold for a fixed price that they were told to use, whereas older sellers more typically adjusted prices in bargaining transactions.

Prior Understandings

The mathematical understandings that sellers brought to bear on the practice—the fourth parameter in Fig. 11.1—were fundamental to the mathematical goals that emerged in a practice. Whether we consider the character of sellers' representational, arithmetic, comparison, or markup goals, in each domain, goals took form in relation to children's mathematical understandings. The means and subgoals that sellers elaborated in each domain depended on these understandings. For instance, a seller who did not understand the relation between wholesale price and retail price did not generate markup goals; or if he did, the mathematical goals in his computation were quite different from the goals of the seller who did.

Sellers' mathematical goals became constituted as they plied their trade. They took form in relation to activity structures, artifacts, social interactions, and prior understandings. In structuring and accomplishing these goals, sellers' mathematics became rooted in both culture and individuals' constructive activities.

Development in the Candy-Selling Practice

In the following analysis of development, I focus on the interplay in development between cultural forms such as currency or a number system and the functions that these forms serve for individuals in their practices. The approach draws on aspects of Werner and Kaplan's (1962) treatment of form–function relations in the development of language, a treatment that I subsequently extended in my own work on cultural practices and children's mathematics (Saxe, 1991, 1996; Saxe, Guberman, & Gearhart, 1987). The formulation also reflects a dominant concern of Vygotsky and other Soviet writers (e.g., Leontiev, 1981; Vygotsky, 1978, 1986), who were interested in identifying analytic units that preserved intrinsic relations between cognitive and sociocultural processes in analyses of development.

Cultural forms vary in the way they afford or are specialized to serve particular functions in practices. For instance, in the domain of arithmetic, the Hindu-Arabic numeration system is highly specialized for computation. Other number systems, like the 27-body-part counting system of the Oksapmin of Papua New Guinea (Saxe, 1982), have been specialized for serving cognitive functions like counting and certain forms of measurement, but not for arithmetic computation. Still other artifacts, such as currency systems, have been specialized for economic exchanges. Next, I target three kinds of development, each of which entails an interplay between form and function in mathematical activities.

Microgenesis

Although forms have evolved over social histories to serve particular functions in practices, in activity, individuals adapt or repurpose forms to accomplish their own goals. Microgenesis[1] refers to this transformative process whereby individuals tailor cultural forms to become means to accomplish goals in practices. To illustrate, consider a seller's activity in the prepare-to-sell phase.

Ten-year-old Luciano was engaged with a markup problem. He paid Cr$7000 at the wholesale store for his 30-unit box of candy bars, and he needed to determine how much to sell the candy for in the street so that his candy moved quickly and he made a good profit. Luciano's approach, like many other sellers, was to first focus on a determination of the price that the box would bring if it were sold at a particular price ratio. He began by considering a price ratio of three bars for Cr$1000. To create a means for accomplishing his computation, he emptied his box on the ground. Then, he replaced bars in the box in groups (see Fig. 11.3). With each placement, he created many-to-one correspondences between the cash price of a Cr$1000 bill and groups of three bars, and incremented his running total by Cr$1000 with each placement. In the end, Luciano compared his calculated street price (Cr$10000) with the wholesale price (Cr$7000) and made use of the *meio-pelo-meio* (half–half) convention as a norm to determine the adequacy of his profit. If he felt he would not earn

---

[1]Some researchers have made use of *microgenesis* to refer to a methodological approach involving the intensive study of shifts in children's strategies and/or cognitive structures over short periods (see, for example, Siegler & Jenkins, 1989). My use of the term is more consistent with earlier treatments of the construct (Vygotsky, 1986; Werner & Kaplan, 1962), in which the very process of schematization of a phenomenon, perceptually or conceptually, is understood as a short-term developmental process. As conceptualized in the present discussion, microgenesis is neither a methodological approach nor a small-scale version of ontogenetic change. Rather, it is a process in which forms with the cognitive functions they afford are transformed into means for accomplishing emerging goals.

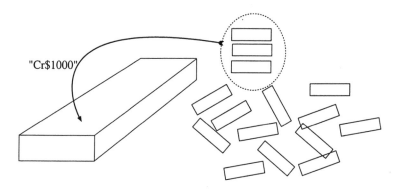

FIG. 11.3. Luciano replaced candies in his box in groups of three, adding "one thousand" to a running total with each placement, until all candies were replaced in his box. This procedure allowed Luciano to determine the gross value of the box, if the price ratio of 3 candies for Cr$1000 was used in sales.

enough profit, he repeated the process with a different grouping and then compared the two results. The method was laborious but reliable.

The three forms with which Luciano worked in his activity—the price-ratio form, the currency, and the candy itself—have emerged over the history of a range of practices to serve culturally valued functions. Commercially packaged candy served as a commodity for trade and consumption; currency served as a common unit of exchange; the price ratio served to mediate sales exchanges between seller and customer. These functions were not fixed. Indeed, in Luciano's markup activity, he adapted and repurposed these forms to achieve his markup goal.

Two features are noteworthy about the microgenesis of these forms into means for accomplishing markup. First, Luciano schematized these forms as mathematical entities and adapted them to serve mathematical functions. Thus, Luciano conceptualized the candy and currency in a relation of many-to-one correspondence—three bars to 1 Cr$1000 bill; then he added Cr$1000 to a running total for each many-to-one correspondence. Thus, in Luciano's activity, these forms became structured as mathematical entities and served mathematical functions.

Second, Luciano deployed the materials strategically. Making use of the properties of candy bars as discrete and movable objects, Luciano emptied the box and replaced the candy in groups of three until none were left on the ground. Thus, he used the materials themselves as an "external" memory to "tell" him when he had exhausted all potential sales. Through this strategy, Luciano insured that no candy was treated as unsold in his summation. In the microgenesis of Luciano's solution, currency and candy became at once the mathematical and physical means to accomplish markup goals, functions that were not given but that emerged in the microgenesis in Luciano's markup.

Ontogenesis

Gaining insight into the development of sellers' mathematics requires an analysis of the epigenesis of sellers' knowledge: Can we identify the origins of 10-year-old Luciano's strategy in younger children's engagement with the practice? Further, can Luciano's strategy be a seed for subsequent, more sophisticated efforts in his own prospective development? To address these questions, I consider first a seller who is younger than Luciano and his use of the candy and price-ratio forms in his activities; then, I turn to a seller older than Luciano and consider the way that Luciano's strategic efforts may serve as seeds for subsequent ontogenetic shifts linked to the practice.

Wilher at 6 Years. In the street, 6-year-old Wilher was observed selling his candy at five packages of lifesavers for Cr$1000. For this 6-year-old seller, the price-ratio form served the cognitive function of mediating exchanges of candy for currency in seller–customer transactions: Wilher exchanged, for instance, one Cr$1000 bill for five candy packs over and over again (as depicted in Fig. 11.4). Thus, like 10-year-old Luciano, Wilher was structuring the price-ratio form as a means of accomplishing an emerging goal, although the means was organized to serve a very different function from markup computation. In fact, for Wilher, issues of price markup were taken care of by others, such as store clerks, older peers, or relatives. Wilher's use of the price ratio—the activity of engaging in the many-to-one exchanges of bills for candy—may well be a critical seed for the kind of strategy we observed with Luciano. Indeed, Luciano appeared to have appropriated the price-ratio form from seller–customer transactions and used it to serve a new function—as a means to refer to potential transactions for the purpose of determining markup.

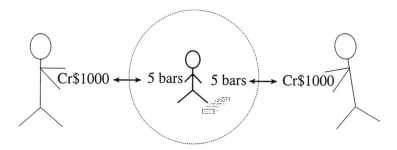

FIG. 11.4. In selling with the price-ratio convention, Wilher creates a series of many-to-one correspondences as he exchanges five candies for each one thousand cruzeiro bill.

Antonio at 14 Years. When we consider a seller older than Luciano, we find evidence that Luciano's strategic efforts at 10 may be the seeds for later shifts in markup strategies. Antonio began his day with a full box of candy bars. The box contained 30 units, and he paid Cr$8000 for the box. He sold the bars at three for Cr$1000. When questioned about how he determined his prices, Antonio explained that he counted each group of three as Cr$1000; each count of three represented one sale, and he counted two groups of three at a time as depicted in Fig. 11.5. Thus, he counted the gross price by stating: "These two (two groups of three) bring Cr$2000; these two (two groups of three) Cr$4000, these two, Cr$6000; . . . these two, Cr$10000. Antonio determined that selling the units for three for Cr$1000 on the street yielded a gross of Cr$10000. He then subtracted the wholesale price of $8000 from the Cr$10000 and determined that he would net Cr$2000. Antonio's calculation as depicted in Fig. 11.5 showed a condensed and abbreviated use of the price ratio to speed computation.

An Epigenetic Sequence. The cross-section of development at 6, 10, and 14 years provides evidence of an epigenetic sequence in which a seller's previous strategic efforts linked to practice participation provided a basis for him to construct new knowledge. In this process, a seller repurposed cultural forms initially used to serve one function as he generated new goals in the course of participating in practices. Thus, the young seller first used the price-ratio form to serve the function of mediating seller–customer exchanges, and he knew that issues of markup would be taken care of by others. The child created many-to-one correspondence between a currency unit—the Cr$1000 bill—and five units of candy. Later, as in the case of 10-year-old Luciano, the seller reconstructed the purpose of

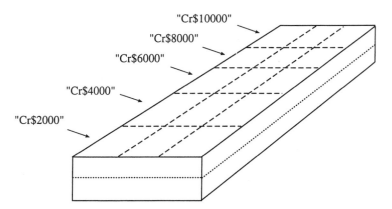

FIG. 11.5. A depiction of Antonio's abbreviated procedure for determining the gross value of his box if the price ratio of 3 candies for Cr$1000 were used in sales.

the price ratio. Luciano used the price ratio referentially: He deployed the ratio as a way to represent potential customer–seller transactions. In his markup computation, he emptied the box on the street and schematized the ratio as a means of representing potential customer–seller transactions. Thus the many-to-one correspondence which had formerly occurred between child and customer was now used to refer to hypothetical customer–seller transactions. This second order use of the ratio allowed the seller to calibrate and recalibrate potential gross prices until he found an appropriate match by using his *meio-pelo-meio* convention as a guide (half the profit for the next box and half for the seller). In the case of the oldest seller, 14-year-old Antonio, we see an abbreviation of means of the hypothetical correspondence between seller and customer. Here, the price-ratio form was hardly discernible in his strategic approach and took the form of a count: "Cr\$2000, Cr\$4000, Cr\$6000, Cr\$8000, Cr\$10000," in a very rapid street price computation.

Sociogenesis

Sociogenesis involves the spread and evolution of means for solving and accomplishing goals. As individuals adapt and repurpose forms into means in practices, these means may be imitated and valued by others to accomplish practice-linked goals. The appropriation and gradual institutionalization of means in a community is central to the dynamics that lead to new cultural forms.

Consider the price ratio as a valued cultural form. In its early genesis in the selling practice, I suspect that older sellers who sold their candy in single units tried using discounting conventions used in other practices— selling a greater volume for a discounted price. The price ratio may then have spread to other sellers and became valued perhaps because it reduced the need for change, served as a convenient way to offer customers a bargain, and possibly increased volume of sales. In addition, and perhaps later, the ratio pricing began serving additional functions. For instance, it became a convenient way of accommodating for inflating prices by lowering numbers of units while retaining the principal currency unit. It also became a popular means of computing markup, as we have seen in the cases of Luciano and Antonio.

The circle is then complete: In individuals' appropriation of forms to accomplish emerging goals in practices, they adapted and repurposed earlier sociogenetic developments through microgenetic processes and built on earlier constructions in ontogenesis. In turn, the microgenetic transformation of forms into means in activity served as a basis for new processes of sociogenesis involving the spread and institutionalization of new cultural forms. Such an interplay between developmental processes pervades cultural practices and roots individual agency and culture in the same dynamic system.

CONCLUDING REMARKS

In various publications, Piaget cited cross-cultural differences in rates of development through his stages as indicators that development was not simply a product of a maturational unfolding. The interplay between sociohistorical and cognitive developmental processes, however, was never a central target of his genetic epistemology, which invariably focused on cognitive structure and principles of self-regulation without a coordinated treatment of practice. Even Piaget's early seminal works that touched on these issues, *The Moral Judgment of the Child* (1932) and *Play, Dreams, and Imitation* (1951), did not elaborate analytic methods for understanding children's constitutive role in the structure of practices and the way that practices in turn frame developmental constructions.

In my brief sketch of a cultural-developmental framework, I have pointed to the importance of integrating accounts of practice and of development in treatments of microgenesis, ontogenesis, and sociogenesis. Such an approach creates needed analytic room for key Piagetian themes like agency and epigenesis in accounts of the socially and historically situated aspects of knowledge. Indeed, an integration of these two tacks—analyses of cultural practice and development—is essential for a systematic treatment of sources of concepts.

ACKNOWLEDGMENTS

The author gratefully acknowledges support from the Spencer Foundation (M890224) and the National Science Foundation (MDR-8855643) during different phases of the research described in this chapter. The opinions expressed in this chapter are my own and not necessarily those of the funding agencies.

REFERENCES

Ball, D. L. (1993). Halves, pieces, and twoths: Constructing representational contexts in teaching fractions. In T. Carpenter, E. Fennema, & T. Romberg (Eds.), *Rational numbers: An integration of research* (pp. 157–195). Hillsdale, NJ: Lawrence Erlbaum Associates.

Berry, J. W. (1966). Temne and Eskimo perceptual skills. *International Journal of Psychology, 1,* 207–229.

Carraher, T. N., Carraher, D., & Schliemann, A. D. (1985). Mathematics in the streets and in schools. *British Journal of Developmental Psychology, 3*(1), 21–29.

Cobb, P. Wood, T., & Yackel, E. (1993). Discourse, mathematical thinking, and classroom practice. In E. A. Forman, N. Minick, & C. A. Stone (Eds.), *Contexts for learning: Sociocultural dynamics in children's development* (pp. 91–119). New York: Oxford University Press.

Fall, J. R. (1997, April). *Capture fractions.* Paper presented at the meeting of the American Educational Research Association, Chicago, IL.

Gearhart, M., Saxe, G. B., Ching, C. C., Nasir, N., Bennett, T., Rhine, S., & Sloan, T. (1997). *When can educational reforms make a difference? Opportunities to learn fractions in elementary mathematics classrooms.* Unpublished manuscript, University of California, Berkeley.

Greenfield, P. M. (in press). Culture change and human development. In E. Turiel (Ed.), *Culture and development. New directions in child development.* San Francisco: Jossey-Bass.

Guberman, S. R., & Rahm, J. (1996, April). *Negotiating boardwalk: Emergent mathematics in children's game play.* Paper presented at the meeting of the American Educational Research Association, New York City.

Iwanaga, J. (1997). *Competitive posture and developmental shifts in the conceptualization of the function of property in Monopoly.* Unpublished manuscript, University of California, Los Angeles.

Lampert, M. (1990). When the problem is not the question and the solution is not the answer: Mathematical knowing and teaching. *American Educational Research Journal, 27,* 29–63.

Leontiev, A. (1981). The problem of activity in psychology. In J. V. Wertsch (Ed.), *The concept of activity in Soviet psychology* (pp. 37–61). Armonk, NY: Sharpe.

Miura, I. T., Okamoto, Y., Kim, C. C., Steer, M., & Fayol, M. (1993). First graders' cognitive representation of number and understanding of place value: Cross-national comparisons—France, Japan, Korea, Sweden, and the United States. *Journal of Educational Psychology, 85*(1), 24–30.

Nasir, N. (1997, April). *Math in basketball play.* Paper presented at the meeting of the International Society for Research in Behavioral Development, Quebec, Canada.

Piaget, J. (1932). *The moral judgment of the child* (M. Gabain, Trans.). New York: Harcourt, Brace & World.

Piaget, J. (1951). *Play, dreams, and imitation in childhood* (C. Gattegno & F. M. Hodgson, Trans.). New York: Norton.

Piaget, J. (1952). *The origins of intelligence in children* (M. Cook, Trans.). New York: International Universities Press.

Piaget, J. (1977). *The development of thought: Equilibration of cognitive structures* (A. Rosin, Trans.). New York: Viking Press.

Price-Williams, D., Gordon, W., & Ramirez, M. (1969). Skill and conservation: A study of pottery-making children. *Developmental Psychology, 1,* 769.

Saxe, G. B. (1982). Developing forms of arithmetic operations among the Oksapmin of Papua New Guinea. *Developmental Psychology, 18*(4), 583–594.

Saxe, G. B. (1991). *Culture and cognitive development: Studies in mathematical understanding.* Hillsdale, NJ: Lawrence Erlbaum Associates.

Saxe, G. B. (1996). Studying cognitive development in sociocultural context. In D. Jessor, A. Colby, & R. Shewder (Eds.), *Ethnographic approaches to the study of human development* (pp. 275–303). Chicago: University of Chicago Press.

Saxe, G. B., & Gearhart, M. (1990). The development of topological concepts in unschooled straw weavers. *British Journal of Developmental Psychology, 8,* 251–258.

Saxe, G. B., Gearhart, M., Note, M., & Paduano, P. (1993). Peer interaction and the development of mathematical understandings: A new framework for research and educational practice. In H. Daniels (Ed.), *Charting the agenda: Vygotskian perspectives* (pp. 107–144). London: Routledge.

Saxe, G. B., Guberman, S. R., & Gearhart, M. (1987). Social processes in early number development. *Monographs of the Society for Research in Child Development, 52*(2, Serial No. 216).

Siegler R., & Jenkins, E. (1989). *How children discover new strategies.* Hillsdale, NJ: Lawrence Erlbaum Associates.

Vygotsky, L. S. (1978). *Mind in society: The development of higher psychological processes.* Cambridge, MA: Harvard University Press.

Vygotsky, L. (1986). *Thought and language.* Cambridge, MA: MIT Press.

Webb, N. M. (1982). Student interaction and learning in small groups. *Review of Educational Research, 52,* 421–445.

Werner, H., & Kaplan, B. (1962). *Symbol formation.* New York: Wiley.

Wertsch, J. V. (1979). From social interaction to higher psychological processes: A clarification and application of Vygotsky's theory. *Human Development, 22,* 1–22.

Wood, D., Bruner, J. S., & Ross, G. (1976). The role of tutoring in problem solving. *Journal of Child Psychology and Psychiatry, 17,* 89–100.

Chapter 12

Levels and Modes of Representation: Issues for the Theory of Conceptual Change and Development

Katherine Nelson
City University of New York Graduate Center

> *Human language is the happy result of bringing together two systems that all higher organisms must have: a representational system and a communication system. A representational system is necessary if an organism is going to move around purposefully in its environment; a communication system is necessary if an organism is going to interact with others of its own kind. . . . Human beings seem to be the only animals in which a single system serves both of these functions*
> —G. A. Miller, 1990, p. 12

> *The advent of language was . . . [a] boon for human beings, a technology that created a whole new class of objects-to-contemplate, verbally embodied surrogates that could be reviewed in any order at any pace. And this opened up a new dimension of self-improvement—all one had to do was to learn to savour one's own mistakes.*
> —Dennett, 1994, p. 177

In this chapter I am concerned to locate language as both a cognitive and a communicative representational system as it develops in the early childhood years. To do so, I consider other modes and levels of representation in phylogenetic and ontogenetic relation to language. I begin with nonlinguistic representational systems, and I present an explicitly *experiential* framework for their development.

REPRESENTATION AND CONCEPTUAL SYSTEMS IN AN EXPERIENTIALIST PERSPECTIVE

First, it is necessary to clarify some of the current terminology that is often conflated with representation or confused with issues of representation. In

269

the psychology of learning systems, representation is taken to be some more or less direct transform of the output of perceptual systems (Gallistel, 1989).[1] Conceptual systems, in contrast, are assumed to arise through constructive cognitive and/or social processes, although in some views, conceptual systems derive from innately designed principles, biases, or constraints in specific content domains. These views merge with notions of *modularity*, when that term is used in Fodor's (1983) sense of modular mechanisms for the analysis of input in specific perceptual systems (Hirschfeld & Gelman, 1994). Modular mechanisms, which surely exist at some level (e.g., the central nervous system), may be either innately prepared (such as the visual, which delivers apparently inescapable visual illusions) or obviously acquired, such as driving skill, reading, or writing. That such modularly organized mechanisms operate in our cognitive systems below the level of awareness seems unexceptional. That they may operate in ways that have some similarity to motor programs in other species (such as spider weaving) is certainly debatable, but irrelevant to the present issues of representation. That their existence tells us anything about representation in relation to conceptual systems is doubtful. For example, to say that the spider's "knowledge" of web weaving is "represented" somewhere in its cognitive or neural system in the same sense as human knowledge is, in my view constitutes a category error. Similarly, the claim that a linguistic grammar is cognitively represented clearly refers to a different kind of representation than the record of one's personal history or organized knowledge of cultural taxonomies (see footnote 1 and following discussion).

Representation here is considered within an experiential framework, that is, in terms of what an organism represents of experience in the world, as well as the mode and function of such representation. The basic experiential idea is that children acquire concepts—of objects, actions, people, as well as more abstract ideas—in the course of their exploration of the world through individual action, through participation in the activities of their social worlds, and through communication with others about their worlds. Their concepts exist within—and are derived from—larger organizations of experientially based knowledge, at the outset within representations of familiar event schemas. Basic questions arise as to how such representations support action in the world and how concepts emerge from this level that have meanings within conventional language systems.

The general idea of the proposed developmental sequence can be conveyed in the following sketch (see Nelson, 1996, for details): The event representation of late infancy connects the simple action schemes of infants

---

[1]A different sense of representation is implied for example in deep structure grammatical representations (Chomsky, 1965), and the term is used broadly to cover conceptual representations, linguistic representations, mental representations, and so on in cognitive psychology generally.

with consequences both social and nonsocial, and thus with representation of whole events. These events are organized by adults, but they include infants as participants; thus the process by which such events are represented is conceived of as *participatory interaction*, in which the child has a role to play as well as the adult. The social world, that is, the other participants in events, conveys meaning within events, first, by arranging environmental settings and activities; second, by interacting with infants around caretaking and other everyday activities; third, by later exchanging communicative signals about the actions and objects therein. For example, children build up "having lunch" scripts that include the other's active parts as well as the possible objects that can occur in the script (Nelson, 1978; Nelson & Gruendel, 1981, 1986). Children need not understand the social and biological significance of such events to represent them. Children's understanding of social events is accomplished through cognitive operations on the initially represented significant event sequences. It is cognitive activity in social events that enables infants to find meaning in the world of people, actions, and objects, even before they can communicate with language.

The experientialist perspective embraces both parts of the biocultural foundation of human development. It views the biological foundations—neuronal organization, action systems, perceptual and cognitive systems—as emerging in developmental systems (Oyama, 1985; chap. 8, this volume) and as continuous with the cultural foundations, rather than seeing one part as natural and the other as added on. Nevertheless, it recognizes that most of what infants and children come to understand about the world is specific to the cultural and historical situation within which each infant exists and survives. Part of the biological given must then be the capacity for *making sense* of these specifics, constructing therefrom conceptual abstractions and generalizations that fit the world as it is encountered; the experiencing infant initially builds models of the world as known, and does not build models of previous worlds, future worlds, or possible worlds. Children's conceptual world models are then based on a history of interactions in real-world situations.

The experientialist perspective is consistent with classic theories such as those of the early American pragmatists, including William James (1950/1890) and especially John Dewey (1961/1916). This tradition continued with theories such as J. J. Gibson's (1986) that sensory systems are designed to pick up information from the environment to which they are evolutionarily adapted and that objects come to be known in terms of their *affordances*. Piaget's (1952) idea that knowledge is constructed on the basis of children's action on objects is experiential to the core. Reed (1993) elaborated Gibson's theory of ecological perception, emphasizing action as the basis of thought, and thus reconciled these two theories often thought to be in conflict. In an important contribution to this line of thinking,

Bickhard (1997) has articulated a foundational theory of interactivism that insists on the predictive value of representations providing the basis for undertaking action in the environment. His account is explicitly experiential—or pragmatic—emphasizing action in the world, the social and cultural world as well as the physical and material one. Hendriks-Jansen (1996) provided a comprehensive account, building on recent models in cognitive science, that also emphasizes situated action in the world and interaction as the basis of human thought and the emergence of language. The ecology of human life is a social-cultural one, and here Vygotsky's (1962) emphasis on the social-cultural and historical specificity of cognition must be recognized as a strong form of experiential theorizing that is echoed today in Bruner's work (e.g., 1986), as well as in that of Cole (1996), Rogoff (1990), and Wertsch (1991). As Reed and Bril (1996) stress, broad cultural variations in what they term the Zone of Promoted Action (see Valsiner, 1987) influence what a child might represent of the world through acting on and in it. All these classic and contemporary contributions assume knowledge based on action in the (social and cultural) world, although not all, if any, would agree with the particulars outlined in what follows here.

In contrast, in addressing what are conceived as foundational issues, other recent theories of development have tended to neglect the social, cultural, and historical frames of action. Most also ignore the symbolic interface where social/cultural experience is carried through. It is the symbolic realm that is so distinctively human, the realm in which children become participants, in ways that take them beyond the action and interaction beginnings of individual representations to the understandings of the shared social and cultural world. The motivation of conceptualizing the world is the same on both the action level and the symbolic level: that is, predicting events in order to act intelligently in them; but the form and content of the representations change. It is these developments that require more explicit theoretical explication while accepting action and activity as the starting points.

The quotation from Miller at the beginning of this chapter asserts that language is the medium of both internal representation and external communication. How do we get to this point from a basically action-oriented system? In human development, representation and communication must become connected; otherwise the nonlinguistic individual would remain in the solipsistic state characteristic of the nonhuman primate or human infant that Dennett refers to in the second quotation at the beginning of this chapter. Vygotsky's idea of social to private to inner speech stands almost alone as an attempt to address this problem (Vygotsky, 1986). Other theorists tend either to treat children as essentially unchanged from the autonomous and even solipsistic status of infants or to assume an unproblematic instantaneous and unobserved move to a symbolic representation system typical of adult human cognizers.

The effect of these unacknowledged assumptions about cognitive development can be seen in the varying models of children's "theory of mind" that have emerged in recent years. This research area is concerned with how we can understand the intentionality of other minds and how children come to take other people's belief states into account in predicting their actions. The test of children's ability to understand other minds is their understanding of false belief in unfamiliar situations with unfamiliar and generally decontexted agents. The tasks used employ language in the form of vignettes conveyed through a combination of visual and verbal presentations. However, the language used is not generally viewed as playing an important role in children's understanding, either in the task situation or in the acquisition of such social knowledge. Rather, children are seen as operating with an innate module (Leslie, 1991), an individually constructed theory (Gopnik, 1993; Wellman, 1990), or a simulation based on self reflection (Harris, 1992).

Recognition of the central role played by language in this domain of knowledge forces a radically different view of the developmental problem. As Dennett put it in the passage from which the opening quotation was taken (1994, p. 177), chimpanzees and other primates "never dispute over attributions, and ask for the grounds for each others' conclusions. No wonder their comprehension is so limited. Ours would be, too, if we had to generate it all on our own." Like chimpanzees, infants and very young children lack just these advantages of human language. Young humans of course are not chimpanzees and are not equivalent to chimpanzees; but they share some of the disadvantages that accrue to those who do not have language, although they operate quite competently in many situations from the intelligent base of event representations based on participatory interactions with knowledgeable adults (Nelson, 1986).

Let me illustrate this problem with a graphic abstraction that is based on the classic semiotic triangle of Ogden and Richards (1946/1923); see Fig. 12.1. At the base of the triangle is the problematic connection between word and object in the world, shown as a dotted line. How does this connection get made? Not, obviously, directly because the connection is arbitrary; the word has no iconic or indexical relation (Peirce, 1960) to the thing it stands in reference to. Rather, the connection is indirect through the concept that stands at the apex of the triangle. The concept exists not in the world but in the minds of language users. But note the problem that arises when there is only one mind and only one language user: The triangle is incomplete. Without another mind, there is no function for the word; the concept–thing relation is complete in itself. The word or other symbolic form is required for conveying a message—a meaning—to another language user. The word is the way to the concept in the mind of the other and reciprocally from the other to one's own mind. This is illustrated in Fig. 12.2, where the original triangle is completed by

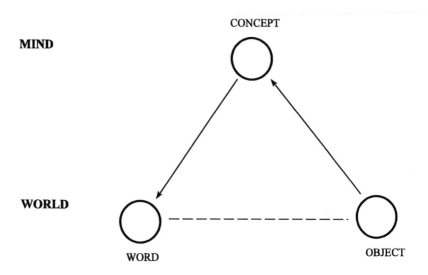

FIG. 12.1. The word–object triangle based on Ogden and Richards (1923).

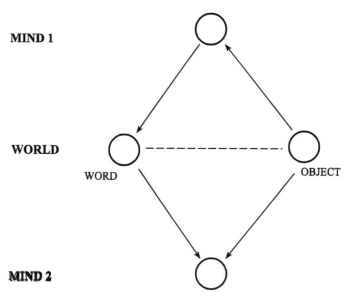

FIG. 12.2. The word–concept–object triangle complement necessary for learning and conveying meaning in words.

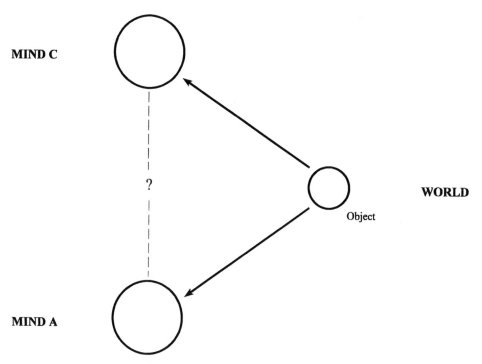

FIG. 12.3. The mind–world triangle complement for learning about and reading mental states.

its complement. In this case, the adult utters a word symbolizing a concept for an object perceived by both adult and child (note the direction of arrows), and the child connects the word with the object through her own concept for the object or constructs a concept in response to the word–object pairing.

The lesson for the theory of mind problem seems relatively clear. For extant theories of theory of mind, the triangle is again incomplete, but it is a different triangle (Fig. 12.3). Here, as in Fig. 12.2, the mind of a child is connected to the thing seen via visual perception, and the mind of an adult is also connected to the state of the world, but from another perspective. There is no direct connection between the child's view and the adult's view and no connection at all between the child's mental state and the adult's mental state. What is missing in this conception is the symbol (word or linguistic expression) that can connect the two: Or more exactly, the use of words in discourse is the missing link (Fig. 12.4). Through discourse about states of the world and related states of mind, a shared symbolic communi- cative system is eventually established that makes it possible for children and adults to exchange and to share perspectives on the world, and for children to gain knowledge from adults, both about the social world in which they

MIND C

WORLD

Word

Object

MIND A

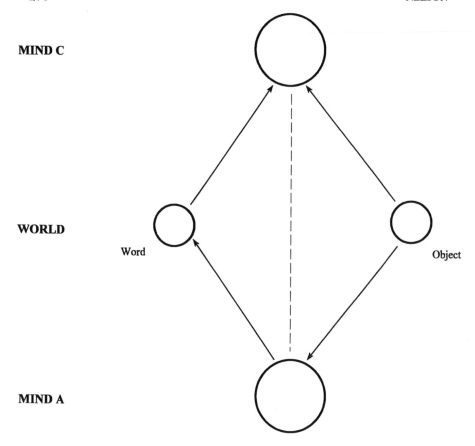

FIG. 12.4.

live and about other possible worlds.[2] Without the possibility of sharing and
exchanging mental views, children can only guess at the meanings and
motivations of others' actions, and the basis for guessing is severely limited
by their own restricted experience in the world.

REPRESENTATION AND COMMUNICATION WITHOUT LANGUAGE

To begin with, the child is in a real sense disconnected from the minds
of others. Many theorists have postulated that the parent–child bond in

---

[2]A number of researchers have begun to investigate the implications of language for
theory of mind (e.g., Bartsch & Wellman, 1995; Dunn et al., 1995; Shatz, 1994; De Villiers,
1996). The broader implications for the relation of language and social cognition remain to
be spelled out.

infancy and toddlerhood establishes a context of intersubjectivity that not only sets the stage for language learning but serves also as the foundation for theory of mind. Although this proposal seems plausible, in my view it rests too much insightful power in the infant mind unaided by the power of a shared symbolic system. Rather, I think we can see a gradual enlightenment taking place through a shared action system that in turn makes possible the interpretation of alternative intentionalities and meaningful messages from other minds.

Beginning with children's understanding of events that they participate in, constructive processes articulate roles and conceptualize objects and categories of objects within events. Subsequently, reenactment of others' roles, shared actions with others, and practice of skilled action on their own become possible. Within these action systems, words become embedded, and within these social activities, discourse is embedded. A system of shared understanding through a shared symbolic system is thereby constructed. It is this system through which children come to interpret others' actions and understanding, including the possibility of their false belief states, as well as their true beliefs, desires, pretenses, emotions, and other mental constructions. These developments must be traced and understood in more detail.

There is now massive evidence that event representations have psychological reality in young children's representational systems. By forming scripts of routine events, children find the meaning in other people's actions, to make sense and to locate their own place in the world of events. The problem is to connect social event knowledge in the form of scripts with concepts that may be the foundation for language and for higher levels of intelligent behavior and thought.

Recent research with infants focused on social development has documented a set of developmental achievements during the 1st year that establish a form of communication between parent and child even before the beginning acquisition of conventional language forms. For some theorists, intersubjectivity is seen to be established in this way and is viewed as a prerequisite both phylogenetically (Byrne, 1995) and ontogenetically (Tomasello, 1992) for the acquisition of language. The important achievements of the latter part of the 1st year and the beginning of the 2nd supporting this view include shared attention to objects between adult and infant, in which the infant follows the adult's gaze and her pointing gesture; social referencing, in which the infant begins to attend to the adult's attitude toward people and objects and to follow suit; and imitation, which develops throughout the 1st year and eventuates in the infant's being able to repeat a remembered action after a delay and thus to begin to engage in what Tomasello and his colleagues consider to be true cultural learning (Tomasello, Kruger, & Ratner, 1993).

The intersubjectivity that contemporary theorists have seen in the latter part of the 1st year is very limited compared to that later seen even in early childhood. Early intersubjectivity depends on children's interpretation of parents' actions and thereby parents' intentions, as well as the reciprocal interpretation of children by parents. Because parents are in general control of events, they are able to set up situations where they can anticipate the desires and beliefs of children; thus in optimal cases, children are led to the reciprocal interpretation of the adult. Of course, this does not always work smoothly; misunderstandings occur. It is no denigration of the child's capacity for following the parent's lead (e.g., following her gaze, adopting her affect) to assert that such following reflects the child's cognitive interpretation of action based on experience rather than cognitive reflection on the parent's mental state. That is, such understanding may reflect interpersonal-activity interpretation, not intersubjectivity per se. Or if you like, it is limited or proto-intersubjectivity, an important step toward, but not the achievement of, intersubjectivity. In this stage of development, children understand reciprocal action roles, such as that you and I have different roles in the same activity; however, children play only their own role. They are like actors in an amateur production of a play, actors who learn only their own lines and the cues for speaking them.[3]

It is interesting and important that the physical knowledge that has been so in focus in infancy studies (e.g., Spelke, Breinlinger, Macomber, & Jakobson, 1992) appears pretty much the same across primate species; for example, monkeys and apes go through stages of acquiring object permanence similar to children and indeed in some cases are precocious in this respect (Antinucci, 1990). In contrast, the social achievements noted in the previous paragraph appear to be unique to human infants (Tomasello, 1998). Human infants and their adult caretakers manage to communicate many messages, involving expressions of affect, desires, and instrumental needs, through vocal and motoric gestures before using conventional language for the purpose. It is now widely accepted that these achievements set the stage for learning language as infants and parents engage in sharing attention and mutually interpreting intentions.

Thus cognitive knowledge of the physical and social world and communication are in place before the onset of language beginning in the 2nd and into the 3rd year of life. Conventional language then succeeds earlier established communicative systems. It is necessary, therefore, to try to understand both the social communicative system and the representation system of 1-year-old children within a single framework. To do this, I invoke the analysis that Donald (1991) presents in the phylogenetic frame linking

---

[3]Imitation at this point, I suggest, does not function to learn another's role, but only to add to one's own repertoire.

action-based communication and representation with later language acquisition. Donald's evolutionary account of human cognition provides insight into these early action-based systems. He has traced the evolution of three transitions in human cognitive history, resulting in the construction of a hybrid representational system incorporating at least four distinct levels among present-day *Homo sapiens*. The first transition, he speculates, took place between early hominids and *Homo erectus*, from representation of events to representation in terms of imitated and reproduced actions, termed *mimesis*. The second transition, during the evolution of *Homo sapiens*, was characterized by the invention of language, resulting in *linguistic representations* of which narratives were the most significant product. The third transition took place in human history and involved *graphic representations*, writing, and all manner of external storage of knowledge systems. According to Donald, this latter transition made possible the development of formal or theoretic thinking.

Donald begins the story with the claim that the basic representational system of nonhuman primate minds is episodic (more or less equivalent to what I term event representations). Thus both phylogenetically and ontogenetically, the theories converge on a nonlinguistic, individual, experientially based representation that guides action in events. If the foregoing analysis of intersubjectivity based in activity is correct, some apes may be able to begin to engage in the level of proto-intersubjectivity that 1-year-old children have achieved (see Byrne & Whiten, 1988), although Tomasello (see Tomasello, 1998) concluded that the great apes are not capable of even this level of intersubjectivity.

Donald's story moves to the *mimetic* stage of the system of representation and communication, involving rhythmic movements, made possible by the human imitative capacity, a capacity that copies and mentally represents exact movements of another (and not just actions oriented toward a goal) and that is accessible to voluntary recall (autocuing). Such a capacity, when turned on itself, enables the practice of motor skills based on the internalization of an action pattern that guides the attempt to achieve better control. At the same time, it enables a new level of communication through modeling and gesturing between group members of new means to goals and thus makes possible both the generation and continuation of cultural forms, or true cultural learning in Tomasello et al.'s (1993) terms.

There are two aspects of the mimetic skills that Donald described as emerging during hominid evolution among *Homo erectus* and still characteristic of a level of our own representational systems. On the one hand, the mimetic capacity enabled individuals to analyze an action into its parts and to reconstitute it for themselves at a different time. This analytic representational capacity may be analogous to the construction of language in terms of words to refer to discrete aspects of the world. On the other hand, the capacity enables the construction of larger wholes, sequences of related actions, carried out both in rhythmic time with a whole group as in dance or in organized reciprocal activities as in games. In both aspects, the capacity is an advance over even social events, in that it involves self and others simultaneously in communicative and representational activity, playing self and other roles alternately as well as simultaneously.

Today we see in the symbolic play of early childhood, which begins in earnest around 2 years of age—play with dolls, trucks, blocks, sand—a reflection of both the event representation (ER) system and the mimetic system. The ER system is organized around children's place in an event— what they know how to do; the mimetic system replays others' roles as well. The two together support not only play but also skilled performance in familiar situations during the early preschool years, and they support as well the acquisition of language in familiar, already understood contexts. Whereas children must take others' roles into account in gaining knowledge about event routines such as the bath, the initial focus is on what to expect in general, that is, on knowledge of the event from the perspective of self. This is true of 2-year-olds in a new day-care setting, for example, as well as infants in their cribs. A different level of knowing comes into play when the role of the other is attended to and used as part of the knowledge base and as an advanced level of interpreting others' intentions, rising to a new level of intersubjectivity. The mode of this level is imitation.

Piaget placed imitation in the important role of internalization of action and thus of representation and symbolization. This aspect of his work has often baffled American cognitive psychologists conditioned to discount imitation as a low-level unproductive process. The importance of imitation in infancy has been brought out by Meltzoff's (1990) empirical studies, and has been subjected to new analysis and given new theoretical significance in developmental work by Tomasello (1990) and colleagues (1993), revealing it as the basis of cultural learning. They point out that true or exact imitation is rare among other primates (although this view has been challenged by some primatologists). For Donald's evolutionary scheme, mimesis, a strong form of precise imitation, is the missing link between action and language in human evolution. In mimesis, individuals attend to and model the actions of others. The model is internalized and becomes a mental representation that can be recalled voluntarily, just as Piaget (1962) posited.

A wide range of motoric and cognitive achievements beyond those discoverable by individual infants becomes possible through mimesis based on displays by other, more skilled actors. Mimesis is thus the basis of skill learning and skill practice, of social games, dance, song, tool use, tool construction, and in general the acquisition of symbolic information through the exchange of imitated action. Early vocal forms are shaped through imitative processes, both in evolution and development, and establish a common form that has the potential to assume and convey stabilized information. Thus mimesis carries individuals beyond self and other into the social group where group activity is engaged and cultural transmission takes place. Mimesis enables knowing others' parts as well as one's own, and through interiorizing others' parts, knowledge is shared in a way that knowledge based solely on individual action in the world cannot be.

When the same system—mimesis or language—serves both external communicative ends and internal representational ends, the way is opened for acquiring shared knowledge, not dependent on individual experience. This way of acquiring knowledge is manifestly true of language (however mysterious the process may be), and it is also true of mimesis, which is not just mimicking others' actions, but incorporating these actions into one's own representational thought processes. The real power of the mimetic representational system is that, like language, it is at once internal and external, both communicative and cognitive.

REPRESENTATION AND COMMUNICATION WITH LANGUAGE

Is language different? Of course. Both structurally and functionally, conventional language goes far beyond what mimesis alone offers. Language makes it feasible to talk about the possible and imagined, about the there and then as well as the here and now. It enables the sharing of points of view and thus goes beyond the perceptual and action sharing of mimesis to thought sharing. Language shapes the concepts derived from individual mental event representations and mimetic representations into stable, conventional, culturally shared concepts.

Yet, each of these higher order levels has its basis in the capacities that event knowledge provides. Event knowledge sets the framework for mimetic practices and for language learning and use. Knowledge grows outward from event knowledge; but from another perspective, event knowledge comes to incorporate within it both mimetic and linguistic forms and later still the graphic and electronic modes of communicating and cognizing that we as adults use today. This is the layered nature of the mature hybrid mind. In this model all representational levels may represent the same experience at the same time but in different ways; they do not compete but complement each other. But each new layer or level also feeds back onto and changes the former; we can never recapture the pure experiential level of infants who apparently live in a timeless world (Nelson, 1989; 1991).

Clearly, one of the most important developments in the postinfancy period is the mastery of language. Yet language plays a peculiar role in general cognitive models, just as it does in theories of cognitive development. Many of those who study adult cognition seem able to overlook the significance of language as well as all social and cultural environmental situatedness. As Wierzbicka (1994, p. 431) commented: "[M]ainstream modern psychology . . . at times seems to behave as if language is irrelevant to the study of mind." The quotations from Dennett and Miller at the beginning of the chapter indicate, however, that this neglect is not total. G. A. Miller's (1990) observation suggests an interpenetration of thought and language, not identity, not determinism, but a moving back and forth from one to the other.[4] It recognizes the importance and uniqueness of language not only as a system in its own right, but as the vehicle of both individual thought and interindividual communication. The challenge is to explicate the important developmental implications of this duality for conceptual thought and to show how such a position articulates with the role of action and interaction in intelligence.

Children begin learning and using conventional language forms around the end of the 1st year. However, in the first few years of language acquisition, language—that is, speech—is being learned and used primarily as a pragmatic operator, as a supplement to ongoing activity, but not as a representer of that activity. When a young child says, "You be the daddy" during play in the housekeeping corner, that child is reflecting his or her own representation of a meal situation and is tacitly assuming that the other child shares the same nonverbal representation. No verbalization of the representation need be called on. In a similar vein, script research (Nelson, 1986) has shown that children can provide verbalizations of knowing about events quite early, but they do not give a full representation of the script through language. When asked to give a script of having lunch or getting dressed, children of 3 years describe one or two actions that stand for the event; when playing out the event, they give evidence of a fuller representation. Thus although they do not at this age represent their knowledge in language, they may do so in action.

In light of these considerations, the phylogenetic sequence that Donald provides is provocative from the developmental perspective. It focuses our attention on the specifically human kinds of intelligent behaviors and capacities that children develop after the infancy period that propel them toward the adult state of human intelligence, using tools, language, and culture. Language, according to Donald, Dennett, and many other contemporary thinkers, made all the difference in enabling humans to engage

---

[4]From another point of view, thought and language are not separate systems; language is just symbolized thought (Tomasello, personal communication, December 7, 1996). But this puts the matter from the inside out only. To function as a system of meaning exchange, the language that expresses the thought of the speaker must be interpreted in terms of the thought of the listener.

in their technology-using, culture-generating ways of living. What difference does it make for children today?

THE DIFFERENCE THAT LANGUAGE MAKES

The contemporary adult world is one in which language reigns. Reality is not measured only in terms of direct experience: Language can change reality. It can bring back events from the past, project events in the future, and invoke events from a different place. It can also be used to express a point of view that is different from the listener's. A 3-year-old is only beginning to come into the kind of knowledge that language makes possible. These advantages come with the practiced use of language in discourse. As Dennett's statement suggests on the phylogenetic level, the cognitive advantage is revolutionary: Language can then be used internally as a representational system for organizing and remembering information. Language then becomes useful as a tool, a medium, and a mediator. As a mediator, language is a vehicle for knowledge gathering. As a medium, language represents knowledge on a level different from that of direct sensorimotor experience or on the level of action-based mimetic models. As a tool, language operates on the represented knowledge. It can thus be seen that Donald's theory of the evolution of human cognition is compatible with Vygotsky's conception of semiotic mediation, from which this description is derived.

From the point of view of the relation between representation and communication, event, mimetic, and linguistic modes differ. Event representations are individual and depend on individual experience—albeit in a social world—for their generation. Communication must be achieved by other means. Mimetic representations may be shared through the internal representation of imitated motoric actions. A representation may be both externalized and internalized but depends on the action systems of individuals. It thus enables sharing external forms, but not internal ones—thoughts, ideas, intentions, explanations. Language allows sharing another's point of view or knowledge through an abstract symbol system rather than via iconic action and thus may enable the construction of other perceptual worlds as well as other worlds of action, intention, and imagination.

This distinctively human level of understanding and entering into the intentional world begins as children acquire language and mimetic forms (games, songs, dance, socially promoted motor skills). Action and ecological perception together constitute individual social event representations; mimesis and symbolic forms of language both internally represent shared forms of knowledge. Language, however, is constituted by socially shared symbols and exists in socially shared symbolic systems. The critical difference is the possibility of sharing not just behavioral schemes but mental schemes as well. Symbols are by definition social: They exist to bring to one mind what is in another (see Figs. 12.2 and 12.3). The generalization to symbolic thought (e.g., private speech) in an individual is essentially that of one mind at one time and place communicating with the same, but now different, mind at a different time and place. As long as one lives in the world in the present (as infants do), there is no point in having symbols for oneself; there is only active reality, although representations of variable interactive possibilities in variable environments are of value. Language takes one simultaneously beyond the present into the past and future and beyond oneself into a socially shared reality. Language goes beyond this. Learning words means achieving a shared *continuing* reality, and it means a shared reality that can be accessed in many different contexts.

In the early years, event representations provide much of the basis for understanding language. Words enter into event representations as component speech acts; they also individuate the parts of the event and establish the parts as stable individual concepts that can be accessed outside the event context. Elena Levy and I (Levy & Nelson, 1994) have traced the uses of some quite abstract words and concepts, in particular causal and temporal language, as they are used by parents and a child over the course of a year. We have shown that temporal and causal terms are first used by the child in phrases borrowed from parents and referring to well-understood daily event routines before they are abstracted from these contexts and used with meaning in novel constructions. In these cases, we can see that the event representation serves as the basis for understanding and using the linguistic form. In a sense, the event representation provides the conceptual potential, but the potential is realized only when the linguistic form gives it a stable, culturally shared existence.[5]

Donald's (1991) account of the change from event to mimetic representation among *Homo erectus* claims that mimetic forms served as a transition to true language, the distinctive achievement of *Homo sapiens*. By this account, language made possible the flowering of culture beginning 30,000 years ago. It enabled the sharing of worldviews within a large social group, views that could be expressed in extended discourse, particularly in narrative forms such as myths and epics. In this conception, language is not primarily an instrument for naming things. It is a higher order capacity with social and cultural value. It ties a cultural group together.

Donald suggested that narrative is "the natural product of language." This idea fits the current emphasis on narrative as a distinctive mode of thought

---

[5]A similar analysis of the use of the mental terms *know* and *think* by mothers and their 2- and 3-year-old children is in progress (Shaw, 1998).

(e.g., Bruner, 1986) and as a particularly effective style of discourse in the socialization and enculturation of young children (P. J. Miller, Potts, Fung, Hoogstra, & Mintz, 1990; Nelson, 1996). Event representations seem to provide the basis from which narratives are expanded to include intentions—Bruner's landscape of consciousness—as well as actions. Young children understand stories because they are based on events; while stories highlight feelings and thoughts in verbal form and thus help to consolidate children's interpretive system for understanding other persons in the social world.

DEVELOPMENTAL IMPLICATIONS OF THE THIRD TRANSITION

Donald posits a further transition in human cognition with the introduction of external symbolic forms, especially alphabetic writing and later, print, in human history. He referred to these forms as external symbol systems (ESS). Like many other writers, he assumes that literacy has made an important change in the modes of human thinking. In particular, he believes that theories based on logical structures became possible only with the onset of external written forms. This part of the argument is too complex to summarize here, and it takes us beyond the achievements of preschool children of today. It is not irrelevant, however, to the consideration of the nature of young children's thought.

According to Donald, modern adult minds are hybrid, with representation levels of each of the kinds identified—basic event models, mimetic models, narrative models, and theoretic models. As a result, children today live in a hybrid culture in which adults, and most children of 7 years and older, read all kinds of materials, including books and newspapers, work on computers, talk on telephones, and so on; they are in fact both orally and literately competent. But small children who know a small amount of oral language, enough to name most of the things in their world and to negotiate basic needs, but not enough to tell what has happened to someone else, to explain what they need, or to say how to do something to someone who does not already know, cannot rely on these external means of representation and communication.

The situation of young children not yet proficient in the interpretation of everyday discourse among strangers is analogous to that of illiterate adults in our literate society who have managed to conceal their illiteracy by use of complex strategies. A 3-year-old in a laboratory test situation often appears very clever and knowledgeable, even when providing incorrect answers to what appear to be simple questions. The intelligent infant has not disappeared, but the intelligence of infancy is not adequate to the demands of the adult world, just as the intelligence of an oral culture is more limited and more context bound than that of a literate culture (Rubin, 1995).

Walter Ong (1982) has discussed the ways of being and thinking in oral cultures, that is, cultures without literate tools. It is provocative to consider that children's thinking in the transitional period from about 3 to 5 years bears many of the marks that Ong noted as characteristic of oral culture. For example, sustained thought in an oral culture is tied to communication, is aggregative rather than analytic, is close to the human life world, and is empathetic and participatory rather than objectively distanced. A number of other characteristics are cited by Ong and others as typical of oral societies, but these four seem to have particular relevance for how we think about children in the preschool years. Children in our literate hybrid culture are not the equivalent of adult nonliterate people in an oral culture, but they appear to share some of the same thought processes. For example, the explicit scaffolding that children need in thinking through a problem may reflect the general nature of thought without external aids. In effect, other people serve as external aids to internal thought processes. That thought is aggregative, piling up ideas—complexive in Vygotsky's terms— rather than analytic also reflects the difficulty of internal manipulation of dynamic concepts realized through speech rather than writing. That it is close to the human life world rather than abstract, and empathetic and participatory rather than distanced are long-recognized characteristics (Cocking & Renniger, 1993; Sigel, 1970) that follows from its basis in experientially derived knowledge systems.

What lies ahead? A 5-year-old, although advanced in comparison to a 2-year-old, is still an oralist in a literate and electronic culture. A child on the verge of the school years has yet to be inducted into literate ways of knowing and thinking. That different and enormously important story extends the account of language in cognitive development up to adulthood and needs to take into account the establishment of new written language skills, skills that Donald argues made possible theoretical constructions in historical time. The implication of this last development is that learning and using oral language, even on an elaborate expressive level, are insufficient for following the complex arguments and ideas of a literate society and for making them one's own. They are insufficient for generating original theoretical constructions or logical arguments, although quite capable of flights of fancy and mythic constructions, told and elaborated in a community. This observation, supported by the work of many scholars (Eisenstein, 1993; Olson, 1994; Ong, 1982; Rubin, 1995) who have studied the structure of oral, written, and printed works, brings into question the attribution of theories to the minds of small children (a now widespread assumption among contemporary cognitive developmentalists, e.g., Carey & Spelke, 1994; Gopnik & Meltzoff, 1996; Gopnik & Wellman, 1994).

Without denigrating the intelligence of young children but also recognizing the limitations of an immature nervous system, restricted experience in the world, little exposure to varied social contexts, and a context-constrained oral vocabulary, we can reasonably doubt the attribution of coherent theoretical constructions as basic representational structures for preschool children, much less infants or toddlers. The fact that children seem to want explanations of their observations of the world does not imply that they are constructing theories, although they may be generating hypotheses and making original associations between observed events. An example from Callanan and Oakes's (1992) study of children's "why" questions is instructive. In this study, mothers kept diaries of the causal questions and explanations that their preschool children exhibited; the following is excerpted from one of these reports.

Situation: Bedtime

Child: Why does Daddy, James (big brother), and me have blue eyes and you have green eyes?

Parent: (Told her she got her eyes from Daddy. Then said goodnight and left the room.)

Child: (Child calls mother back 5 minutes later.) I like Pee Wee Herman and I have blue eyes. Daddy likes Pee Wee Herman and he has blue eyes. James likes Pee Wee Herman and he has blue eyes. If you liked Pee Wee Herman you could get blue eyes too.

Parent: (I told her it would take more than my liking Pee Wee Herman to make my eyes blue. I realized that she didn't understand me, so I explained that God gave me this color and that they couldn't be changed.)

Child: Could you try to like Pee Wee Herman so we could see if your eyes turn blue?

Parent: (I said I would think about it, but if my eyes stayed green it was ok.) (Callanan & Oakes, 1992, 221–222)

Although this example indicates creative causal thinking, it violates in the most extreme way the boundary between basic biological and symbolic cultural domains and hardly suggests the possession of systematically organized, causally related knowledge (i.e., theories) in either domain.

How does this bear on the problem of children's theory of mind that I raised earlier? If we bring together Donald's claim that narrative is the natural product of language, Bruner's positing of the "landscape of consciousness" (intentionality) as the essential ingredient of narrative, and the observation of children's intuitive understanding of story and easy acquisition of narrative form (P. J. Miller, 1990), we have an attractive alternative source of children's emerging understanding of others' psychological states. From this perspective, children do not construct *theories of mind,* nor do they acquire theories of mind. They enter into the cultural world models instantiated in stories—real and fictional, personal and social—wherein actions are motivated and explained in terms of the emotions, desires, and beliefs of the characters who act. Thus, the representational claims of Donald and the intentionality claims of Bruner come full circle into the developmental story of layered representations that support children's emergence into the cultural way of making human sense.

From this perspective, we may reconstruct the theory of mind problem as the problem of the construction of self and other through the co-construction of the initially missing symbolic link (see Figs. 12.2 & 12.3). The full story is then one of collaboration and integration. Children begin with basic event knowledge followed late in the 1st year and into the 2nd by coordinated action mimetic schemes. The communicated perspectives and knowledge of others are sources through which children elaborate and transform their earlier experiential representations at the same time that the event knowledge provides the source of conceptual knowledge structures with the potential to take on the new meanings implicated in the language of the cultural community. Among these cultural knowledge systems are the folk theories of mental entities that lie behind and seem to explain human action. These and other folk theories (of biology, cosmology, and so on) are incorporated in the categories of the language (as asserted by Whorf, 1956) and are displayed causally in the discourse of adults. Like language itself, they are complex systems elaborated and extended over generations of human cultural histories. They are not invented by young children on their own but are reconstructed anew in each generation through the marvelous social exchange tool that we call language.

In the end, we come back to the dual role that language plays: at once an individual representation system and a shared communicative system, each with enormous power. Individual children always contribute to any communicative exchange a unique representation based on a unique experiential history. Thus the construction of knowledge through language must be thought of as a collaborative process, neither the product of the social other nor of an individual child, but a collaboration between the two. As Ong noted with regard to oral culture, sustained thought is tied to communication. For this purpose, we need to conceive, not of a closed system mind interacting with a passive world or of an open mind receiving knowledge like a sponge, but of a constructive, generative mind in continual, active exchange with the social world, collaboratively working on models of the lived experience as well as representations of the unexperienced and newly constructed or conceived.

REFERENCES

Antinucci, F. (1990). The comparative study of cognitive ontogeny in four primate species. In S. Parker & K. R. Gibson (Eds.), *"Language" and intelligence in monkeys and apes: Comparative developmental perspectives* (pp. 157–171). New York: Cambridge University Press.

Bartsch, K., & Wellman, H. M. (1995). *Children talk about the mind.* New York: Oxford University Press.

Bickhard, M. H. (1997). Is cognition an autonomous subsystem? In S. O'Nuallain, P. McKevitt, & B. MacAogain (Eds.), *Two sciences of mind* (pp. 115–131). Amsterdam: John Benjamins.

Bruner, J. S. (1986). *Actual minds, possible worlds.* Cambridge, MA: Harvard University Press.

Byrne, R. (1995). *The thinking ape: Evolutionary origins of intelligence.* New York: Oxford University Press.

Byrne, R., & Whiten, A. (Eds.). (1988). *Machiavellian intelligence.* Oxford, England: Oxford University Press.

Callanan, M. A., & Oakes, L. M. (1992). Preschoolers' questions and parents' explanations: Causal thinking in everyday activity. *Cognitive Development, 7,* 213–233.

Carey, S., & Spelke, E. (1994). Domain-specific knowledge and conceptual change. In L. A. Hirschfeld & S. A. Gelman (Eds.), *Mapping the mind: Domain specificity in cognition and culture* (pp. 169–200). New York: Cambridge University Press.

Chomsky, N. (1965). *Aspects of a theory of syntax.* Cambridge, MA: MIT Press.

Cocking, R. R., & Renninger, K. A. (Eds.). (1993). *The development and meaning of psychological distance.* Hillsdale, NJ: Lawrence Erlbaum Associates.

Cole, M. (1996). *Cultural psychology: A once and future discipline.* Cambridge, MA: Harvard University Press.

Dennett, D. (1994). Language and intelligence. In J. Khafa (Ed.), *What is intelligence?* (pp. 161–178). Cambridge, MA: Cambridge University Press.

DeVilliers, J. (1996, October). *Complementing cognition: The relationship between language and theory of mind.* Paper presented at the Boston University Child Language Conference, Boston.

Dewey, J. (1961). *Democracy and education.* New York: Macmillan. (Original work published 1916)

Donald, M. (1991). *Origins of the modern mind.* Cambridge, MA: Harvard University Press.

Eisenstein, E. (1993). *The printing revolution in early modern Europe.* New York: Cambridge University Press.

Fodor, J. (1983). *Modularity of mind.* Cambridge, MA: MIT Press.

Gallistel, C. R. (1989). Animal cognition: The representation of space, time and number. In M. R. Rosenzwig & L. W. Porter (Eds.), *Annual review of psychology* (Vol. 40, pp. 155–189). Palo Alto, CA: Annual Reviews.

Gibson, J. J. (1986). *The ecological approach to visual perception.* Hillsdale, NJ: Lawrence Erlbaum Associates.

Gopnik, A. (1993). How we know our minds: The illusion of first-person knowledge of intentionality. *Behavioral and Brain Sciences, 16,* 1–14.

Gopnik, A., & Meltzoff, A. (1996). *Words, thoughts, and theories.* Cambridge, MA: MIT Press.

Gopnik, A., & Wellman, H. M. (1994). The theory theory. In L. A. Hirschfeld & S. A. Gelman (Eds.), *Mapping the mind: Domain specificity in cognition and culture* (pp. 257–293). New York: Cambridge University Press.

Harris, P. L. (1992). From simulation to folk psychology: The case for development. *Mind and Language, 7,* 120–144.

Hendriks-Jansen, H. (1996). *Catching ourselves in the act: Situated activity, interactive emergence, evolution, and human thought.* Cambridge, MA: MIT Press.

Hirschfeld, L. A., & Gelman, S. A. (Eds.). (1994). *Mapping the mind: Domain specificity in cognition and culture.* New York: Cambridge University Press.

James, W. (1950). *The principles of psychology.* New York: Dover. (Original work published 1890)

Leslie, A. M. (1991). The theory of mind impairment in autism: Evidence for a modular mechanism of development? In A. Whiten (Ed.), *Natural theories of mind* (pp. 63–78). Oxford, England: Basil Blackwell.

Levy, E., & Nelson, K. (1994). Words in discourse: A dialectical approach to the acquisition of meaning and use. *Journal of Child Language, 21,* 367–390.

Meltzoff, A. N. (1990). Foundations for developing a concept of self. In D. Cicchetti & M. Beeghly (Eds.), *The self in transition* (pp. 139–164). Chicago: University of Chicago Press.

Meltzoff, A. N., & Gopnik, A. (1993). The role of imitation in understanding persons and developing theories of mind. In S. Baron-Cohen, H. Tager-Flusberg, & D. Cohen (Eds.), *Understanding other minds: Perspectives from autism* (pp. 335–366). New York: Oxford University Press.

Miller, G. A. (1990). The place of language in a scientific psychology. *Psychological Sciences, 1,* 7–14.

Miller, P. J., Potts, R., Fung, H., Hoogstra, L., & Mintz, J. (1990). Narrative practices and the social construction of self in childhood. *American Ethnologist, 17,* 292–311.

Nelson, K. (1978). How young children represent knowledge of their world in and out of language. In R. S. Siegler (Ed.), *Children's thinking: What develops?* (pp. 225–273). Hillsdale, NJ: Lawrence Erlbaum Associates.

Nelson, K. (1986). *Event knowledge: Structure and function in development.* Hillsdale, NJ: Lawrence Erlbaum Associates.

Nelson, K. (1989). Monologue as construction of self in time. In K. Nelson (Ed.), *Narratives from the crib* (pp. 284–308). Cambridge, MA: Harvard University Press.

Nelson, K. (1991). The matter of time: Interdependencies between language and thought in development. In S. A. Gelman & J. P. Byrnes (Eds.), *Perspectives on language and cognition: Interrelations in development* (pp. 278–318). New York: Cambridge University Press.

Nelson, K. (1996). *Language in cognitive development: The emergence of the mediated mind.* New York: Cambridge University Press.

Nelson, K., & Gruendel, J. (1981). Generalized event representations: Basic building blocks of cognitive development. In M. Lamb & A. Brown (Eds.), *Advances in developmental psychology* (Vol. 1, pp. 131–158). Hillsdale, NJ: Lawrence Erlbaum Associates.

Nelson, K., & Gruendel, J. (1986). Children's scripts. In K. Nelson (Ed.), *Event knowledge: Structure and function in development* (pp. 21–46). Hillsdale, NJ: Lawrence Erlbaum Associates.

Ogden, C. K., & Richards, I. A. (1946). *The meaning of meaning* (8th ed.). London: Routledge & Kegan Paul. (Original work published 1923)

Olson, D. R. (1994). *The world on paper.* New York: Cambridge University Press.

Ong, W. J. (1982). *Orality and literacy: The technologizing of the word.* New York: Routledge.

Oyama, S. (1985). *The ontogeny of information: Developmental systems and evolution.* New York: Cambridge University Press.

Peirce, C. S. (1960). *The collected papers of Charles Sanders Peirce* (C. Hartshorne & P. Weiss, Eds.). Cambridge, MA: Harvard University Press.

Piaget, J. (1952). *The origins of intelligence in children.* New York: Norton.

Piaget, J. (1962). *Play, dreams and imitation in childhood.* New York: Norton.

Reed, E. S. (1993). *The ecological approach to language development: A radical solution to Chomsky's and Quine's problems.* Unpublished manuscript.

Reed, E. S., & Bril, B. (1996). The primacy of action in development. In M. Latash & M. Turvey (Eds.), *Dexterity and its development.* Hillsdale, NJ: Lawrence Erlbaum Associates.

Rogoff, B. (1990). *Apprenticeship in thinking: Cognitive development in social context.* New York: Oxford University Press.

Rubin, D. (1995). *Memory in oral traditions.* New York: Oxford University Press.

Shatz, M. (1994). Theory of mind and the development of social-linguistic intelligence in early childhood. In C. Lewis & P. Mitchell (Eds.), *Children's early understanding of mind: Origins and development* (pp. 311–330). Hillsdale, NJ: Lawrence Erlbaum Associates.

Shaw, L. K. (1998). *Meaning of mental state terms in context of use by mothers and young children.* Doctoral dissertation in preparation, City University of New York Graduate Center.

Sigel, I. E. (1970). The distancing hypothesis: A causal hypothesis for the acquisition of representational thought. In M. R. Jones (Ed.), *Miami symposium on the prediction of behavior, 1968; Effects of early experience* (pp. 99–118). Coral Gables, FL: University of Miami Press.

Spelke, E. S., Breinlinger, K., Macomber, J., & Jacobson, K. (1992). Origins of knowledge. *Psychological Review, 99,* 605–632.

Tomasello, M. (1990). Cultural transmission in the tool use and communicatory signaling of chimpanzees? In S. T. Parker & K. R. Gibson (Eds.), *"Language" and intelligence in monkeys and apes* (pp. 274–311). New York: Cambridge University Press.

Tomasello, M. (1992). The social bases of language acquisition. *Social Development, 1,* 67–87.

Tomasello, M. (1998). Uniquely primate, uniquely human. *Developmental Science, 1,* 1–16.

Tomasello, M., Kruger, A. C., & Ratner, . (1993). Cultural learning. *Behavioral and Brain Sciences,* 495–552.

Valsiner, J. (1987). *Culture and the development of children's action.* New York: Wiley.

Vygotsky, L. (1986). *Thought and language.* Cambridge, MA: MIT Press.

Wellman, H. M. (1990). *The child's theory of mind.* Cambridge, MA: MIT Press.

Wertsch, J. (1991). *Voices in the mind.* Cambridge, MA: Harvard University Press.

Whorf, B. L. (1956). *Language, thought and reality: Selected writings of Benjamin Lee Whorf.* Cambridge, MA: MIT Press.

Wierzbicka, A. (1994). Cognitive domains and the structure of the lexicon: The case of the emotions. In L. A. Hirschfeld & S. A. Gelman (Eds.), *Mapping the mind* (pp. 431–452). New York: Cambridge University Press.

Chapter 13

Sources of Conceptual Change

Susan Carey
New York University

THE VERY NOTION OF CONCEPTUAL CHANGE

Accounting for the emergence of novelty, of the genuinely *new*, is among the deepest mysteries facing students of development. Cognitive development consists, in part, of the acquisition of new representational resources, such as natural languages, written languages, mathematical and logical notations. Cognitive development also consists, in part, of the acquisition of new systems of concepts that allow the expression of thoughts previously unthinkable. This latter kind of novelty arises whenever knowledge acquisition involves conceptual change, and conceptual change concerns me here.

Conceptual change must be distinguished from cognitive development in general. Three expressions are often used interchangeably: *knowledge acquisition, cognitive development,* and *conceptual change.* In scientific discourse, we can adopt whatever terminology we wish as long as we are clear, but it is theoretically useful to distinguish among the three expressions and to give *conceptual change* the meaning that it receives in the literature on history and philosophy of science. *Cognitive development* is the broadest of the three: Strategy development, skill development, maturationally driven increases in information-processing capacity or executive function, knowledge acquisition all fall in the domain of the study of cognitive development. *Knowledge acquisition* is more focused: All changes in beliefs, mastery of new facts, and increases in implicit and explicit understanding exemplify knowledge acquisition. Finally, *conceptual change* is the most specific: It is (as it says) change at the level of individual concepts. Conceptual change belongs in the domain of knowledge acquisition, but it occurs only rarely as children construct understanding of the world. As Piaget insisted, sometimes knowledge acquisition involves knowledge restructuring. Conceptual change is part of the process of knowledge restructuring.

Although there are many knowledge structures worthy of study (scripts, schemata, prototypes, the integer list representation of number, the alphabet), many students of cognitive development have assumed that one kind of knowledge structure, intuitive theories, plays a particularly important role in cognitive architecture (Carey, 1985b; Gopnik & Meltzoff, 1997; Keil, 1989; Wellman & Gelman, 1992). I endorse this assumption, and here I focus on what Wellman and Gelman (1992) called framework theories. This class of intuitive theories grounds the deepest ontological commitments and the most general explanatory principles in terms of which we understand our world. One task (but by no means the only task) in the study of cognitive development is accounting for the acquisition of framework theories.

It is worth stepping back and considering what is presupposed by the choice of the term *intuitive theory* rather than the neutral *cognitive structure*. Intuitive theories play several unique roles in mental life. These include determining a concept's core (the properties seen as essential to membership in a concept's extension), representing causal and explanatory knowledge, and supporting explanation-based inference. As Gopnik and Meltzoff (1997) emphasized, the mechanisms underlying theory development differ from those underlying the acquisition of different conceptual structures. It is an empirical question whether children represent intuitive theories and whether knowledge acquisition in childhood involves the process of theory change. Those who talk of intuitive theories and framework theories are explicitly committing themselves to an affirmative answer to these empirical questions. This commitment does not deny that there are important differences between children as theorizers and adult scientists (hence the qualifier "intuitive theories"). Children are not metaconceptually aware theory builders (e.g., D. Kuhn, Amsel, & O'Loughlin, 1988). In spite of these differences, the research enterprise in which this work is placed presupposes that questions can be asked, literally, of both scientific theories and intuitive theories and that the answers are the same in both cases. The merit of this presupposition depends on the fruitfulness of the research that it generates. See, for example, the explicit comparison of conceptual change in thermal concepts in the history of science and of conceptual change in concepts of matter in middle childhood (Carey, 1991; Smith, Carey, & Wiser, 1985; Wiser & Carey, 1983). The present chapter is a case study framed in this research tradition.

Conceptual change is implicated in cases of theory development that involve incommensurability. A given theory at Time 1, Theory 1 ($T1$), and the descendent of that theory at Time 2, Theory 2 (*T*2), are incommensurable insofar as the beliefs of one cannot be formulated over the concepts of the other, that is, insofar as the two are not mutually translatable. Not all theory development involves conceptual change; theories are often merely enriched as new knowledge accumulates about the phenomena in the domain of the theory. Theory enrichment consists of the acquisition of new beliefs formulated over a constant conceptual repertoire. I (Carey, 1991) provided a summary of related analyses of conceptual change in the philosophical literature (Hacking, 1993; Kitcher, 1978; T. S. Kuhn, 1962, 1982), as well as a defense of the claim that normal cognitive development involves theory changes that implicate incommensurability.

Conceptual changes take several forms. Perhaps the most common is differentiation. In conceptual differentiations involving incommensurability, the undifferentiated parent concept from *T*1 no longer plays any role in *T*2. Examples include Galileo's differentiation of *average* from *instantaneous velocity* (T. S. Kuhn, 1977), Black's differentiation of *heat* from *temperature* (Wiser & Carey, 1983), and a child's differentiation of *weight* from *density* (Carey, 1991; Smith et al., 1985). Another common type is coalescence. In coalescences involving incommensurability, entities considered ontologically distinct in *T*1 are subsumed under a single concept in *T*2. Examples include Galileo's abandonment of Aristotle's distinction between *natural* and *artificial motions* (T. S. Kuhn, 1977) and children's uniting of *animal* and *plant* into the new concept *living thing* (Carey, 1985b). Conceptual change may also involve the reanalysis of a concept's basic structure (such as the Newtonian reanalysis of *weight* from a property of objects to a relation between objects). Finally, on the common treatment of concepts as having a core–periphery structure, changes in the concept's core constitute examples of conceptual change (Kitcher, 1988; see Carey [1988, 1991] for examples of each of these conceptual changes in the course of normal cognitive development).

I want to dispel, at the outset, several misunderstandings about the claim that cognitive development involves conceptual change. It is important to note that the difference between knowledge enrichment and conceptual change is not sharp: There are many intermediate cases. Also, the analysis of conceptual change endorsed here is not that of T. S. Kuhn (1962) and Feyerabend (1962). These writers were committed to the existence of radical incommensurability, in which theories before and after conceptual change share no conceptual machinery. The incommensurability occurring in the historical and developmental theory building that I have examined is what T. S. Kuhn (1982) called *local incommensurability*, incommensurability that implicates only some of the concepts that articulate successive theories. Finally, conceptual change does not occur suddenly: There is not one moment of gestalt shift. It takes time for concepts to change, sometimes centuries in the history of science, always years for the individual scientist or student or child engaged in knowledge restructuring (Carey, 1985b, 1991; Chi, 1992; Gruber [on Darwin], 1974; T. S. Kuhn, 1977; Nersessian [on Maxwell], 1992).

WHAT IS AT STAKE

The distinction between conceptual change and knowledge enrichment, along with the existence of conceptual change in childhood, raises a fundamental descriptive question for those of us who study cognitive development: Which cases of knowledge acquisition involve incommensurability? Another way of putting the same descriptive question is: When are children's beliefs formulated over concepts incommensurable with ours? A preschool child tells us the sun is alive or that buttons are alive because they keep up pants. A preschool child tells us that it *cannot* be that statues are not alive, because we can see them. How are we to interpret these bizarre beliefs? Is the child saying something false, in terms of concepts shared with us? Is the child saying something true, formulated over concepts different from those expressed by our use of the same terms? If the latter, are the child's concepts locally incommensurable with ours?

Furthermore, the existence of conceptual change, both in childhood and in the history of science, raises some of the very toughest challenges to an understanding of the sources of cognitive development. Many classes of learning mechanisms, which account for a major share of knowledge acquisition, consist of selection or concatenation over an existing conceptual base. These classes include hypothesis testing, parameter setting, association, and correlation detection, among others. Additional learning mechanisms of some other sort must be implicated in conceptual change.

CONCEPTUAL CHANGE IN CHILDHOOD:
INTUITIVE BIOLOGY

The literature contains myriad case studies of conceptual change. Many case studies are historical and document changes from $T1$ to $T2$ over decades or centuries. These include the often mined case of the change from the phlogiston theory to the oxygen theory of burning (Kitcher, 1978; T. S. Kuhn, 1962, 1982; Thagard, 1992), the change from Aristotle's to Galileo's physics (T. S. Kuhn, 1977), the construction of the concept of the gene in the 20th century (Kitcher, 1993), and changes in thermal concepts in the 17th century (Wiser & Carey, 1983). Other case studies focus on theory construction by individual scientists, such as Gruber's

(1974) classic study of Darwin's shift from a monad theory of evolution to the theory of natural selection and Nersessian's (1992) study of the process through which Maxwell formulated electromagnetic theory. Finally, there have been several studies of conceptual change in childhood. In an earlier Piaget Society volume, I sketched evidence for conceptual change in elementary school-aged students' intuitive theory of matter (Carey, 1991; see Piaget & Inhelder, 1941; Smith et al., 1985); see also Vosniadu & Brewer's (1992) study of changes in concepts such as *earth, sun, moon,* which occur over the same age range.

Here, I focus on the conceptual change that is part of the development of a framework theory of intuitive biology, a case I have described in detail elsewhere (Carey, 1985b, 1988, 1995). Consider, to begin with, the changes in the ontologically central concepts of *person* and *animal* between ages 4 and 10. Young infants and preschoolers have an elaborate concept of *person.* Even young infants distinguish people from nonpeople and have different expectations about the two classes of entities (cf. Leslie, 1994; Spelke, Phillips, & Woodward, 1995; Wellman & Gelman, 1992). Young preschool children, even infants, also have a concept of *animal* that serves as the basis for the accumulation of extensive encyclopedic knowledge about different kinds of animals (Carey, 1985b; Mandler, Bauer, & McDonough, 1991; Wellman & Gelman, 1992). Young preschoolers distinguish animals from nonanimals and use this distinction productively in similarity-based inductive reasoning. Nevertheless, there is ample evidence that preschoolers' concepts of *animal* and *person* differ from 10-year-olds and are embedded in very different framework theories (Carey, 1985b, 1988, 1995).

I have argued that the core of preschoolers' concept of *animal* is that of a behaving being, in essence a simplified variant of the prototypical behaving being—people. That people and animals are capable of self-generated, goal-directed, attention-guided motion is at the core of these concepts. The attribution of goal directedness (e.g., Gergely, Nasdasdy, Csibra, & Biro, 1995; Meltzoff, 1995) and attention guidedness (Johnson, Slaughter, & Carey, 1998) provides the explanatory structure to older infants' and young preschoolers' understanding of people's and animals' behavior. That is, preschoolers' framework theory (*T*1) in which the concepts of *person* and *animal* are embedded is a theory of mind or intuitive psychology rather than an intuitive biology. Some researchers have disagreed and have characterized *T*1 as an intuitive biology, organized around central explanatory concepts such as essentialism or functional explanation (Gelman, Coley, & Gottfried, 1994; Keil, 1994). In either characterization of *T*1, preschoolers' extensive encyclopedic knowledge about animals includes many facts not yet integrated into any causal framework (Carey, 1985b, 1995). By age 10 (recent workers have revised this estimate downward, closer to age 7 or even younger; see the following discussion and Carey, 1995, for a review), children have constructed a new intuitive theory of biology (*T*2), with *animal* and *plant* coalesced into the single core ontological kind of *living thing* (Carey, 1985b; Keil, 1979) organized around the life cycle and the function of bodily parts in the service of maintaining life rather than supporting behavior. Inagaki and Hatano (1993) characterized this new biology as a vitalist biology. Crider (1981) characterized it as the container theory of the body. Here, I call this new framework theory *T*2, by which I mean an intuitive biology organized around core concepts of the life cycle of organisms, as well as a view of bodily function in the support of maintaining life.

For it to be true that there are conceptual changes in the concepts of *person* and *animal* over these years, there must be conceptual changes in a host of interrelated concepts. Other changes include the differentiation of preschoolers' concept of *not alive* into adults' concept of *dead, inanimate, unreal,* and *nonexistent* (Carey, 1985b, 1988; Laurendeau & Pinard, 1962; Piaget, 1929) and the differentiation of children's concept of *family* into separate concepts of *biological family* and *social family* (Solomon, Johnson, Zaitchik, & Carey, 1996). Others include the reanalysis of *death* from a behavioral interpretation to include the collapse of the bodily machine (Carey, 1985b; Koocher, 1974; Nagy, 1948, 1953; Slaughter, Jaakkola, & Carey, in press) and the reanalysis of *baby* from small, helpless animal to reproductive offspring (Callanan, Perez, McCarrell, & Latzke, 1992; Carey, 1985b, 1988). The core features of the concept of *species kind* shift from physical and behavioral characteristics toward origins of the animal (Johnson & Solomon, 1997; Keil, 1989). Finally, the concept of *person* is reanalyzed from *prototypical behaving being* to *one-animal-among-many* (Carey, 1985b).

CONCEPTUAL CHANGE IN INTUITIVE BIOLOGY: THE EVIDENCE

There are many types of evidence for emergence of a vitalist biology in the early school years, the core of which is the concept of *life*, and for the absence of this concept earlier in the preschool years. The earliest and most abundant source of data is the Piagetian clinical interview, which has been used in the realm of intuitive biology to explore children's understanding of the nature of life and what things are alive (the animism interview, e.g., Carey, 1985b; Hatano et al., 1993; Laurendau & Pinard, 1962; Piaget, 1929; Safier, 1964), their understanding of death (e.g., Koocher, 1973; Nagy, 1948; Speece & Brent, 1992; Slaughter et al., in press; White, Elsom, & Prawat, 1978), illness (e.g., Au & Romo, 1996; Bibace & Walsh, 1981), reproduction (e.g., Bernstein & Cowan, 1975; Goldman &

Goldman, 1982), and bodily organs (e.g., Crider, 1981; Nagy, 1953; Slaughter et al., in press; see Carey, 1985b, chap. 2, for a review of this literature).

The animism interview provides simple, straightforward evidence that preschool children have not differentiated the biological concept of *life* from other concepts, namely *activity, existence,* and *reality*. Preschool children judge some inanimate objects alive (some children judge everything that exists or is real to be alive and justify their judgments with comments such as "You can see it"; others judge only some inanimate active, useful things or some inanimate things that move or move on their own to be alive). Only at the end of elementary school do children restrict life to animals and plants and justify their choices by reference to biological criteria (growth, need for food and air, death; Carey, 1985b; Hatano et al., 1993; Laurendau & Pinard, 1962). My (Carey, 1985b) version of the animism interview provides a clear reflection of preschoolers' undifferentiated concept of *alive* via an analysis of children's examples of things that are not alive. Preschoolers do not reply with examples of inanimate objects; rather, they give examples of dead, imaginary, unreal entities, such as their grandpa, George Washington, dinosaurs, gremlins, cartoon figures, or pictures on television (Carey, 1985b, chap. 1).

Understanding the source of preschoolers' undifferentiated concept of life has two parts—a positive characterization of what concepts they have and what input they have received as well as a characterization of concepts they have not yet constructed (lack of differentiation is always relative to subsequent, differentiated concepts). First, their concept of living things is supported by adult use of the word *alive*. Young children hear this word applied to people and animals; thus it inherits its ontological status from the fact that it can be predicated of (Keil 1979) what are fundamentally behaving beings. In addition, monsters, representations, and dead things are contrasted with living things, often to reassure children. That is, adults do not restrict the alive-not alive contrast to the contrast between biological and nonbiological material entities. Second, preschoolers have not yet constructed a biological concept of life and death and do not have these differentiated concepts available as possible meanings for the lexical contrast alive-not alive.

As an aside on the form of argument I am developing here, I make three uses of preschoolers' alleged undifferentiated concept of *alive*. First, I offer it as part of the evidence that preschoolers have not yet constructed *T*2. Second, I claim that it is, itself, part of the source of *T*2. And finally, I use the lack of *T*2 (a lack supported by much convergent evidence) as part of an explanation for why preschoolers have not mapped *alive* onto the biological concept of *living thing*.

Evidence that preschoolers have not yet constructed a biological concept of death also derives from clinical interviews (e.g., Koocher, 1973; Nagy,

1948; Slaughter et al., in press; Speece & Brent, 1992; White, Elsom, & Prawat, 1978). The interviews probed children's views about what entities can die, what happens to a person or an animal when it dies, whether death is inevitable, whether death is reversible, and what causes death. Preschool children understand death as continued existence in altered circumstances, someplace else (under the ground, in heaven). They analogize it to sleep (because dead people are lying down, motionless, and have their eyes closed). They often do not consider death inevitable or final and understand its causes to be avoidable (when asked to state the causes of death, one of the most common preschooler suggestion is poison) and external. In a recent addition to the standard interview, Slaughter et al. (in press) asked 4- to 6-year-olds whether dead people need food, air, and water, need to go to the bathroom, and move and dream, and whether a cut on a dead person's body would heal. More than half of those children who had not yet begun to construct a vitalistic understanding of bodily function answered these questions affirmatively except that they judged that dead people do not move.

Preschoolers' concept of death is intimately intertwined with their concept of life: Children learn from adult usage that death is opposed to life (to be dead is to be not alive) and that people and animals die. If they see a dead animal, they see that to be dead is to have fallen down and to be motionless. Lack of motion is particularly salient, because activity and behavior are at the core of preschoolers' concept of animals. Naturally, children construct their concept of death from the elements available to them. Thus for preschoolers, death is the negative of the undifferentiated concept of life: To be dead is to be not alive, to be inactive, unreal, nonexistent, absent. A full analysis of how their concept differs from adults' requires attention to what they lack. Because they have not yet constructed the vitalist understanding of the bodily machine, they are not in a position to understand the causes of death in terms of its breakdown or to understand death as the inevitable, irreversible, terminus of every living thing's life cycle. Death is opposed to life for all of us, but without a differentiated, biological concept of life, a biological concept of death is impossible for preschool children to achieve. The clinical interview literature reviewed here indicates that this process is not complete until the end of the elementary school years.

The evidence that preschool children have not yet constructed an understanding of the bodily machine also derives from interview studies (Crider, 1981; Nagy, 1953; Slaughter et al., in press). When asked what is inside the human body, preschool children are, not astonishingly, remarkably ignorant: They respond "Bones, blood," and sometimes "heart." Simons and Keil (1995) dramatically confirmed that preschool children are completely ignorant of the internal structure of animal bodies. When asked to pick from three pictures that came from inside a body, 4-year-olds were as likely to pick a picture of gears and other metal devices as to pick pictures of actual bodily organs or other biological-looking possible parts. Furthermore, the clinical interview literature confirms that preschoolers are ignorant of the functions of those bodily organs that they do know about. They tend to offer very general functions (e.g., "The heart is for your body"), and if they offer any specific functions, it is on a "one organ–one function basis," such that the functions are not coordinated in any way (the heart is for beating or making blood, the stomach is for food, the lungs are for air, and the brain is for thinking), just as external organs can be assigned a function (the eyes are for seeing, the hands for holding things, the legs for walking).

The clinical interview studies show that by age 10 children have constructed what Crider (1981) called a container theory of the body. This theory is that certain crucial substances are needed to support body maintenance (air, food, water), that the lungs and stomach are the containers for these substances as they are taken in from the environment, and that the blood takes them from these initial containers and distributes them throughout the body. This theory is the vitalist biology more recently and more fully described by Inagaki and Hatano (1993): Bodily function supports life, which requires certain substances (food, air, water) for its constant replenishment. Each bodily organ is assigned a causal role in the intake and processing of these life-sustaining necessities. Any breakdown of this system (the person fails to eat, drink or breathe, the heart stops beating, etc.) causes death.

The clinical interview methodology taps explicit, formulatable knowledge and has been criticized for underestimating what children know. Young children certainly represent concepts they cannot explicitly define, and their inferences are constrained by knowledge they cannot formulate. More sensitive methodologies have placed the construction of the vitalist biology closer to age 6 than to age 10. Inagaki and Hatano (1993) gave children an explanation choice task, in which they were presented with different types of explanations for bodily processes (e.g., why do we bleed when we cut ourselves, why do cuts heal, why do we eat food?). Six-, eight-, and ten-year-old children chose what they considered the best explanation from among three offered for each question. For the eating question, for example, the choices were an intentional explanation (we eat because we like tasty food), a vitalist explanation (we eat because we get vital energy from the food), and a mechanistic explanation (we eat because we need the substance to build new muscle and bone as we grow). They found that children of all these ages rejected the intentional explanation. Six-year-olds preferred the vitalist explanations, ten-year-olds the mechanistic explanations. From these data, they argued that the first biology that children construct is a vitalist biology and that between ages 6 and 10 there is a shift to a mechanist biology.

Jaakkola (1997) recently offered a friendly amendment to these findings as well as her interpretation. She added a 4-year-old group and adapted the procedure so that younger children could do the task. She also made the three types of explanations more comparable in complexity. She found that 4-year-olds had no preference for any of the types of explanations. Control tasks, in which the explanation choices concerned mechanical causality, showed that 4-year-olds could manage the explanation choice methodology; their failure in the bodily process version reflected no preference as to what type of explanation was valid in these cases. In addition, she confirmed that by age 6 children preferred vitalistic explanations to intentional ones, but they equally preferred mechanistic ones. She argued that Inagaki and Hatano's mechanistic explanations also reflected a vitalist biology, one in which more details of the bodily processes have been filled in.

Jaakkola's findings added credence to the claim that 4-year-olds have not yet constructed a vitalist biology in which important vital substances must be obtained from the world to subserve the maintenance of life. In support of this conclusion, Jaakkola (1997) also looked at a modified clinical interview on body parts. She asked 4-, 6-, and 8-year-old children what various parts of the body were for and what would happen if a person didn't have the relevant part (e.g., didn't have eyes, hands, a heart, a brain.) Four-year-olds were in general unable to offer any specific bodily functions for most internal organs, although they were able to reply appropriately for external body parts (e.g., eyes are for seeing; hands are for picking things up). Explicit teleological reasoning did not defeat them, and the functions they offered for external body parts were generated from their understanding of people as intentional, behaving beings. Jaakkola added a further finding to this picture of ignorance of biological teleological functions for internal body parts: Between ages 4 and 6, children became "life theorizers," in the very weak sense that they began to appeal to life as the teleological goal of body parts. That is, in response to questions about what internal body parts were for or what happened without them, they began to provide general (and uninformative with respect to specific bodily process) answers such as, "You need a heart to live" or "Without a heart, you'd die." This change between ages 4 and 6 is consistent with the claim that a skeletal vitalist biology is constructed over these years.

The clinical interview literature reviewed here shows marked development in each of these domains throughout the elementary school years. As just reviewed, however, recent, more focused studies, in contrast, seem to contradict the findings of this literature. The clinical interview literature places the construction of T2, a vitalist theory of the body, with the biological concepts of *life* and *death* at its core, at the end of the elementary school years, but Inagaki and Hatano (1993), Jaakkola (Jaakkola, 1997), and Slaughter et al. (in press) provided evidence of *T2* by age 6. Part of the resolution of this apparent contradiction is methodological. The clinical interview tasks are more open ended than those of the more recent literature: More constrained tasks are more sensitive to partial, less robust knowledge. Even with the more constrained explanation choice methods, with more focused questions, the newer literature did not show *T2* to be completely in place by age 6 (e.g., Inagaki & Hatano, 1993; Jaakola, 1997; Slaughter et al., in press). Conceptual change takes time, and is ongoing throughout the elementary school years, a process that explains the gradual diminishment of animistic responses and *T1* responses on clinical animism and death interviews.

Other recent literature seems even to contradict the claim that preschoolers are in the grips of *T1*. Preschool children are said to understand biological inheritance (e.g., Hirschfeld, 1995; Springer, 1992, 1995), illness (e.g., Keil, 1994), and bodily functions such as growth (Rosengren, Gelman, Kalish, & McCormick, 1991), death (Inagaki & Hatano, 1996), and the capacity for bodily self-repair (Backscheider, Shatz, & Gelman, 1993). For instance, Inagaki and Hatano (1996, Experiment 3) reported that 4- to 5-year-old preschool children in Japan recognize that animals and plants die as well as grow and need to eat. In their experiment, they tried to elicit childrens recognition that animals and plants are similar by asking the following question: "A squirrel or an alligator can die. Do you think anything similar to this occurs with a tulip or a pine tree?" They reported that 80% of preschoolers asserted that plants could die; only 13% asserted that inanimate objects (a chair or a pay phone) could die.

To fully review this apparently contradictory literature is beyond the scope of the present chapter, but here I would like to make three related points. First, in view of the robust results from the clinical interview literature on death, we must ask what preschool children mean by the assertion "Plants die." If the claims about incommensurability are correct, then this sentence means something different to them than it does to an adult. Second, as argued next, many of these studies tapped the earliest acquisition of knowledge, formulated in the concepts of *T1*, that provide the material from which *T2* is constructed. And third, as shown next, the transition between *T1* and the earliest appearance of *T2* takes place in the years up to age 6; some 4- and 5-year-olds have already made it.

These studies provided evidence for preschoolers' undifferentiated concepts of *alive/real/existent/active* and *dead/unreal/nonexistent/absent* and for their differentiation of the biological concepts of *life* and *death* from these as part of the construction of a vitalist biology around age 6. Finally, this construction allows children to coalesce the previously ontologically distinct concepts of *animal* and *plant* into a single concept of *living thing* (Carey, 1985b; Inagaki & Hatano, 1996).

Organizing our understanding of animals around the concept of the life cycle entails more than constructing a vitalist biology in terms of which death is reconceptualized and animals and plants reconceptualized as a single kind. It also entails understanding birth as the origin of each animal's life cycle and as part of the process of biological reproduction, in turn a crucial part of understanding the source of an animal's species and many of its individual properties. These aspects of folk biology also begin to emerge around age 6 or 7 (e.g., Keil, 1989; Solomon et al., 1996; Springer & Keil, 1989), with continued development over the elementary school years, and provide examples of two further types of changes at the level of individual concepts: changes in a concept's core and changes in a concept's type.

Keil's (1989) transformation studies provide elegant data in support of the claim that there are changes in the core of children's concept of animal kind between ages 4 and 7. In two related paradigms, Keil showed children photographs of an animal like a skunk and then told them stories that challenged them to consider whether this individual was a skunk or a raccoon. In one paradigm, children were shown transformations, after which the animal looked just like a raccoon. The question was which transformations, if any, change the "essence" of the animal that makes it a skunk. For preschool children, any transformation that changed the body of the animal was sufficient to lead a child to say that it was now a raccoon. In one such transformation, a plastic surgeon changes the shape of the skunk's head, adds some bulk to the body, and dies its fur brown with stripes, such that it ends up looking exactly like a raccoon (the child is shown a picture of a raccoon). In another transformation, a veterinarian mistakenly gives a baby skunk a shot that causes it to grow into an animal that looks like a raccoon (again, the child is shown a picture of a raccoon.) By ages 7 to 9, children told the first scenario judge that the animal is still a skunk, and older children judge that the raccoon-looking animal in the second scenario is still a skunk. Apparently, what makes something a raccoon for a preschool child is that its body is that of a raccoon; it does not matter how it got that way. For an older child, what matters is the origin of the bodily features; the animal must have obtained them through a process of growth or, still later, must have been born with them.

That preschoolers do not see birth as relevant to the fixing of species kind is confirmed in the second of Keil's paradigms. Here too children are first shown a photograph of an animal like a skunk, and again they assert that it is a skunk. They are then told that scientists had discovered that the parents of this animal were these (photographs of raccoons) and that its babies were these (photographs of raccoons) and they are asked whether the animal is a skunk or a raccoon. Preschool children assert that it is a skunk, raccoon parents and babies notwithstanding. By ages 7 to 9, the same ages that the children pass the surgery-transformation version of the task, children assert that it is a raccoon. Again, we see evidence of the change of the core of species kind, from characteristic bodily features and characteristic behaviors to considerations of the origins of the animal.

Finally, the construction of an understanding of birth and biological reproduction supports a change in the concept of *baby* from a property of some animals to a relation among animals. Several sources of data have shown that for young preschoolers, babies are fundamentally small, help-less, behaviorally impoverished animals or people, whereas by age 6 or so they are conceived as the reproductive offspring of other animals (see Carey, 1985b, 1988). Perhaps the clearest recent demonstration of this change comes from the work of Callanan et al. (1992). She showed children pictures of a full-size animal such as a grown horse, labeled as the mother horse. The child was then given two choices for the horse's baby, another full-size horse or a puppy. Preschoolers chose the puppy; older children, like adults, chose the full-size horse.

My goal in this sketch has been to give a flavor of the data that support the claim that conceptual change occurs in the course of normal cognitive development. These data show that the changes between the two theories of animals involve local incommensurability, as there are changes in con-ceptual cores, the right types of differentiations and coalescences, and changes in underlying concept types.

PROCESSES UNDERLYING CONCEPTUAL CHANGE—THREE FALSE STARTS

The challenge to understand the transition from *T*1 to *T*2 derives from the incommensurability of these two theories. *T*1 (preschoolers' theory of animals and people) does not have the representational resources to ex-press the concepts, beliefs, and explanatory structure of *T*2 (6- to 10-year-olds' vitalist biology). *T*1 does not include the concepts of living thing, life cycle, death, birth, biological inheritance, or bodily machine. How do the children construct such concepts and build explanations of a wide range of phenomena in terms of a vitalist theory of the body?

Several accounts of theory construction, although not wrong, fail to fully engage the problem. These include: *T*2 is socially constructed, both historically and by an individual child's participation in society; the tran-sition between *T*1 and *T*2 is achieved via a variety of processes of dise-quilibration; domain general cognitive development yields resources that children can draw on for theory construction.

T2 Is Socially Constructed

First, there is no doubt that *T2* was originally socially constructed (like much culturally important knowledge) and that children acquire it via social processes. They learn it from adults, through making sense of adult language, through making sense of the artifacts made possible by *T2* (e.g., medicinal, dietary, and fertility practices), and as the result of explicit teaching. Although this explanation is certainly true, it does not solve the basic problem of how each child comes to master a set of concepts that are incommensurable with those they currently command.

How do children learn facts and causal accounts they do not have the concepts to express? This is, of course, the basic problem of science education. Consider the problem of how children construct the concept of *living thing*, superordinate to animals and plants. Children can certainly learn, if explicitly told or by merely noting adult language use, that plants as well as animals are alive. They must, however, represent this newly learned fact in terms of their concept of *alive*, which is undifferentiated between *real, existent, active,* or *living*. Initial learning of new facts, by necessity, must be formulated over the available conceptual repertoire.

Disequilibration Is the Engine That Underlies Conceptual Change

Without doubt, the process of disequilibration is an important part of the process of conceptual change. Children notice failed predictions and internal contradictions among their beliefs. Learning that plants are alive contains the seeds of a contradiction: Plants are not notably active. My daughter, age 4, in the throes of *T1*, said to me: "That's funny, statues are not alive, but you can still see them." Asked what was funny about that, she said, "Well, Grampa's dead, and that's sad because we can't see him anymore." In view of her lack of differentiation between *nonexistent, absent, dead, unreal,* or *inactive*, the properties of statues posed several contradictions. They were indeed not real, in the sense that they were representations. They were certainly inactive. So far so good, as far as being not alive. They were, however, both existent and present (hence we can see them). How can this be, she asked? When I tried to explain to her that *dead* is different from *inanimate* and that statues, like tables and chairs, were not alive in the latter sense, I only confused her. Her last words were: "Right, isn't it funny, tables and chairs are not alive, but we can still see them!"

Noting inconsistencies in beliefs serves a motivational role, even for preschool children, and also pinpoints the cracks in *T1* (in the statue example, in the concept *not alive*). It does not, however, provide an answer to the question of where *T2* comes from. How is the biological concept of death constructed to enable children to differentiate the sense of *not alive* that applies to statues from the sense of *not alive* that applies to Eliza's grandfather? Appeals to disequilibration do not begin to provide an answer to this question.

Domain-General Cognitive Development

Six-year-olds have many cognitive resources that four-year-olds do not, resources that play a role in their capacity for theory development. These resources were Piaget's focus in his work on the transition from preoperational to concrete operational thought. Although such changes may have been reconceptualized in various ways since Piaget's classic work, they are undoubtedly important to the process of conceptual change. Increases in information-processing capacity allow children to consider more aspects of a phenomenon at once, so as to notice contradictions and failed predictions. Increased metaconceptual understanding of the nature of knowledge allows children to monitor their comprehension of phenomena (e.g., Flavell, Speer, Green, & August, 1981; Markman, 1977), which also contributes to knowledge restructuring. Older children continue to construct more sophisticated epistemologies of science, which almost certainly play a role in the process of theory construction (e.g. Carey, Evans, Honda, Unger, & Jay, 1989; Carey & Smith, 1993; D. Kuhn et al., 1988).

Although domain-general cognitive development yields new resources for theory development, it is obvious that these resources cannot be the sources of *T2*. The concepts of *T2* are domain specific; they are constitutive of a particular theory, embody its ontological commitments, and articulate the explanations that it provides for the phenomena in its, and only its, domain. Greater metaconceptual understanding of the nature of knowledge, of theories, of learning, of evidence, and of the importance of belief consistency, in addition to increased information-processing resources and tools of wide application (Carey, 1985a) such as logicomathematical concepts and formalisms, cannot by themselves provide children with a concept of *dead* differentiated from *inanimate*.

SOURCES OF *T2*; BEGINNING POINTS

What then *are* the sources of *T2*? Very young children, even infants, bring more to conceptual development than was recognized by Piaget, including both domain-general and domain-specific cognitive resources. Many domain-general representational capacities that support theory building in all domains are available early in the preschool years. These include an essentialist conceptualization of kinds and a capacity for causal analysis, including command of the general causal schemata first characterized by

Aristotle (see T. S. Kuhn, 1978). Further, there is domain-specific support for *T*2 in the form of ancestor concepts. These include the concepts of one of the core domains (core domains are those conceptual domains for which there is innate support; see Carey & Spelke, 1996) and of *T*1 itself, which by the preschool years yields *animal* as an entrenched concept embedded in a rich theory.

Domain-General Support for Theory Construction

Essentialist Construal of Kinds. At the minimum, an essentialist construal of a kind involves a commitment to there being some nonobvious property of its members determining kind membership, causing the observable properties of kind members, and licensing the rich inductive potential derived from categorization of an entity as a member of a kind. As Atran (1994), Keil (1994), and others have pointed out, folk biology universally includes essentialist reasoning about animal kinds, and indeed T2 does so as well (Keil, 1989; cf. the skunk–raccoon studies reviewed earlier; Johnson & Solomon, 1997). Preschoolers also reason in an essentialist manner about animal kinds (Gelman et al., 1994; Johnson & Solomon, in press). Some have taken preschoolers' essentialism about animal kinds to mean that *T*1 is an autonomous biology (e.g., Keil, 1994). Whether essentialism with respect to animal kinds implies autonomous biology depends on two further considerations: first, whether only biological kinds are reasoned about essentially and second, whether the essentialist commitments for animals are in any way biological.

A moment's reflection reveals that not only biological kinds are reasoned about essentially; at the minimum, all natural kinds have essences (Schwartz, 1977), and young children reason essentially about substance natural kinds as well as animal natural kinds (Gelman & Markman, 1986, 1987; Keil, 1989). Furthermore, there is some plausibility to the claim that we reason about *all* genuine kinds according to the principle of psychological essentialism (Markman, 1989; Medin & Ortony, 1989), that is, the distinction between kind concepts and predicates comes down to the distinction between concepts that fall under psychological essentialism and those that do not. Many natural languages make a distinction between concepts lexicalized as count nouns (called *sortal* concepts in the semantics literature; Carey & Xu, in press; Hirsch, 1982; Macnamara, 1987; Wiggins, 1967, 1980) and those lexicalized as adjectives and verbs (predicate concepts). Sortal concepts provide criteria for individuation and numerical identity (sameness in the sense of *same one*). We can trace an individual through time, in spite of all manner of changes in surface appearance. This capacity, already in place by 12 months of age, presupposes a distinction between superficial properties and identity-determining ones (Xu & Carey, 1996).

It seems, then, that the human conceptual system distinguishes between concepts for which we adopt psychological essentialism (i.e., make a commitment to the existence of hidden properties that determine the entity's kind, its properties, and its continued existence through time) and those for which we do not. Most kinds lexicalized as substance sortals (sortals that trace identity through an entity's whole existence, such as *dog, table, sun,* as opposed to stage sortals such as *pet, baby, passenger*) fall under the assumption of psychological essentialism.

An essentialist construal of kinds aids in theory building in all domains. Any evidence that entities fall under a single kind (e.g., discovery of richly intercorrelated properties, of distinctive causal and functional implications, of being lexicalized by a single count noun) is an invitation to search for essential properties, the causally deepest properties that determine the kind. Intuitive theories are those conceptual structures in which causally deep properties are represented. If this line of reasoning is correct, then psychological essentialism is not part of just one domain, biology, but is an important component to all theory building, including *T2*.

The particular essences posited by *T2*, tied to the origins of animals as they are, are domain-specific, biological essences, just as every theory determines domain-specific essences for the kinds that fall under it. The assumption that there are essences of kinds is an aid to theory building, but theory building is still required to discover the actual essences that nature provides.

Capacity for Causal Analysis; the Aristotelian Explanation Categories. Causation, like essentialism, is at the core of all theories. Theories are individuated by their causal commitments (*Tx* is a *different* theory from *Ty* just because it posits *different* causal and explanatory mechanisms). Specific *causes*, like specific *essences*, are thus domain specific and vary from theory to theory. Nonetheless, the capacity to reason causally is domain general and is an important component to the theory-building capabilities of human beings.

There are two quite distinct traditions in the psychological and philosophical analyses of causation (see Sperber, Premack, & Premack, 1995, for work in both traditions). The first concerns the inference of causality from patterns of covariation and thus is obviously domain general. All manner of moderately evolved creatures and computational algorithms are exquisite covariation detectors (rats, connectionist algorithms), and if Gallistel (1990) is right, classical and operant conditioning both reflect computations that posit causation from covariation. However, not until late in childhood or in adulthood do people acquire explicit metaconceptual control of the principles of warrant for imputing causal relations among variables as a function of their statistical relations to each other (e.g., D. Kuhn et al., 1988).

The second tradition in the study of causal reasoning analyzes causal mechanism. Some philosophers (e.g., Salmon, 1989) argued that there is never full warrant for causal inference from statistical data; we must always appeal to theory-licensed mechanism in the end. Be this as it may, the study of mental representations of causal mechanism is an important part of the study of causal cognition. Although each theory licenses its own causal mechanism, these fall into four very general classes, the Aristotelian categories (formal, efficient, material, and final). Roughly, final cause is exploited in teleological explanation; efficient cause is that in which one event causes a subsequent event; material cause is that in which phenomena are explained in terms of properties of the substances from which the entities involved are made. It is likely that preschool children have at least three of the four causal schemas available to them; they reason about artifacts and biological kinds in terms of functional or teleological explanation, and want–belief explanation is also a type of final cause; we explain a behavior in terms of the goals of the actor. Preschool children also reason in terms of efficient causation; the causal mechanisms studied by Shultz (1982) are examples, as is the Michotte causality that is part of the core domain of mechanics. Callanan and Oakes (1992) studied the why questions of 3- to 5-year-olds and classified their questions and the answers provided by their parents. They found both efficient and final causal schemata amply represented even at the youngest ages. Finally, Au (1994) showed that preschool children relied on material cause in reasoning about hidden properties of substances.

The Aristotelian categories of causal analysis are domain general. As T. S. Kuhn (1997), pointed out, there is no one to one fit between theoretical domain and Aristotelian category of causation. Indeed, as theories change, their commitments to allowable types of causality change (e.g., Aristotelian physics made heavy use of final cause reasoning, a type of mechanism ruled out in Newtonian physics, in which only efficient causality is seen as valid).

The conclusions from a consideration of causal reasoning are parallel to those from our consideration of essentialist reasoning. Very young children have extensive cognitive resources that support causal reasoning, and these play an important role in theory building, including *T*2, for theories are just those conceptual structures that embody causal knowledge. As these resources are domain general, they do not solve the problem of how the particular biological causal mechanisms that articulate *T*2 are constructed.

Domain-Specific Support for *T*2

We still seek the sources of the concepts and causal schemata that are specific to *T*2. Preschool children are not resourceless in this regard, either. Ancestor concepts to those of *T*2 are found even in infancy.

Core Domains. Fifteen years of research on infant cognition has established that infants possess much richer knowledge than was previously believed. Although there is no agreement as to the *nature* of infant knowledge (perceptual or conceptual, implicit or explicit), on my reading of the literature, its existence is beyond doubt. This literature has led Spelke, Brelinger, Macomber, and Jacobson (1992), Leslie (1994), and others to formulate the "core knowledge" hypothesis. They hypothesized that the acquisition of at least some infant knowledge was guided by innate, domain-specific principles that determine a few basic ontological distinctions and provide skeletal constraints on causal attribution (see Carey & Spelke, 1994, 1996, for a review of the evidence for core knowledge).

By 12 months of age, infants represent concepts in at least three core domains: intuitive mechanics, with *physical object* the central ontological kind and *contact causality* the basic causal principle (e.g., Leslie, 1994; Spelke et al., 1992), intuitive psychology, with *person* as the central ontological kind and *intentional causality* the basic causal principle (Johnson, Slaughter, & Carey, 1998; Leslie, 1994; Spelke et al., 1995); and number, with *individuated entity, set, numerical equivalence* at its core (Wynn, 1992, 1996).

As Carey and Spelke (1997) argued, core domains differ from later theories in several respects. First, they have substantial innate support; the process through which they are acquired is different. Second, they are close to the perceptual data; the criteria that enable children to identify a physical object, for example, are spatiotemporal (objects are bounded, coherent wholes that trace spatiotemporally continuous paths and obey the no action at a distance principle). These same spatiotemporal principles exhaust the inferences that infants make about objects (e.g., that objects continue to exist behind a screen follows from spatiotemporal continuity, that one object causes another to move only if hit follows from contact causality). Later theories, including *T2*, have much more inferential depth between the phenomena in their domains and their explanatory principles.

Although core domains differ from later theories in several respects, they are also theory like. They are the structures that determine the cores of ontologically important concepts, they embody causal and explanatory principles, and they support inferences. One of the core domains, intuitive psychology, includes the ancestor concepts of *T1*. It allows babies to interpret some behaviors as goal directed and guided by perception (i.e., as intentional), and thus to interpret the behavers as intentional. This first theory grounds infants' concept of *animal.*

T1 Itself. Early in the toddler years, children understand animals to be behaving beings, (capable of self-generated motion, goal-directed behavior, and perception), and by ages 3½ to 4 they have constructed full-blown want/belief intentional causality (Perner, 1991; Wellman, 1990). In addition, preschool children have elaborated a wide network of beliefs grounded in the concepts of *T*1. They know that there are kinds of animals (elephants, cows, dogs, cats, lizards, birds) and that members of families resemble each other (Springer, 1992). They know that animals grow, that they need to eat to grow, that germs cause disease. These are one-step causal facts (that is, children know no mechanisms that underlie these facts), and they are formulated in terms of *T*1's concepts (e.g., *family* is undifferentiated between *birth family* and *social family*). Still, this vast network of knowledge provides a basis for the construction of *T*2.

Not only does *T*1 provide an entrenched concept of *animal*, as R. Gelman (1990) pointed out, the undifferentiated concept of *alive* contains a notion that is a direct ancestor to the biological concept of life, which Gelman called the *innards principle*. That animals are capable of self-generated motion means that there is an internal causal force that is also the source of growth, and of growth in one direction rather than another (i.e., it is because of something inside them that puppies grow up to be dogs rather than cats). The innards principle is co-opted into the vitalistic concept of *life* early in the elementary school years.

WHAT ELSE IS NEEDED?

To reiterate what we are looking for: We seek the processes by which new domain-specific concepts, new explanatory mechanisms come into being. We must not lose sight of the problems posed by the local incommensurability of the core concepts of *T*2 with those of *T*1. The new concepts of *T*2 are not definable in terms of those available to *T*1.

Analogical Mapping

We are searching for sources of genuine conceptual novelty. One process often implicated in conceptual change is analogical mapping, a process that uses the conceptual resources from one domain as a source of conceptual structure in another. This process has been well described in historical studies, especially historical studies of diaries of individual scientists in the process of conceptual change (e.g., Gruber, 1974 [on Darwin]; Nersessian, 1992 [on Maxwell]).

As Nersessian pointed out, Maxwell's use of analogical reasoning was systematic, deliberate, and crucial to his success in formulating electromagnetic theory. Maxwell began with the electromagnetic phenomena discovered by Faraday, and self-consciously tried to map them onto the mathematics of Newtonian mechanics. He assumed that analogical forces were involved in each domain. He used what he called a visual analogy, deploying spatial representations that he knew were isomorphic to the Newtonian mathematics, because these were easier to think with than were the formalisms. By the end of this process, which extended over several years of solid work, Maxwell had invented a mathematics that was more powerful than Newton's and had formulated electrodynamic theory, a theory incommensurable with Newtonian mechanics. Exploring the mapping entailed changes in the representations of both the target and base domains.

An analogical mapping process structurally identical to that employed by Maxwell has been shown to be effective in facilitating conceptual change in a science education setting (e.g., Smith, Snir, & Grosslight, 1992; Smith & Unger, 1997; Wiser, 1995). Wiser employed visual analogies that embodied the mathematics of intensive-extensive quantities as a source domain to facilitate high school students' differentiation of heat and temperature, and Smith et al. used similar visual analogies to facilitate middle school students' differentiation of weight and density. The two extensive quantities in the source domain were number of dots and number of boxes, and the intensive quantity was density or number of dots per box. Both research groups found that curricula that involved constructing a mapping between this source domain and the physics of heat and matter, respectively, were more effective than were comparable curricula that did not make use of visual analogies.

Whereas analogical mapping is certainly one source of conceptual change, exactly how the process works is not fully understood. In cases of conceptual change, a person at first does not have the concepts in the target domain to map onto the relevant concepts of the source domain, and it is not obvious which concepts most fruitfully map onto which. When Maxwell began, he did not have the concepts of electrodynamic theory, and children at first do not have differentiated concepts of weight and density (Carey, 1991; Smith et al., 1985) or heat and temperature (Wiser, 1988, 1995). If children have not yet differentiated weight from density (heavy from heavy kind of stuff), how are they to map weight onto total number of dots and density of material onto number of dots per box? This problem is deep and explains why the process takes so long; years in Maxwell's case, as he was constructing the mapping for the first time, and months in the science education case, in which children are guided by curricula designed by people who already understand the target theory and the mapping between it and the source domain.

Smith and her colleagues (Smith et al., 1992; Smith & Unger, 1997) provided an account of how the dots per box source domain facilitates conceptual change in middle school children's theory of matter. Youngsters of this age conceive of weight as felt weight, undifferentiated between the extensive notion of heaviness and the intensive notion of heavy for a given size (Carey, 1991; Smith et al., 1985). The curriculum begins with thought experiments and limiting case analyses that point the way toward an extensive concept of weight. For example, children with the beginning, undifferentiated conception of weight think that a single grain of rice weighs nothing at all, zero grams. They participated in an experiment in which 50 grains of rice are sufficient to topple a card balanced on a wide fulcrum, and they explained this by the weight of the rice. Ten grains of rice are sufficient to topple a card balanced on a narrower fulcrum, and one grain of rice is sufficient to topple a card delicately balanced on a thin fulcrum. They were asked to reflect on this fact and to square it with their belief that a single grain of rice weighs zero grams. They were also asked to reflect how 50 grams of rice can weigh something if each grain weighs nothing. These exercises played a disequilibrating role by pointing out a problem area in their current theory of matter and in their current concept of weight.

Students were then introduced to the source domain—dots per box, number of boxes, number of dots. They saw that they can predict the third variable from any two. For example, they can predict how many dots a figure contains if they know how many boxes and how many dots per box. They used the model to explain why there is a linear relation between number of boxes and number of dots, given a common density. After they explored the source model, they explored several phenomena in the do-main of matter. These could include the linear relation between weight and volume given a constant material, the fact that two objects that are the same size might weigh different amounts, and the phenomena of sinking and floating. They then began to try to map the target domain of matter onto the source domain. They were guided to map weight onto number of dots, volume onto number of boxes. Density is visible in the model in the form of dots per box. What remained was for them to see that there is an explanatory physical magnitude that corresponds to dots per box. They could use the mapping to explain why two objects that are the same size might weigh different amounts, why the relation between weight and volume is linear given a single density, what relevant variables explain sinking and floating, and so on.

There are three crucial ingredients to such curricula. First, children must master phenomena in the target domain for which an explanation depends on the differentiated concepts. Second, they must see the analogy between these phenomena and the corresponding phenomena in the source domain. Finally, the visual analogy provides an anchor for the distinct roles of each differentiated concept in understanding these phenomena.

This process is not magic. Not all children going through this process succeed in making the mapping. The limiting case analysis and a measure-ment procedure for weight can give children a beginning inkling of the extensive concept of weight, and if they map this notion onto the extensive concept of number of dots, they are already part way there in distinguishing it from density. It remains for them to grasp that there is a distinct physical variable in the domain of matter corresponding to the variable dots per box, and the curriculum provides activities that support this insight.

It is likely that analogies contribute to the construction of vitalist biology, the *T*2 that concerns us here. Parents often use plant analogies to help children understand reproduction, and several researchers have shown that these analogies actually play a role in children's understanding of this crucial piece of *T*2 (Bernstein & Cowan, 1975; Goldman & Goldman, 1982). It is also likely that children analogize the eating and drinking of animals to plants needing water (Inagaki & Hatano, 1996). Both these analogies between the plant and animal world play a role in constructing the concept of *living thing* encompassing animals and plants and excluding entities that do not grow or reproduce.

Although analogical mapping between domains is certainly an important source of conceptual change and probably is part of the process of constructing *T*2, it probably plays a relatively minor role in the construction of a vitalist biology by 6- to 10-year olds. Most important, and most obvious, there is no source domain that has the same structure as vitalist biology. Second, the analogical mapping processes used in the science curriculum, or by scientists themselves, are under metaconceptual control. The curriculum sketched previously contains many activities that explore what models are and how they help to understand phenomena. Children in these curricula, just like the scientists, know they are systematically exploring an analogical model. *T*2, in contrast, is not explicitly taught, and 6- to 7-year-olds do not have the metaconceptual understanding of the nature of scientific knowledge to support the relevant, explicit understanding of models (Grosslight, Unger, Jay, & Smith, 1991).

In sum, although we have some ingredients in place for children's construction of vitalist biology, we still need to look elsewhere in our search for a full account of the process.

Coherence, Causal Networks, Entrenchment, and Neurath's Boat

Analogical mapping is a bootstrapping process; the target domain never has exactly the same structure as the source domain. In analogical mapping, the structure that provides a partial skeleton for the new theory is borrowed from a different domain, but not all bootstrapping processes are of this sort. In others, *T*2 is bootstrapped entirely from *T*1 itself, via a skeletal structure of interconnected propositions formulated in terms of concepts available in *T*1.

Facing the problem of local incommensurability, writers have almost always appealed to bootstrapping metaphors in their attempts to explain how conceptual change is possible. These attempts have both captured the problem and provided a metaphor for its solution. One famous image is Neurath's boat, in which theory construction is seen as a process of building a boat while in the middle of the ocean (Neurath, quoted in Quine, 1960). Neurath's metaphor vividly portrayed the dilemma of theory construction in cases implicating conceptual change. In those cases, the new theory was not grounded at all (hence it is represented as a boat); one builds a structure that works while already afloat. Other common bootstrapping images have included constructing a ladder grounded in the concepts of $T1$, getting to a new place, and then kicking the ladder out from under. Again, the destination achieved was not grounded in the old (hence the image of kicking the ladder out from under), but, by necessity, the process must begin there.

Bootstrapping processes depend on knowledge: of the materials of the boat, of the ladder. Theory construction requires knowledge of the phenomena that provide fodder for disequilibration and are in the domain of $T2$, that is, are ultimately explained by the concepts and causal schema of $T2$. If children do not know that animals grow, that eating causes growth, that people get sick, that sickness sometimes causes death, if they do not know about some internal body parts and myriad other facts, they do not know about the phenomena that $T2$ integrates. Acquiring such knowledge is entirely unproblematic insofar as it is couched in concepts that are constant between $T1$ and $T2$. The incommensurability between $T1$ and $T2$ is what Kuhn (1982) termed *local incommensurability*; many of the concepts that articulate the two theories remain unchanged in the course of theory change. Other facts are articulated, initially, in the concepts of $T1$, facts that are locally incommensurable with those of $T2$. In these cases, because of the inherent contradictions in $T1$ from the point of view of $T2$, these facts (such as the fact that both plants and animals are alive) are fodder for disequilibration. They become articulated in the concepts of $T2$, internal contradictions resolved, when the ladder is kicked out from under.

$T2$ emerges from patterns of coherent interrelations among these newly learned facts. Some facts are particularly important, these one-step causal relations that children learn—that is, causal relations between events for which children as yet know no intervening causal mechanism. Causal knowledge is particularly salient (to children of all ages; see the "why" questions of preschoolers, Callanan & Oakes, 1992). Examples of one-step causal facts that play a role in the bootstrapping of $T2$ from $T1$ include germs causing illness, eating vegetables keeps you healthy, needing food to grow, to stay healthy, and to stay alive, plants needing water to stay alive and to grow, and so on for hundreds more. These facts are articulated in the concepts of $T1$ and thus sometimes represent different beliefs than they do when *T*1 has been replaced with *T*2. For example, preschoolers' belief that animals die if they do not eat means something different from 8- to 10-year-olds' belief articulated in the same words, in view of the conceptual change in the concept of *death* over these years.

Causal knowledge of this sort is important for two reasons. First, it serves a placeholder role, an invitation to construct theories that provide causal mechanisms. One can know that germs cause illness without having the slightest idea of what a germ is or by what mechanism germs cause illness (Au & Romo, 1996; Solomon & Cassimites, in press), the state of affairs for preschool children. This causal belief anchors a theory of illness as children begin to fill it in. The second role that such causal knowledge plays derives from the coherent patterns it falls into. For example, children learn as one-step causal facts that many things are necessary for life: food, especially healthy food, water, air, sleep. They also learn that largely the same things are necessary for growth. They learn that plants as well as animals grow and that water is necessary for plants to stay alive and to grow. As Inagaki and Hatano (1996) pointed out, this overlapping structure of causal facts promotes differentiating a concept of *living thing* that applies only to animals and plants, from the undifferentiated concept of *alive, real, active.* The construction of the differentiated concept of *living thing* becomes more complete as children learn the container theory that is the role of internal parts and substances in moving these precious substances around the body. These facts rule out as living (in this sense of living) those entities that do not grow and do not eat, breathe, or take in water.

Such systems of causal facts serve not only as placeholders for mechanisms, but also as means of entrenching the concept that unites the causal network. In this process, cores of concepts change during theory construction. Not only does *animal, plant life* become differentiated from the undifferentiated concept, it also becomes the core of children's concept of animal and plant kinds as it anchors an increasingly rich interconnected causal structure.

In the construction of *T*2, there are several such systems of causal facts that are originally formulated over the concepts of *T*1. These include the facts of reproduction, which become part of a theory of inheritance, the differentiation of biological and social family, and a change in the core of animal such that origins are taken as determining essences (see Solomon & Johnson, in press, for a teaching intervention based on coherence of causal facts and an explicit placeholder; see also Springer, 1995). Another system concerns the construction of a coherent theory of disease (see Au & Romo, 1996). Still another concerns the construction of a vitalist theory of bodily function, in terms of which the differentiated concepts of *life* and *death* are constructed (Inagaki & Hatano, 1993, 1996; Slaughter et al., in press).

A WORKED EXAMPLE: THE CONSTRUCTION OF *T2*
(A SKELETAL VITALIST BIOLOGY)

Inagaki and Hatano (1996) provided a sketch of how *T2* might be boot-strapped from *T1*. Building on Backscheider et al. (1993), they showed that by age 5 children are clear that animals and plants, but not inanimate objects, get bigger over time. Growth, in the sense of increase in size, is a concept neutral between *T1* and *T2*, and the generalization can be learned by observation and direct adult description. Obviously, children's own growth is a salient fact. Knowledge of growth is unlikely to be part of core knowledge; indeed, 3- and 4-year-olds are far from categorical in their knowledge that all animals grow and that nonanimals do not (Backscheider et al., 1993; Carey, 1985b; Inagaki & Hatano, 1996).

Inagaki and Hatano (1996) further suggested that by age 5, children have constructed the beginnings of a coherent, interrelated set of beliefs that begin to unite animals and plants into a single category of *living things* (as opposed to merely *growing things*). They studied children's inductive projection of several biological properties from people to other entities. The properties were growth, sometimes becoming ill, breathing, eating, taking in food and water, and defecating. The properties were introduced as properties of people, and children were asked whether a series of ani-mals, plants, and inanimate objects also had each property. The crucial manipulation was whether the property was introduced with a short vitalistic explanation context or not. For example: (No context) "A person needs water and/or food. Then, does X need water and/or food?" And (Context) "A person needs water and/or food. If he does not take in energy or vital power from water and/or food, he dies. Then, does X need water and/or food?" Five-year-olds attributed several of these properties to all animals and plants and to no inanimate objects; in some cases (attribution of growth, taking ill, and taking food and water), the "living thing" pattern was greater when the vitalist context was provided.

Inagaki and Hatano believed that these results show that their 5-year-olds have already constructed the concept of *living thing*, which is activated by the vitalist context. This conclusion goes beyond these data, for the context that is provided also supports property–property induction. That is, if chil-dren know that people need food and water and that plants need food and water, then the vitalist context makes salient the similarities between people and plants and makes the attribution of growth to plants more likely. The important point here, however, is not whether these data show that 5-year-olds already have a vitalist biology (see next), but that they show that 5-year-olds have begun to interrelate the properties of growth on the one hand and taking in food and water on the other, in a coherent structure of beliefs. This pattern of beliefs that can be formulated in terms of concepts of *T1* at least provides a skeletal structure that a vitalist biology fills in. As Inagaki and Hatano (1996) rightly emphasized, this skeletal structure supports the uniting of animals and plants into a single category, differentiated from other kinds of things.

When does the category of *food or water needing entity* or *growing entity* become the category of *living entity*? As reviewed earlier, there is good evidence that a vitalist biology is in place at age 6, not at age 4 (Inagaki & Hatano, 1993; Jaakkola & Carey, 1998). Consistent with *T2* emerging, at least in skeletal form, between ages 4 and 6 is Jaakkola's (1997) finding that 100% of 6-year-olds were "life theorizers" on a clinical interview on the functions of internal body parts, whereas only 33% of 4-year-olds consistently appealed to the maintenance of life or the avoidance of death as the function of eating, breathing, hearts, blood, lungs. Such appeals on an open-ended clinical interview suggest that the concept of *life* has begun to organize children's searches for causal mechanisms by age 6.

If *T2* emerges between ages 4 and 6, we should be able to study the process by examining larger samples of 4- and 5-year-olds. A recent study by Slaughter, Jaakkola, & Carey (in press) looked for coherence in a body interview and a death interview. Thirty-eight children were given two different interviews, one probing the function of several internal and external body parts and the other probing their conception of death (what things in the world die, whether death is inevitable and irreversible, the causes of death, and whether bodily function ceases on death). We predicted that children who were life theorizers on the body interview would show more articulated and specific knowledge of bodily function for internal organs and be less likely to provide the living-on-in-altered circumstances pattern of responses on the death interview.

Eighteen of the children (mean age 4:11) were classified as non-life-theorizers (they did not appeal to maintaining life or avoiding death as a function of internal body parts), whereas 20 were classified as life-theorizers, a finding confirming that this transition occurs during the late preschool years. As predicted, life-theorizers had significantly greater knowledge of specific bodily function, knowledge articulated in vitalist terms (the stomach is for holding food when we eat; without food we die). The mean body-knowledge score for life-theorizers was 2.65 (of a possible 5), whereas that for non-life-theorizers was 1.33 (between groups ANOVA $F(1, 36) = 11.70$; $p < .001$).

This difference between the two groups in canonical functional knowledge of the body holds in spite of the fact that the two were of approximately the same age. What distinguishes the two groups is whether or not a child used *life* as a central construct in understanding the human body. Non-life-theorizers had almost no knowledge of canonical body function. The body scores for the life-theorizers was well below the maximum of five canonical function responses.

The association between life theorizing and knowledge of bodily function has two possible interpretations. Learning about the canonical purposes of just a few specific vital organs, in conjunction with the coherent association of growth, needing food, and so on, may provide a causal schema in which life is the ultimate teleological goal of bodily function. This schema in turn is the beginning of the differentiated vitalist concept of life, which serves as a placeholder goal for other, as yet unknown, specific purposes of internal body parts. Alternatively, there may be some other source of life-theorizers' concept of life, such as extending the schema connecting food to growth, growth to aging, and aging or lack of food to death; this development may be required for children to even begin to understand the body in vitalist terms, as the strikingly low body scores of the non-life-theorizers might suggest. That is, without the concept of life to organize reasoning about the body, children might not have the conceptual resources to understand bodily organs in terms of their biological functions. It is not necessary to choose between these two alternative interpretations of the correlation. The developments occur simultaneously and coherently, such that acquiring knowledge about the body and having *life* at the core of a vitalist theory of the body are ultimately mutually defining.

Similarly, on several of the component sections of the death interview, the life-theorizers outperformed the non-life theorizers (applicability—restricting death to animals and plants; cessation—knowledge that dead people do not need food, air, etc; inevitability—judging that all people die; and irreversibility—judging that a doctor cannot bring a dead person back to life). Furthermore, on a composite score (range 0–6), the average death score for life-theorizers was 3.6, compared to 1.2 for non-life-theorizers (between groups ANOVA $F(1, 36) = 31.49$; $p < .001$). Those children who spontaneously organize their understanding of the functions of internal body organs in terms of the concept of *life* are also farther along in construction a biological understanding of death as the inevitable, irreversible cessation of the working of the bodily machine.

A final analysis investigated the relation between children's knowledge of body function and their knowledge of death. We computed Pearson correlations between children's body scores and their death scores. For all the children combined, there was a significant relation between knowledge of the body and knowledge about death: $r(36) = .543$, $p < .001$. Next, we looked at the correlations between body scores and death scores for the life-theorists and the non-life-theorists separately. For the life-theorists, the correlation was not significant ($r(18) = .228$, *ns*); for the non-life-theorists, the correlation was significant ($r(16) = .475$, $p < .05$).

This pattern was unexpected. It appears to indicate that for non-life-theorists, those children who are accumulating specific knowledge about body function are also more likely to be constructing a biological understanding of death. For the life-theorists, in contrast, detailed biological knowledge of the body is not related to understanding death. Why would this be? It seems likely that the life-theorists have acquired the basic coherent structure of the vitalist theory—that the maintenance of life is the goal of bodily function and that death is the cessation of life, which is itself the cessation of body function. Beyond that, we suggest that the life-theorists are individually acquiring various aspects of body or death knowledge, such that there is no longer a linear relation between how much they know about the body and how much they know about death. That is, once children have constructed the coherent foundation of the working vitalist theory, then the details of body function and death may develop in a piecemeal fashion depending on the particular interests and experiences of the individual children.

It is important to emphasize that these data confirm the literature on preschool performance on the body and death interviews. Taken all together, the children in our study showed very little understanding of bodily function and provided typical preschool responses on the death interview. Even life-theorizers were far from ceiling on each task; in particular, many of their response were consistent with nonbiological understanding of some components of the death interview.

Nonetheless, this pattern of data confirms and extends the argument of Inagaki and Hatano (1996) and of Jaakkola and Carey (1998) about the construction of a vitalist biology between ages 4 and 6. The cluster of concepts—needing food, growth, death—forms the skeleton placeholder to be filled in with causal mechanisms at the body level. This structure supports the differentiation of *death* from the $T1$ concept of *absent, nonexistent, inactive, asleep* and the construction of the core vitalistic concept *life*. The correlation between bodily function scores and death scores among non-life-theorizers can be interpreted in terms of a process by which mutually reinforcing knowledge, formulated initially in $T1$ concepts, is being built up. Apparently, this process both supports the construction of a differentiated concept of life and its entrenchment until a certain threshold is reached, signified in these data by becoming a life-theorizer. At this point, the differentiated concepts, embedded in a skeletal vitalist biology ($T2$), direct further learning, which accrues relatively easily and quickly, as opportunity affords; further learning is no longer so closely correlated, as it no longer plays the role of bootstrapping the new theory from the old.

CONCLUSION

In conclusion, I want to emphasize that neither analogical mapping nor in-domain bootstrapping is an algorithmic process. It is unlikely that a computational mechanism can unfailingly yield conceptual change. Theory development, including that requiring conceptual change, proceeds by trial and error and involves processes such as abduction and inference to best explanation. Moves that work—that fill in causal mechanisms for causal placeholders, that provide insight into the essences of already identified kinds, that add to coherence and consistency of beliefs—become entrenched, until, that is, the weight of remaining problems accumulates and the bootstrapping processes begin again.

REFERENCES

Atran, S. (1994). Core domains versus scientific theories: Evidence from systematics and Itza–Maya folkbiology. In L. A. Hirschfeld & S. A. Gelman (Eds.), *Mapping the mind: Domain specificity in cognition and culture* (pp. 316–340). New York: Cambridge University Press.

Au, T. K. (1994). Developing an intuitive understanding of substance kinds. *Cognitive Psychology, 27*, 71–111.

Au, T. K., & Romo, L. (1996). Building a coherent conception of HIV transmission: A new approach to AIDS education. *Psychology of Learning and Motivation, 35*, 193–241.

Backscheider, A. G., Schatz, M., & Gelman, S. A. (1993). Preschoolers' ability to distinguish living kinds as a function of regrowth. *Child Development, 64*, 1242–1257.

Bernstein, A. C., & Cowan, P. A. (1975). Children's concepts of how people get babies. *Child Development, 46*, 77–91.

Bibace, R., & Walsh, M. (1981). *Children's conceptions of health, illness, and bodily functions.* San Francisco: Jossey-Bass.

Callanan, M., & Oakes, L. (1992). Preschoolers' questions and parents' explanations: Causal thinking in every day activity. *Cognitive Development, 7*, 213–233.

Callanan, M., Perez, D., McCarrell, N., & Latzke, M. (1992, August). *Children's concepts of baby animals.* Paper presented at the annual meeting of the American Psychological Association.

Carey, S. (1985a). Are children fundamentally different thinkers and learners from adults? In S. F. Chipman, J. W. Segal, & R. Glaser (Eds.), *Thinking and learning skills* (Vol. 2, pp. 485–517). Hillsdale, NJ: Lawrence Erlbaum Associates.

Carey, S. (1985b). *Conceptual change in childhood.* Cambridge, MA: MIT Press.

Carey, S. (1988). Conceptual differences between children and adults. *Mind and Language, 3*, 167–181.

Carey, S. (1991). Knowledge acquisition: Enrichment or conceptual change? In S. Carey & R. Gelman (Eds.), *The Epigenesis of mind: Essays in biology and cognition* (pp. 257–291). Hillsdale, NJ: Lawrence Erlbaum Associates.

Carey, S. (1995). On the origins of causal understanding. In D. Sperber, D. Premack, & A. J. Premack (Eds.), *Causal cognition* (pp. 268–308). Oxford, England: Clarendon Press.

Carey, S., Evans, R., Honda, M., Unger, C., & Jay, E. (1989). An experiment is when you try and see if it works: Middle school conception of science. *International Journal of Science Education, 11*, 514–529.

Carey, S., & Smith, C. (1993). On understanding the nature of scientific knowledge. *Educational Psychologist, 28*, 235–251.

Carey, S., & Spelke, E. S. (1994). Domain specific knowledge and conceptual change. In L. Hirschfeld & S. Gelman (Eds.), *Mapping the mind: Domain specificity in cognition and culture* (pp. 169–200). Cambridge, England: Cambridge University Press.

Carey, S., & Spelke, E. S. (1996). Science and core knowledge. *Journal of Philosophy of Science, 63*(4), 515–533.

Carey, S., & Xu, F. (in press). Sortals & kinds: An appreciation of John Macnamara. In R. Jackendoff, P. Bloom, & K. Wynn (Eds.), *John Macnamara: On the border.* Cambridge, MA: MIT Press.

Chi, M. T. H. (1992). Conceptual change within and across ontological categories: Examples from learning and discovery in science. In R. Giere (Ed.), *Cognitive models of Science: Minnesota studies in the philosophy of science* (pp. 129–186). Minneapolis: University of Minnesota Press.

Crider, C. (1981). *Children's conceptions of health, illness, and bodily functions.* San Francisco: Jossey-Bass.

Feyerabend, P. (1962). Explanation, reduction, empiricism. In H. Feigl & G. Maxwell (Eds.), *Minnesota studies in the philosophy of science* (Vol. 3, pp. 41–87). Minneapolis: University of Minnesota Press.

Flavell, J. H., Speer, J. R., Green, F. L., & August, D. L. (1981). The development of comprehension monitoring and knowledge about communication. *Monographs of the Society for Research in Child Development, 46* (5, Serial No. 192).

Gallistel, C. R. (1990). *The organization of learning.* Cambridge, MA: MIT Press.

Gelman, R. (1990). First principles organize attention to and learning about relevant data: Number and the animate-inanimate distinction as examples. *Cognitive Science, 14,* 79–106.

Gelman, S. A., Coley, J. D., & Gottfried, G. M. (1994). Essentialist beliefs in children: The acquisition of concepts and theories. In L. A. Hirschfeld & S. A. Gelman (Eds.), *Mapping the mind: Domain specificity in cognition and culture* (pp. 341–366). New York: Cambridge University Press.

Gelman, S. A., & Markman, E. M. (1986). Categories and induction in young children. *Cognition, 23,* 183–208.

Gelman, S. A., & Markman, E. M. (1987). Young children's inductions from natural kinds: The role of categories and appearances. *Child Development, 58,* 1532–1541.

Gergely, G., Nadasdy, Z., Csibra, G., & Biro, S. (1995). Taking the intentional stance at 12 months of age. *Cognition, 56,* 165–193.

Goldman, R., & Goldman, J. (1982). How children perceive the origin of babies and the roles of mothers and fathers in procreation: A cross-national study. *Child Development, 53,* 491–504.

Gopnik, A., & Meltzoff, A. N. (1997). *Words, thoughts, and theories.* Cambridge, MA: MIT Press.

Grosslight, L., Unger, C. M., Jay, E., & Smith, C. (1991). Understanding models and their use in science: Conceptions of middle and high school students and experts. *Journal of Research in Science Teaching, 28,* 799–822.

Gruber, H. (1974). *Darwin on man: A psychological study of scientific creativity.* London: Wildwood House.

Hacking, I. (1993). Working in a new world: The taxonomic solution. In P. Horwich & J. Thomson (Eds.), *World changes* (pp. 275–310). Cambridge, MA: MIT Press.

Hatano, G., Siegler, R., Richards, D., Inagaki, K., Stavy, R., & Wax, N. (1993). The development of biological knowledge: A multi-national study. *Cognitive Development, 8,* 47–62.

Hirsch, E. (1982). *The concept of identity.* New York: Oxford University Press.

Hirschfeld, L. (1995). Do children have a theory of race? *Cognition, 54,* 209–252.

Inagaki, K., & Hatano, G. (1993). Children's understanding of mind–body distinction. *Child Development, 64,* 5, 1534–1549.

Inagaki, K., & Hatano, G. (1996). Young children's recognition of commonalities between animals and plants. *Child Development, 67,* 2823–2840.

Jaakkola, R. (1997). *The development of scientific understanding: Children's construction of their first biological theory.* Unpublished doctoral dissertation, Massachusetts Institute of Technology, Boston.

Johnson, S., Slaughter, V., & Carey S. (1998). Whose gaze would infants follow? The elicitation of gaze following in 12-month-olds. *Developmental Science, 1,* 233–238.

Johnson, S. C., & Solomon, G. E. A. (1997). Why dogs have puppies and cats have kittens: Young children's understanding of biological origins, *Child Development, 68,* 404–419.

Keil, F. C. (1979). *Semantic and conceptual development: An ontological perspective.* Cambridge, MA: Harvard University Press.

Keil, F. C. (1989). *Concepts, kinds, and cognitive development.* Cambridge, MA: MIT Press.

Keil, F. C. (1994). The birth and nurturance of concepts by domains: The origins of concepts of living things. In L. A. Hirschfeld & S. A. Gelman (Eds.), *Mapping the mind: Domain specifity in cognition and culture* (pp. 234–254). New York: Cambridge University Press.

Kitcher, P. (1978). Theories, theorists and theoretical change. *Philosophical Review, 87,* 519–547.

Kitcher, P. (1988). The child as parent of the scientist. *Mind and Language, 3,* 217–227.

Kitcher, P. (1993). *The advancement of science: Science without legend, objectivity without illusions.* New York: Oxford University Press.

Koocher, G. P. (1973). Childhood, death and cognitive development. *Developmental Psychology, 9,* 369–375.

Koocher, G. P. (1974). Talking with children about death. *American Journal of Orthopsychiatria, 44,* 404–410.

Kuhn, D., Amsel, E., & O'Loughlin, M. (1998). *The development of scientific thinking skills.* San Diego, CA: Academic Press.

Kuhn, T. S. (1962). *The structure of scientific revolutions.* Chicago: University of Chicago Press.

Kuhn, T. S. (1977). *The essential tension: Selected studies in scientific tradition and change.* Chicago: University of Chicago Press.

Kuhn, T. S. (1982). Commensurability, comparability, communicability. *PSA 1982* (Vol. 2, pp. 669–688). East Lansing, MI: Philosophy of Science Association.

Laurendeau, M., & Pinard, A. (1962). *Causal thinking in the child: A genetic and experimental approach.* New York: International Universities Press.

Leslie, A. M. (1994). ToMM, ToBy, and agency: Core architecture and domain specificity. In L. Hirschfeld & S. Gelman (Eds.), *Mapping the mind: Domain specificity in cognition and culture* (pp. 119–148). New York: Cambridge University Press.

Macnamara, J. (1987). *A border dispute: The place of logic in psychology.* Cambridge, MA: MIT Press.

Mandler, J., Bauer, P., & McDonough, L. (1991). Separating the sheep from the goats: Differentiating global categories. *Cognitive Psychology, 23*(2), 263–298.

Markman, E. M. (1977). Realizing that you don't understand: A preliminary investigation. *Child Development, 48,* 986–992.

Markman, E. M. (1989). *Categorization and naming in children: Problems of inductions.* Cambridge, MA: MIT Press.

Medin, D., & Ortony, A. (1989). Psychological essentialism. In S. Vosniadou & A. Ortony (Eds.), *Similarity and analogical reasoning* (pp. 179–195). New York: Cambridge University Press.

Meltzoff, A. (1995). Understanding the intentions of others: Re-enactment of intended acts by 18-month-olds. *Developmental Psychology, 31,* 838–850.

Nagy, M. H. (1948). The child's theories concerning death. *Journal of Genetic Psychology, 73,* 3–27.

Nagy, M. H. (1953). Children's conceptions of some bodily functions. *Journal of Genetic Psychology, 83,* 199–216.

Nersessian, N. J. (1992). How do scientists think? Capturing the dynamics of conceptual change in science. In R. N. Giere (Ed.), *Cognitive models of science: Minnesota studies in the philosophy of science* (Vol. 15, pp. 3–44). Minneapolis: University of Minnesota Press.

Perner, J. (1991). *Understanding the representational mind.* Cambridge, MA: MIT Press.

Piaget, J. (1929). *The child's conception of the world.* London: Routledge & Kegan Paul.

Piaget, J., & Inhelder, B. (1941). *The child's construction of quantities: Conservation and atomism* (A. J. Pomerans, Trans.) New York: Basic Books.

Quine, W. V. O. (1960). *Word and object.* Cambridge, MA: MIT Press.

Rosengren, K. S., Gelman, S. A., Kalish, C. W., & McCormick, M. (1991). As time goes by: Children's early understanding of growth in animals. *Child Development, 62,* 1302–1320.

Safier, G. (1964). A study in relationships between the life and death concepts in children. *Journal of Genetic Psychology, 105,* 283–294.

Salmon, W. C. (1989). *Four decades of scientific exploration.* Minneapolis: University of Minnesota Press.

Schwartz, S. P. (1977). Introduction. In S. P. Schwartz (Ed.), *Naming, necessity and naturalness.* Ithaca, NY: Cornell University Press.

Shultz, T. R. (1982). *Rules of causal attribution.* (Monographs for the Society for Research in Child Development). Chicago: University of Chicago Press.

Simons, D. J., & Keil, F. C. (1995). An abstract to concrete shift in the development of biological thought: The insider story. *Cognition, 56,* 129–163.

Slaughter, V., Jaakkola, K., & Carey, S. (in press). Constructing a coherent theory: Children's biological understanding of life and death. In M. Siegel & C. Petersen (Eds.), *Children's understanding of biology and health.* Cambridge, England: Cambridge University Press.

Smith, C., Carey, S., & Wiser, M. (1985). On differentiation: A case study of the development of the concepts of size, weight, and density. *Cognition, 21,* 177–237.

Smith, C., Snir, J., & Grosslight, L. (1992). Using conceptual models to facilitate conceptual change: The case of weight–density differentiation. *Cognition and Instruction, 9,* 221–283.

Smith, C., & Unger, C. (1997). What's in dots-per-box? Conceptual boot-strapping with stripped-down visual analogs. *Journal of the Learning Sciences, 6,* 143–181.

Solomon, G. E. A., & Cassamites, N. (in press). On the evidence that young children's understanding of germs implies a naive theory of biology. *Developmental Psychology.*

Solomon, G. E. A., & Johnson, S. C. (in press). Conceptual change in the classroom: Teaching young children to understand biological inheritance. *British Journal of Developmental Psychology.*

Solomon, G. E. A., Johnson, S. C., Zaitchik, D., & Carey, S. (1996). Like father, like son: Young children's understanding of how and why offspring resemble their parents. *Child Development, 67,* 151–171.

Speece, M., & Brent, S. (1992). The acquisition of a mature understanding of three components of the concept of death. *Death Studies, 16*(3), 211–229.

Spelke, E. S., Breinlinger, K., Macomber, J., & Jacobson, K. (1992). Origins of knowledge. *Psychological Review, 99,* 605–632.

Spelke, E. S., Phillips, A., & Woodward, A. L. (1995). Infants' knowledge of object motion and human action. In D. Sperber, D. Premack, & A. J. Premack (Eds.), *Causal cognition: A multidisciplinary debate.* Oxford, England: Clarendon Press.

Sperber, D., Premack, D., & Premack, A. J., (Eds.). (1995). *Casual cognition: A multidisciplinary debate.* Oxford, England: Clarendon Press.

Springer, K. (1992). Children's beliefs about the biological implications of kinship. *Child Development, 63,* 950–959.

Springer, K. (1995). Acquiring a naive theory through inference. *Child Development, 66,* 547–558.

Springer, K., & Keil, F. (1989). On the development of biologically specific beliefs: The case of inheritance. *Child Development, 60,* 637–648.

Thagard, P. (1992). *Conceptual revolutions.* Princeton, NJ: Princeton University Press.

Vosniadou, S., & Brewer, W. F. (1992). Mental models of the earth: A study of conceptual change in childhood. *Cognitive Psychology, 24,* 535–585.

Wellman, H. M. (1990). *The child's theory of mind.* Cambridge, MA: MIT Press.

Wellman, H. M., & Gelman, S. A. (1992). Cognitive development: Foundational theories of core domains. *Annual Review of Psychology, 43,* 337–375.

White, E., Elsom, B., & Prawat, R. (1978). Children's conceptions of death. *Child Development,* *49,* 307–310.

Wiggins, D. (1967). *Identity and spatio-temporal continuity.* Oxford, England: Basil Blackwell.

Wiggins, D. (1980). *Sameness and substance.* Oxford, England: Basil Blackwell.

Wiser, M. (1988). The differentiation of heat and temperature: History of science and novice–expert shift. In S. Strauss (Ed.), *Ontogeny, phylogeny, and the history of science* (pp. 28–48). Norwood, NJ: Ablex.

Wiser, M. (1995). Use of history of science to understand and remedy students' misconceptions about heat and temperature. In D. Perkins, J. Schwartz, M. West, & M. Wiske (Eds.), *Software goes to school* (pp. 23–38). New York: Oxford University Press.

Wiser, M., & Carey, S. (1983). When heat and temperature were one. In D. Gentner & A. Stevens (Eds.), *Mental models* (pp. 267–297). Hillsdale, NJ: Lawrence Erlbaum Associates.

Wynn, K. (1992). Addition and subtraction by human infants. *Nature, 358,* 749–750.

Wynn, K. (1996). Infants' individuation and enumeration of physical actions. *Psychological Science, 7,* 164–169.

Xu, F., & Carey, S. (1996). Infants' metaphysics: The case of numerical identity. *Cognitive Psychology, 30,* 111–153.

Author Index

Subject Index